Congress of the United States

begun and held at the City of New-York, on
Wednesday the fourth of March, one thousand seven hundred and eighty nine

THE Conventions of number of the States, having at the time of their adopting the Constitution, expressed a desire, in order to prevent misconstruction or abuse of its powers, that further declaratory and restrictive clauses should be added; And as extending the ground of public confidence in the Government, will best ensure the beneficent ends of its institution.

RESOLVED by the Senate and House of Representatives of the United States of America, in Congress assembled, two thirds of both Houses concurring, that the following Articles be proposed to the Legislatures of the several States, as amendments to the Constitution of the United States, all, or any of which Articles, when ratified by three fourths of the said Legislatures, to be valid to all intents and purposes, as part of the said Constitution; viz.

ARTICLES in addition to, and Amendment of the Constitution of the United States of America, proposed by Congress, and ratified by the Legislatures of the several States, pursuant to the fifth Article of the original Constitution.

Article the first..... After the first enumeration required by the first Article of the Constitution, there shall be one Representative for every thirty thousand, until the number shall amount to one hundred, after which the proportion shall be so regulated by Congress, that there shall be not less than one hundred Representatives, nor less than one Representative for every forty thousand persons, until the number of Representatives shall amount to two hundred, after which the proportion shall be so regulated by Congress, that there shall not be less than two hundred Representatives, nor more than one Representative for every fifty thousand persons.

Article the second... No law, varying the compensation for the services of the Senators and Representatives, shall take effect, until an election of Representatives shall have intervened.

Article the third... Congress shall make no law respecting an establishment of religion, or prohibiting the free exercise thereof; or abridging the freedom of speech, or of the press; or the right of the people peaceably to assemble, and to petition the Government for a redress of grievances.

Article the fourth... A well regulated Militia, being necessary to the security of a free State, the right of the people to keep and bear arms, shall not be infringed.

Article the fifth... No Soldier shall, in time of peace be quartered in any house, without the consent of the owner, nor in time of war, but in a manner to be prescribed by law.

Article the sixth... The right of the people to be secure in their persons, houses, papers, and effects, against unreasonable searches and seizures, shall not be violated, and no Warrants shall issue, but upon probable cause, supported by oath or affirmation, and particularly describing the place to be searched, and the persons or things to be seized.

Article the seventh... No person shall be held to answer for a capital, or otherwise infamous crime, unless on a presentment or indictment of a Grand Jury, except in cases arising in the land or naval forces, or in the Militia, when in actual service in time of War or public danger; nor shall any person be subject for the same offence to be twice put in jeopardy of life or limb; nor shall be compelled in any criminal case to be a witness against himself, nor be deprived of life, liberty, or property, without due process of law; nor shall private property be taken for public use, without just compensation.

Article the eighth... In all criminal prosecutions, the accused shall enjoy the right to a speedy and public trial, by an impartial jury of the State and district wherein the crime shall have been committed, which district shall have been previously ascertained by law, and to be informed of the nature and cause of the accusation; to be confronted with the witnesses against him; to have compulsory process for obtaining witnesses in his favor, and to have the assistance of Counsel for his defence.

Article the ninth... In suits at common law, where the value in controversy shall exceed twenty dollars, the right of trial by jury shall be preserved, and no fact tried by a jury, shall be otherwise re-examined in any Court of the United States, than according to the rules of the common law.

Article the tenth... Excessive bail shall not be required, nor excessive fines imposed, nor cruel and unusual punishments inflicted.

Article the eleventh... The enumeration in the Constitution, of certain rights, shall not be construed to deny or disparage others retained by the people.

Article the twelfth... The powers not delegated to the United States by the Constitution, nor prohibited by it to the States, are reserved to the States respectively, or to the people.

ATTEST,

Frederick Augustus Muhlenberg, Speaker of the House of Representatives.

John Adams, Vice-President of the United States, and President of the Senate.

John Beckley, Clerk of the House of Representatives.
Sam. A. Otis Secretary of the Senate.

IN OUR DEFENSE

To Bonnie and Les

Caroline Kennedy
Ellen Alderman

IN OUR DEFENSE

The Bill of Rights in Action

ELLEN ALDERMAN
CAROLINE KENNEDY

WILLIAM MORROW AND COMPANY, INC.

New York

Library of Congress Cataloging-in-Publication Data

Alderman, Ellen.
    In our defense : the Bill of Rights in action / Ellen Alderman and Caroline Kennedy.
        p.   cm.
    ISBN 0-688-07801-X
    1. Civil rights—United States—Popular works. 2. United States—Constitution—Amendments—1st–10th—Popular works. 3. Civil rights—United States—Cases. I. Kennedy, Caroline. II. Title.
KF4750.A43   1990
342.73'085—dc20
[347.30285]
                                                                90-48844
                                                                     CIP

Printed in the United States of America

              6   7   8   9   10

BOOK DESIGN BY PAUL CHEVANNES

To
Edwin, Rose, Tatiana, and John

Mark, Sue, John, Nancy, David, and Laurie

And to our parents

Acknowledgments

There are many people whose help has made this book possible. Most important are those whose experiences have defined our freedom, both those whose stories are told in this book and many whose are not. To the people who have allowed and helped us to tell their stories, and who have been so generous with their time and their materials, we are especially grateful. They are:

Lyng v. Northwest Indian Cemetery Protective Association
Rodney Hamblin, Jeanerette Jacobs-Johnny, Jimmie James, Walter Lara, Susie Long, Marilyn Miles, and Lawrence O'Rourke

Missouri Knights of the Ku Klux Klan v. Kansas City
Reverend Emanuel Cleaver, Joanne Collins, William Geary, Stuart Gold, Leonard Hersh, Dennis Mahon, Stephen Pevar, and John Sharp

United States v. The Progressive
Terry Adamson, Hon. Griffin Bell, John Griffin, Erwin Knoll, Thomas Martin, Howard Morland, Duane Sewell, Hon. Robert Warren, and Brady Williamson

Hobson v. Wilson
Sammie Abbott, Charles Brennan, Reverend David Eaton, Tina Hobson, Anne Pilsbury, Daniel Schember, Ralph Temple, Arthur Waskow, and David White

Quilici v. Morton Grove
Martin Ashman, Don Bennett, Neil Cashman, Dan Perry, Maureen Piszczor, Isaiah Stroud, Christopher Walsh, Terry Walsh, Gregory Youstra, and Jim Zangrilli

McSurely v. McClellan
Raymond Battochi, Margaret Haring, Philip Lacovara, Alan McSurely, Mellie Nelson, Thomas Ratliff, and Morton Stavis

"Linares"
Daniel Coyne, Rodolfo Linares, Tamara Linares, and Scott Nelson

Green v. United States
George Blow

Baltimore City Department of Social Services v. Bouknight
José Anderson, Jacqueline Bouknight, George Burns, M. Cristina Gutierrez, George Lipman, Mitchell Merviss, Robin Parsons, and Ralph Tyler

Fuentes v. Shevin
Robert Shevin and Rosa Bell Andrews Washington

Poletown Neighborhood Council v. Detroit
George Fox, General Motors Corporation, Walter and Josephine Jakubowski, Isaac Jones, Michael Krowlewski, Emmett Moten, Dick O'Brien, Tom Olechowski, Ronald Reosti, Reverend Frank Skalski, Stan Stachowicz, United Auto Workers, and Hon. Coleman Young

Machetti v. Linahan
Jack Boger, Susan Boleyn, Bill Gifford, Rebecca Machetti, and Maryann Oakley

Coy v. Iowa
The two girls and their families, Bruce Ingham, Gary Rolfes, and Jack Wolfe

In re Myron Farber
Floyd Abrams, Myron Farber, and Henry Furst

United States v. Cronic
Chris Colston, Harrison Cronic, Steven Duke, Hon. John Green, and Gary Peterson

Tison v. Arizona
Michael Beers, Alan Dershowitz, Cynthia Hamilton, David Heller, Mike Piccaretta, Hon. William Shafer, Stephen Sublett, Raymond Tison, and Ricky Tison

Although their cases did not end up in the book, we would also like to thank Marie Deans, Joe Giarratano, Richard Gorman, Robert Harris, David and Debbie Klebanoff, Steve Landers, Jordan Lawrence, John Payton, Earl Washington, Johnny Watkins, and Gerald Zerkin.

There are a number of other people who provided valuable guidance at various stages, including Jeff Blattner, Jack Boger, Richard Burr, Herbert J. Miller, Jr., F. Richard Pappas, Joseph Rauh, Nicole Seligman, and most especially, Gary Ginsburg.

For their careful review of the manuscript, and assistance with the endnotes, we would like to thank Peter Critchell, R. Townsend Davis, Robert deBy, Lisa Markoff, and Greg Naron.

We would also like to thank the faculty of the Columbia Law School for encouragement of this project, especially Vivian Berger, Vincent Blasi, Jack Greenberg, Eben Moglen, and Richard Uviller. Our thanks as well to the staff of the Columbia Law School Library. We are also grateful to the firm of Paul, Weiss, Rifkind, Wharton & Garrison.

Finally, this book would not have been possible without the dedicated editorial assistance of Janet Hulstrand. We are also grateful to Michele Bocchi for her painstaking typing and transcription.

For their general all-around help, our thanks to Arthur Cohen, Janet Coviello, Elaine Kennelly, Amelia North, Marta Sgubin, Maria Torres, Stewart Wallace, and Barbara Wilder, and to Lisa Drew and Bob Shuman.

Contents

Authors' Note

A 1987 newspaper poll showed that 59 percent of Americans could not identify the Bill of Rights. At the time, we were in law school, discovering a world of complicated people, complex situations, and compelling principles. It seemed to us that an unfortunate gulf exists between those who know about the law and those who do not. The law has its own language and its own rules, both of which operate to exclude the uninitiated.

But to lawyers, for whom the technical rules and procedure are no longer a barrier, the law becomes, as Oliver Wendell Holmes wrote, "a magic mirror," in which "we see reflected not only our own lives, but the lives of all men that have been." The study of the law becomes the stories of human nature. And many of the most compelling stories are those that have shaped the freedoms we Americans so take for granted that we cannot even name them.

We wanted to write a book that would tell some of these stories and introduce some of the fundamental principles of the Bill of Rights. We decided to begin with the people, traveling the country to meet and talk with them. Because the law evolves in tiny increments of *Plaintiff v. Defendant*, we decided to tell the stories of their cases.

In these stories, majestic principles of liberty and justice are played out in the lives of ordinary Americans, some heroic and some malevolent. For as one Supreme Court justice wrote, "It is a fair summary of history to say that the safeguards of liberty have frequently been forged in controversies involving not very nice people."

The stories were chosen for many reasons. Some illustrate why the Founding Fathers protected these individual rights against the power of the government, and why we still need them today. Others show how far we have come in two hundred years. Still others raise difficult questions for the future.

This book is not intended to, nor could it ever, explain the entire Bill of Rights, or analyze the current state of the law covered by these ten amendments. It is a subjective slice of an enormous subject. But if we succeeded in what we set out to do, you may share our belief that, as the Bill of Rights enters its third century, it is only by fighting for those rights, win or lose, that they will continue, in our defense.

Historical Note

Considered together, the ten amendments in the Bill of Rights outline the most comprehensive protection of individual freedom ever written. But originally they were not even part of the Constitution.

After the Revolution, the states adopted their own constitutions, many of which contained Bills of Rights. But Americans still faced the challenge of creating a central government for their new nation. In 1777 the Continental Congress adopted the Articles of Confederation, which were ratified by 1781. Under the Articles, the states retained their "sovereignty, freedom and independence," while the national government was kept weak and subordinate. Over the next few years it became obvious that this system of government was not equal to the challenge of settling and defending the frontier, regulating trade, currency, and commerce, and organizing thirteen states into one union.

So in the summer of 1787 delegates from twelve states convened in Philadelphia to draft a new Constitution (Rhode Island did not send any delegates). They proposed a strong national government that would assume many powers previously exercised by the states.

Because of this strong federal authority, the Constitution faced much opposition when it was submitted for the required approval from three quarters of the state legislatures. People objected that because the liberties they had fought for in the Revolution were not protected by the Constitution, these rights could be disregarded by the federal government. Those who opposed the Constitution's broad grant of powers to the new federal government were called Anti-Federalists; those who supported it were called Federalists. The Anti-Federalists called for another convention to draft a Bill of Rights *before* the Constitution was approved. The Federalists, fearing that the process would unravel completely, urged immediate ratification, with consideration of a Bill of Rights to come later. Eventually, the Federalists prevailed. By 1788, eleven states had ratified the Constitution. Six states, however, sent Congress proposals for amendments, modeled on their state constitutions and designed to protect individual rights.

James Madison realized that the public desire for a Bill of Rights could not be ignored. In 1789, after reviewing the state-proposed amendments and state Bills of Rights, he proposed nine amendments to be considered by Congress for insertion into the text of the Constitution. After consideration, debate, and some alterations, the House and Senate voted to add the amendments on at the end of the Constitution and sent twelve amendments to the states for ratification. Only ten were ratified—the ten we know as the Bill of Rights. (The two that failed dealt with the apportionment of representatives and salary increases for Congress.)

As ratified in 1791, the Bill of Rights protected individual rights from violation by the *federal* government. For example, the First Amendment begins, *"Congress* shall make no law . . ."* Madison's original draft had contained a proposal that would have also prohibited state governments from violating the Bill of Rights, but it was deleted by the Senate.

So it was not until the Thirteenth, Fourteenth, and Fifteenth amendments were enacted, after the Civil War, that the federal Constitution began to protect individuals against the states. The Fourteenth Amendment has been the principal means by which this protection has been accomplished. It reads, in part, "No *State* shall . . . deprive any person of life, liberty, or property, without due process of law." The Supreme Court has interpreted this guarantee of liberty to embrace the fundamental liberties in the Bill of Rights, meaning that state governments must observe and protect them to the same extent as the federal government. In legal parlance, this process is called incorporation. The amendments in the Bill of Rights are said to be incorporated against the states through the due process clause of the Fourteenth Amendment. There has been an ongoing debate on the Supreme Court about the scope of incorporation, and whether the entire Bill of Rights, or only some of its guarantees, should be incorporated against the states.

In any event, the process of incorporation did not begin until the twentieth century. Most rights were not incorporated until the 1960s, which explains why most constitutional litigation has taken place only within the last twenty-five years. As of now, the few rights not incorporated against the states include the Second Amendment right to keep and bear arms, the Fifth Amendment right to a grand jury indictment, the Sixth Amendment requirement of twelve jurors on a criminal jury, and the Seventh Amendment right to a civil jury. The Supreme Court has held various state procedures adequate to protect the values inherent in those constitutional rights. All the rest of the fundamental freedoms in the Bill of Rights have been incorporated and may not be infringed by the federal government or by the states.

The sacred rights of mankind are not
to be rummaged for among old parchments, or
musty records. They are written, as with a
sunbeam, in the whole volume of human nature
by the hand of the divinity itself; and can
never be erased or obscured by mortal power.

—Alexander Hamilton

FIRST AMENDMENT

"Congress shall make no law respecting an establishment of religion, or prohibiting the free exercise thereof; or abridging the freedom of speech, or of the press; or the right of the people peaceably to assemble, and to petition the Government for a redress of grievances."

Dennis Mahon, Imperial Dragon, Missouri Knights of the Ku Klux Klan and host of the television program "Klansas City Kable"

REPRINTED BY PERMISSION OF THE KANSAS CITY STAR

Reverend Emanuel Cleaver, who opposed the Klan program

PHOTO BY STEVE GONZALES; REPRINTED BY PERMISSION OF THE KANSAS CITY STAR

Freedom of Speech:
Missouri Knights of the Ku Klux Klan v. Kansas City

"Congress shall make no law abridging the freedom of speech."

Q: Are black genes as good as white genes?
A: Not when it comes to intelligence. Not when it comes to building society. The blacks are very emotional people and they don't reason. This is why for thousands of years the blacks had nothing in Africa except the mud hut. They're eating their brothers. They live worse than the caveman did.

T HESE ARE THE WORDS OF DEN-nis Mahon, a former hydraulic mechanic for Trans World Airlines, and Imperial Dragon of the Missouri Knights of the Ku Klux Klan. Mahon ignited a national controversy in August 1987, when he and Exalted Cyclops J. Allan Moran requested air time on Kansas City's public access cable television channel in an exercise of their First Amendment right to free speech. Channel 20, the public access channel, was available to all on a first-come, first-serve basis, free of any editorial control from the cable company. Mahon and Moran planned to air weekly episodes of "Race and Reason," a program produced by Tom Metzger, former

Klansman and present leader of the White Aryan Resistance (WAR). "Race and Reason" had been on cable television for five years, reaching over fifty cities nationwide.

But in Kansas City, a community attempting to address problematic race relations, local leaders and the cable company did not simply accept the claim to a First Amendment right. In their judgment, racist diatribes were more than people should have to endure, particularly in their own homes, on their own televisions, and on a public access channel they paid a monthly fee to support. Some black ministers and politicians found it hard to believe that the First Amendment, which had protected them and their leaders throughout the civil rights movement, would now require them to be exposed to Klan propaganda.

Mahon and his fellow Klansmen marched in full Klan regalia to the cable company, American Cablevision, to present their formal request. At first the request was denied because company regulations required that programming on channel 20 be produced locally. The Klan was undeterred. Instead of airing "Race and Reason," it agreed to produce a local show. The program would be called "Klansas City Kable." Its host would be Imperial Dragon Dennis Mahon. American Cablevision then said its regulations required that at least six Klan members receive training in video production. The Klan was happy to oblige.

According to Mahon, a majority of "Klansas City Kable" shows would deal with racial issues. Other episodes would expose government and corporate bureaucracy. "Our show is based on the white working class," he says. "We are going to expose the filthy rich for what they are and most of them are white." There were also plans to interview black nationalists and black separatists, "who do not believe in racial interaction." According to Mahon, "They are just like Klansmen except they're black. Basically we get along with those men very, very well. In fact, we're all for them getting self-determination back in Africa."

But in Kansas City, the cable company studio is located in a neighborhood that is 95 percent black. American Cablevision was concerned that violence would occur. It was also afraid that many viewers would cancel their subscriptions. The sight of Klansmen marching to the studio in their robes was disturbing to many residents. And the idea of them marching into his living room on public access TV was intolerable to Reverend Emanuel

Cleaver, pastor of the Saint James–Paseo United Methodist Church and a member of the Kansas City Council.

Reverend Cleaver grew up in Waxahachie, Texas. At the time, in the early 1960s, many communities in the South were still completely segregated and black social life centered around the church. In 1964, when he was fifteen, Cleaver led his first civil rights march to desegregate three downtown movie theaters, though it was not until he had graduated from college that Cleaver saw a movie in his own home town. In 1968, he moved to Kansas City, where he received his master of divinity degree, became a pastor, a board member of the local chapter of the American Civil Liberties Union (ACLU), a national vice-president of Reverend Martin Luther King, Jr.'s Southern Christian Leadership Conference, and in 1979, a member of the city council. One year later his family was awakened by the sound of shattering glass. A Molotov cocktail had been thrown through one of their windows, and outside a cross burned on their lawn. Though the FBI investigated the incident, no one was ever charged.

As in many big cities in the 1980s, race relations in Kansas City remained tense. The Kansas City School District is among the most segregated in the country. According to Cleaver, there have been racially motivated cross burnings and graffiti, black homeowners have been run out of white neighborhoods, and after a period of relative dormancy, the Ku Klux Klan has been trying for a comeback in the area.

According to Dennis Mahon, its principal state organizer, the Klan has become more sophisticated in its recruiting techniques. It now exploits a full range of media options in an exercise of its First Amendment rights. The Klan's newsletter is mailed to about five hundred recipients, each of whom is responsible for photocopying and distributing ten copies. Call-in telephone numbers with answering machines deliver the Klan's "racialist" message and seek contributions. Klan members appear on radio talk shows and, more important, are beginning to use television to spread their views and recruit new members.

Reverend Cleaver, however, did not see "Klansas City Kable" as an exercise in free speech. "My problem is that I never saw this as a First Amendment issue. I saw this as a terrorist organization attempting to use the airwaves to create an atmosphere where terror could thrive. I felt that they were trying to plant the seeds of racial intolerance in a community where the problems already existed, and I felt that those seeds in many instances would germinate and would blossom. I don't believe that we should restrict people in terms of their First Amendment rights, as long as that right does not interfere with the right of other groups to exist. These are terrorists, they're murderers. History—recorded history—in this country will show that they have killed thousands of my people. Thousands."

On the Supreme Court, the struggle between the fear of violence provoked by speech and the promise of the First Amendment produced perhaps the most famous principle in all of constitutional law: the "clear and present danger" test. The idea that government cannot punish speech unless it creates a clear and present danger was originally developed by Supreme Court Justices Oliver Wendell Holmes and Louis Brandeis at the time of World War I. Although the rhetoric was always ringing in support of the right to speak freely, in practice it proved difficult for the Court to determine when the danger was "clear" enough, how remote it could be and yet still be considered "present," and exactly how perilous the "danger" had to be to justify suppressing speech.

Perhaps because free speech is so vital to American public life, free speech decisions often reflect larger social changes. In the early cases brought under the Espionage Act of 1917, the Supreme Court construed freedom of speech quite narrowly. Such men as labor leader Eugene Debs were jailed for opposing World War I and advocating socialism. Debs, who had run for president four times on the Socialist ticket, addressed an outdoor rally in Chicago on a Sunday afternoon in June 1918. He had just come from visiting a local jail where three "loyal comrades" were imprisoned for obstructing the draft. Debs said he was proud of his comrades and went on to criticize capitalist plutocrats, praise the working man, and prophesy the ultimate triumph of the Socialist crusade. He exhorted the crowd, "You need to know you are fit for something better than slavery and cannon fodder."

Debs was convicted of causing and inciting insubordination, disloyalty, mutiny, refusal of duty in the military forces and obstructing the recruitment service of the United States. At his trial, he addressed the jury himself. "I have been accused of obstructing the war. I admit it. Gentlemen, I abhor war. I would oppose the war if I stood alone." Debs was found guilty and sentenced to two concurrent ten-year prison terms. The Supreme Court upheld the conviction and the sentence. As one First Amendment scholar has written, "It is somewhat as though George McGovern had been sent to prison for his criticism of the [Vietnam] war."

Then, during the 1950s, faced with a number of cases involving the Communist party, the Supreme Court struggled to distinguish advocacy of organized violent action, which is within the government's power to prohibit, from advocacy of belief, which is not. In a 1951 case, the Court upheld the convictions of Communist party leaders for participating in a conspiracy to advocate the overthrow of the government. Six years later, the Court reversed the convictions of fourteen second-string party leaders, finding their teaching of Communist party doctrine, though it included advocacy of the overthrow of the U.S. government, to be more like advocacy of belief. (In other words, the danger it presented was not clear and present enough to justify suppression.)

In 1969, the Supreme Court reformulated the clear and present danger test. By this time, society generally, and the Supreme Court in particular, were prepared not only to tolerate, but to protect speech that would have astounded the justices who upheld Eugene Debs's conviction. In *Brandenburg v. Ohio*, the Court held that government can restrict speech only when it advocates the use of violence directed toward inciting imminent and likely lawless action.

Under the *Brandenburg* standard, unless Reverend Cleaver could show that "Klansas City Kable" would trigger violence that was both imminent and likely, not just hypothetically possible, he could not keep it off the air, no matter how offensive it would be to channel 20's viewers. Because the cable studio's neighbors had said they would fight to prevent the Klan from marching to the studio, Cleaver thought he could show that violence was likely. And Mahon, though often conciliatory when speaking to the media, did not rule out violence either. "We will go to war to have our show on the air. We will kill and we will take a chance of getting killed for freedom of speech. We are going to have our show on the air whether they like it or not."

But because no episodes of "Klansas City Kable" were available, and no air date had been set, Cleaver and his allies on the

city council were not sure they could prove violence was imminent. In that case, they could not keep the Klan from exercising
its constitutional right to speak. They decided to invoke another
constitutional principle instead.

In addition to speech, the First Amendment protects writing,
demonstrating, parading, leafletting, and certain forms of symbolic expression (such as wearing black armbands in school to
protest a war). Confronted with cases where local governments
have tried to restrict, or accommodate, these various kinds of
speech, the Supreme Court has developed the principle that government can place reasonable regulations on when, where, and
how speakers may express themselves. Under the Constitution,
however, these regulations must not be motivated by an effort to
restrict the *content* of what the speaker has to say. In legal terms,
the right of free speech is subject to "reasonable time, manner,
and place" regulations, as long as these regulations are "content-
neutral." Therefore, a city government may require a parade permit or limit the ability to demonstrate in certain places in order
to protect public safety, but the restrictions must apply
evenhandedly to all speakers, regardless of the message they wish
to convey.

So when the Village of Skokie, Illinois, home to thousands of
Holocaust survivors, refused to issue a permit to Nazis to parade
in front of the village hall, a federal court held that the town
officials had violated the Nazis' right to free speech. Their refusal
to allow the parade was not motivated by a fear of imminent,
likely violence, but was content-based discrimination, prohibited
by the First Amendment. The court wrote, "Any shock effect must
be attributed to the content of the ideas expressed. Public expression of ideas may not be prohibited merely because the ideas are
themselves offensive to some of their hearers."

The context in which the speech is delivered may affect the
application of these principles. Speech is most protected (that is,
speakers are most free to say what they like) in streets, parks, and
public places, which have "immemorially been held in trust for
the use of the public and, time out of mind, have been used for
purposes of assembly, communicating thoughts between citizens,
and discussing public questions." These places are called public
forums. Once established, a public forum cannot be eliminated by
the government in order to silence speech. In essence, it belongs

to the people. According to Stephen Pevar, the ACLU attorney who represented the Klan, "The public access channel today is what the speaker's soap box was two hundred years ago. It is the poor person's forum. It is one of the few ways in which someone with little means can reach a wide audience in today's technological age."

At the other end of the spectrum is private property. The right to exclude others from one's property is a basic organizing principle of U.S. society, and homeowners are free to forbid speech in their house or demonstrations in their front yard. Reverend Cleaver and the cable company argued that the public access channel was the private property of American Cablevision, not a public forum.

After consulting with the city's law department, Reverend Cleaver and his allies on the city council proposed a resolution eliminating the public access channel altogether. Many believed that the resolution was motivated by Cleaver's desire to keep the Klan from reaching a large television audience. But because the resolution would keep all producers of public access programming, not just the Klan, off the air, Cleaver was satisfied it was evenhanded, content-neutral, and would pass the First Amendment test.

Thus the Kansas City dispute raised the question: Is a public access channel the "soap box of the future," a public forum where speakers enjoy broad First Amendment protection? Or is it more like private property, where the cable company owner has control? The Klan's request was bringing the faded parchment of the First Amendment into the electronic age.

On June 16, 1988, the city council of Kansas City passed Resolution 62655 authorizing American Cablevision to drop the public access channel. The vote was nine to two.

One of the two votes against the resolution was cast by Joanne Collins, a native Kansas Citian who had served on the city council for sixteen years. A fifty-four-year-old grandmother married to a former schoolteacher, Collins got a lot of attention for her vote because she is black. Collins says, "I hate some of the things [the Klan] has done, I hate some of the things that they say, but I don't hate the person. . . . I come from a philosophy that you learn by education and you don't withhold information. . . . I have learned from even the most negative person, and because I don't agree with him doesn't mean that he shouldn't be heard, or I shouldn't listen. I believe right will always prevail."

Collins's remarks echo the classic defense of free speech that dates back to John Milton, a belief in the importance of dialogue and faith in the power of reason and truth to emerge victorious. As Milton wrote in 1644, "And though all the winds of doctrine were let loose to play upon the earth, so Truth be in the field, we do injuriously, by licensing and prohibiting, to misdoubt her strength. Let her and Falsehood grapple; who ever knew Truth put to the worst, in a free and open encounter?"

In this century, Justice Holmes shifted the metaphor from the battlefield to the marketplace: "When men have realized that time has upset many fighting faiths, they may come to believe even more than they believe the very foundations of their own conduct that the ultimate good desired is better reached by free trade in ideas—that the best test of truth is the power of the thought to get itself accepted in the competition of the market, and that truth is the only ground upon which their wishes safely can be carried out.

This model of the "marketplace of ideas" gives rise to the theory that the proper response to offensive speech is not to prohibit it, but to combat it with counterspeech. Those who follow Holmes's view believe that the strength of the First Amendment depends on a shared idealism and respect for the principle of free speech itself, if not for the views it permits to be expressed. When the voices of hate and intolerance grow louder, when the Klan holds rallies in Georgia and skinheads camp out in California, the most effective rebuttal, in this view, is to see them outnumbered by those who abhor racism and believe in peaceful pluralism.

As Justice Brandeis wrote in his famous defense of free speech: "Those who won our independence believed that the final end of the state was to make men free to develop their faculties; and in its government the deliberative forces should prevail over the arbitrary . . . they knew . . . that it is hazardous to discourage thought, hope, and imagination; that fear breeds repression; that repression breeds hate; that hate menaces stable government; that the path of safety lies in the opportunity to discuss freely supposed grievances and proposed remedies; and that the fitting remedy for evil counsels is good ones."

According to the theory of counterspeech, the proper remedy

he says,
. You've

he First
ion. If it
petrator
erring to
oppressed
violence,
tion. It's
nce. The
free kill-
and that

l issues
ke Rev-
that the
ndment
if they
used to
nk that,
flawed.
ion be-
ealizing
ething I
Amer-

a of the
ourt on
Kansas
nst the
public
ight to
e First
t also
grams.
d that
at the
com-

s for Reverend Cleaver and others to
w exposing the errors of the Klan's
decide for themselves to reject the
ould do so based on an informed de-
les of the issue. The rejection of the
d therefore be more secure and long-

er, disputes this solution. He is not
ch is effective, and he feels society
or truth to prevail in the marketplace.
have a responsibility to challenge
us. We may lose in court every day.
sit passively and watch people who
eive a prominent spot on television."
hen Pevar says, "Free speech has to
peech for unpopular views as well as
ssibly make distinctions between ac-
cceptable speech] and remain a free
would prevent the Klan from appear-
e prevented Martin Luther King, Jr.,
' Listening to offensive speech is one
"when we just have to nod our head
ve pay for liberty.'"
Why should we tolerate and grant free
, were they in power, would deny free
's own admission, a nation run by the
speech as we know it under the First
ck people do not return to Africa, Ma-
a white nation in five states in the
dents of the area who did not wish to
nation would be paid to leave. Mahon
n free speech will be allowed only as
s with the government. "First of all,
ecause it will be a white nation. They
o say, but we will not allow treason
e will pay them to leave. We will not
starts yelling at the white race, some-
heir block off."
s in the fact that U.S. society strives to
eals, to be different from such a total-

itarian regime. "If you don't give them free speech,
"then the era that you're afraid of has already arriv
created it."

According to Pevar, Mahon's talk is exactly what
Amendment protects, precisely because it is talk, not a
were action, and a crime were committed, then the p
would be prosecuted in the criminal justice system. R
the Supreme Court's test, which allows speech to be s
only when it creates the danger of imminent likely
Pevar says, "There is a difference between speech and
a fundamental difference and it's a constitutional diffe
Constitution guarantees free speech, it doesn't guarant
ing. So [the Klan] can talk about killing all they want t
is constitutionally protected."

But today when public debate is often angry, and ra
continue to divide communities like Kansas City, some
erend Cleaver, question such a system. "I don't believ
Framers of the Bill of Rights ever intended the First A
to be so ubiquitous that it tolerated everything. Beca
really believed that, then the First Amendment could
dismantle everything they put together," he says. "I
like the Bible, like life, like love, the First Amendmen
The older this nation becomes, the more mature this
comes, the more comfortable we are going to become i
that we do need to develop some exceptions. It's not s
think will damage or destroy America. In fact, it may
ica."

When the city council voted to authorize the elimina
public access channel, Pevar filed suit in federal distri
behalf of the Klan: *Missouri Knights of the Ku Klux Kla
City*. The suit alleged that the city had discriminated
Klan on the basis of the content of its speech, that
access channel was a public forum that the city had
eliminate, and that in doing so the city violated not on
Amendment rights of the Klan and other producer
those of viewers who have a right to watch uncensored

The city tried to have the lawsuit dismissed. It cl
the resolution dropping the channel was content-neutr
public access channel was not a public forum but the

pany's private property, and that the Klan was not deprived of its right to free speech. The city argued that the Klan, like any other speaker, was not entitled to its first choice of a means by which to spread its message. The city pointed out that the Klan could still solicit over the telephone, hold rallies, distribute leaflets, appear on radio or TV talk shows when invited, or march down "Main Street."

On May 26, 1989, the district court ruled against the city on all counts. It found that if the Klan succeeded in proving its allegations, it could win at trial and therefore should be given an opportunity to try. A trial date was set for September.

In June, the U.S. Supreme Court decided two cases that made the city even more pessimistic about its chances of prevailing. The Court held that burning the American flag in political protest and certain telephone Dial-a-Porn services were protected by the First Amendment. If the First Amendment was broad enough to protect those forms of offensive speech, the city's lawyers concluded, it could also protect the Klan's television program. After all, race relations are a subject of vital public debate in the United States and of crucial political significance. As such, they lie close to the core of the First Amendment.

The city council also knew that its lawyers estimated they had completed less than a quarter of the amount of work necessary to prepare for trial, yet had already amassed a large legal fee. The Klan's ACLU lawyers had accrued expenses of a hundred thousand dollars. If the city lost at trial, it could be liable for the ACLU's expenses as well as its own. Kansas City was in the midst of a budget crisis; there was a freeze on hiring and it was an election year.

The city offered to settle. It suggested an open-microphone format where anyone could come in and talk for fifteen minutes at a time. The Klan rejected the offer. Pevar set forth two conditions for any settlement: the public access channel had to be reinstated, and the city had to develop new regulations to ensure that the free speech rights of all public access producers would be protected.

The vote to reinstate the public access channel came before the city council on July 13, 1989. Reverend Cleaver moved for a public hearing on the issue. The motion failed. But Kansas Citians demanded to be heard. A group of ministers, both black and white, gathered at the railing separating the public area of the council chamber from the council members' desks. They asked repeatedly to be allowed to speak. Finally, the mayor agreed to allow them ten minutes. In a series of emotional speeches, each minister preached as if to a huge congregation.

A half hour later, the mayor called for order and a vote. The ministers kept speaking. The mayor called for the room to be cleared. The ministers and their followers began to sing an old spiritual with new words:

> Keep the Klan off TV.
> We shall not be moved.
> Like a tree that grows by the water
> We shall not be moved.

The mayor banged his gavel and again called for a roll call. The ministers were joined by others who, hearing what was happening in the council chamber, began to crowd the room. The chorus launched into "We Shall Overcome," then "The Star Spangled Banner," followed by "God Bless America." The singing was interrupted by a prayer asking God to touch the council members and make them understand that they should vote against the public access channel. An attempt was made to clear the room. It did not work. The mayor, now visibly impatient, again called for a vote. The ministers refused to leave; they began to pray. During the entire roll call and vote by the thirteen council members the ministers sang and then quietly recited the Lord's Prayer. "Our father Who art in heaven . . . hallowed be Thy name . . . forgive us our trespasses, as we forgive those who trespass against us." The vote was announced by the mayor: seven to three. The public access channel was to be resurrected with new guidelines protecting free speech.

The first episode of "Klansas City Kable" aired April 3, 1990.

SANDERS, THE MILWAUKEE JOURNAL

Freedom of the Press:
United States v. The Progressive

"Congress shall make no law abridging the freedom of the press."

What you are about to learn is a secret—a secret that the United States and four other nations, the makers of hydrogen weapons, have gone to extraordinary lengths to protect. . . . [A secret] that initially eluded the physicists of the United States, the Soviet Union, Britain, France and China; that they discovered independently and kept tenaciously to themselves, and that may not yet have occurred to the weapon makers of a dozen other nations bent on building the hydrogen bomb.

I discovered it simply by reading and asking questions, without the benefit of security clearance or access to classified materials. . . .

Why am I telling you?

It's not because I want to help you build an H-bomb. Have no fear; that would be far beyond your capability—unless you have the resources of at least a medium-sized government.

Nor is it because I want India, or Israel, or Pakistan, or South Africa to get the H-bomb sooner than they otherwise would, even though it is conceivable that the information will be helpful to them. . . .

I am telling the secret to make a basic point as forcefully as I can: Secrecy itself, especially the power of a few designated "experts" to declare some topics off limits, contributes to a political climate in which the nuclear establishment can conduct business as usual, protecting and perpetuating the production of these horror weapons.

T HE TITLE OF THE ARTICLE JUST
quoted is "The H-Bomb Secret." Written by an antinuclear activist,
Howard Morland, it was scheduled to be the cover story of the April
1979 issue of *The Progressive,* a small monthly magazine published
in Madison, Wisconsin. Morland insisted that absolutely none of his
material was classified. He, a layperson, had uncovered the secret
by reading materials in the public domain, interviewing people on
the inside of the "nuclear fraternity," and using his own ingenuity
to piece the puzzle together. Nonetheless, an alarmed MIT professor
sent an early draft of the article to the Department of Energy.

Duane Sewell was assistant secretary for the Defense Program
in the Department of Energy and the man in charge of keeping
secret information about nuclear weapons secret. This was the
first time Sewell had seen the H-bomb secret in the "outside
world." He showed the Morland article to James Schlesinger, secretary of energy, and to members of the Department of State and
the Arms Control and Disarmament Agency. They agreed that not
only was some of the information in the Morland article classified, but also that publication would harm the security of the
United States. Word went out to the Justice Department that the
Progressive had to be stopped.

There was a problem, however: under the First Amendment,
the government did not just "stop" the press. Hard-fought cases
had set guidelines for punishment *after* publication of certain
kinds of information. But it was well established that if the First
Amendment means anything, it means the government may not
impose a *prior* restraint on the press. Censorship was not only
distinctly unpopular in the United States, it was also notoriously
unsuccessful. Indeed, just a few years earlier the government had
suffered a well-publicized defeat in attempting to restrain the
press in the Pentagon Papers case. Many of the staff members of
the emergency litigation division were uneasy.

Secretary James Schlesinger personally presented the *Progressive* controversy to Attorney General Griffin Bell. Schlesinger
told Bell that the data in the Morland article provided foreign
nations with a "map and a shortcut" to designing thermonuclear
weapons. He explained that even if pieces of the secret design of
thermonuclear weapons had seeped into the public sector, as Mor-

land claimed, no publication had ever put all the pieces together in one place, in easy-to-understand language, as the Morland article did. According to Bell, "No cabinet secretary in my tenure ever pushed us harder to move in court."

And so a district court judge in Madison, Wisconsin, came to work one day to find the Department of Justice on his doorstep and, through affidavits, three cabinet secretaries and half the nation's Nobel laureates talking about nuclear holocaust. The case was *United States of America v. The Progressive*, Inc. "It was an uneven match," says Erwin Knoll, editor of *The Progressive*. "We had the government licked from the beginning and we knew it."

The Progressive, a so-called alternative magazine, was founded in 1909 by Robert "Fighting Bob" La Follette, Sr., governor of Wisconsin, U.S. senator, and presidential candidate for the Progressive party. According to Knoll, *The Progressive* is "devoted to certain fundamental principles that were very important in the early Progressive movement . . . an opposition to militarism and war, a very strong commitment to civil rights and civil liberties, a strong commitment to environmental protection, and a profound suspicion of big corporations and what they do." In 1979, *The Progressive* had a circulation of between thirty-five and forty thousand across the United States.

The previous year, Samuel H. Day, Jr., former editor of the *Bulletin of Atomic Scientists*, became the managing editor of *The Progressive*. He had a fresh idea for a series of articles on the nuclear weapons industry—the articles would be based on actual tours of nuclear plants across the country. One of Day's pieces, "The Nicest People Make the Bomb," appeared in the October 1978 issue. While researching his series, Day met Howard Morland.

Morland grew up in the 1950s in Chattanooga, Tennessee, ninety miles downriver from Oak Ridge, a major nuclear research center established during World War II's Manhattan Project. Growing up, Morland did not know that Oak Ridge still bore its wartime code name, Y-12, and would one day be in the business, at least according to Morland, of "turn[ing] out H-bomb components as routinely as General Motors turns out automobiles." Even so, the sprawling complex cast an impressive shadow across Morland's home town. "In some parts of the country children say, 'If you're so smart, why aren't you rich?' In my part of the country, eastern Tennessee, where the atomic bomb was born, they used to say, 'If you're so smart, why aren't you a nuclear physicist?'"

At Emory University in Atlanta, Morland took several physics courses but decided against making a career of it. Instead, he joined the air force and flew cargo planes between California and Vietnam, "going over with this and that and coming back with dead bodies in aluminum boxes." In the air force, Morland also got his first look at a real hydrogen bomb. It indeed looked quite bomblike, a streamlined missile shape with a point at one end and fins at the other. But Morland was taken aback by how small an H-bomb was—only six to eight feet long and a foot and a half in diameter. Somehow, the realization that a bomb one thousand times the strength of the one that hit Hiroshima could come in such a small package made the whole concept more terrifying to Morland. "They could be mishandled or abused so easily," he says, prompting him to ponder his childhood interest in the bomb.

To Morland, that meant pondering not only why, but how, *precisely* how, a nation went about building such things. It was the way Morland looked at the world. He is, according to one observer, "the sort of person who would not drive a car unless he knew how it worked." Thus when Morland became passionate about the antinuclear cause, it was natural that he would turn his considerable energy toward the technical workings of the nuclear armament.

He was also a natural for Sam Day and Erwin Knoll's new series for their magazine. Morland and the editors of *The Progressive* believed that the government had shrouded the H-bomb in secrecy for decades to keep Americans from questioning the nuclear arms race. Morland's assignment was to determine how much justification there was for such secrecy. On July 7, 1978, Morland wrote to *The Progressive:* "We agree[d] that nuclear weapons production has prospered too long in an atmosphere of freedom from public scrutiny. . . . I hope to know as much as it is legal to know—and possible for a layman to understand—about thermonuclear warhead design. I will then trace each major component through its fabrication process, starting with the mineral ore and ending with final assembly of the warhead. . . . Some of the needed information is classified, of course, and holes in the story will have to be filled by educated speculation." *The Progressive* advanced Morland five hundred dollars and helped him obtain permission to tour nuclear facilities.

Morland's first stop was Germantown, Maryland, where he met with Charles Gilbert, deputy director of the Division of Military Applications at the Department of Energy. Gilbert laid out the ground rules for Morland's research. Because Morland did not know what information was classified, he obviously did not know what questions he could and could not ask. They agreed that Morland should ask whatever he wanted, with the understanding that he might not get an answer. According to Morland, only once was he flatly told he was treading into classified territory.

Morland began to read, obsessively, about the H-bomb. He pulled out his old college textbooks, scoured public libraries from Boston to Los Alamos, and pored over the *Congressional Record*. He also toured nuclear facilities around the country, including Oak Ridge, and talked to everyone he could who was a member of the nuclear fraternity. To get scientists to open up, Morland used a standard journalistic technique—pretending to know more than he did. He would slip a concept into a conversation and wait for the frown, nod, or look of surprise that would tell him whether he was on the right track. "Of course you know," a subject would begin, and Morland, who of course did not know, would nod in encouragement, mentally rearranging his theories to accommodate each new piece of information.

As Morland came closer to what he believed to be the H-bomb secret, he was surprised to realize he had heard it before. A few months earlier, he had been lecturing on nuclear disarmament in a dormitory at the University of Alabama in Tuscaloosa. At the end of his lecture Morland asked, mostly in jest, if anyone knew the secret of the H-bomb. A young man in the back of the room raised his hand. "Sure, I know," the student said. "The secret is in the radiation reflectors." The young man explained that he knew people who worked at Oak Ridge. They had told him that the key was to reflect gamma and X rays in a way that would ignite the H-bomb fuel.

Morland did not think twice about the concept at the time, but after months of dogged research he became convinced that the college student did indeed have the secret concept. More important, Morland became convinced, as he had suspected all along, that it was not really secret at all. According to him, anyone with a basic knowledge of physics, and time and tenacity, could pull disparate public sources together into a coherent explanation of the workings of the hydrogen bomb.

The secret, Morland wrote in his article, is in the coupling mechanism that enables a fission, or atomic bomb, to trigger the far deadlier fusion or hydrogen bomb. "The physical pressure and heat generated by x- and gamma radiation moving outward from the trigger at the speed of light bounces against the weapon's inner wall and is reflected with enormous force into the sides of a carrot-shaped 'pencil' which contains the fusion fuel." That, Morland wrote, "within the limits of a single sentence," is the essence of the secret.

Morland insisted in his article that it was not dangerous for him to tell how a hydrogen bomb is made. First, he wrote, the article "falls far short of providing a blueprint for nuclear weapons." In addition, the money and technical resources needed to build an H-bomb were far beyond the capabilities of most nations. An atomic bomb was needed just to start the process. Finally, Morland explained, all of the information was already in the public domain, there for the taking by anyone with some basic science education and the desire "to put two and two together."

"The weapons are harder to believe than to understand," he wrote. Morland's ten-page article included seven diagrams of a thermonuclear weapon to help the nonscientist understand.

On March 2, 1979, Duane Sewell, other Department of Energy staff, and members of the Department of Justice were in *The Progressive*'s offices in Madison. Erwin Knoll and Sam Day insisted that all of the information in Morland's article came from public sources. They wanted to know exactly what in the article was classified. The answer, Duane Sewell explained, was classified as well. Instead, the Department of Energy offered to do a rewrite. Knoll's reaction to that proposal was expressed in a "few blunt expletives." *The Progressive*'s attorneys told Sewell that the government's offer was "more than objectionable" and requested a few days to decide what to do.

That same day, Attorney General Griffin Bell sent a memorandum to President Carter on the *Progressive* controversy. He explained that they were negotiating with the magazine to prevent publication, but failing that, he recommended immediate legal action. "While we cannot assure you that we will prevail in this suit," the attorney general wrote, "the potentially grave consequences to the security of the U.S. and the world itself resulting from the disclosure of the data are obvious and frightening." President Carter responded in longhand across the top of the memo: "Good move—proceed. J."

On March 7, attorneys for *The Progressive* notified the Department of Energy that the magazine intended to publish the article without alteration. The next day, the government filed suit before Judge Robert W. Warren in the Western District of Wisconsin to stop publication. *The Progressive* refused to give in, claiming it had a First Amendment right to publish.

Indeed, the First Amendment was the product of a long history of opposition to government censorship. Elaborate seventeenth-century licensing schemes prompted one of the most famous and impassioned arguments against prior restraint of the press. In *Areopagitica—a Speech for the Liberty of Unlicensed Printing*, John Milton wrote, "Truth and understanding are not such wares as to be monopolized and traded in by tickets and statutes and standards." To Milton, censorship was the "greatest discouragement and affront that can be offered to learning and to learned men." Furthermore, Milton wrote, human nature being what it is, there is simply no point in trying to stop the free flow of ideas and information through suppression of the press. "Evil manners," he warned, "are as perfectly learnt without books a thousand other ways which cannot be stopped."

Although licensing schemes had largely been abolished by 1700, the colonists in the New World developed an abhorrence of censorship and a firm conviction that a free press was essential to a free people. Since the First Amendment was drafted, there has been debate on whether it was intended to abolish prosecution of the press for libel and invasion of privacy, but there has been little doubt that the First Amendment was intended to prohibit censorship. In the first major Supreme Court case to consider the issue, *Near v. Minnesota* (1931), the Court stated, "It is the chief purpose of [liberty of the press] to prevent previous restraints upon publication." In *Near*, the state had permanently enjoined publication of a local newspaper on the grounds that it was a public nuisance. Although by all accounts the paper was a malicious scandal-mongering rag, the Court held that it could not be censored. Subsequent punishment, under libel or other laws, was the appropriate remedy under the First Amendment.

There has also always been debate on whether and the extent to which the First Amendment protects artistic, scientific, and commercial expression, but there has been no question that the First Amendment protects expression on matters of public import. In *New York Times v. Sullivan* (1964), the Supreme Court wrote of a "profound national commitment to the principle that debate on public issues should be uninhibited, robust, and wide-open."

Thus the *Progressive* case challenged fundamental beliefs about the First Amendment and questioned just how "uninhibited" the press can be in determining the form the public debate will take. The Constitution charges the executive branch with maintaining national security. Yet as Thomas Jefferson wrote just one year after the Bill of Rights became law, the First Amendment contemplates that "the only security of all is in a free press."

Under one view, there should be no limit, at least not from the government, on the press. This absolutist view holds that under the First Amendment, government censorship of the press can never be justified. Erwin Knoll is a staunch absolutist. He says that during the *Progressive* controversy he listened in amazement as an editor of the *San Francisco Examiner* delivered what was, at least in Knoll's eyes, "an impassioned defense of censorship."

"If I am sitting down there in the Rosebud Bar one afternoon," the editor said to Knoll, "and a drunken Marine Corps colonel tells me that he has marching orders the next day to invade Lebanon, *you're goddamn right* I want the government to stop me from printing it."

Knoll replied, "Do you mean to tell me that if you were sitting in the Rosebud Bar and you learned that in violation of the Constitution of the United States, the government was about to go to war without a declaration of Congress, you wouldn't regard that as news? I would. Oh, you bet I would publish that."

Would Knoll publish the name of a U.S. agent working in a foreign country? "It depends on what the agent is doing. . . . If there is an agent in another country undermining democracy in my name and at my expense, I sure would want everybody to know."

Even if revealing the agent's identity would cost him his life? "Sure, that's their job, they understand the risks. A guy who works on electric poles knows that he might fall or get a shock. A guy who becomes a CIA agent knows that he might get killed. That's an occupational hazard." Knoll says he may or may not publish such information, depending on whether he considers it "news"; but the decision is up to him, not the government.

In support of his position, Knoll looks to the words of the First Amendment itself. In this, he has from time to time had the support of members of the Supreme Court. Justice Hugo Black, for example, argued, "Madison and the other Framers of the First Amendment, able men that they were, wrote in language they earnestly believed could never be misunderstood: 'Congress shall make *no law* . . . abridging the freedom . . . of the press.'"

The absolutists, however, have never commanded a majority of the Court. In an important passage in *Near*, the Court stated, "The protection even as to prior restraint is not absolutely unlimited." Thus the Court created what has come to be known as the national security exception to the presumption against prior restraint. "No one would question," the Court wrote, "but that a government might prevent actual obstruction to its recruiting service or the publication of the sailing dates of transports or the number and location of troops."

Despite the Supreme Court's wording, this passage seems to have raised nothing but questions. As Justice Potter Stewart noted, the national security exception creates a "dilemma." By definition, areas of national security are dominated by the executive branch, often without the customary checks and balances from the other two branches of government. "For this reason," Justice Stewart wrote, "it is perhaps here that a press that is alert, aware, and free most vitally serves the basic purpose of the First Amendment." Yet it is elementary that successful diplomacy and defense require "both confidentiality and secrecy," and thus may require restraint of the press. Hence the dilemma.

In seeking to resolve the dilemma, courts cannot always rely on traditional free press principles. The national security exception founders when viewed in light of one of the bedrock concepts of the First Amendment—debate should be "robust and wide open," and through the free "marketplace of ideas" truth shall emerge. Here it is the very *disclosure* that is supposed to cause harm. The rules for robust debate cannot apply when the whole point is that one dare not speak.

In fact, one of the ironies of this aspect of freedom of the press is that because the right is so cherished, there is little guidance as to how to proceed. The presumption against prior restraint is so strong, there are very few cases on the subject. In the rare instance when the government does seek to impose a prior restraint, the case is hurried through the judicial process in an uncharacteristically feverish fashion, leaving important issues in somewhat of a blur.

Not until almost four decades after *Near* did the Supreme Court again have occasion to consider the question of government censorship of the press. It was the famed Pentagon Papers case in which Daniel Ellsberg leaked to *The New York Times* and *The Washington Post* admittedly classified information regarding events leading up to U.S. involvement in Vietnam. That case produced four different lower-court opinions and nine separate Supreme Court opinions—all in a matter of weeks. In fact, Chief Justice Burger refused to decide the issues raised by the Pentagon Papers case because it had zoomed up to the Court so rapidly that "we literally do not know what we are acting on." In the end, the Court voted six to three against the government's attempt to stop publication of the Pentagon Papers. Out of the confusion of nine separate opinions, a standard of sorts emerged. Two justices agreed that the government may not restrain the press unless it can prove that "publication must inevitably, directly, and immediately cause the occurrence of an event kindred to imperiling the safety of a transport already at sea." Whether this is indeed the legal standard in the clash between national security and the press is not completely clear. Whether the standard is appropriate in a case like the *Progressive* is even less clear.

How meaningful is a standard of "direct and immediate" harm in the area of thermonuclear weapons? When the harm alleged is, as the government claimed in the *Progressive* case, "potential destruction in a nuclear holocaust," how significant is the difference between a few days, months, or years? The enormity of the potential harm involved in the *Progressive* case threatened to overwhelm the usual rules of constitutional law.

On the other hand, attorneys for *The Progressive* argued that in the area of science, even thermonuclear science, the "dilemma" is easier, not harder, to resolve. In science, they said, the whole concept of secrecy is optimistic but outmoded. In support of their position, they cited no less an authority than Albert Einstein. In a January 22, 1947, letter (appealing for support for the Emergency Committee of Atomic Scientists), Einstein wrote:

> Through the release of atomic energy, our generation has brought into the world the most revolutionary force since prehistoric man's discovery of fire. This basic power of the universe cannot be fitted into the outmoded concept of narrow nationalisms. For there is no secret and there is no defense; there is no possibility of control except through the aroused understanding and insistence of the peoples of the world.

In addition, *The Progressive* had marshaled an array of leading nuclear scientists in support of its position. Many of *The Progressive*'s experts did not agree with the magazine's reasons for publishing the Morland article. Like the government, they did not think technical information was essential to an informed debate on nuclear weapons. They also felt Morland's science was sloppy. Nonetheless, they submitted affidavits stating that Morland's information was no longer a secret and that its publication could cause no harm.

The government, however, submitted affidavits from the secretaries of state, energy, and defense, the directors of most major nuclear weapon design laboratories, and Nobel laureate Hans Bethe. These experts stated that the Morland article contained crucial information not publicly available, which if published "would irreparably damage the national security of the United States by aiding foreign nations in developing thermonuclear weapons and so increasing the risk of thermonuclear war." The threatened harm was considerably more alarming than that alleged in the Pentagon Papers case. And the government had something else it did not have in the Pentagon Papers case—a statute authorizing it to stop the press.

The suit was brought under the Atomic Energy Act of 1954, an extraordinary statute designed to deal with an extraordinary subject. It is one of the few U.S. statutes that specifically grants the government the power of censorship. If nothing else, it shows that a government attempt to restrain the U.S. press is a most peculiar business.

Under the act, the government may sue to enjoin anyone who is about to disclose "restricted data." Restricted data includes all data concerning "the design, manufacture, or utilization of atomic weapons or the production of special nuclear material . . . *but shall not include data declassified or removed from the Restricted Data category.*" In other words, all such information is classified until it is declassified by the government. In government parlance, the information is "classified at birth." It does not matter whether the information is produced by a government employee toiling away in a laboratory or dreamed up by a private citizen sitting in his or her living room. The moment a formula, a design, an *idea* in the designated area is born, it is classified. Therefore, the government argued, even if Howard Morland did find all of his information in the public domain, the manner in which he put it together was classified until the government decided it was not.

The Atomic Energy Act also provides criminal sanctions. During the *Progressive* controversy, disclosure of restricted data was punishable by a fine of not more than ten thousand dollars or imprisonment for not more than ten years, or both. The good news, Erwin Knoll wrote at the time, was that the act no longer carried the death penalty.

Finally, a case brought under the Atomic Energy Act inevitably has a behind-the-looking-glass quality to it. On the one hand, the defendants in the *Progressive* case were forbidden to discuss or disclose any restricted data. On the other hand, they were not allowed to know what the restricted data was. They did not know what information in Morland's article, in the court papers, or in the whole universe of things was restricted. Morland, Knoll, and Day were under siege by a media full of questions, yet they could not respond.

Furthermore, any information introduced into court was in danger of being swept into the secrecy net. In support of his contention that he used no classified information, Morland prepared a voluminous affidavit citing his public sources. One source Morland submitted to the court was his college physics book with some passages underlined. The government said the textbook had to be kept secret until Morland's underlining was erased. Morland tried to explain that he had done the underlining as a college freshman in preparation for class, but by now the book had taken on a new character: it was a clue to the H-bomb secret.

Morland's affidavit also included a well-known *Encyclopedia Americana* article by Edward Teller, the "father of the H-Bomb." As one journalist later reported, "[The] Justice [Department] declared that Dr. Teller's article in the *Encyclopedia Americana* was secret, the affidavits by which it was introduced were secret, arguments over whether it was secret were secret, and the court's opinion about these secrets was secret."

When *The Progressive* objected to the government's censorship of its affidavits, some in the government said they objected to *The Progressive*'s use of the word *censorship*. "I have been told that the United States Attorney . . . prefers 'deletion,'" said Erwin Knoll. "I don't care if the government calls it banana cream pie. It's still censorship."

Judge Warren certainly recognized it as such. In a candid admission about his position as judge in the *Progressive* case, he wrote, "If a preliminary injunction is issued, it will constitute the first instance of prior restraint against a publication in this fashion in the history of this country, to this court's knowledge. Such notoriety is not to be sought."

On March 26, 1979, Judge Warren issued his opinion. First, he distinguished the case from that of the Pentagon Papers. Unlike the Pentagon Papers case, in which the executive branch was acting on its own in trying to stop the press, here Congress had passed a statute, the Atomic Energy Act, granting the power to enjoin. Judge Warren found that the statute was neither too vague nor overbroad under the First Amendment. He also found it significant that the Pentagon Papers case, in contrast to the *Progressive* case, involved only "historical data" relating to events some three to twenty years previously.

Finally, Judge Warren looked at the risk. "While it may be true in the long run, as Patrick Henry instructs us, that one would prefer death to life without liberty, nonetheless, in the short run, one cannot enjoy freedom of speech, freedom to worship or freedom of the press unless one first enjoys the freedom to live," he wrote. "A mistake in ruling against the United States could pave the way for thermonuclear annihilation for us all. In that event, our right to life is extinguished and the right to publish becomes moot." Judge Warren "regretfully" issued the historic prior restraint.

The Progressive immediately appealed, vowing, indeed hoping, to go to the Supreme Court. A few weeks later the government's case began to unravel.

On May 9, 1979, Dimitri Rotow, an amateur nuclear weapons designer and ACLU investigator working on behalf of *The Progressive*, walked into the Los Alamos Scientific Laboratory public library, looked in the card catalogue under "weapons," and pulled UCRL-4725 from the shelf. It turned out that the document contained much of the same "secret" restricted data that was in the Morland article. The government claimed UCRL-4725 had been declassified by mistake. It had somehow been overlooked in a review of the library just a year previously, prompted by another, unrelated, incident in which Rotow had found supposedly classified material sitting on the public shelf.

Because of Rotow's finding, many in the Justice Department wanted to drop the case. But intelligence sources assured the attorney general that, regardless of the Los Alamos incident and Morland's claims, the information in the article had not reached "sensitive" foreign powers. Attorney General Bell exhorted his staff, "The public interest and the Atomic Energy Act require that we do our best . . . some disclosure does not mandate full disclosure."

The *Progressive* case was, however, fast proving John Milton right. His three-hundred-year-old argument against prior restraint was based in part on the belief that, in the end, it simply does not work. "Evil manners," it seems, are indeed as "perfectly learnt" in a thousand ways that cannot be stopped . . . at least in this instance. The government had become, as Milton predicted, "like that gallant man who thought to pound up the crows by shutting the park gate."

Some reporters deliberately set out to duplicate Morland's feat and, using their public libraries, came fairly close. Other journalists, in trying to cover the *Progressive* case, apparently kept bumping into the H-bomb secret. "Quite by accident," the *Columbia Journalism Review* reported, "we have stumbled onto what we believe to be the 'secret' of the H-bomb." Then a California man named Chuck Hansen entered the fray.

Hansen, who has been described as a "nuclear hobbyist" or "H-bomb fan," mounted a campaign against the government's action in the *Progressive* case. He blanketed the Department of Energy and his congressman with letters of protest. He launched an

"H-bomb design contest"—the first entry to be classified by the Department of Energy would be the winner. Then, in the fall of 1979, he sent a letter to Senator Charles Percy outlining his own version of the H-bomb secret in terms similar to those in Morland's article. He helpfully sent the letter along to several newspapers across the country.

On September 16, a small Wisconsin newspaper, the *Madison Press Connection*, published the Hansen letter. The next day, the government dropped its case against *The Progressive*. Finally, they felt the secret was out. "The printing of the Hansen letter by one publication, an action that was reported throughout the world, made pointless any effort to restrain publication by others," says Griffin Bell.

The November 1979 issue of *The Progressive* carried the full-page headline "THE H-BOMB SECRET. HOW WE GOT IT—WHY WE'RE TELLING IT." It was the original cover designed for the April issue. Inside, Howard Morland's article was printed in full. Although during the lawsuit Morland had discovered that his article contained some technical errors, "not a word, not a comma" was changed. (Morland added a one-page correction at the end.)

"Read Howard Morland's article," Erwin Knoll wrote in an introductory comment. "Feel free to challenge his facts or the conclusions he draws from them. Feel free to question our editing of the article, our judgment in publishing it. But most of all, *feel free*—more free than any of us were for the six months and nineteen days when the article could not be printed by us or read by you."

Some say that the *Progressive* case has forever changed the face of the First Amendment. It is not impregnable; a prior restraint can be had. Conversely, others argue that the case, especially coming on the heels of the Pentagon Papers case, only proves the futility and embarrassment of government attempts to restrain the U.S. press.

For his part, Griffin Bell says, "I don't think prior restraint does work [in cases like the *Progressive*]." Nonetheless, he still firmly believes that the magazine was wrong to publish the H-bomb article and that the government was right to try to stop it. Charged with the responsibility of protecting national security and given the same set of facts, Griffin Bell says he would do the same again. Erwin Knoll, on the other hand, says he would do things quite differently. He would not have held up publication of the article and he would not have obeyed the court's order of silence regarding restricted data during the trial. "I would have tried to find out what I could," says Knoll, "and published it."

A decade after publication of "The H-Bomb Secret," it is difficult to determine the extent to which the government's predictions of terrible harm have come true. To the average American there is no discernible effect. But according to some government officials, publication of the article did harm the national security of the United States. The exact nature of the harm, however, is a secret.

Lawrence "Tiger" O'Rourke, a member of the Yurok Indian tribe, who tried to stop the government highway
CAROLINE KENNEDY

Walter "Black Snake" Lara, Yurok chairman of the Northwest Indian Cemetery Protective Association, standing at the entrance to the proposed G-O Road
CAROLINE KENNEDY

Freedom of Religion: *Lyng v. Northwest Indian Cemetery Protective Association*

"Congress shall make no law respecting an establishment of religion, or prohibiting the free exercise thereof . . ."

W<small>HEN THE DOGWOOD TREE</small> blossomed twice and a whale swam into the mouth of the Klamath River, the Yurok medicine man knew it was time for the tribe to perform the White Deer Skin Dance. He knew that these natural signs were messengers sent by the Great Spirit to tell the people things were out of balance in the world. The White Deer Skin Dance and Jump Dance are part of the World Renewal Ceremonies of the Yurok, Karok, Tolowa, and Hoopa Indian tribes of northern California. The World Renewal Ceremonies are performed to protect the earth from catastrophe and humanity from disease and to bring the physical and spiritual world back in balance. Preparations for the ceremonies begin far up in the mountains, in the wilderness known to the Indians as the sacred "high country."

According to Indian mythology, the World Renewal Ceremonies were initiated by the *woge*, spirits that inhabited the earth before the coming of man. The *woge* gave culture and all living things to humanity, and the ceremonies are held at sites along the river where these gifts were given. The *woge* then became afraid of human contamination and retreated to the mountains before ascending into a hole in the sky. Because the mountains were the *woge*'s last refuge on earth, they are the source of great spiritual power.

In recent years, there has been a quiet resurgence of traditional Indian religion in the high country. Young Indians who left to find jobs on the "other side of the mountain" are returning to their ancestral grounds. Lawrence "Tiger" O'Rourke, a thirty-two-year-old member of the Yurok tribe, worked for eight years around the state as a building contractor before returning to raise fish in the traditional Indian way.

"In the white man's world . . . you just spend all of your lifetime making money and gathering up things around you and it doesn't really have any value," Tiger says. "Here, the Spirit is still in everything—the trees, the rocks, the river . . . the different kinds of people. It's got a life spirit, so we're all connected. . . . The concrete world, it's kind of dead. It feels like something's missing and the people are afraid. . . . So this place is just right for me, I guess."

There are about five thousand others who, like Tiger, are happy to live in isolation from the "white man's world"; indeed the spiritual life of the high country depends on it. But when the U.S. Forest Service announced plans to build a logging road through the heart of the high country, many of the Yurok tribe decided they could not remain quiet any longer.

They went to court, claiming that the logging road would violate their First Amendment right to freely exercise their religion. They said it was like building a "highway through the Vatican." What the Indians wanted the courts to understand was that the salmon-filled creeks, singing pines, and mountain trails of the high country were their Vatican.

To prepare for the World Renewal Ceremony, the medicine man first notifies the dance givers that it is time. According to Indian law, only certain families are allowed to give dances and to own dance regalia. The privilege and the responsibility are passed down from generation to generation.

"In the beginning," says Tiger, a member of such a family, "the Spirit came up the river and he stayed at different people's houses. He only knocked and went in where he knew the people would take care of him. They would have a responsibility to the people, and the world, and the universe to make the ceremony, and they would always do it. It's a lot of work. You have to live a good life, you have to live with truth. Not everybody could do it."

The dance giver is also responsible for paying up all debts before the dance. Indian law puts a price on everything, and by paying the price the social balance is restored. If you insult someone, you owe that person a certain amount; if you kill a person, you must pay that person's family. Payment prevents hatred and anger from spreading to infect the community and brings the world back into harmony.

Next, the medicine man must prepare for the World Renewal Ceremony. He must cleanse and purify himself to receive the "power" from the Spirit. Without it, the dance will fail. He must fast for ten days, eating only enough acorn gruel to prevent dehydration. He must cook and eat alone, for he cannot make eye contact with any impure person who might pollute his medicine.

Once purified, the medicine man ascends into the high country to receive the power. Known in Indian language as *wagay*, which translates roughly as "way out there," the high country is a remote area five to seven thousand feet up in northern California's Siskiyou Mountains, about twenty miles east of the Pacific Ocean and thirty miles south of the Oregon border. Today, it is part of Six Rivers National Forest.

The most sacred area of the high country is known as Medicine Mountain, a ridge dominated by the peaks of Doctor Rock, Peak 8, and Chimney Rock. Chimney Rock, a majestic outcropping of pinkish basalt, rises sixty-seven hundred feet above sea level. From its summit, views of receding blue waves of mountain ridges fade into the horizon in all directions. On a clear day, the shimmer of the Pacific Ocean gleams at the end of the winding silver ribbon of the Smith River below.

Once the medicine man reaches Chimney Rock he uses Rhythm Sticks to enter a trancelike state in which he will communicate with the Spirit World. He may remain on the rock all night, or for a number of days and nights, until he receives a sign from the Creator that the ceremonies may begin.

Indian doctors, primarily women, also use the high country for training and to gather medicinal herbs. They train at Doctor Rock, another lower outcropping on Medicine Mountain. Doctors must also purify themselves by fasting, and may spend days or nights dancing and singing on Doctor Rock's prayer seat, a stone slab enclosed on three sides with an opening facing the dawn. The connection between doctoring and the high country is particularly strong because the doctors draw their healing powers from the *woge*. When they die, doctors' souls follow the *woge* to the mountains, adding to the power that can be obtained there.

Although only a few medicine men and Indian doctors actively use the sacred sites of the high country, the spiritual well-being of the entire tribe depends on performance of the ancient rituals. Despite more than a half century during which the government removed Indians from their villages and prohibited them from speaking their own language or practicing their religion, a few elderly Indians never left or gave up the old ways. Some young Indians, like Tiger, are returning to their homeland. And others, like Walter "Black Snake" Lara, are trying to balance the old world with the new.

Black Snake works felling trees. He says it is an honorable job in many parts of the lush California forests, but not in the high country. Of the sacred grounds he says, "The Creator fixed it that way for us. We're responsible for it."

Tiger, Black Snake, and others are struggling to maintain their fragile way of life. They are succeeding in part because the steep mountains, dense forests, and nonnavigable streams have protected their cemeteries, villages, and high country from encroachment by the "concrete" world. To them, the proposed highway was more than just a symbol of that concrete world. By the Forest Service's own estimates, each day it would bring about seventy-two diesel logging trucks and ninety other vehicles within a half mile of Chimney Rock.

Actually, the Forest Service started constructing a logging road through the Six Rivers National Forest in the 1930s. It began at either end, in the lumber-mill towns of Gasquet to the north and Orleans to the south, thus becoming known as the G-O Road. Under the Forest Service's management plan, once the road was completed, the towns would be connected and timber could be hauled to mills at either end of the forest. In the meantime, as construction inched toward Chimney Rock, new areas of timber were opened up to logging. "They snuck that road in from both sides," says Black Snake.

By the 1970s, the two segments of the seventy-five-mile road dead-ended in the forest. Black pavement simply gave way to gravel and dirt, and then the side of a mountain. The final six-mile section needed to complete the road was known as the Chimney Rock section of the G-O Road.

The Indians feared that if the road was built it would destroy the sanctity of the high country forever. As Sam Jones, a full-blooded Yurok dance giver put it, "When the medicine lady goes out there to pray, she stands on these rocks and meditates. The forest is there looking out. [She] talks to the trees and rocks, whatever is out there. After they get through praying, their answer comes from the mountain. Our people talk in their language to them and if it's all logged off and all bald there, they can't meditate at all. They have nothing to talk to."

An influx of tree fellers, logging trucks, tourists, and campers would also destroy the ability to make medicine in the high country. The consequences were grave; if the medicine man could not bring back the power for the World Renewal Ceremonies, the people's religious existence would be threatened. And because the land itself is considered holy by the Indians, they could not move their "church" to another location. "People don't understand about our place," Black Snake says, "because they can build a church and worship wherever they want."

The Indians filed a lawsuit in federal district court in San Francisco: *Northwest Indian Cemetery Protective Association v. Peterson.* (R. Max Peterson was named as defendant in his capacity as chief of the U.S. Forest Service.) They claimed that construction of the G-O Road would destroy the solitude, privacy, and undisturbed natural setting necessary to Indian religious practices, thereby violating their First Amendment right to freely exercise their religion.

By invoking the First Amendment, the Indians joined those before them who had sought religious freedom in America. After all, many colonists came to the New World to escape religious persecution in the Old, establishing colonies that reflected the varied beliefs of their inhabitants. The Puritans of Massachusetts sought to build their "City on a Hill," Lord Baltimore founded Maryland as a colony where Catholics and Protestants would live together and prosper, William Penn led the Quakers to Philadelphia, and the Virginia planters were strong supporters of the Church of England.

The reality of religious life in the colonies, however, often did not fulfill these ideals. Those who did not share the beliefs of the dominant group were often banished, imprisoned, fined, and persecuted. They were also taxed and compelled to attend government-sponsored churches whose ministers preached inflammatory sermons designed to bolster the established religion by stirring hatred against dissenters. By the time of the American Revolution, every colonial government imposed religious tests for public office, and eight of the thirteen colonies had established an official religion.

After Independence, though the United States remained essentially a Protestant nation, state-established religion met with increasing opposition. New immigrants, growing numbers of Baptists and Presbyterians, and those who resented restrictions on the promise of freedom that had brought them to America, joined forces to oppose the state systems. This resistance culminated in a battle waged by Thomas Jefferson and James Madison against Patrick Henry's 1784 bill proposing tax-supported religion in Virginia. Madison led the opposition with his famous "Memorial and Remonstrance Against Religious Assessments," circulated in 1785, in which he set forth his conviction that a man's spiritual life is no concern of his political governors.

> The Religion then of every man must be left to the conviction and conscience of every man; and it is the right of every man to exercise it as these may dictate. This right is in its nature an unalienable right . . . because the opinions of men, depending only on the evidence contemplated by their own minds, cannot follow the dictates of other men. . . . Before any man can be considered as a member of Civil Society, he must be considered as a subject of the Governor of the Universe. . . . We maintain therefore that in matters of Religion, no man's right is abridged by the institution of Civil Society, and that Religion is wholly exempt from its cognizance.

Madison and his allies succeeded in postponing consideration of the bill while opposition mounted. In 1786, he reintroduced Thomas Jefferson's "Bill for Establishing Religious Freedom," which had previously been shelved by the legislature. Instead of tax-supported religion, Jefferson's bill proclaimed religious freedom, banned compulsory attendance or support of any religious institution, and forbade religious tests for office. It also declared that any reversal of its provisions would infringe the "natural rights of mankind." This time it passed by an overwhelming majority.

Jefferson's statute served as one of Madison's models for the First Amendment, which, as adopted and ratified, has two components: the establishment clause and the free exercise clause. In general terms, according to the Supreme Court, the "establishment of religion clause of the First Amendment means at least this: Neither a state nor the Federal Government can set up a church. Neither can pass laws which aid one religion, aid all religions, or prefer one religion over another. . . . In the words of Jefferson, the clause against establishment of religion by law was intended to erect 'a wall of separation between church and State.'" Courts have relied on the establishment clause to strike down state support for parochial schools, statutes mandating school prayer, and the erection of religious displays (for example, nativity scenes or menorahs) on public property.

In contrast, the free exercise clause forbids the government from outlawing religious belief. It also forbids the government from unduly burdening the exercise of a religious belief. However, some regulation of conduct expressing belief is permitted. If a person claims that a government action violates his right to freely exercise his religion, courts must first determine if the asserted religious belief is "sincerely held." If so, then the burden on individual worship must be balanced against the state's interest in proceeding with the challenged action. Only if the state's interest is "compelling" will it outweigh the individual's right to the free exercise of religion.

In the two hundred years since the First Amendment was ratified, the free exercise clause has protected many whose religious beliefs have differed from those of the majority. For example, the Supreme Court has held that unemployment benefits could not be denied to a Seventh-Day Adventist fired for refusing to work on Saturday, her sabbath; nor to a Jehovah's Witness who quit his job in a weapons production factory for religious reasons. Forcing these individuals to choose between receiving benefits and following their respective religious practices violated their right to the free exercise of religion.

In 1983, the Federal District Court for the Northern District of California held that completion of the G-O Road would violate the Northwest Indians' right to freely exercise their religion. The court concluded that the G-O Road would unconstitutionally burden their exercise of sincerely held religious beliefs, and the government's interest in building the road was not compelling enough to override the Indians' interest. Therefore, the court enjoined, or blocked, the Forest Service from completing the road. When the decision was announced, the group of fifty to a hundred Indians who had traveled south to attend the trial were convinced that their medicine had been successful.

The government appealed the decision to the Ninth Circuit Court of Appeals. While the case was pending, Congress passed the California Wilderness Act, which designated much of the sacred high country as a wilderness area. Thus all commercial activity, including mining or timber harvesting, was forever banned. But as part of a compromise worked out to secure passage of the act, Congress exempted a twelve-hundred-foot-wide corridor from the wilderness, just enough to complete the G-O Road. So although the surrounding area could not be destroyed, the road could still be built. That decision was left to the Forest Service. The medicine was still working, however; in July 1986, the Ninth Circuit affirmed the district court's decision and barred completion of the road.

The government then appealed the case to the U.S. Supreme Court. It filed a "petition for certiorari," a request that the Court hear the case. The Supreme Court receives thousands of these "cert" petitions each year, but accepts only about 150 for argument and decision. In order to take the case, four justices must vote to grant "cert." If they do not, the lower-court ruling stands. Because freedom of religion is so important in the constitutional scheme, and because the case involved principles affecting the management of vast tracts of federal land, *Northwest Indian Cemetery Protective Association* was one of the 150 cases accepted.

The Indians based their Supreme Court arguments on their victories in the lower courts and on a landmark 1972 Supreme Court case, *Wisconsin v. Yoder*. In *Yoder*, three Amish parents claimed that sending their children to public high school, as required by law, violated their right to free exercise of religion. They explained that the Old Order Amish religion was devoted to a simple life in harmony with nature and the soil, untainted by influence from the contemporary world. The Amish said that public schools emphasized intellectual accomplishment, individual distinction, competition, and social life. In contrast, "Amish society emphasize[d] informal learning-through-doing; a life of 'goodness,' rather than a life of intellect; wisdom, rather than technical knowledge; community welfare, rather than competition; and separation from, rather than integration with, contemporary worldly society." The Amish said that forcing their children out of the Amish community into a world undeniably at odds with their fundamental beliefs threatened their eternal salvation. Therefore, they claimed, state compulsory education laws violated their right to freely exercise their religion. The Supreme Court agreed.

If the Supreme Court could find that freedom of religion outweighed the state's interest in compulsory education, the Indians believed that the Constitution would make room for them too. After all, Chief Justice Warren Burger had written in *Yoder*, "A way of life that is odd or even erratic but interferes with no rights or interests of others is not to be condemned because it is different." The Indians argued that, like the Amish, they wanted only to be left alone to worship, as they had for thousands of years.

But the Forest Service argued that the Indians were seeking something fundamentally different from what the Amish had won. Whereas the exemption from a government program in *Yoder* affected only the Amish, and "interfere[d] with no rights or interests of others," the Indians were trying to stop the government from managing its own resources. From the government's point of view, if the courts allowed these Indians to block the G-O Road, it would open the door for other religious groups to interfere with government action on government lands everywhere. (It did not matter to the government that the Indians considered the high country to be *their* land.) The Forest Service produced a map marked to indicate sacred religious sites in California; the red markers nearly covered the state. Giving the Indians veto power over federal land management decisions was not, in the government's view, what the free exercise clause was intended to protect. As Justice William O. Douglas once wrote, "The Free Exercise Clause is written in terms of what the government cannot do to the individual, not in terms of what the individual can exact from the government."

The singing pines, soaring eagles, and endless mountain vistas of northern California are about as far from the white marble Supreme Court on Capitol Hill as it is possible to get in the United States. Yet like thousands of Americans before them, a small group of Indians came in November 1987 to watch their case argued before the highest court in the land. Though the Indians had never put much faith in any branch of the government, they had come to believe that if the justices could see the case through "brown eyes," they would finally make room in the Bill of Rights for the "first Americans."

Some did not realize that by the time a case reaches the Supreme Court, it no longer involves only those individuals whose struggle initiated it, but has enduring repercussions throughout the country. Unlike a legal code or statute that is written with specificity, "a constitution," wrote Chief Justice John Marshall, "is framed for ages to come, and is designed to approach immortality, as nearly as human institutions can approach it." When the Supreme Court decides a case based on the Bill of Rights, it enunciates principles that become the Supreme Law of the Land, and are used by lower courts across the United States to guide their decisions.

The Indians lost by one vote. "The Constitution simply does not provide a principle that could justify upholding [the Indians'] legal claims," Justice Sandra Day O'Connor wrote for the majority. "However much we wish that it were otherwise, government simply could not operate if it were required to satisfy every citizen's religious needs and desires."

The Court accepted that the G-O Road could have "devastating effects on traditional Indian religious practices." Nonetheless, it held that the G-O Road case differed from *Yoder* because here, the government was not *coercing* the Indians to act contrary to their religious beliefs. In what may prove to be an important development in the law, the Court concluded that unless the government *coerces* individuals to act in a manner that violates their religious beliefs, the free exercise clause is not implicated, and the government does not have to provide a compelling reason for its actions.

The Court also noted the broad ramifications of upholding the

Indians' free exercise claim. While the Indians did not "at present" object to others using the high country, their claim was based on a need for privacy in the area. According to the Court, under the Indians' reasoning there was nothing to prevent them, or others like them, from seeking to exclude all human activity but their own from land they held sacred. "No disrespect for the [Indian] practices is implied when one notes that such beliefs could easily require *de facto* beneficial ownership of some rather spacious tracts of public property," the Court wrote.

Justice William Brennan's emotional dissent rejected the Court's reasoning and result. The religious freedom remaining to the Indians after the Supreme Court's decision, according to Justice Brennan, "amounts to nothing more than the right to believe that their religion will be destroyed . . . the safeguarding of such a hollow freedom . . . fails utterly to accord with the dictates of the First Amendment." Justice Brennan and the two justices who joined him, Thurgood Marshall and Harry Blackmun, rejected the Court's new "coercion test."

"The Court . . . concludes that even where the Government uses federal land in a manner that threatens the very existence of a Native American religion, the Government is simply not 'doing' anything to the practitioners of that faith," Justice Brennan wrote. "Ultimately the Court's coercion test turns on a distinction between government actions that compel affirmative conduct inconsistent with religious belief, and those governmental actions that prevent conduct consistent with religious belief. In my view, such a distinction is without constitutional significance." The dissenters believed instead that the Indians' religion would be severely burdened, indeed made "impossible," by the government's actions, and that the government had not shown a compelling interest in completing the road.

"They might as well rewrite the Constitution. They teach us we have freedom of religion and freedom of speech, but it's not true," says Tiger O'Rourke. "This was our place first time, our home. It's still our home, but we don't have the same rights as other Americans."

Currently, the G-O Road is stalled. The Indians are challenging the Forest Service on environmental grounds and attempting to get Congress to add the G-O Road corridor to the existing, protected wilderness area.

Like many Americans, Tiger and Black Snake say they never thought much about the Constitution until it touched their lives directly. Among the tribes of northern California, defeat has fired a new fight for their way of life, spurred intertribal outreach and educational efforts, and brought a new awareness of the legal system. "We *have* to understand the Constitution now," says Tiger O'Rourke. "We still need our line of warriors, but now they've got to be legal warriors. That's the war now, and it's the only way we're going to survive."

*   *   *

N.B. On October 28, 1990, the last day of its session, the 101st Congress passed legislation adding the G-O Road corridor to the Siskiyou Wilderness. This legislation ensures that the logging road will not be completed; its two spurs will remain dead-ended in the forest beneath Chimney Rock. Because the area was protected to preserve the environment rather than the Indians' religion, the Indians found their victory bittersweet. "It's all right for us. We'll use the area as we always have," says Black Snake. "But we didn't accomplish what we set out to accomplish for other tribes. [We] can't win one on beliefs." But, he adds, "maybe it's the Creator's way of seeing just how sincere we are."

J ulius and Tina Hobson at a press conference in Washington, D.C., 1971

THE WASHINGTON POST; *REPRINTED BY PERMISSION OF THE D.C. PUBLIC LIBRARY*

Freedom of Assembly:
Hobson v. Wilson

"Congress shall make no law abridging the right of
the people peaceably to assemble, and to petition the
Government for a redress of grievances."

By August of 1969, Abe Bloom
and Arthur Waskow were spending almost every night planning a
massive demonstration against the Vietnam War scheduled for
November 15 in Washington, D.C. Bloom, an electronics engineer
by training, was treasurer of the New Mobilization Committee to
End the War in Vietnam (New Mobe). Waskow, a Ph.D. historian
and scholar, was a member of the New Mobe Steering Committee. Like Bloom, he had attended or spoken at every major demonstration in Washington in the 1960s, including one where he
was arrested for chaining himself to the door of the Selective Service building to protest the draft.

One of the New Mobe's biggest challenges was to get the local
black community to participate. Though many black leaders condemned the war, the local black community often had other concerns. "At that particular time blacks were struggling for things
like decent housing and decent job opportunities," says Reverend
David Eaton, the senior minister at All Souls Church, who was
active in both the civil rights movement and the peace movement. "The liberal white community seemed to be only interested

in the Vietnam War situation. So you had a difference in priorities [which] did generate some animosity."

The New Mobe had secured a commitment from Coretta Scott King to lead the November march, and New Mobe volunteers were actively recruiting local black leaders such as Eaton and Julius Hobson. Although not nationally well known, Julius Hobson was a central figure in Washington's black community. A statistician for the Department of Health, Education, and Welfare (HEW) for most of his working life, Julius Hobson led the effort to desegregate Washington, D.C. He successfully sued the school system in 1962, led demonstrations to desegregate housing and hospitals in Washington, and as president of the Congress of Racial Equality (CORE) from 1960 to 1964, he organized more than eighty picket lines on downtown retail stores, resulting in the initial employment of five thousand black citizens. In the fall of 1969, Julius Hobson was engaged to marry Tina Lower, a divorced white mother of two who worked at the Civil Service Commission. Hobson was perhaps the most prominent local black leader to oppose the Vietnam War. Along with Mrs. King, he was scheduled to speak at the New Mobe demonstration on November 15.

The New Mobe was also anxious to have the participation of the Black United Front (BUF), a local organization whose founders included Julius Hobson and Reverend David Eaton. But some members of the BUF, including Reverend Doug Moore, were less than enthusiastic. Moore felt that Washington, D.C., a city with a large black population, spent too much of its resources on white demonstrators. The huge protests, often organized by predominantly white groups like the New Mobe, required extra work by city administrators, police, traffic control, and the department of sanitation. Moore floated the idea of asking the New Mobe to donate money to the black community to offset the expenses of the demonstrations.

In August, the BUF set up a meeting with the New Mobe Steering Committee to discuss Moore's proposal. Both Abe Bloom and Arthur Waskow attended. Moore suggested that the New Mobe pay a one-dollar-per-demonstrator fee to the BUF. The idea became known as the "head tax." According to Bloom, the proposal "immediately created a split in the [New Mobe] because all the people were participants in various civil rights activities. They related to the black community, they wanted to get participation from the black community, and many of them felt we should honor such a request. On the other hand, there was a feeling that the right to demonstrate . . . was inherent . . . and should not be taxed in any way."

Within the BUF the idea also faced opposition. Julius Hobson was furious at the attempt to charge money. "He strongly believed that as Washington is the center of the government, this is where demonstrations should happen," says Tina Hobson.

Arthur Waskow, however, thought the idea had merit. Largely at his urging, the New Mobe was still debating the proposal when Abe Bloom received a typewritten letter signed "Rev. Moore," demanding that the New Mobe make an immediate contribution of twenty-five thousand dollars to the BUF. People at the New Mobe found the tone of the letter "incredibly offensive" says Waskow. "The initial [proposal], whether one agreed with it or not, was an authentic proposal to be negotiated. It was the letter which made enormous trouble."

This was exactly what the FBI had in mind. Although the Hobsons, Waskow, Eaton, and Bloom did not know it, the letter did not come from Reverend Doug Moore at all. It was written by an agent in the Washington Field Office (WFO) of the FBI as part of a secret counterintelligence program known internally as COIN-TELPRO.

FBI agents assigned to COINTELPRO were directed to investigate groups and individuals that the Bureau perceived as dangerous. They were also ordered to thwart the efforts of these targets through disruption, interference, and harassment. Antiwar and civil rights groups were targeted by two branches of COINTELPRO: COINTELPRO–New Left and COINTELPRO–Black Nationalist.

COINTELPRO–New Left was established in May 1968. A memo from Charles Brennan, chief of the Internal Security Section of the FBI, recommended a counterintelligence program "to expose, disrupt, and otherwise neutralize" those in the antiwar movement.

> Our Nation is undergoing an era of violence and disruption caused to a large extent by various individuals generally connected with the New Left. Some of these activists urge revolution in America and call for the defeat of the United States in Vietnam. They

continually and falsely allege police brutality and do not hesitate to utilize unlawful acts of violence to further their so-called causes. The New Left has on many occasions viciously and scurrilously attacked the Director and the Bureau in an attempt to hamper our investigation of it and drive us off the college campuses.

The memo was initialed "O.K. H" on the bottom, signifying that J. Edgar Hoover approved.

Five days later, a three-page letter was sent to FBI field offices around the country informing them of the new program and exhorting them to take action.

> The purpose of this program is to expose, disrupt, and otherwise neutralize the activities of the various New Left organizations, their leadership and adherents. . . . In every instance, consideration should be given to disrupting the organized activity of these groups and no opportunity should be missed to capitalize on organizational and personal conflicts of their leadership.

COINTELPRO–Black Nationalist was established in response to increasing militancy in the civil rights and black power movements after the Newark and Detroit riots of 1967. An "airtel," or FBI medium-priority communication, sent by headquarters to FBI field offices around the country, set forth the five major goals of COINTELPRO–Black Nationalist:

> 1. Prevent the *coalition* of militant black nationalist groups (an effective coalition of black nationalist groups might be the first step toward a real "Mau Mau" in America, the beginning of a true black revolution).
> 2. Prevent the *rise of a "messiah"* who could unify, and electrify, the militant black nationalist movement.
> 3. Prevent *violence* on the part of black nationalist groups. Through counterintelligence it should be possible to pinpoint potential troublemakers and neutralize them before they exercise their potential for violence.
> 4. Prevent militant black nationalist groups and leaders from gaining *respectability*, by discrediting them to three separate segments of the community. . . . First, to the responsible Negro community, second . . . to the white community, both the responsible community and to "liberals" who have vestiges of sympathy for militant black nationalists simply because they are Negroes. Third . . . in the eyes of Negro radicals.
> 5. Prevent the long-range *growth* of militant black nationalist organizations especially among youth.

Both COINTELPROS were to be kept completely secret. FBI memos repeatedly stressed that no counterintelligence action was to be initiated by field offices without specific authorization from headquarters in Washington, and "under no circumstances should the existence of the program be made known outside the Bureau."

A rift over the head-tax issue between antiwar activists and the black community was tailor-made for the FBI. In fact, on August 21, 1969, an airtel outlining the controversy between the New Mobe and the BUF was sent from FBI headquarters to field offices in eight cities where the New Mobe had representatives. It stated, "The Washington Field Office has recommended, and the Bureau concurs that this is an ideal situation to exploit through the counterintelligence program. . . . Recipient offices are to furnish recommendations for such action without fail. . . . The [New Mobe] can be accused of racism in refusing to go along with this demand."

In late September, Julius Hobson informed the New Mobe that he refused to sit on the podium or speak at the November 15 demonstration if any money was collected for the head tax.

By October 1, a special agent in the FBI's Washington Field Office had drafted a news release to be provided to a "friendly" news source for publication a week before the demonstration. It was titled "Members of the BUF Express Shock at Hobson Stand." According to the FBI's own cover memo, the release was intended to embarrass the BUF, cause Black leaders to view each other with suspicion, and discredit Julius Hobson, possibly forcing him to resign from the BUF. The release claimed that an unidentified BUF official felt Hobson's refusal to speak at the November 15 demonstration "clearly revealed him to be an Uncle Tom, willing to sell out the interests of the black community to white intellectuals, thus exposing his black brothers to a violent confrontation with the police should disorders take place during peace movement demonstrations." It was a total fabrication.

Meanwhile, Doug Moore, who had never seen the letter the FBI sent to Bloom over his name, was waiting for a reply to his original proposal for a head tax. On October 10, the FBI's New York Field Office proposed sending a leaflet that would appear to be the New Mobe response. In accordance with headquarters' instructions, the leaflet was designed to widen the rift between the

New Mobe and the BUF. Five days later, headquarters approved the plan. The authorization said, "Take all necessary steps to protect the identity of the Bureau as the source of these leaflets."

In early November, Doug Moore received the FBI's leaflet. It was yellow. It had a black monkey on it, and it was titled "Give them Bananas!" (opposite). The leaflet was signed "Sid," whom Moore presumed to be Sidney Peck, another member of the New Mobe Steering Committee.

After the leaflet was received, the atmosphere between the groups became one of hostility and "mutual disgust," says Tina Hobson. Communication between the organizations was practically nonexistent.

Despite the widening rift between the black and white groups, the mass rally was still set for Saturday, November 15. Three days before, there was a March Against Death. The forty-hour candlelight procession began at Arlington National Cemetery, where demonstrators picked up placards bearing the names of GIs killed in Vietnam, carried them past the White House, where they called out the names of the dead soldiers, then continued on to the Capitol, where each sign was placed in a coffin.

The November 15 demonstration also went ahead as planned. The New Mobe's efforts had paid off. In spite of freezing temperatures and a cold north wind, it was the biggest rally ever held in Washington until that time. More than three hundred thousand demonstrators marched up Pennsylvania Avenue, then down Fifteenth Street to a rally at the Washington Monument. Demonstrators bearing forty coffins filled with the names of the war dead led the march, followed by a large banner that read "SILENT MAJORITY FOR PEACE." Senators Eugene McCarthy and George McGovern, along with Coretta King, Dick Gregory, and Julius Hobson, linked arms to lead the parade. It lasted into the afternoon and the rally continued until dark.

Although black leaders participated in the march, the campaign to encourage black involvement did not succeed. According to Tina Hobson, "[Our] efforts to get black people to march were not effective. We were disappointed that there weren't more black citizens that participated."

It is impossible to know how the demonstration would have been different, or if the BUF and the New Mobe would have ever united without FBI interference, but both sides trace the hostility

Give them BANANAS!

We see where the New Mobilization Committee - organizing group for the march on Washington November 15th - has had the blocks thrown to it by the so-called BLACK UNITED FRONT, which demands much bread for any peace activity in the Amerikan capital.

BUF leader, the Rev. Douglas Moore, at first requested the modest sum of a buck a head - hoping to blast a hundred grand out of poor old NMC. Later, he asked for a mere $25,000. Right now the Zulu King would settle for two-bits if it came from the blood and sweat of the movement. Mr. Moore, whose brain is as sharp as a limp dishrag, is nothing but a black blackmailer.....his stock in trade is the color of his skin. His built in prejudices against whites are typical of those arising from the festering sores of ignorance and lack of intelligence. We might mention Mr. Moore's fantastic grasp of the English language - sometimes his grunts actually make sense. Not a bad fellow, really for he does like colored balls and old   automobile tires.

Well, to get back   to the BUF blackmail ploy. The march for peace   will go on as scheduled in spite of any blackbirds who try   to shit on it. Mr. Moore and his pack or herd or pride   or whatever you call a group of bloodsucking   animals, are in for a shock. We say: if they must   get something in return for their non-violence   towards NMC during these days of demonstrations, give them BANANAS - all they can eat.

We'll be in Washington on November 15th, Douglas. You can mark that on your calendar in RED, pal. If you won't join us you're against us. It's as simple as that. We consider you and your kind as black bandits and the most dangerous of the elements eating away at the movement.

The Steering Committee of NMC can feed you all the shit they want, Mr. Moore but lip-service isn't money...none that you'll ever see.

Suck on your bananas, brother and someday you might learn how to make fire or build a wheel.

Affectionately,

Sid

between them back to the head-tax episode. The FBI continued to
capitalize on it. Four months later, the Bureau was still sending
anonymous memos referring to the head tax to New Mobe Steering Committee members. And FBI agents continued to produce
phony press releases and leaflets designed to split the New Mobe
leadership. The FBI also tried to take advantage of religious tension within the New Left. In September 1970, Abe Bloom and
Arthur Waskow, both Jewish, were among the recipients of a *New
York Times* article titled "Jews Fear Anti-Zionism of New Left,"
reprinted in pamphlet form and mailed by the FBI.

Then, on March 8, 1971, an FBI field office in Media, Pennsylvania, was burglarized. One of the stolen documents bore the
heading "COINTELPRO–New Left." On April 27, at J. Edgar
Hoover's direction, a memo went to FBI field offices around the
country immediately terminating all COINTELPROS. At the time
there were five: New Left, Black Nationalist, White Hate Groups,
Espionage, and Communist Party, USA. In exceptional instances,
the memo announced, counterintelligence actions would still be
considered on an individual basis.

Actually, COINTELPRO's existence did not become widely known
until four years later, when information about FBI practices was
made public during the 1975 Senate hearings of the Select Committee to Study Governmental Operation with Respect to Intelligence Activities (known as the Church Committee, after its
chairman, Senator Frank Church). Extensive coverage in the
Washington media detailed the use of agents provocateurs placed
by the intelligence agencies to disrupt demonstrations, as well as
widespread electronic eavesdropping, mail interception, bank account monitoring, and "trash covers" (the FBI systematically
goes through a person's trash).

Reading the newspapers, Abe Bloom and Julius and Tina Hobson realized that they had been active in events and organizations targeted by the FBI. They joined forces, brought in Arthur
Waskow and David Eaton, among others, and decided to file suit.
They also recruited Anne Pilsbury and Dan Schember, two young
lawyers who would stay with the case, *Hobson v. Wilson*, for the
next twelve years.

The complaint was filed in July 1976. When filing a lawsuit,
the plaintiff must allege specific injuries that will be proven at
trial. But because of the secret nature of COINTELPRO, the plain-

tiffs did not have specific information. Although they had heard generally about COINTELPRO, the plaintiffs had no idea how extensive the program was or whether they had actually been among its targets. And they had no idea who within the FBI was responsible.

Originally, the plaintiffs sued ten defendants, mostly people whose names had appeared in the papers during the Church Committee hearings and other "unnamed agents." They later added twenty-eight more names, but dropped all but five by the time of trial. The men who were finally charged were Charles Brennan, George Moore, Cortland Jones, Gerald Grimaldi, and Gerould Pangburn.

From 1966 to 1970, Charles Brennan had been chief of the Internal Security Section in FBI headquarters, where he supervised COINTELPRO–New Left. In 1970–71, Brennan was assistant director in charge of the Domestic Intelligence Division. He supervised both COINTELPRO–New Left and COINTELPRO–Black Nationalist. Brennan apparently wrote the memos announcing both the creation and termination of COINTELPRO–New Left. The plaintiffs' lawyers obtained Brennan's name as a result of his testimony before the Church Committee.

George Moore had also testified. Moore was chief of the Racial Intelligence Section in FBI headquarters from 1967 to 1974. The section supervised field office implementation of COINTELPRO–Black Nationalist. The memo setting forth the goals of COINTELPRO–Black Nationalist went out over his name.

Cortland Jones had been the special agent in charge of the Washington Field Office, a liaison position between the WFO and FBI headquarters. From 1964 to 1974, he was WFO security coordinator, supervising nine squads, including squads 5 and 7. Squad 5 handled racial matters and COINTELPRO–Black Nationalist. Squad 7 was responsible for the New Left and COINTELPRO–New Left.

Gerald Grimaldi was a special agent in the WFO from 1956 to 1971. He was a member of squad 7, then became the WFO's COINTELPRO–New Left coordinator and later squad 5 supervisor. He was the author of the *Rational Observer*, a phony student newspaper that attacked student antiwar activities. It was published by the FBI and distributed at American University in Washington, D.C.

Gerould Pangburn, a WFO agent, succeeded in splitting his case from the others and would eventually receive a separate trial on the issue of damages.

The plaintiffs chose these five men as defendants because their initials appeared on FBI documents relating to COINTELPRO generally (Brennan and Moore), the WFO's participation in the program (Jones), or specific COINTELPRO actions (Grimaldi and Pangburn).

The plaintiffs also sued the District of Columbia and members of the Metropolitan Police Department (MPD). (Jerry Wilson, chief of the MPD at the time, was listed as the first defendant.) The case was brought under a federal civil rights conspiracy statute. The plaintiffs claimed that the FBI defendants conspired with one another, and with members of the Metropolitan Police Department, to violate their First Amendment right to "peaceably assemble and petition the government for a redress of grievances."

In guaranteeing the fundamental right of assembly, the Supreme Court has recognized that protecting individual rights in times of stability and social harmony is easy. It becomes more difficult in times of crisis, but that is precisely when the right to assemble, to speak out, and to disagree with the prevailing orthodoxy must be most vigilantly protected. In 1937, Chief Justice Charles Evans Hughes wrote, "The greater the importance of safeguarding the community from incitements to the overthrow of our institutions by force and violence, the more imperative is the need to preserve inviolate the constitutional rights of free speech, free press, and free assembly in order . . . that changes, if desired, may be obtained by peaceful means. Therein lies the security of the Republic, the very foundation of constitutional government."

From this basic right to assemble peaceably, the Supreme Court developed the broader concept of freedom of association, the right to join with others for the purpose of political expression. This is what Abe Bloom, Arthur Waskow, Tina and Julius Hobson, David Eaton, and their respective organizations claimed they were trying to do.

The plaintiffs' first move in the pretrial discovery process was to request their FBI files under the recently passed Freedom of Information Act. Although the plaintiffs suspected that they had been under surveillance, it was only upon receiving their files that they were sure. In all, they received over thirteen thousand pages of documents. The files showed that their phones had been tapped and that FBI agents had listened to both their business and personal conversations. The FBI had also monitored their bank accounts; copies of the plaintiffs' checks and bank statements were in the files. Their business associates, neighbors, and friends had been questioned by the FBI and reports of the conversations written up for the files. The FBI had requested additional background checks and investigations on Tina Hobson from the Civil Service Commission during the period when she and Julius were engaged.

The plaintiffs also discovered that the FBI had planted informants in the New Mobe, the BUF, and other political organizations. The files, however, did not mention any COINTELPRO actions. Huge passages had been deleted by the FBI, and Pilsbury and Schember thought references to COINTELPRO must have been in those portions. After more than a year of battling over the redactions, Dan Schember went to the FBI reading room to review some COINTELPRO files that had recently been made available under another Freedom of Information Act lawsuit. Only then did he discover that under the FBI filing system, in order to ensure additional secrecy, a COINTELPRO action taken against a particular person would not appear in that person's file. It would only appear in the COINTELPRO files.

Reading COINTELPRO files, Schember discovered documents relating to the plaintiffs, including those regarding the head-tax issue and the November 15 demonstration, and first read of COINTELPRO–Black Nationalist. He also discovered a secret world of government surveillance, counterintelligence, disruption, and interference dating back to the 1950s.

J. Edgar Hoover built the FBI and trained its agents in the post–World War II period when communism was perceived as one of the greatest threats to the American way of life. In 1956, Hoover authorized the first COINTELPRO against the Communist party. In 1961, a counterintelligence operation was authorized against the Socialist Workers party. Covert actions in these two COINTELPROS averaged one hundred per year in the period between 1956 and 1971.

Then, in 1964, during a period of increasingly violent reaction to the civil rights movement, the FBI instituted a COINTELPRO against the Ku Klux Klan and other "White Hate" organizations, such as the American Nazi party and the National States Rights party. Covert actions in this category averaged forty per year until 1971. According to the FBI, these COINTELPROS were designed to prevent violence. The Klan program was a success, according to Charles Brennan, "because of the money factor. We were able to buy so many informants in the Klan that we got to the point where we were running some of the chapters." Brennan says that the FBI was then able to dissuade Klan members from violence by proposing alternative action or additional planning.

COINTELPRO–Black Nationalist and COINTELPRO–New Left followed in 1967 and 1968.

In the late 1960s, in Washington, the FBI felt besieged. One of its prime responsibilities was to ensure that the government and residents of Washington were prepared and protected. Yet hundreds of thousands of demonstrators were "marching on Washington" four or five times annually, with many smaller rallies taking place at the Pentagon, the Selective Service building, the Capitol, and the White House throughout the year. It was the FBI's belief that radical groups would use these events for their own purposes of disruption. In advance of most demonstrations, rumors and rhetoric were flying. Most protestors wanted to march peacefully, but some wanted to block traffic into the city, enter the Pentagon, or climb the White House fence. There were a more militant few who advocated burning bridges, throwing bombs, and killing police. It was hard for the FBI to know which threats, if any, to take seriously.

Looking back on that time, Brennan says, "I think it is [difficult] to understand the nature of the problem we were facing, unless you lived through that period and experienced the disorder, the disruption, and the bombings. The pressure on the FBI was just intense. From the White House to the FBI; from Congress to the FBI; from Hoover down to agents within the FBI, because pressure was being put on him. He would call and say, 'I had a call from the president this afternoon, and he's concerned. He wants some answers and he wants a memorandum on his desk tomorrow morning.' You were bombarded."

To provide those answers, the FBI needed accurate information. COINTELPRO was supposed to provide it. But the FBI was having trouble defining its targets, especially within the New Left movement. During the *Hobson* trial, Brennan described "New Left" as "an amorphous grouping . . . a broad spectrum of individuals who were engaged in social dissent, whose central feature was advocacy of violence to smash the existing system." He went on to say that the New Left also included those who did not advocate violence, but whose activities would open them to Communist infiltration. As a result of this lack of definition, the FBI continually expanded its counterintelligence operation to include a widening range of people and groups. The Church Committee found that FBI headquarters developed over five hundred thousand domestic intelligence files, sixty-five thousand of which were opened in 1972 alone.

Names of people considered "potentially dangerous to the national defense of public safety of the United States" were placed on lists for dissemination to U.S. attorneys around the country. In a national emergency, a U.S. marshal would be sent to arrest them. Although such lists had been kept since the end of World War II, the growth of the lists in the 1960s and 1970s reflected the same inability to define the target group. In 1970, Charles Brennan reorganized the lists so the FBI could "zero in on the most dangerous individuals and 'lop off' the top level immediately." According to the FBI, Priority I included "individuals who have shown the greatest propensity for violence" and those with "special training in sabotage, espionage, guerilla warfare, etc." According to Arthur Waskow, it meant "all but shoot on sight." It turned out Waskow was Priority I, though he did not learn of this until after the *Hobson* lawsuit was under way.

In addition to gathering information, COINTELPRO–New Left and Black Nationalist, like their predecessors, were designed to prevent violence. Under the FBI rationale, disrupting targeted groups would make them less effective and therefore less violent. Brennan explains: "All of the movements I saw went from a passive stage through a more active stage up to a violent stage. We had to consider, 'How the hell can we stop it?' [The New Left] was a massive movement and the only way that you could possibly affect it would be [to] divide and conquer."

Hobson and the other plaintiffs argued that in targeting people whom it had no reason to believe were engaged in violence or illegal activities, and actively interfering with their lawful efforts for political change, the FBI exceeded its mandate. The scope of this mandate had been clearly articulated as early as 1924 by Attorney General (later Chief Justice) Harlan Fiske Stone: "The Bureau of Investigation is not concerned with the political or other opinions of individuals. It is concerned only with their conduct, and then only as such conduct is forbidden by the laws of the United States." When asked by the Church Committee "whether anybody at any time during the course of [COINTELPRO activity] ever discussed [its] constitutionality or legal authority," George Moore replied, "No, we never gave it a thought."

"We just went one step further and that one step was generated by the problems confronting us," says Charles Brennan. "We took that extra step because we felt that we had God protecting us. He was sitting up there on the fifth floor saying 'Go Get 'Em.'"

But by the time the *Hobson* case came to trial, in November 1981, J. Edgar Hoover had been dead for nearly ten years. At trial, the plaintiffs introduced the "Bananas" leaflet, the *Rational Observer* (a phony student newspaper published by the FBI), and evidence of FBI efforts to disrupt the November 15 demonstration. The plaintiffs also detailed FBI interference with other demonstrations. For example, during one protest, FBI agents intercepted demonstrators' CB transmissions and directed them to march outside the approved parade route, knowing they would be arrested. In preparation for another demonstration, the FBI filled in housing forms with fictitious addresses, causing thousands of out-of-town participants to arrive in Washington only to find they had no place to sleep. The evidence of surveillance, harassment, and disruption was extensive.

The plaintiffs faced a major problem, however. In order to recover damages they had to prove that they had suffered actual injury as a result of the FBI's activities. Under the law, it was not enough that they felt what the FBI did was wrong, or even that they could prove it was unconstitutional.

According to the plaintiffs' attorney, Anne Pilsbury, "The judge made it real clear that we had to show that the FBI's improper goal had been carried out and it had affected these people, either emotionally or financially. That was the hard part, because these were all normal, happy, well-balanced individuals. A lot of it was water off their backs. They were damned if they were going to be deterred, and they were very apt to say so too." It seemed ironic to Pilsbury that because the plaintiffs were so committed to their political beliefs, and therefore unlikely to be daunted by harassment, they faced the risk of not being able to prove harm.

The issue of harm was certainly not artificial to the FBI defendants. Under the law of conspiracy, as long as each of them knew the general scope and essential nature of COINTELPRO, and as long as one of them had acted to further its general objectives, each of them could be held liable for *all* COINTELPRO actions. Furthermore, in 1971, the Supreme Court had made it possible to sue individual members of the government personally for their official actions, and to try the case in front of jurors who could award damages as they saw fit. (Previously, it had only been possible to sue a government agency or the U.S. government itself, and the amount of the recovery was fixed by law.)

Each of the FBI agents stood to lose a substantial part of his life savings for allegedly violating the First Amendment rights of people who had not been aware of the FBI's activities, and who by their own admission were not deterred. After all, three hundred thousand people had assembled peaceably in the November 15 demonstration led by Coretta King and Julius Hobson. Charles Brennan believes that the plaintiffs "weren't able to show any damage. We weren't going around chopping people's heads off or doing really nasty dirty stuff. This was a get-even suit."

The FBI agents also argued they were unfairly selected as defendants, chosen because of their positions rather than their actions. They claimed that their names were obtained randomly, making it unfair to hold them personally responsible. Brennan's and Moore's names came from their Church Committee testimony, and the names of the others were obtained from files selectively released by the FBI. Had documents bearing other names been released, they argued, other men would have been sued. In addition, they claimed, because all five lived in the Washington area they were easy targets. They pointed out that others who were more difficult to locate (the New York agent who wrote the "Bananas" leaflet, for example) were not brought to court.

Brennan and his co-defendants also felt that the FBI itself should have been sued instead of the agents. They argued that they received approval for each COINTELPRO action and remained within the guidelines set down by J. Edgar Hoover. When this argument failed, they asserted that, as public employees, they were immune from liability. Under the law at the time of trial, the judge told the jury they could find a defendant immune only if he sincerely and reasonably believed his officially approved conduct was lawful.

Apparently, the jury did not believe anyone could consider CO-INTELPRO's actions lawful. After five days of deliberations, they awarded a total of $711,937.50 to eight plaintiffs. Abe Bloom and Arthur Waskow each were awarded $93,700. Tina Hobson and David Eaton each were awarded $81,062.50.

"The jury got it," says Waskow. "They really got it. That was pretty amazing. Totally aside from the massive amount of money, they got the sense that the Constitution does matter. There are rights, and you can say people are damaged if their rights are taken away, even if they can't figure out how to say they lost money on it. That felt really good."

On appeal, the U.S. Court of Appeals for the D.C. Circuit upheld the jury's verdict against the FBI defendants. It wrote, "The extraordinary nature of these charges makes this an easy case. Whatever authority the Government may have to interfere with a group engaged in unlawful activity . . . it is *never* permissible to impede or deter lawful civil rights/political organization, expression or protest with no other direct purpose and no other immediate objective than to counter the influence of the target associations."

The Court continued: "Government action, taken with the intent to disrupt or destroy lawful organizations, or to deter membership in those groups, is absolutely unconstitutional. The Government could not constitutionally make such participation unlawful; consequently it may not surreptitiously undertake to do what it cannot do publicly. Nor can we fathom any conceivably legitimate governmental interest in such an undertaking."

The court found, however, that there was insufficient evidence of a conspiracy between the FBI and the Metropolitan Police Department, or between the police and the District of Columbia. It also ruled that the claims of Abe Bloom and three other plaintiffs were barred by the statute of limitations. Consequently, the court found the jury's damage awards against each defendant excessive and ordered the trial court to redetermine the amounts.

The FBI defendants were all retired by this time, facing per-

sonal financial ruin. "Working in the FBI is a great job, but you
don't get rich," says Brennan. "No way [was] anybody going to
dig $130,000 out of me." But he had faith that somehow the FBI
would take care of them. After all, they had grown up in the FBI,
each of them had at least twenty years of service.

A settlement was finally negotiated in 1986. The plaintiffs accepted $46,000 in full satisfaction of their claims. Attorney Gen-
eral Edwin Meese agreed that the FBI would indemnify its agents
and pay the sum.

Arthur Waskow received a total of $8,000: $4,000 for emotional
distress, intimidation, and fear resulting from FBI exploitation of
his religious background, and from the discovery that he was priority I on the security index; $2,250 for being subject to three
years of "extensive and intrusive investigation"; $1,250 for emo-
tional distress and injury to his reputation caused by the FBI's
extensive questioning of his neighbors; $350 for injury to his rep-
utation caused by being one of the purported authors of the "Bananas" leaflet; and $150 for emotional distress from the leaflet
itself.

The Reverend David Eaton received a total of $7,500: $3,000
for emotional distress and injury to his reputation resulting from
a COINTELPRO letter threatening death to each member of the BUF
Board of Convenors, except Eaton, unless the BUF ceased its
efforts to combat drug sales in the black community; $2,500 for
the head-tax controversy and the "Bananas" leaflet; $2,000 for
being listed on the agitator index and having reports about his
behavior circulated to other federal agencies.

Julius Hobson died in 1977. Tina Hobson received $8,500:
$3,500 as compensation for humiliation and embarrassment re-
sulting from FBI inquiries into her personal premarital relations
with a prominent black leader; and $5,000 for FBI intrusion into
her employment.

Tina Hobson split the money among her children and Julius's
children, because she felt they had suffered the most from the
FBI's interference into their family life. Arthur Waskow has used
his money "for good politics," and Reverend David Eaton's
money is helping to put his children through college.

When it comes to the future, "I am inclined to guarantee that
you will never see a resumption of that type of activity by the FBI
again," Charles Brennan said at trial. "The delineation of what

the FBI can or can't do is very clear, and the Department of Justice has taken much firmer control over the FBI so that it is not going to operate in the autonomous manner that it did under Mr. Hoover."

Tina Hobson is not so sanguine. "I think that since our case is over, somebody else better follow. You have to try to create a government that's close to your heart's desire. If you don't do it, somebody else will."

SECOND AMENDMENT

"A well regulated Militia, being necessary to the security of a free State, the right of the people to keep and bear Arms, shall not be infringed."

Maureen Piszczor of Oak Park, Illinois, whose husband was killed by an assailant with a handgun
REPRINTED BY PERMISSION

Don Bennett, an Oak Park gas station owner, arrested for possession of a handgun after using it to deter robbers
CAROLINE KENNEDY

The Right to Keep and Bear Arms:
Quilici v. Morton Grove

"YOU KNOW, MOST PEOPLE HAVE
this John Wayne 'You've got to have a gun, it's your right to have
a gun, this is America' syndrome. If you ask people on the street
whether they have a right to have a gun under the Constitution,
most people would say, 'You betcha!'" says Greg Youstra, a
trustee of the Village of Morton Grove, Illinois, at the time it became the first town in the United States to ban the possession of
handguns.

In constitutional terms, it is known as the right to keep and
bear arms. It is rooted in the Second Amendment, which provides, "A well-regulated Militia, being necessary to the security of
a free State, the right of the people to keep and bear Arms, shall
not be infringed." And although the gun lobby and certain scholars are convinced that citizens have a constitutional right to pack
a gun, the courts have not supported this interpretation.

On March 30, 1981, John Hinckley attempted to kill President
Ronald Reagan with a gun. Six weeks later, on May 13, Pope
John Paul II was shot in Saint Peter's Square. Two weeks after

that, Geoffrey LaGioia applied for a permit to open a gun store in a small shopping mall in the Chicago suburb of Morton Grove. "People didn't like the idea," says Martin Ashman, the village's attorney. "They didn't like the idea of a gun shop where children could watch people buy guns and window-shop for guns. This was in an all-night convenience food mart; the walls weren't very secure. Anyone could break in and take a whole load of guns."

Neil Cashman, the longest-serving village trustee and father of nine, was also troubled. He called Ashman, told him that the trustees were concerned about having a gun shop in town, and asked Ashman what they could do about it. After some legal research, Ashman concluded that a town could ban the *sale* of guns. He called Cashman on the Thursday before a Monday trustees meeting and told him, "We could keep these people out. We can pass a law which bans the sale of all guns in Morton Grove."

Ashman continues: "As an aside I said, 'You know, if you want to ban the *possession* of handguns you probably can get away with that too. I'm not sure, because nobody has done it.' Cashman said, 'I think I may want to propose that.' I said, 'Well, you better think real hard, because you don't want to go way out on a limb. Check with people before you do it.' Cashman replied, 'I will. Over the weekend I will.' But he didn't."

At the trustees' Monday meeting, the chambers were full of people against the gun shop. A proposal that Ashman draft an ordinance banning the sale of guns passed easily. Then, "out of the clear blue," Ashman says, "Neil Cashman proposed a law banning the private possession of handguns. There was a long moment of silence. And finally Don Sneider, another trustee, seconded the motion."

The proposal was tabled until the next meeting, at which time the trustees voted to have a public hearing on the ordinance, to allow each side to air its views. As the trustees lined up, there were two in favor of the ordinance banning handguns, Cashman and Sneider; two opposed, Joan Dechert and Dick Hohs; and two undecided, Lou Greenberg and Greg Youstra. All of them realized that Morton Grove would be the first town in the United States to ban the private possession of handguns.

So did the National Rifle Association (NRA), the powerful gun lobbying group, nearly three million strong. The NRA began to campaign publicly against the ordinance, deluging Morton Grove with pamphlets and calling residents who were opposed to the ordinance, specifically targeting American Legion members, veterans, and registered gun owners. The NRA also encouraged its out-of-town members to travel to Morton Grove to speak at the public hearing. Greg Youstra, a black belt in karate, high school physical education teacher, and recreational gun user, says, "I'd owned guns for years, but I never gave it any thought. All of a sudden I'm inundated from both sides; do it, don't do it. [People] would call, they wanted coffee, they wanted dinner, they wanted to start seeing me. Suddenly I was getting the rush from everybody."

In addition to pressure from the people in town, Morton Grove became a focus of both the Chicago and the national media. Editorials appeared in the local paper, the churches in town began to stake out their positions. The trustees were barraged with phone calls, requests for interviews, and appearances on television talk shows. Both sides held rallies in the junior high school auditorium and petitions circulated through town.

On the evening of June 8, 1981, it was raining lightly. The police department had canceled all vacations; they were expecting a large crowd. At the public hearing, the council chambers were packed. A closed-circuit television hookup enabled the hundreds of people gathered outside to see what was going on inside the room. The networks were there carrying the story, excerpts of the hearing were shown on the "MacNeil-Lehrer NewsHour," and the debate was reenacted on "Nightline." Correspondents from as far away as Japan and Australia converged on the usually tranquil bedroom community. Ashman, Cashman, and Youstra agree that most of the people in the crowd were not locals. "The night of the vote, the NRA trucked them in by truck, bus, car; American flags all over the place, John Deere hats. It looked like rural America was here," says Youstra.

"They were hollering and yelling and everything. 'Taking away our rights. Taking away our rights,'" says Cashman.

"I mean, they surrounded the village hall where it was fifty deep," adds Youstra. "This guy doesn't scare very easily, but I was scared that night. I was afraid I was going to get shot."

Because the purpose of the hearing was to give Morton Grove's residents a chance to express their opinions to the trustees, persons wishing to speak had first to give their name and address.

After these were checked against the town water registry, people were permitted to approach the microphone. The mayor of Morton Grove had decided that each person who wanted to speak would be allowed. "There were some pretty irrational arguments," Neil Cashman says. "It was four and a half hours of Archie Bunker. I was called everything in the book. And the more names they called me the more determined I was."

At 1:30 A.M. a vote was called. No one knew how it would go. Youstra's was the last vote. "When they mentioned my name, that it was going to be Greg Youstra's vote, a cheer went up from outside, like you know, Caesar Augustus. They were all out there saying, 'There's no way in the world the guy is going to vote for this thing.' And when I said, 'I vote for the ordinance,' [there were] boos and 'You sold us out, you dirty commie.' It was unbelievable."

By a vote of four to two Morton Grove became the first town in the United States to prohibit the possession of handguns in the home. "I hope we saved a couple of lives," Neil Cashman says. "I guess I'll never see the complete ban of handguns. I don't know whether my Patty [his daughter] will ever see it, but I sure hope that little Emily and Patrick and Sean [his grandchildren] do see the complete ban of guns. That's my wish."

Martin Ashman had worked on the ordinance for over a month to ensure that it would stand up to a legal challenge. "I knew that if it passed it was going to go to the U.S. Supreme Court, and I knew from what was happening—the media attention was intense—that I had better do it right."

Morton Grove's ordinance actually prohibited possession of bludgeons, blackjacks, slug shots, sand clubs, sandbags, metal knuckles, switchblades, sawed-off shotguns, bombs, Molotov cocktails, and *any handgun unless it had been rendered permanently inoperative.* Exceptions were made for peace officers, prison wardens, members of the armed forces or the National Guard carrying a gun on-duty, private security guards, licensed gun collectors, licensed gun clubs, and antique firearms. Transporting guns through Morton Grove, provided they were dismantled or were being transported for the purpose of competitive target shooting, was also allowed.

Any person who owned a handgun was required to turn it in to the police department. Those found with a gun after the ordinance took effect faced a fine of up to five hundred dollars (later raised to a thousand dollars). Gun owners wishing to use their weapons for recreational shooting could store them at their gun clubs.

The morning after the ordinance was passed the media deluge began again. Hate mail started coming in. The trustees who had voted for the ordinance and Ashman received threats to themselves and their families. Those eventually stopped. The real attack came from Victor Quilici, a lawyer and gun-owning resident of Morton Grove, who filed a lawsuit challenging the ordinance. Quilici claimed it violated his Second Amendment right to keep and bear arms.

The lawsuit and the controversy over the right to arms center on whether the right belongs to the individual or to the people as a group. Does the Constitution protect a person's right to have a gun for hunting and self-defense, or does it provide a collective right to defend the state?

The Second Amendment debate turns traditional constitutional arguments inside out. Some scholars who usually favor restricting individual rights and a narrow construction of the Constitution believe that the Second Amendment should be interpreted broadly. In contrast, those who often argue for an expansive reading of the Constitution with strong protection for individual rights, argue that the Second Amendment applies only to the federal government's right to raise a militia, and does not provide an individual the right to keep and bear arms.

The arguments begin with the language of the Second Amendment itself. Proponents of the individual-right theory argue that the first clause of the Second Amendment, "a well regulated Militia being necessary to the security of a free State," is an amplifying clause intended to illustrate one application of the right to bear arms, but not the only one. Next, they claim that "the right of the people" means the right of each person, just as it does in the First Amendment or the Fourth Amendment. Finally, they argue that "to keep and bear arms" means precisely what it says: to keep arms in one's home and to bear them in self-defense, or in defense of the state.

These textual arguments are rebutted by the collective-right advocates, who claim that the Second Amendment must be read as a whole, not split into phrases that, when read separately, distort its meaning. To them, its meaning is clear. The Framers included the first clause to justify and explain the right at issue: "A well regulated Militia being necessary to the security of a free State . . ." They maintain that this clause qualifies, rather than amplifies, the right to arms, restricting it to activities that the state determines are necessary to maintain a militia.

In addition to arguments based on the language of the Constitution, each side makes a number of historical arguments to support its position. These are based on English common law, the English Bill of Rights, the American colonial experience, and debates over the ratification of the American Bill of Rights.

Individual-right advocates argue that the Framers intended to protect a personal right to bear arms when they wrote the Bill of Rights because such a right was widely accepted in the eighteenth century, having been recognized in English common law since before the Norman Conquest in 1066. Not only were English citizens allowed to possess arms, they were required to do so because England depended for its defense on a citizen's militia, not a royal army. Englishmen were also required to respond with their weapons in good condition when summoned by the sheriff in local disturbances and to take turns keeping watch over their villages at night. The progun side interprets the historical record to support an underlying and implicit right to keep and bear arms.

Gun control proponents respond that the common law right to keep and bear arms was not an individual right to keep weapons, but existed primarily for the defense of the state and community. Furthermore, they argue, it was never an absolute right; as early as 1328, Parliament placed limits on the right. The early restrictions prohibited carrying weapons in public; later, Parliament restricted gun ownership to the wealthy. During and after the English Civil War in the seventeenth century, the Stuart kings further limited gun ownership, allowing only their religious or political supporters to possess weapons. To gun control advocates, these repeated efforts to regulate, restrict, and disarm segments of the population do not support an underlying right to arms, but rather prove the validity of legislative attempts to restrict it, including modern gun control laws.

The historical debate then crosses the ocean to the United

States. Under the Articles of Confederation, the states had maintained their "sovereignty, freedom and independence" at the expense of a weak central government. Each state was required to keep a "well regulated and disciplined militia, sufficiently armed and accoutred." These militias required men between the ages of approximately sixteen and sixty to keep weapons and be ready to defend their state. Congress's military powers, on the other hand, were severely limited. The federal government could not maintain any army at all without the consent of nine of the thirteen states.

The delegates to the Constitutional Convention in the summer of 1787 debated the relative merits of the militia system and a national standing army. The tyranny of the British army during colonial times had made Americans intensely suspicious of military power not subject to civilian control. In spite of this distrust of standing armies, however, the American experience in the Revolutionary War and under the Articles of Confederation had convinced most delegates that Congress needed the authority to raise and support an army to protect the frontier, the national government, and the nation itself.

As part of the system of checks and balances, they came up with a compromise that divided the military power between the federal government and the states. Under the Constitution, Congress has the authority to declare war, raise an army, and call up the militia, but the states keep the power to appoint militia officers and train militia members, subject to the instructions of Congress.

The progun side in the *Morton Grove* case interpreted the Framers' support for the militia as evidence of their acceptance of private possession of firearms and their intent to secure an individual right to keep and bear arms.

First, Quilici argued that as a general matter, guns played an important role in eighteenth-century America. At that time, guns were an everyday tool used to procure food, pursue livelihoods, and protect settlements in a hostile frontier.

Quilici also argued that the right to bear arms was essential to a man's ability to serve (with his own weapon) in the militia, which, in turn, is necessary to the national defense. He argued that after the gun ban, citizens of Morton Grove would be unable to respond if called as part of the reserve militia in a national emergency or foreign invasion.

The gun control side rejected this contention as absurd. They argued that private weapons are unnecessary for reserve militia duty because the state of Illinois provides weapons for its militia, and, in any event, residents could keep their weapons at a club, collect them, and report for duty in case of an emergency. To gun control advocates, the Framers' solution prevents the federal government's usurpation of the state's power to control its militia. It does not protect an individual right to keep and bear arms. As they are quick to point out, there was no mention of individual arms ownership, hunting, or even self-defense in the debates over the ratification of the Bill of Rights.

The courts have overwhelmingly supported the collective-rights interpretation. The federal courts in the *Morton Grove* case were no exception. The district court held that Morton Grove's ordinance did not violate the Illinois Constitution or the Second Amendment. It based its holding on the fact that the Second Amendment has never been incorporated into the Fourteenth and made applicable against the states. The Second Amendment, therefore, acts only as a restriction on the federal government, keeping it from passing legislation that would infringe on a state's right to arm and train its militia. State legislatures remain free to regulate or restrict state militias. Municipalities may also limit private access to weapons under their power to provide for the public health and safety. "Since the Second Amendment does not apply to the States and localities," the court held, "it is not infringed by the Morton Grove ordinance."

On December 6, 1982, the U.S. Court of Appeals for the Seventh Circuit affirmed. It agreed that the Second Amendment does not apply to the states. To the court, the words of the Second Amendment made clear that the right to bear arms is "inextricably connected to the preservation of a militia." Under the controlling authority of the only Supreme Court case to address the scope of the Second Amendment, *U.S. v. Miller*, the court concluded that "the right to keep and bear handguns is not guaranteed by the Second Amendment." The U.S. Supreme Court declined to hear the case, letting the lower-court rulings stand.

Gun control advocates were on a roll. They envisioned a movement sweeping across the United States town by town. Nearby was another Chicago suburb, Evanston, a liberal, affluent college town. In Evanston, a gun control ordinance was introduced by the Board of Trustees and passed with little fanfare.

The next town to try was Skokie, which lies between Morton Grove and Evanston. Skokie's population includes a large number of Holocaust survivors, some of whom had lived through the Warsaw uprising. They vowed to themselves and their children, "Never again." They were afraid that if disarmed, they would be vulnerable once more, and at an emotional town meeting the gun control ordinance was defeated. But the tough questions and policy debate were revived in Oak Park, the fourth Chicago suburb to consider a ban on handguns.

Maureen and Jim Piszczor used to read the newspaper together at the end of the day after they put their kids to bed. Jim was a lawyer in Chicago. The young couple had met and married while Jim was in law school, then settled in the integrated suburban community of Oak Park. Though they had never been politically active, one Thursday night they discussed an article about the upcoming weekend's annual march against handgun violence.

The next morning, October 21, 1983, Jim was shot in a Chicago courtroom by the ex-husband of a woman he was representing in a postdivorce proceeding. Still conscious as he was wheeled into the hospital, Jim repeated Maureen's name over and over, and the image inundated the local newscasts. Jim died that night.

A few hours after his death, Maureen asked Jim's best friend, Chris Walsh, to write a statement encouraging people to support the gun control march because, she says, "I knew what kind of person Jim was, I remembered him talking about the march, and I just kept thinking about it. People were so upset and angry, everything was so negative and sad, and I just felt this need to somehow reach out in his memory for something more positive."

Neither Maureen nor Chris Walsh had ever been particularly interested in gun control before, but by December Jim's friends had decided that as their memorial to Jim, they wanted his community, Oak Park, to pass an ordinance banning the possession of handguns. By then they had researched the issue, formed the Oak Park Citizen's Committee for Handgun Control, and joined with other Oak Park residents. But most of the others had never been politically active either, and only one even knew the names of the village trustees. Chris Walsh describes their early meetings: "I remember going to bed at night and thinking, how will we ever do this? We don't know anybody. Nobody knows who we are. We decided that we had to do a petition drive to demonstrate that the issue was not one that was simply of interest to a small group of people who knew and loved Jim Piszczor, but was rather a matter of widespread concern throughout the community."

By February, the other side was ready. The Oak Park Freedom Committee, led by tax accountants Jim Zangrilli and Isaiah Stroud, began circulating petitions against the ban. They pointed out that a gun ban would not have saved Jim Piszczor's life, and argued that just as the remedy for drunk driving is not to confiscate cars, the remedy for handgun violence is not to ban guns. They argued that safety education and increased public awareness were the solutions. In March, the Freedom Committee lobbied the trustees to put the issue before the people in an advisory referendum, rather than allowing it to be decided by a trustees-only vote.

In April, the Oak Park trustees voted four to three in favor of an ordinance like Morton Grove's, which banned the possession of handguns. The Freedom Committee, not wanting to leave the decision in the hands of a few trustees, immediately filed petitions demanding a referendum. As a result of their efforts, the Oak Park trustees agreed to place a question on the ballot in the local school board election. The question asked Oak Park voters whether the ban should be repealed, making Oak Park the first community in the nation to put a gun ban to a vote by the people.

Both sides swung into high gear. Maureen Piszczor and Chris Walsh concentrated on door-to-door, precinct-by-precinct, standing-at-the-el-at-rush-hour efforts. "This story is as much about the First Amendment as it is about the Second Amendment," says Chris Walsh, "because it was really people assembling to petition the government." The progun side outspent them more than two to one, but when the votes were tallied, Maureen and Chris had won: 8,031 to 6,368.

Some hard questions remained for both sides, however. Most important was the question of self-defense. Two days after the ban went into effect, Don Bennett, a gas station owner, was held up at gunpoint. Before the ban, he had always worn a gun at work, making sure it was conspicuous because he had been robbed a number of times. But Bennett had taken it off to appear to be in compliance with the law. The robbers held a gun to his head, forced him to empty his cash register and pockets, and left. Bennett ran outside and grabbed his gun from his car. According to Bennett, the robbers shot at him and he returned five shots into the back of their station wagon. Then he went inside to call the police. When they arrived, the police confiscated Bennett's gun and arrested him for violating the ordinance. The robbers were never caught.

To Jim Zangrilli, Bennett's story illustrates the misguided emphasis of the ordinance. Zangrilli argues that the ordinance penalizes the victim, not the criminal, putting law-abiding citizens on trial for exercising their right to self-defense. To Zangrilli, personal security is exactly what the Constitution should protect, or else we risk losing the ability to enforce our other rights.

Chris Walsh argues that Zangrilli and his fellow believers are wrong. "Their anger comes from their belief that a handgun will protect them, and by taking that handgun away you're taking away their right to defend themselves. My anger comes from the fact that I don't have my best friend around to talk to anymore. Maureen doesn't have her husband around to talk to anymore and Rachel and Bob don't have a father. And the reality is that our case is a lot more common than their case. . . . My neighbor's gun threatens my life."

THIRD AMENDMENT

"No Soldier shall, in time of peace be quartered in any house, without the consent of the Owner, nor in time of war, but in a manner to be prescribed by law."

CONGRESS of the UNITED STATES.

In the HOUSE *of* REPRESENTATIVES,

Tuesday, the 28th of July, 1789.

MR. VINING, *from the Committee of eleven, to whom it was referred to take the subject of* AMENDMENTS *to the* CONSTITUTION *of the* UNITED STATES, *generally into their consideration, and to report thereupon, made a report, which was read, and is as followeth:*

IN the introductory paragraph before the words, " *We the people,*" add, " Government being intended for the benefit of the people, and the right-
" ful establishment thereof being derived from their authority alone."

ART. 1, SEC. 2, PAR. 3—Strike out all between the words, "*direct*" and " *and until such,*" and instead thereof insert, " After the first enumeration there shall
" be one representative for every thirty thousand until the number shall
" amount to one hundred ; after which the proportion shall be so regulated
" by Congress that the number of Representatives shall never be less than
" one hundred, nor more than one hundred and seventy-five, but each
" State shall always have at least one Representative."

ART. 1, SEC. 6—Between the words "*United States,*" and "*shall in all cases,*"
strike out "*they,*" and insert, " But no law varying the compensation shall take
" effect until an election of Representatives shall have intervened. The
" members."

ART. 1, SEC. 9—Between PAR. 2 and 3 insert, " No religion shall be
" established by law, nor shall the equal rights of conscience be infringed."

" The freedom of speech, and of the press, and the right of the people
peaceably to assemble and consult for their common good, and to apply to
the government for redress of grievances, shall not be infringed."

" A well regulated militia, composed of the body of the people, being the
best security of a free State, the right of the people to keep and bear arms
shall not be infringed, but no person religiously scrupulous shall be compelled to bear arms."

" No soldier shall in time of peace be quartered in any house without
the consent of the owner, nor in time of war but in a manner to be prescribed by law."

" No person shall be subject, except in case of impeachment, to more than
one trial or one punishment for the same offence, nor shall be compelled
to be a witness against himself, nor be deprived of life, liberty, or property
without due process of law ; nor shall private property be taken for public use without just compensation."

" Excessive bail shall not be required, nor excessive fines imposed, nor cruel
and unusual punishments inflicted."

" The right of the people to be secure in their person, houses, papers and
effects, shall not be violated by warrants issuing, without probable cause

An early draft of the Third Amendment, appearing here in Article 1, Section 9

Quartering Troops:
Engblom v. Carey

Between one of the most controversial amendments, the Second, and one of the most heavily litigated, the Fourth, is the forgotten amendment. Even people who know all sorts of things about the Bill of Rights ask, "What's the third one again?" The "third one" prevents the government from quartering troops in your home. Specifically, the government may not lodge a single soldier in a home during peacetime without the owner's consent and, during wartime, may do so only if a special law is passed. The Third Amendment is a reminder that although the Constitution was "framed for ages to come and . . . designed to approach immortality," it was also written to address real and immediate grievances suffered by its authors.

In 1765, the British Parliament passed the first Quartering Act, requiring American colonists to bear the cost of sheltering and feeding British troops in the colonies. If there was insufficient room for the soldiers in the barracks, the act provided that they be quartered in livery stables, inns, and alehouses. In response, Benjamin Franklin helpfully suggested, "Let [the British] first try the effects of quartering soldiers on butchers, bakers, or other private houses [in England] and then transport the measure to America. Parental example may provide filial obedience."

Nine years later, in the aftermath of the Boston Tea Party, the British Parliament enacted an even harsher law, the Quartering Act of 1774. The law was one of the "intolerable acts" and authorized British troops to be quartered wherever necessary, including in private homes. As one colonist wrote at the time, "What a handle such conduct as this gives to the Tories! . . . besides, it is downright and intolerably wrong." The quartering of British soldiers in colonial homes was an economic burden, an invasion of all sense of privacy and repose, and considering England was rapidly changing from mother country to enemy, a constant source of tension and wild rumors of spying.

Thus the Declaration of Independence lists as a specific grievance against the king, "He has kept among us, in times of peace, Standing Armies, without the Consent of our legislatures" and "quarter[ed] large bodies of armed troops among us." A decade later, one of the objections to the recently drafted Constitution was that it did not prevent the new U.S. government from perpetrating this "intolerable wrong" on the people. In the debates in the Virginia ratifying convention, on June 16, 1788, Patrick Henry argued, "One of our first complaints, under the former government, was the quartering of troops among us. This was one of the principal reasons for dissolving the connection with Great Britain. Here we may have troops in time of peace. They may be billeted in any manner—to tyrannize, oppress, and crush us." When Madison submitted his draft of the Bill of Rights for debate, the quartering troops provision passed with little discussion.

Since its glory days in the late eighteenth century, however, the Third Amendment has languished. The changing economics and practicalities of waging war have left little for it to do. Over time, as the other amendments in the Bill of Rights became flashpoints for important public controversies and benchmarks of great societal change, the Third trundled along on its own peculiar path.

First, after lying dormant for nearly two centuries, it began cropping up in the oddest cases. The president of a bankrupt securities corporation claimed that a subpoena to produce business records was a violation of, among other things, his Third Amendment rights. A bewildered New York court dismissed the claim in a footnote. An army reservist who complained that orders to participate in a veteran's parade violated his Third Amendment rights suffered a similar fate.

The goofiest attempt to invoke the amendment came in a case brought under the 1947 Housing and Rent Act. The defendant claimed that the act "is and always was the incubator and hatchery of swarms of bureaucrats to be quartered as storm troopers upon the people in violation of Amendment III of the United States Constitution." A California court quoted the conclusion from defendant's brief that "this challenge has not been heretofore made or adjudged by any court, insofar as our research discloses" and responded, "We accept counsel's statement as to the results of his research, but find this challenge without merit."

Then, in 1979, in the small upstate hamlet of Warwick, New York, it appeared the Third Amendment would finally be called to duty. Marianne E. Engblom and Charles E. Palmer were corrections officers at the Mid-Orange Correctional Facility in Warwick. They and several other corrections officers lived on the grounds of the facility in dormitory-style housing owned by the state. The rooms had a private or semiprivate bath and common kitchen areas. The prison provided standard fixtures and a bed and dresser. The occupants supplied all other furnishings and accessories "from curtains to toilet paper and light bulbs." Thirty-six dollars a month was deducted from their paychecks to cover the rent.

In April 1979, most of the corrections officers at Mid-Orange, including Engblom and Palmer, walked off the job as part of a statewide strike. Governor Hugh Carey mobilized the National Guard, ordering guardsmen to provide security in New York's prisons. At Mid-Orange, the striking corrections officers were locked out of their living space and some of the guardsmen housed there during the three-week emergency. Engblom and Palmer were among those who were locked out while guardsmen lived in their rooms without their consent. They sued Governor Carey and various prison officials for damages under the Third Amendment.

A New York federal district court judge declared, "In an extraordinary demonstration of the vitality and versatility of our Constitution, [a Third Amendment] claim is here made for the first time." The court noted the silly cases brought previously, which it said did not count, and pointed out that when the Third

Amendment had been mentioned seriously in other cases, it was in the context of a larger discussion about the spirit of the Bill of Rights. It was clear that of all the provisions in the Bill of Rights, the Third was the only one left untouched, that is, uninterpreted by the courts, since the Revolution. The court's opinion in *Engblom* is an illustration of the fundamental but sometimes overlooked fact that construing basic English, especially in a constitutional provision, is not nearly as simple as it appears.

The court began with the underlying principle of the Third Amendment as its guide to interpreting the text. Most scholars accepted Justice Joseph Story's brief explication of the amendment in his nineteenth-century *Commentaries on the Constitution:* "This provision speaks for itself. Its plain object is to secure the perfect enjoyment of that great right of the common law, that a man's house shall be his own castle, privileged against all civil and military intrusion. The billeting of soldiers in time of peace upon the people has been a common resort of arbitrary princes, and is full of inconvenience and peril."

The two troublesome words in the text were *Soldier* and *house.* The court concluded that the National Guard is the modern-day successor to the militia and therefore guardsmen should be considered soldiers under the Third Amendment. *House*, however, was trickier.

The court decided that in keeping with the spirit of the provision as set forth by Justice Story, *house* should not be limited to the traditional abode with a mortgage. On the other hand, the court did not feel the amendment should be read so broadly as to protect just any place where one happened to live. It noted that Engblom's and Palmer's occupancy of the dormitory-style units would last only as long as their jobs, and that the prison administration retained strict control over the housing, including a right to enter the premises at any time and a broad power to evict. Therefore, the court held, Engblom's and Palmer's "possessory interest in the premises did not entitle them to Third Amendment protection, particularly since the State, the only 'owner' of the 'house' in question here, consented to the quartering." The district court held that, as a matter of law, there was no need for a trial on the Third Amendment issue. Therefore, it did not find it necessary to consider the defenses raised by Governor Carey and the prison officials.

On appeal in 1982, the Second Circuit reversed. Looking to property and landlord-tenant law, as well as cases dealing with privacy interests under other amendments, the appellate court held that it was too early to say that the Third Amendment's protection of house did not include Engblom's and Palmer's somewhat unique dwelling. A majority of the Second Circuit panel thought there should be a trial on the issue. One judge dissented, stating that the dormitorylike housing at Mid-Orange "simply bears no resemblance to the kind of oasis of privacy our Forefathers undoubtedly envisioned when they fashioned the Third Amendment. The majority's willingness to seriously entertain a 'quartering of troops' claim holds us up to derision."

Nonetheless, *Engblom* went back to the district court in what was now surely the longest judicial journey ever for the Third Amendment. This time, the court had to look at the defense raised by Governor Carey and the other defendants. They relied on the doctrine of "qualified immunity," developed to protect public officials from lawsuits regarding action taken in the course of their public duties. Just a year earlier, in the wake of a flood of Watergate suits, the Supreme Court had completely revamped the law of qualified immunity. The Court held that the new test of whether a public official is immune from suit is: Did the conduct of the official "violate clearly established statutory or constitutional rights of which a reasonable person would have known"? The question focuses on the state of the law at the time of the alleged violation, in Engblom's and Palmer's case, April and May 1979.

Sometimes determining whether a right was "clearly established" at the time of the alleged violation is difficult. Here, however, the parties were dealing with a law, a constitutional amendment no less, that had never been brought to trial and therefore had never been interpreted by the courts. It would, in fact, be impossible to find a right that was *less* clearly established. In a brief opinion, the district court held that the defendants were protected by qualified immunity and therefore *Engblom* had to be dismissed.

For the first time in the two-hundred-year history of the Republic, someone had brought an arguably bona fide claim under the Third Amendment. But the case could not proceed *because* it was the first time in the two-hundred-year history of the Republic that someone had brought an arguably bona fide claim under the amendment. The strange saga of the Third Amendment continues.

FOURTH AMENDMENT

"The right of the people to be secure in their persons, houses, papers, and effects, against unreasonable searches and seizures, shall not be violated, and no Warrants shall issue, but upon probable cause, supported by Oath or affirmation, and particularly describing the place to be searched, and the persons or things to be seized."

Margaret and Alan McSurely with their son, Victor, in Kentucky, 1968, a year after their home was raided
LES JORDAN

Unreasonable Search and Seizure:
McSurely v. McClellan

O<small>N A HOT SUMMER NIGHT, AU-</small>
gust 11, 1967, in Pike County, Kentucky, in an old farmhouse in
the foothills of the Appalachian Mountains, two young civil rights
workers, Alan and Margaret McSurely, were settling in for the
evening. Alan was in a spare room writing at a makeshift desk
and Margaret was in the kitchen cooking some squash for dinner.
From the kitchen window Margaret spotted a dozen or so armed
men making their way through the tall grass behind their house.
Fearing that the men were looking for an escaped convict, Margaret called out to her husband. He was already up out of his
chair and on his way to the front of the house.

"I walked up to the door and reached my hand out to open the
door, [it] opened in on me and about five guys came running
right by me up into the living room and the first guy said, 'Where
is Alan McSurely?' They had gone right by me, I was back by the
door. I said, 'I'm right here.'"

The sheriff announced to Alan that he was under arrest for sedition against the Commonwealth of Kentucky and read aloud an
arrest warrant and search warrant. "As soon as [the sheriff] fin-

ished reading these to me there was a moment when it was clear nobody knew what to do . . . [then] some more guys come walking in the front door . . . in their uniforms with their guns drawn, and there was this guy with a business suit on and a tie. I recognized him as Thomas Ratliff."

The McSurelys and Thomas Ratliff had never met before that night, but what happened next in the McSurely home would lock them into a seventeen-year battle involving a powerful U.S. senator, his feud with a celebrated columnist, and more than eleven trips to five different courts.

Margaret Haring was born in Ashland, Kentucky, in 1936. The daughter of a well-to-do Baptist minister, Margaret was schooled in traditional southern ways and had little interest in politics or the seeds of social unrest beginning to take root around her. Rather, she left college to marry a young army man and promptly had two sons. When her husband was transferred, Margaret moved the family to Washington, D.C., and when her husband decided to pursue a career in medicine, Margaret went looking for secretarial work to help put him through school.

It soon became apparent, however, that neither her marriage nor her job was working out. Margaret and her husband began an unhappy series of separations and, on her own, Margaret was bored and frustrated with her secretarial work on Capitol Hill. She turned to a friend for help and the friend, in turn, put Margaret in touch with Drew Pearson, the Washington columnist.

At the time, Pearson was one of the most famous, some would say infamous, journalists in the country. With Jack Anderson, he wrote a syndicated newspaper column, "The Washington Merry-Go-Round." Part gossip, part political commentary, the column went after public officials for their personal as well as professional shortcomings. The combination of his wide audience and no-holds-barred approach made Pearson a man to be feared, especially on Capitol Hill.

In 1962, Margaret was one of Pearson's four secretaries. At the age of twenty-six, just as her marriage was ending, her political and social education began. For Pearson was not just a muckraker but, according to some, a "muckraker-crusader." People from all over the country wrote trying to get the columnist to champion, or at least mention, their cause. Screening Pearson's mail, Margaret was finally introduced to "the movement" that had begun to unsettle the country.

She became particularly interested in the Student Nonviolent Coordinating Committee (SNCC), which had been mounting voter registration drives among the black population in the South. "They got turned away and beaten up for trying to vote," Margaret says. "So I tried to get [Pearson] to write something about it."

Pearson also introduced Margaret, literally, to "inside" Washington. He would take her to parties or invite her to his home, where she met congressmen, senators, and the vice-president. She also typed Pearson's personal correspondence and even his diary. Within a few months, Margaret began an affair with her boss, who was then nearing seventy.

For a time, Margaret was happy with her role as secretary and mistress. "I was really struck by the power that this man had. This was before the women's movement and I knew nothing about being somebody in my own right. I was raised to think that a woman was support staff for a man, for somebody that was going to be something.

"Then he made the mistake of taking me to the Democratic Convention in '64."

At the convention, Margaret met face to face with the people behind Pearson's mail. "I met all these SNCC people. And I will never forget, an old black man was going around asking people if they had eaten. And it never occurred to me that there was a problem with people being hungry at that convention because here I was in a nice hotel. So I just started to really look at myself and what I was doing with my life. I volunteered to go to Mississippi.

"I . . . walked out of my house and [my ex-husband] got the kids. I'm not really a rash person, but either history is being made and I can be a part of it or I can choose to be on the sidelines. So I decided to go."

Margaret eventually returned to Washington in 1966, but she did not see Pearson. Instead, she took a job with the United Planning Organization (UPO), a program funded by the Office of Economic Opportunity (OEO) and designed to implement the Johnson administration's War on Poverty. At the UPO offices, Margaret worked down the hall from Alan McSurely.

Alan was born in Ohio in 1936 but grew up in the Washington suburbs. Like Margaret, he had married and separated young. Unlike Margaret, however, he had always been interested in political and social causes. At the time, Alan was doing probation work with the local juvenile court when he was offered a job at the UPO. There he worked with Margaret on the UPO's Neighborhood Youth Development Program, organizing summer activities for children in the slums of Washington. They soon fell in love.

Alan and Margaret discovered that they shared not only a passion for the same work, but also a similar philosophy. They believed that it was a mistake to structure programs around white people helping poor blacks. Rather, they felt that blacks should work with the black poor and whites with the white poor. So they left their work in the inner city and turned to Appalachia.

Alan was offered a job with the Appalachian Volunteers (AVs), another program funded by the OEO. He was to train the AV fieldworkers who would go into the mountains to work with the poor. The AVs were setting up new offices in Pikeville, located in Pike County, Kentucky, and they asked Alan to come down.

Pike is the largest county in the state of Kentucky. Although it is roughly the size of Rhode Island, in 1967 it had a population of only eighty thousand. About five thousand people lived in Pikeville, the largest and only city of consequence in the county. The rest of the population was scattered across the valley, up in the "hollers" and deep in the Appalachian Mountains of east Kentucky. Many were in great need of assistance. For although the coal-rich earth of Pike County had long been a bonanza for the mining industry, in the late 1960s nearly a quarter of the adult population was illiterate and nearly half of the families were living in poverty.

But needing outside assistance is one thing; desiring it is quite another. Many families had been in Pikeville for two centuries, able to perpetuate a close-knit and insular community by not traveling far from the hollers of their hometown. Suspicion and fear of outsiders was inbred and intractable.

Thomas Ratliff was fairly well known in Pike County. He first had a small law practice and then a successful career in the coal-mining business, eventually becoming a wealthy man. In 1964, he was elected to a six-year term as commonwealth attorney for the thirty-fifth judicial district of Kentucky, which included all of Pike County. In 1967, he was a Republican candidate for lieutenant governor of the state.

Alan and Margaret moved to Pike County on April 1, 1967. They rented a large frame house on a hill from a local gas contractor and truck driver, James Madison Compton. As soon as Alan's divorce became final, they were married.

Margaret took a job with the Southern Conference Educational Fund (SCEF), a civil rights organization founded in 1938, for which she researched the local coal-mining industry and its effects on the mountain people. That spring, Alan and Margaret went to Nashville to attend a meeting of the boards of SCEF, SNCC, and the Southern Students Organizing Committee. Although they had no way of knowing it at the time, this trip would later provide the basis for turning a backwoods controversy into a confrontation with the U.S. Senate.

At the meeting, a young man named Stokely Carmichael spoke. Carmichael was one of several emerging black leaders who had begun to shake the foundations of the civil rights movement and organizations such as SNCC. He spoke of a new kind of movement, grounded in the new and, to some, scary concept of "black power."

Carmichael attended the Nashville meeting, then left to spend a few days speaking on college campuses in Tennessee. In one college town, a small riot broke out after Carmichael gave a speech there. Depending on the source, the riot was either caused by Carmichael's inflammatory speech or was wholly unrelated to Carmichael and instead the result of a barroom fight. Either way, the McSurelys had long since returned to Pike County to resume their work.

Alan's job with the AVs, however, lasted less than a month. Not content to merely organize fieldworkers, he began speaking out about sweeping political and social reform. Some regarded Alan's political activism as harmless egotistical ramblings, some were frightened by it, and some simply did not like the impression it made. For one or all of these reasons, the AVs fired him.

Undaunted, Alan began helping Margaret with her SCEF work. The couple also joined picketers at the county courthouse to protest strip mining in the mountains. Certainly none of their activities was designed to ingratiate themselves with the establishment in Pike County. There was also some question as to whether the people the McSurelys had come to help, the poor and the uneducated, were even interested in the kind of assistance the movement had to give.

Margaret began to despair. She still believed in the war on poverty, but even for a war that by its definition is fought on the fringes, Pike County was an outpost. Perhaps because she herself was a Kentuckian, Margaret more than Alan sensed the wide chasm between themselves and the locals. "I knew the people didn't want us there, and wouldn't listen. And I was afraid, too. They kill you in those mountains for less than Al was doing."

The locals, too, it seems, were becoming afraid. Around the beginning of August, the McSurelys' landlord suddenly told them that they would have to leave. James Madison Compton said that his sister was coming up from Florida and needed the house. He wanted the McSurelys to move within the week. Alan and Margaret thought the request rather sudden, but began packing their things. Compton later admitted that although his sister was in fact arriving from Florida, he had used her arrival as an "excuse." "I was getting phone calls from my neighbors and customers asking me why I was letting Communists live on my land, and I wanted to be rid of them."

Alan asked his landlord to come up the hill and inspect the house to see that no damage had been done. Compton did not want to bother, but Alan insisted. So Compton, accompanied by his father, two of his sisters, and his brother-in-law, finally went up the hill. The McSurelys, in the process of moving, were not in at the time. The house was nearly empty. The furniture, dishes, pots, and pans were already moved. All that was left, stacked the length of a wall, were materials related to the McSurelys' work: books, pamphlets, brochures, photographs, posters, reels of films, and correspondence. The Comptons had never seen anything like it.

"Some were so surprised and excited about it, they wanted to leave the house," Compton said. He, however, stayed to look through the material and would later testify as to what he saw.

A: I saw a number of photos of blacks and whites mixed. . . . Everything I seen was hate literature. . . . What few clippings I read was just literature that you see from these radicals throughout the United States that had the marches.

Q: Who were they hating?

A: I would say the American people.

Q: Do you remember any piece of literature that you saw?

A: No, I don't really, just to say the exact words, I don't. I just gazed at them. I don't know if I read any completely.

Q: Did you read any of them incompletely?

A: Partly, yes.

Q: Please help me out if you possibly can, Mr. Compton. Can you recall anything about it?

A: Well, I seen some of the literature on that [Selma] march they had down South. . . .

Q: It was [literature] about the racial question in the South?

A: Right. Not necessarily in the South, but where these colleges had their problems. I believe there was some in Berkeley, California, I am not sure about that . . . I just glanced at them and read maybe a paragraph or two . . . to me, I thought it was a Communist-based deal.

Q: Now, I want to make sure that I understand what it was that led you to that conclusion. You have thus far described the pictures and the literature about Selma and Berkeley. What else was there that made you draw that conclusion?

A: I believe there were some books there with Communistic titles to them that gave me that impression.

Q: Do you remember what they were?

A: Right off, I don't. I never read a Communist book in my life that I know of.

Q: You knew these books were Communist books?

A: Yes, I did.

Q: How could you tell?

A: I knew that China was Communist, I knew that Russia was Communist, I knew that Cuba was Communist.

Q: And there were some books there about China?

A: I'm pretty sure there were.

Q: And there were some books there about Cuba?

A: I think there was some books there about Castro.

Q: Do you know whether it was for or against Castro?

A: No, I don't know that.

Q: And do you know whether it was for or against Russia?

A: No, I don't.

Q: Do you know whether it was for or against China?

A: No, I don't.

Q: You just knew that the book was about China?

A: That's right. I didn't find nothing about America or the United States or freedom.

James Madison Compton called his high school friend Perry Justice. An embalmer and funeral director by trade, Justice had recently been elected to a four-year term as sheriff of Pike County.

Compton said of that conversation, "I told him that we had a nest of Communists among us that should be checked out."

On August 11, Sheriff Justice called and asked Compton and his son to attend the fiscal court meeting that day. Justice also called Thomas Ratliff, Marrs Alan May, the local county prosecutor, and John Burke, special agent for the FBI assigned to Pike County, requesting that they all attend the meeting too.

The Pike County fiscal court meeting, held in the local courthouse, was open to the public and lasted most of the day. It was, as one local explains it, a place for townspeople to air their grievances, "to come and say my road needs fixing, or I got chicken thieves in the area," or, as on this day, that some of the neighbors up the holler were planning a revolution.

On August 11, the fiscal court passed a new school budget and assessed taxes to support it. What happened next is open to some dispute. Thomas Ratliff says he arrived late to the meeting and "sat there sort of in the background and listened." John Burke said Thomas Ratliff ran the meeting.

"Ratliff took over and said something to the effect that 'We are finally going to take action.' . . . The FBI normally does not take part in joint ventures with local departments. So I couldn't see what purpose I had in being there. . . . He got obviously perturbed and said something to the effect, 'If you can't come with us, then please tell us what you know about the McSurelys.' I said, 'I cannot tell you anything.' . . . And then [Ratliff] said, 'You are American, the FBI is an American agency, you have to assist us.' I said, 'I am sorry, I can't give you any assistance.'"

Thomas Ratliff and Marrs Allen May went across the hall to look through the state laws, or Kentucky Revised Statutes (KRS). They found KRS 432.40, Kentucky's antisedition law. The statute, passed in 1920 in the aftermath of World War I and the Bolshevik Revolution in Russia, was amended slightly in 1922 but otherwise had remained unchanged for more than half a century. Under the statute, the crime of sedition was punishable by up to twenty-one years in prison or a fine of up to ten thousand dollars, or both.

According to Burke, "Mr. Ratliff stated that undoubtedly a Pike County, Kentucky, jury would convict McSurely of sedition. He stated that he expected the American Civil Liberties Union, ACLU, would probably be able to overrule convictions with appeals to superior courts, but his purposes would be accomplished by the initial conviction."

"He was mistaken about that," Thomas Ratliff says. "He had me confused with Marrs Allen May."

In any event, Ratliff explains, "People were fed up. . . . Hanoi Jane is one thing. But when they move into your neighborhood, and they've got $1 million of your tax money to do it with . . . These people had weaseled their way into these federal programs . . . [and] there were some moral things involved. There were accusations of all kinds of sex going on up there. . . . In that period of time, we're talking about some serious business. We're talking about cities that were on fire in this country. We're talking about college students who were shot by the National Guard. . . . The people were aware of it and they were bothered by it. . . . It was an affront to their patriotism, it was an affront to a lot of things they believed in."

An arrest warrant was prepared for Alan McSurely and a search warrant prepared for the McSurely home, directing the searchers to seize "seditious matter or printing press or other machinery to print or circulate seditious matter."

The McSurelys' new home was about a mile north of Pikeville, a small, one-story wood frame house, thirty-five by thirty-five feet square, with a living room, bedroom, study, kitchen, and bath. Because the McSurelys had moved in just a week before, the house was wall-to-wall with still packed boxes and cartons. They had little furniture and fewer clothes. They had, however, an overflow of books and papers. In addition to the materials for their work, the McSurelys had hundreds of books and stacks of correspondence. They typed all of their letters and always kept carbons. They also kept all of the mail they received. The packed cartons were filled and the house crammed with a written record of Alan's and Margaret's lives.

On the night of August 11, Sheriff Justice and his men were the first to arrive at the McSurely home. The sheriff led several deputies through the front door while another group surprised Margaret in the kitchen; they ushered her into the living room, where Alan had just been placed under arrest for sedition.

"They grabbed me," Alan says. "They searched me and then they put me over on the couch and they said don't move." Margaret, who was obviously several months pregnant, was left alone.

Then Thomas Ratliff arrived with Marrs Allen May, and the deputies who had remained outside to secure the house were called inside. According to Alan, "Ratliff got this director's chair that we had in the living room and pulled it over in front of the bookcase . . . he pulled books out, thumbed through them while these deputies were bringing stuff to him. . . . He had two stacks at his feet and he put some over on one side and some over on the other side."

More than a dozen men swarmed through the tiny house. They took every book from the shelves. They pulled drawers from the desks and dressers and emptied their contents on the floor. They hauled boxes and clothes from the closets and rummaged through the kitchen cabinets. They took the sheets off the mattress, the mattress off the bed frame, and then took the bed frame apart. "I don't know why they did that," says Margaret. "But they left it that way."

It was a sweltering August night, but Alan was shivering on the couch. "I was scared shitless," he says.

Margaret went over to the couch and sat beside her husband. "I tried to reassure Al that if we could just make it through the night and get word to the outside what was going on . . . it was then this [deputy] in a yellow windbreaker came up."

The deputy pulled Alan's arms behind his back and said, "Hold your head up high. I want to see how you look when you hang."

"It was at that moment that I realized we were in extreme danger," Margaret says. "So I stood up tall and said, 'Well look, I'm pregnant and I've got to go to the bathroom and I'm going.'"

On the way, Margaret picked up the phone. Thomas Ratliff called out to the deputies not to stop her. She called a local lawyer, who said he would meet them at the jail.

While Margaret was on the phone, someone found papers detailing her work for SNCC. An arrest warrant was drafted on the spot and she too was placed under arrest. Then the character of the search began to change.

"[Ratliff] wasn't careful at all about what he was doing from then on," Alan says. "He just said bring the stuff . . . he would thumb through it and put it down. There were no longer two stacks, it was just one big stack."

The deputies brought to the pile the McSurelys' phone bills, utilities bills, tax returns and canceled checks, their letters, journals and notebooks, their marriage certificate and old college exams. They also added all 564 of the McSurelys' books. Two hundred and ninety-six of them were copies of the same work, *False Witness* by Harvey Matuso. *Guerrilla Warfare* by Ché Guevara, *Das Kapital* by Karl Marx, *The Teachings of Karl Marx* by Lenin, and the collected works of Mao Tse-tung went into the pile, along with the works of Frederick Douglass; fiction by Albert Camus, John Updike, and Dostoyevsky; poetry by W. B. Yeats; a book called *Tricks and Training for Cats;* and a copy of the Washington, D.C., telephone directory.

Thomas Ratliff, Alan says, was "constantly urging people to hurry up, bring him the stuff, get it in the living room."

"I didn't intend to spend the night there," Ratliff later said. "Now, you know it's easy for someone in a courtroom to say in hindsight . . . why did you take this volume or that volume. Or why were there clothes under the books in the bottom of a box. I mean, this was the real world we were dealing with, not an ivory tower in Washington, D.C., in the federal courthouse. It was a dark night. I sure didn't want to hang around. I'm sure the sheriff didn't either. The McSurelys—their things were as precious as mine, I'm not saying they're not. But, you know, there's a real world out there. All of our rights to some degree are watered down to live in the real world."

A few deputies went to a neighbor's house to borrow a pickup truck. All of the McSurelys' belongings were packed into the truck and hauled away.

Alan and Margaret were jailed that evening. Bail was set at five thousand dollars for Alan, two thousand for Margaret. The couple soon got word that friends were trying to raise bail and had also enlisted the aid of William Kunstler and Morton Stavis in New York. Kunstler and Stavis were two lawyers who had recently formed the Center for Constitutional Rights and would take on cases like the McSurelys' for little or no fee. Now in contact with the outside world, the McSurelys' concern over their physical safety began to give way to a new fear.

It was clear that the search party had taken everything the McSurelys had. That included boxes packed in haste and still unopened, filled with papers they had not looked at for years.

Things accumulate; the McSurelys could not be sure what had been seized. Their biggest fear was that their lists of contacts would now somehow put their friends and co-workers in danger.

Margaret was even more concerned than Alan. She had seen one of the men take her diary, which detailed not only her private thoughts, but also her relationships and affairs with various men in her life. She also knew that among her papers was every love letter she had received, including those from Drew Pearson. Through friends in Washington, she alerted the columnist and asked for help in making bail.

The McSurelys spent a week in jail before friends from Louisville raised bail. A Pike County grand jury hearing was set for September 5 to determine whether the McSurelys would be indicted for sedition. In the meantime, William Kunstler and Morton Stavis set up a legal leg race of sorts. They petitioned the federal courts to declare the Kentucky sedition statute unconstitutional. They hoped to have it struck down before the local grand jury could act.

Margaret, privately, was still trying to reach Pearson. On the back of an SCEF press release about their case she wrote:

Dear D.P.

Thanks anyway about the bail. It's O.K. But if you had any sense you would do everything you could to get this case into the federal courts immediately and out of the hands of Pike Co. officials who stole everything and will use it. The 3-judge fed. panel must be convened before the grand jury hearing.

Margaret

Pearson never responded to Margaret's note; indeed he never contacted her again.

On September 11, a Pike County grand jury indicted Alan and Margaret on charges of sedition pursuant to the Kentucky statute. Three days later, the U.S. District Court for the Eastern District of Kentucky declared, "It is difficult to believe that capable lawyers could seriously contend that this statute is constitutional.

"[The statute] contravenes the First Amendment . . . because it unduly prohibits freedom of speech, freedom of the press, and the right of assembly," the court wrote. "It fails to distinguish between the advocacy of ideas and the advocacy of action. . . . It imposes the penalty of imprisonment for advocating an unpopular political belief." The court permanently enjoined the Commonwealth of Kentucky from proceeding further with the sedition charges against the McSurelys, or from bringing such charges against anyone else.

Then, in a paragraph that would be read ragged over the next seventeen years, the court directed that Thomas Ratliff hold the seized materials in "safekeeping," pending a possible appeal: "It is further ordered that all books, papers, documents or other material now in the custody of the Commonwealth Attorney of Pike County, Ratliff, reflected by the Inventory filed in this action continue to be held by him in safe keeping until final disposition of the case by appeal or otherwise." Thus, the McSurelys found themselves in the peculiar position of having been freed while their possessions were still locked away.

In a bizarre coincidence, on August 11, 1967, the same day that the McSurelys' home was raided, the U.S. Senate approved Resolution 150 of the Ninetieth Congress. The resolution grew out of a Senate study that reported that approximately 166 riots and major civil disturbances occurred between the beginning of 1965 and mid-1968, resulting in 189 people killed, 7,615 people reported injured, and an estimated $158 million in property damage. Thus, Resolution 150 authorized the Senate Committee on Government Operations to investigate the disturbances and propose measures to preserve "law and order and . . . domestic tranquility within the United States."

The Permanent Subcommittee on Investigations, headed by the powerful Arkansas senator John L. McClellan, was chosen to run the investigations. McClellan had been a member of the Senate since 1943, serving on some of its most high-profile and important committees. He had also been a longtime target in Drew Pearson's column.

Through the Washington grapevine, the subcommittee learned of the McSurelys' papers. On October 8, 1967, John Brick, an investigator for the subcommittee, traveled to Pikeville and spoke with Thomas Ratliff. He examined photocopies of 234 of the McSurelys' documents and then went home to report on what he had found. Four days later, Brick made another trip to Pike

County. When he returned to Washington, he had copies of the 234 documents with him.

According to court records, "the 234 documents were maintained by order of Senator McClellan in Brick's personal file under lock and key, and . . . [a] personal letter to Margaret McSurely from Drew Pearson was displayed to Senator McClellan and then placed in a sealed envelope to be opened only by John Brick, J. S. Adams, General Counsel, and Senator McClellan."

A week later, on October 18, John Brick arrived at the McSurelys' house. He told Alan and Margaret that the subcommittee was investigating the riot that occurred after the Nashville meeting they had attended. Brick served each of them with a subpoena from the subcommittee.

As it turned out, the Senate subcommittee was interested not in the McSurelys themselves, but in their belongings, still locked away in the Pike County jail. Alan and Margaret had no intention of making their papers available to the subcommittee; they also had no idea that the subcommittee already had them. That same day, the McSurelys' attorneys asked the district court for an order directing that documents be returned and for an injunction prohibiting the release of the documents to the Senate. A court hearing was set for the beginning of December. Alan and Margaret felt confident that they could protect their papers this time because, they say, "We had a better sense of these people from Washington than we did of the people from Pikeville."

Their confidence began to falter, however, after they read about themselves in the *New York Times*. A November 1, 1967, article was headlined "SENATE UNIT GETS MILITANTS' FILE." The article referred to a "Kentucky raid" and stated, "Field investigators of the Senate Permanent Investigating Subcommittee . . . have gained access to a large file of 'important' correspondence and papers. . . . The Subcommittee's method in obtaining the material is being challenged in the federal courts, but many of the documents apparently have already been placed in the investigators' hands."

The McSurelys thought it had to be a mistake. Why would the subcommittee have sent the subpoena if it already had their papers? Alan and Margaret had thought that once their side of the story was fully told, they would succeed in having the subpoena quashed. Now they were not so sure.

At the December 5 district court hearing, the McSurelys were represented by Morton Stavis. Also present were John Brick, Donald O'Donnell, the subcommittee's chief counsel, and attorneys from the Justice Department. First, the court instructed the lawyers to draw up a "stipulation of facts." So the two sets of attorneys went to one side of the courtroom, parsed through the convoluted series of events, and agreed on one list of undisputed facts. They then showed the stipulation to their clients for confirmation.

"I read it over very carefully," Alan says, "and there was a lot of new information in it about Mr. Brick coming down and talking to Mr. Ratliff and inspecting the documents and going back up to Washington and coming back down. And then finally bringing down the subpoenas in the middle of October. But it said absolutely nothing about the fact that he had already taken the documents up to Washington. . . . So I said, 'Let's go back over there and find out whether they got any of our stuff.'"

Morton Stavis went back to the other side of the room, this time with his clients. He asked the attorneys for the subcommittee whether the Senate already had some of the McSurelys' papers in Washington. Brick and O'Donnell looked at each other in silence for a moment and then asked to confer in private. When they came back, they told Stavis and the McSurelys that, yes, some documents were taken from their pile of possessions and brought up to the Senate. The stipulation of facts was amended accordingly.

Margaret was in a panic. Both she and Alan had been fearful all along for their friends and co-workers. They were certain if anything was taken to Washington it was the lists of names, addresses, and organizations they had built up over the years. But Margaret, privately, was panicked about what else the Senate might have. She knew her diary had been taken from her house, but did not know whether it—or any other private papers—had been turned over to the subcommittee.

The district court denied the McSurelys' motion to have their documents returned and ordered Ratliff and the McSurelys to comply with the subpoena. Months later, the U.S. Court of Appeals for the Sixth Circuit reversed the district court on the issue of the return of the documents. The Sixth Circuit explained that the "safekeeping order" had been issued so the documents would be preserved for appeal. Since time for appeal in the sedition case had run out, the documents must be returned. The court, however, declined to address the McSurelys' constitutional arguments regarding the subpoenas. Therefore, the court ordered that the documents be returned, but left the subcommittee free to enforce the subpoenas.

More than a year after the raid, the McSurelys would finally get their possessions back. On the morning of November 8, 1968, Alan and Margaret drove to the Pikeville Federal Building. Inside, stored in two jail cells in stacks several feet high, were the books, letters, pamphlets, papers, and clothing taken from the McSurely home. "It was ridiculous," Margaret says. "Our stuff was in jail."

Among the men overseeing the return of the documents was John Brick. He called Alan aside to talk. Brick was holding an inventory, fourteen pages long, labeled "A List of 234 Items." It was a list of the documents he had copied and taken to Washington. He also had two cartons; one contained the original 234 items taken from the McSurely home and the other contained photocopies of those items. Brick asked Alan to go through each document, one at a time, comparing the original to the copy, to ensure that the McSurelys received everything.

"We started with number one on this list," says Alan, "and I started just skimming through them to make sure they were the same as the originals. When I got down to number six on the list . . . I realized that this was the famous diary that we heard about. I had never seen it before. . . . It was the most intimate details of her relationship with Mr. Pearson, and I wasn't stunned by what I was reading but I was stunned by the fact that . . . it just dropped on me like a pipe, a lead pipe right on my shoulders. These guys, this guy standing right here in front of me . . . had taken this stuff . . . up to the Senate and kept it there for a year, and said that they were investigating riots.

"I couldn't hardly think or feel, I was just totally numb by that. I looked at him, and he . . . knew which thing I was reading and he wouldn't look at me, he would look out the window and look down. . . . I put those aside and I started reading a couple more and got to somewhere in the 11, 12, 13, and these were very romantic, beautifully written love letters that Margaret had gotten from . . . a friend of mine, that she was going with when she went south and worked with SNCC.

"I had never known about this affair. I didn't have any right to know about it, it happened a long time before I met her, but I felt, you know, like an intruder, like I was getting into reading something that I had no business to read about Margaret. If she wanted to tell me about that, it was her business, but she apparently hadn't wanted to . . . up until then.

"And then the thought . . . these things have been passed around and looked at by no telling how many old men up in the Senate, plus, of course . . . Ratliff and his troops had been looking at this stuff for a year and a half, too.

"So I said to Brick, 'This is the kind of stuff that you took to Washington?' . . . He never looked me in the eye the whole time. He kept his eyes down like this, and he said, 'Just keep on reading.' So I kept moving through this list of stuff. There was a letter, number 140, which started out, 'Dear Young Lady.' It was a short letter from Drew Pearson to Margaret when she was in Mississippi. It was written in this tone of half-father, half-lover, jilted-lover, 'What are you doing down there, we can do much more good if you are up here with me,' et cetera. 'Please come back' and that sort of thing.

"I felt embarrassed for Drew Pearson for a minute . . . but then I realized . . . how it could have been used in the hands of somebody that didn't like Drew Pearson, and I felt very, very concerned, and a little bit guilty that we had done anything in any way that might have caused problems for him.

"We got to 201, and this was another letter that Pearson had written to Margaret when she was in Mississippi, in October of '64, and it was addressed, 'Dearest Cucumber,' which I had never heard her called before. . . . He told her how much he respected what she was doing and everything, and talked about how much he loved her. . . .

"When I finished reading this letter, Brick [looked] away, and I said something about, 'Did this help you investigate the riots?' and he wouldn't say a word.

"As he handed me these letters, he had this smile on his face . . . it was a sense of like two men, that we were looking at some, you know, sexy picture or something like that. 'We are the boys and we can look at this stuff.'

"It made me sick. I was so furious that I really couldn't concentrate. . . . My basic thought was to smash him in the face. . . . I have been trained as a psychologist and to be cool and to help people figure out ways of expressing their hostility in a constructive manner, et cetera, but at that time the only thing I could think about was to hit this guy."

"I was trying to look over their shoulders," Margaret says. "I saw they had taken some love letters of mine and I was really embarrassed. I couldn't believe that they would do anything that dirty."

"In the back of my mind, it wasn't just him," Alan says, "it was like a gang rape, he had raped my wife right there in front of me."

At home, Alan separated Margaret's papers from his own. "I took my stuff in another room because I didn't want anybody else to see me," says Margaret. "I ran through and saw what they had taken and I was devastated. . . . I knew that these things had to be destroyed."

Alan, parsing through his own papers in the other room, was beginning to think the same. The McSurelys were convinced that there was no way to keep their papers safe from anyone who might want to take them. "They hadn't been safe from the orders of a federal judge and they certainly couldn't be safe in our house," Margaret says.

At first, Alan and Margaret were going to discuss the idea with Morton Stavis. "But [a lawyer] would be obliged to tell us not to do it, so we decided not to tell Morty—he's never forgiven me," Margaret says with a grin.

The McSurelys burned all of the "234 Items" in their backyard that evening. Alan and Margaret knew the bonfire ensured they would be cited for contempt of Congress, because now they could not possibly comply with the subpoena. They also knew that they were losing, irretrievably, a large part of the record of their lives that they had built up over the years. "It was really sad to me," Margaret says, "having to destroy something that is very precious. But it had been contaminated."

"Whenever you shall find a painter, male or female, I pray you to suggest a scene and a subject for the pencil," former President John Adams wrote to a friend who had asked him about the origins of the American Revolution. "The scene is the Council Chamber in the old Town House in Boston. The date is in the month of

February, 1761. . . . In this chamber, round a great fire, were seated five Judges . . . all arrayed in their new, fresh, rich robes of scarlet, English broadcloth; in their large cambric bands, and immense judicial wigs. In this chamber were seated at a long table all the barristers at law of Boston, and of the neighboring county of Middlesex." One of the lawyers at the table was Adams, then twenty-five and just admitted to the bar of the Massachusetts Bay Colony.

The case before the superior court involved a writ of assistance or "general warrant." Such a writ gave an officer of the Crown the authority to enter anyone's property at any time to search simply for "smuggled goods." In England, notorious abuse of the writs provoked such public condemnation that by the mid-1700s their use was largely restricted to one kind of case only—sedition.

In America, however, when the colonists began to revolt against the enormous taxes imposed on them by the Acts of Trade, the writs were resurrected. Parliament authorized use of writs of assistance "to command all sheriffs and constables, &c., to . . . [break] open houses, stores, shops, cellars, ships, bales, trunks, chests, casks, packages of all sorts, to search for goods . . . which had been imported . . . without paying the taxes imposed by . . . the acts of trade."

The merchants of Boston demanded a hearing before the superior court on use of the writs. They were represented by James Otis, Jr., who had resigned his prestigious post as advocate general of the admiralty court to take on the cause. As reconstructed by Adams, Otis's argument before the superior court laid the foundation for the Fourth Amendment's prohibition against unreasonable searches and seizures.

"In the first place," Otis began, "may it please your Honors, I will admit that writs of one kind may be legal; that is, special writs directed to special officers, to search certain houses and so on specially set forth in the writ." The evil of the writs of assistance, however, was the arbitrary power they granted by leaving it up to officials conducting the search to decide who, where, when, and what to search. "It is a power," Otis said, "that places the liberty of every man in the hands of every petty officer." Such power threatened the right of privacy, the simple right to be left alone. "A man's house is his castle, and whilst he is quiet he is as well guarded as a prince in his castle," Otis declared. "This writ,

if it should be declared legal, would totally annihilate this privilege."

For five hours Otis railed against the writs of assistance. "Otis
was a flame of fire!" Adams wrote. "With a promptitude of classical allusions, a depth of research, a rapid summary of historical
events and dates, a profusion of legal authorities, a prophetic
glance of his eye to futurity, and a torrent of impetuous elo-
quence, he hurried away every thing before him.

"Every man of a crowded audience appeared to me to go away,
as I did, ready to take arms against writs of assistance. Then and
there was the first scene of the first act of opposition to the arbitrary claims of Great Britain. Then and there the child Independence was born. In fifteen years, namely in 1776, he grew up to
manhood, and declared himself free."

At the heart of the Fourth Amendment is the phrase "unreasonable search." To be brought within the amendment, an act by a
government official must first be deemed a "search." Advances in
law enforcement and technology have made this determination
far more difficult than the Framers could ever have envisioned. If
a police officer looks through your pockets, you have been
"searched" within the meaning of the Fourth Amendment. But
what if the officer tests samples of your blood or urine? What if
the government places a wiretap on your telephone line? Have
you been the subject of a Fourth Amendment search?

In answer, the Supreme Court looks to the rights sought to be
protected by the Fourth Amendment. In 1928, Justice Brandeis, in
dissent, wrote:

> The makers of our Constitution undertook to secure conditions
> favorable to the pursuit of happiness. They recognized the signifi-
> cance of man's spiritual nature, of his feelings and of his intellect.
> They knew that only a part of the pain, pleasure and satisfactions
> of life are to be found in material things. They sought to protect
> Americans in their beliefs, their thoughts, their emotions and their
> sensations. They conferred, as against the Government, the right to
> be let alone—the most comprehensive of rights and the right most
> valued by civilized men. To protect that right, every unjustifiable
> intrusion by the Government upon the privacy of the individual,
> whatever the means employed, must be deemed a violation of the
> Fourth Amendment.

Nearly a half century later, the Supreme Court adopted the

Brandeis reading of the Fourth Amendment. The government con-
ducts a search, and therefore must adhere to Fourth Amendment
restrictions, if a public official intrudes on an individual's "reasonable expectation of privacy." (In the examples above, taking blood
and urine and wiretapping are all Fourth Amendment searches.)

But once an act of a government official is deemed to be a search,
the next question is an even thornier one: Was it "reasonable"? The
Fourth Amendment starts with the presumption that before a
search is conducted, government officials must first obtain a warrant describing precisely the person, place, or thing to be searched,
and that once the search is under way, the officials must comply
with the warrant. Some believe the exigencies of law enforcement,
however, often make such rules unworkable. So the Supreme Court
has carved out exceptions to the warrant rule. For example,
searches conducted immediately after the "hot pursuit" of a suspected felon do not require warrants. Whether conducted pursuant
to the warrant rule or one of its exceptions, all Fourth Amendment
searches are governed by the command of reasonableness.

The McSurelys felt that neither the local Kentucky officials nor
members of the Senate subcommittee had obtained their documents in a reasonable manner. Indeed, Alan and Margaret were
convinced that they had been caught in the middle of a feud between Senator McClellan and Drew Pearson. They knew Pearson
had frequently attacked McClellan in his column. They also knew
that the senator had singled out from their hundreds of papers a
love letter from Drew Pearson to Margaret. They thought Senator
McClellan and his aides had conspired with Thomas Ratliff to
obtain incriminating information about the columnist.

On the other hand, Morton Stavis was never really convinced
of the conspiracy theory. He says, "I think Brick just went over
the materials and said, 'Wow.' He brought them back to the boss
and McClellan picks this one letter, 'Dearest Cucumber,' and says
to keep it under lock and key. I think it was just a glorious find."

Stavis did, however, think that the subcommittee had violated
the McSurelys' constitutional rights. So on the same day that Alan
and Margaret were to appear before Senator McClellan, their lawyer filed a civil suit for damages against the subcommittee's members. Immediately afterward, the McSurelys walked over to the
new Senate Office Building, stood before Senator McClellan's subcommittee, and stated that they refused to comply with the sub-

poenas. Soon after, the McSurelys were prosecuted for contempt of Congress. Faced only with the question of whether the McSurelys had complied with the subpoenas, a D.C. jury convicted Alan and Margaret of contempt of Congress. Alan was sentenced to one year and Margaret to three months in prison.

On appeal to the U.S. Court of Appeals for the D.C. Circuit, the McSurelys claimed that their contempt convictions should be reversed because they were based on evidence seized in an illegal search. To ensure compliance with the Fourth Amendment, the Supreme Court had fashioned the "exclusionary rule." The Court held that evidence seized in an illegal search could not be introduced at trial as evidence against the person whose Fourth Amendment rights were violated. Convictions based on such evidence must be set aside.

The most basic aspect of a traditional Fourth Amendment search is that it must be pursuant to a warrant that is based on "probable cause" and describes with particularity "the place to be searched, and the persons or things to be seized." The person who makes these determinations must be a "neutral and detached magistrate," not the police officer who is in the business of ferreting out crime.

The warrant issued for the search of the McSurely home was based on an affidavit by James Marion Compton. Compton stated only that one James Madison Compton (his father), "a reputable citizen of Pike County, Kentucky," on August 4, 1967, "did observe certain seditious materials . . . at or on the above described premises." James Marion swore to the existence of materials that his father, not he, had seen.

The Court of Appeals found that the affidavit did not support a search warrant for several reasons. There was nothing in the affidavit to indicate James Marion's connection to the McSurely investigation. Furthermore, the affidavit was not based on James Marion's own observations, but on hearsay. Finally, the affidavit mentioned only "seditious material." Even assuming that the Kentucky sedition statute was valid, there was nothing in the affidavit by which the magistrate could make an independent determination that the material was indeed seditious and therefore in violation of the law.

The warrant itself directed officials to seize "seditious matter or printing press or other machinery to print or circulate seditious matter." Again, there was no particularized description of what materials could be seized. It was "so vague and broad as to be the very antithesis of the 'particularity' required by the Fourth Amendment." Two centuries after Otis's historic argument, the Pike County officials had, in effect, resurrected the notorious writ of assistance.

Indeed, during the trial of the McSurelys' civil suit for damages, some of those who conducted the search testified about the role the Fourth Amendment played. The sheriff of Pike County, Perry Justice, was asked:

Q: Did you ever, in the course of your years as a sheriff, look at the Fourth Amendment to the Constitution?
A: No, sir.
Q: Did you know that there is anything in the Fourth Amendment about how to conduct searches and seizures?
A: Not that I recall, sir, no.
Q: Did anybody ever advise you that there was something in the Constitution about searches and seizures?
A: Not specifically, no, sir. . . .
Q: Do you know what a general warrant is?
A: A general warrant?
Q: Yes.
A: No, sir. I couldn't distinguish. I just don't know what you are talking about, sir. . . .
Q: . . . Isn't there in fact one specific thing mentioned there [in the warrant] to be seized?
A: Printing press and other machinery to print or circulate seditious matter.
Q: You saw a mimeograph machine which might be considered a printing press, right?
A: Yes.
Q: You didn't take that?
A: No, sir.
Q: You saw a machine which was a typewriter?
A: Yes, sir.
Q: You didn't take that?
A: No, sir.
Q: Is there anything else that if you saw you could identify as being required by that warrant?
A: In my opinion, sir, what I took was what I considered seditious.
Q: You mean everything you took was seditious?
A: I did not examine all of it, sir.
Q: Then how do you know that it was seditious if you didn't examine it?
A: I just took it.

The U.S. Court of Appeals for the D.C. Circuit held that the search of the McSurely home was a classic example of a general search in violation of the Fourth Amendment. The documents on which the subpoenas and thus the contempt convictions were based were the product of that illegal search. The subpoenas should have been suppressed. Therefore, the court held, the contempt convictions had to be reversed.

There remained, however, the McSurelys' civil suit against the Senate subcommittee members. Alan and Margaret amended the complaint to add John Brick and Thomas Ratliff to tie in with their theory that the federal defendants had conspired with Thomas "for the purpose of harassing and intimidating the McSurelys . . . or carrying out a 'personal vendetta' of [Senator] McClellan." The McSurelys wanted vindication, in one suit, for all of the events that stemmed from the night of August 11.

The Senate defendants immediately moved to dismiss the case, claiming that they had absolute immunity under the speech and debate clause of the U.S. Constitution (Article I, section 6). That clause was designed to preserve the independence and integrity of the legislative branch by ensuring that its members would not be subject to suit based on their legislative acts.

The full Court of Appeals for the D.C. Circuit, ten judges, many of whom had by now become familiar with Alan and Margaret, Ratliff, and the senator, heard arguments on the immunity issue. All agreed that if any members of the subcommittee had disseminated copies of the documents outside of Congress, then such action would not be protected by the speech and debate clause. All ten judges also agreed that, regardless of how the documents came to be in the possession of the Senate subcommittee and staff, what those members did with the documents in the course of their legislative duties was protected by the speech and debate clause. Therefore, Brick, O'Donnell, Adlerman, and McClellan all had absolute immunity with respect to their inspection of the documents, as well as their issuance of subpoenas and contempt citations.

The Fourth Amendment, however, tripped up any neat disposition of the remaining issue regarding Brick's acts of inspecting the documents and transporting them back to Washington. Information gathering in preparation for a congressional hearing is protected by the speech and debate clause. Unlike activities performed within the halls of Congress, however, investigative field-work is not given absolute immunity; the investigator is protected from suit *unless* he violates the Fourth Amendment in the process. Thus the ten judges focused on the issue of whether Brick's inspection and transportation of the McSurelys' papers was a "search and seizure" within the meaning of the Fourth Amendment. They split right down the middle, five to five.

In the federal courts, a split decision affirms the decision of the court below. Here, the lower court had held that the McSurelys made a strong enough argument that Brick's inspection and transportation of the documents *was* a Fourth Amendment search (and therefore not protected by the speech and debate clause) to at least withstand a motion to dismiss. Therefore, this issue would proceed to trial.

Usually, once a party wins on an issue, particularly in the early stages, such as here, that's it; no one remembers that the vote was close. But in this instance, the split would prove to be impor-tant, finally providing the key to closing the door on the McSurely case.

In the meantime, Thomas Ratliff was making his own motion to dismiss on grounds of immunity. As a local prosecutor, Ratliff could not claim the protection of the speech and debate clause. He could, however, rely on the doctrine of qualified immunity. At the time, the test of whether a public official should be immune from suit was whether his conduct "violate[d] clearly established statutory or constitutional rights of which a reasonable person would have known."

Using this standard, the Court of Appeals for the D.C. Circuit concluded that it was "surely at least arguable" that Thomas Ratliff should have known that the Compton affidavit upon which the search warrant was based was inadequate, and that the search as carried out exceeded the scope of the warrant. The court also concluded that the McSurelys should have an oppor-tunity to prove that a reasonable person would have known that the documents protected by the safekeeping order could not be turned over to the subcommittee. Thus the case against Thomas Ratliff, too, would proceed to trial.

The trial began in front of a jury in a federal district court in Washington, D.C. It was November 1982, fifteen years after the night on which the McSurelys met Thomas Ratliff and the Senate

passed Resolution 150. Alan and Margaret, now divorced, sat together at the plaintiffs' table with Morton Stavis, who continued
to represent them. The lawsuit, however, had outlasted most of
the other participants. Drew Pearson had died years before, never
having spoken publicly about the case. Senator McClellan, Brick,
and Adlerman had also died. Their estates were substituted as
defendants and all were represented by the Justice Department.
Thomas Ratliff, represented by his own attorney, was the only
live defendant in the courtroom.

Ratliff testified that he was familiar with the Fourth Amendment and that he considered the search warrant to be sufficient
under the law. He also testified that his role in the whole episode
had been merely an advisory one. Under Kentucky law, he said,
the commonwealth attorney did not have authority until an indictment had been handed down. With respect to the safekeeping
order, Ratliff testified that he interpreted the order as a preservation, not a secrecy, order. He pointed out that the documents had
not been "sealed"—the standard procedure for ensuring the confidentiality of court papers. Finally, Ratliff testified that as soon
as he was contacted by the subcommittee, he tried to reach the
three judges who had issued the safekeeping order. He succeeded
in reaching only one, who told him "not to get into a confrontation with the United States Senate."

Ratliff also testified as to his opinion of the McSurelys, Margaret in particular. "Also among [the] evidence was a diary of
Mrs. McSurely which I considered an important part of the evidence. . . . I got a picture of the lives and careers of these two
people. . . . Mrs. McSurely was very generous with her sexual
favors. . . . She would rate her sexual partners by—well, by their
anatomy. . . . If you were a good performer, you were 'beef
stroganoff.' If you were less skillful as a sexual partner, you
would get a different rating based on a different food. . . . She
abandoned her husband. . . . She sought the help of a psychiatrist
and that was detailed in her diary."

Morton Stavis did not interrupt Ratliff's lengthy recounting of
the intimate details from Margaret's diary. "It was absolutely incredible," Stavis says. "He had to have his head examined. I
would say that particular scene cost him a fortune. Just a fortune."

Indeed, the jury of five women and one man returned a verdict imposing $1.6 million in damages against Thomas Ratliff. The jury also assessed damages of approximately $200,000 against McClellan, $84,000 against Adlerman, and $105,000 against Brick.

The Justice Department, on behalf of the Senate defendants, immediately appealed. Thomas Ratliff hired a new attorney and also began his appeal. Faced, however, with the possibility of the million-dollar verdict being upheld, as well as his mounting legal fees, Ratliff decided to settle with the McSurelys. "I couldn't afford the victory," he says.

On the other hand, the Justice Department, armed with the qualified immunity standard pressed on. Thus the McSurelys were once again before the Court of Appeals for the D.C. Circuit. The court again set forth the standard by which government officials claiming immunity are to be measured: Did their conduct violate clearly established constitutional or statutory rights? The court noted that the last time the question of the Senate defendants' liability under the Fourth Amendment was before these same judges, they split down the middle, five to five. Thus it could hardly be said that the law at the time of the Senate defendants' actions was "clearly established." The Fourth Amendment claims against the Senate defendants were dismissed.

The court did find, however, that the manner in which Brick returned the 234 documents, including Margaret's private papers, violated the McSurelys' right to privacy under the common law of Kentucky and was not protected by immunity. "Converting what should have been the simple physical return of documents to their respective owners into the sadistic and voyeuristic exercise described at trial cannot fall under the mantle of necessary legislative conduct," the court declared. A portion of the damages assessed against Brick would stand.

Then, with a nod to Abraham Lincoln, the court finally put an end to the case of *McSurely v. McClellan:* "The curtain ought to be drawn. The legal world will little note nor long remember the fine lines that have been drawn in this opinion or in any of the four previous opinions rendered by this court. It will be enough if our opinion finally ends this sorry chapter of investigative excess. The McSurelys cannot be made whole, nor can they be vindicated. Those parts of the district court's judgment that we uphold today can only stand as a small reaffirmation of the proposition that there are bounds to the interference that citizens must tolerate from the agents of their government—even when such agents invoke the mighty shield of the Constitution and claim official purpose to their conduct."

The settlement decree between the McSurelys and Thomas Ratliff stipulates that the amount of the settlement remain confidential. "But," Morton Stavis says, "it was enough money to change Alan and Margaret's lives." Alan quit his job as a postal service employee, went to law school, remarried, and began raising a new family. Margaret went back to college and got her degree, spending her last semester studying in Florence, Italy. Morton Stavis used his fee to make a down payment on a New York condominium for offices for the Center for Constitutional Rights. Thomas Ratliff retired and moved to Florida.

FIFTH AMENDMENT

"No person shall be held to answer for a capital, or otherwise infamous crime, unless on a presentment or indictment of a Grand Jury, except in cases arising in the land or naval forces, or in the Militia, when in actual service in time of War or public danger; nor shall any person be subject for the same offence to be twice put in jeopardy of life or limb; nor shall be compelled in any criminal case to be a witness against himself, nor be deprived of life, liberty, or property, without due process of law; nor shall private property be taken for public use, without just compensation."

Rudy and Tammy Linares walking through Chicago's Criminal Court Building, where Tammy testified before a grand jury about the death of their son, 1989
REPRINTED BY PERMISSION OF AP/WIDE WORLD PHOTOS

Right to a Grand Jury Indictment: Rudy Linares

"No person shall be held to answer for a capital, or otherwise infamous crime, unless on a presentment or indictment of a Grand Jury."

ON APRIL 26, 1989, AT ABOUT 1:00 A.M., Rudy and Tammy Linares went to visit their baby son, Sammy, at Rush-Presbyterian-St. Luke's Medical Center in Chicago. Sammy was in the pediatric intensive care unit. He was in an irreversible coma, hooked up to a respirator, with tubes coming out of his nose and mouth. He had permanent brain damage but he was not brain dead. He had been that way for nine months, since August 2, when he choked on a piece of a yellow birthday balloon which burst as it was being blown up. The balloon fragment got stuck in Sammy's windpipe, cutting off the oxygen supply to his brain. He was six months old at the time.

Rudy had tried to revive Sammy with mouth-to-mouth resuscitation, but it did not work. When Sammy began turning blue, Rudy scooped him up and ran to a nearby fire station hoping someone there could help. Paramedics rushed Sammy to the hospital, where he was put on life support and his heartbeat restored. Sammy's condition was critical. Based on the high acidity levels in his blood, doctors thought he would die. But given the enormous and unpredictable recovery powers of children, they made every effort to save his life. Had Rudy and Tammy known then what Sammy would go through for the next nine months, they say they would never have wanted him to be kept alive.

"You'd touch him, he'd curl up, he'd start shaking. Fluids out of the nose, out of the mouth," Rudy says. "The worst [way] you can see a kid, that's how you'd see him. There was nothing left." Not only were they watching Sammy suffer, without much hope of improving, but "it was just tearing apart the whole family."

After a few months, Rudy and Tammy tried to have Sammy removed from life support but were told by hospital personnel they would need a court order to do so. They were also told that judges hardly ever issued such orders. Rudy, twenty-three, was a high school dropout, working as a "striper," painting lines in parking lots. Tammy, twenty-one, had married him when she was fifteen. They had no money and no experience with the legal system. Rudy and Tammy tried, but could not find or afford a lawyer to help them.

Finally, in April, one of the nurses at the hospital gave the Linareses the name of a lawyer she knew who would be willing to take the case for free. The Linareses made an appointment for Friday morning, April 28. But on the Tuesday before, they were told Sammy would be transferred to Sycamore Hospital, a long-term care facility two hours away. They would not be able to visit him as often, and they had seen Sycamore before. All the children there were like Sammy, all on respirators.

Rudy decided that no one was going to "warehouse" his baby to die. "If he's going to die, he's going to die in my arms 'cause he died in my arms one time already and he's not going to die someplace strange."

When they went to see Sammy on Wednesday night, without telling Tammy, Rudy hid a .357 Magnum under his coat. In the unit they each held Sammy. They were both in tears about the prospect of their baby being moved to Sycamore. Tammy left the room around 1:30 A.M. Rudy stayed behind, as he often did, to talk to his son alone. But this time Rudy pulled out the gun, ordered the nurses out of the room, unhooked Sammy's respirator, and gathered the baby in his arms.

When a nurse attempted to reconnect Sammy to the respirator, Rudy cocked the trigger and told her to get out. He pointed the gun at Sammy's head and said no one would get hurt unless they tried to stop him. Rudy sat cradling Sammy in his arms and sobbing for about a half hour, until the baby stopped breathing. Sammy Linares was pronounced dead at 2:05 A.M. Rudy then turned the gun over to police waiting outside the unit and surrendered himself into their custody. He was arrested and taken to the police station. To reporters gathered outside, Rudy explained, "I did it because I loved my son, all right?"

But the Cook County state's attorney saw it differently and declared, "No one has the right to take the law into his own hands." He charged Rudy with first-degree murder.

In Illinois, "murder one" is defined as intentional killing, or killing with the knowledge that one's actions create a strong probability of death or great bodily harm. Scott Nelson, assistant state's attorney in charge of the Homicide–Sex Crimes Division and the prosecutor responsible for the Linares case, said, "Someone, somewhere may not think this is a real murder case. But if you read the letter of the law, it unquestionably—in my mind at least—is."

Tammy was subpoenaed to testify before a grand jury on Wednesday, one week after Sammy's death and two days after his funeral. Other subpoenas were issued to Rudy's mother, Maria, his brother, Robert, Sammy's doctor, the Cook County medical examiner, and the police officer who investigated the incident. The purpose of the grand jury investigation was to determine if there was enough evidence—or probable cause—to indict Rudy and require him to stand trial.

In Illinois, probable cause is not defined to the grand jurors, but the process of indictment is explained. The grand jurors are told that if a majority of them find there is probable cause to believe the accused committed the crime with which he is charged, they should vote to indict him. On the other hand, they are told that if a majority find the evidence is insufficient, they should return a "no true bill," meaning they refuse to indict. Requiring the state to convince a grand jury that there are sufficient grounds for a trial is intended to serve as a restraint on the otherwise unbridled power of the prosecutor by requiring the approval of a neutral body of citizens before the state can move against the accused.

In the past, the grand jury had the power to conduct investigations on its own initiative, and it still possesses the broad subpoena powers of the court. But today the grand jury depends heavily on the prosecutor. An Illinois grand jury, for example, sits for a one-month term and investigates approximately fifteen hundred cases. Its role is largely confined to evaluating the evidence the prosecutor places before it. Still, the ultimate decision to indict remains the grand jurors' alone. If they indict, the accused goes to trial. If they do not, the accused goes free.

At first Tammy was reluctant to testify. Her lawyers were afraid she too might be charged with Sammy's murder. They tried to have the subpoena quashed on the grounds that the law protects one spouse from testifying against the other. They were overruled and Tammy was ordered to appear. Tammy then decided to cooperate, believing that if the grand jury heard the Linareses' side of the story from her, perhaps it would help Rudy. Tammy knew a little bit about the grand jury from watching television, but she had never been in a courtroom before.

As it turned out, the Cook County grand jury room looks exactly the way Tammy feared it would. Built in the 1920s, it is an imposing room, shaped like a small auditorium, with high painted ceilings and dark wood-paneled walls. The witness sits in a chair, front and center, facing sixteen grand jurors in four rows of raised seats. Directly across from the witness in the center of the front row sits the prosecutor, asking questions. The grand jurors may also ask their own questions directly.

Tammy answered the prosecutor's questions for twenty-five minutes, but she says it felt like hours. "They all stare at you. They want to see your reaction and how you're saying everything. I was scared and crying and I cried through the whole thing."

Though appearing before a grand jury may seem like yet another ordeal for a witness, historically the grand jury developed as one of a citizen's greatest protectors. Its origins can be traced back to the twelfth century, when juries of twelve freemen reported to the king's traveling judges the names of those locally suspected of committing crimes. Originally, these same men would then determine whether the person they had accused was actually guilty. This procedure was challenged as unfair, and by the end of the fourteenth century the system had evolved to provide two juries: one to accuse, and another to determine guilt at trial. The accusing jury consisted of twenty-three members (double the number of the trial jury minus one to prevent a tie vote) and became known as "le graunde inquest" or the grand jury.

In colonial America, the grand jury became an increasingly independent institution. Its members were future Americans, while colonial officials and prosecutors were the king's representatives. In one celebrated instance in 1735, a grand jury twice refused to issue an indictment for seditious libel against John Peter Zenger, a German immigrant printer whose weekly newspaper attacked the greedy, high-handed royal governor of New York. The government finally brought Zenger to trial through a prosecutor's information, another type of charging document that requires no community approval; it is screened only by a magistrate or judge. Zenger's eventual acquittal was not only a great victory for freedom of the press in America, but it elevated the grand jury into a bulwark against oppressive prosecution. Gouverneur Morris, one of the men who drafted the Constitution, called Zenger's trial "the germ of American freedom—the morning star of that liberty which subsequently revolutionized America."

It is no surprise, therefore, that Madison included the right to have one's case screened by a grand jury among the basic protections to be included in the federal Bill of Rights. Although the Fifth Amendment right to a grand jury indictment has not been incorporated into the Fourteenth Amendment to apply to the states, every state constitution provides some form of screening before a person can be tried for a felony. Roughly one-third of the states use a grand jury system, while in the other two-thirds the prosecutor may choose to proceed either by grand jury indictment or by information.

Today, an information results from a preliminary hearing, which differs from a grand jury proceeding in that it is adversarial. The accused is present and is represented by a lawyer who can cross-examine witnesses. The proceeding is conducted in public, in front of a judge who decides whether there is sufficient evidence to put the accused on trial. If there is, the prosecutor then files an information.

The grand jury proceeding, on the other hand, is secret. A witness's testimony is not made public and the names of the jurors are not disclosed. The secrecy is to ensure that witnesses reveal as much information as possible, and that the grand jurors feel free to vote their consciences. Though critics have likened the grand jury to an inquisition precisely because of its secrecy, Tammy Linares says, "I was thankful I didn't have anybody looking at me, like lawyers and reporters, and everybody else. Staring at me like they're gonna write all this stuff in the papers." But the most important difference between a preliminary hearing and a grand jury indictment system is that ordinary citizens sit on the grand jury and evaluate the evidence against the accused.

Still, the grand jury system today often comes under attack. Many defense attorneys feel that the grand jury system is unfair to the accused because they are not allowed to present a defense, or even, in some states, to speak on their own behalf. Federal grand juries also are allowed to consider evidence, such as hearsay, that cannot be admitted at trial. Indeed, many claim that the grand jury of today has lost its historic independence and become a "rubber stamp" for the prosecution. According to the chief judge of New York State, a prosecutor could get a grand jury to "indict a ham sandwich" if he wanted to.

In Illinois, as in most states, after all the witnesses have been questioned and all the evidence has been presented to the grand jurors, the prosecutor and the court reporter leave the room. The grand jury then begins its secret deliberations. According to Scott Nelson, "The [grand] jury is given the facts, and enough knowledge of the law, then we count on these people to do the right thing."

On May 18, 1989, the members of the grand jury returned a "no true bill," refusing to indict Rudy for first-degree murder.

Rudy says he did not know what a grand jury was before his case was submitted to one. Even though he did not appear to tell his side of the story, he thought he would be better off with a grand jury instead of a judge. "The way I had it figured they're people just like I am, and they're bound to have kids." Rudy says he fully expected to be prosecuted for murder when he left the hospital, but he now believes "the grand jury didn't want to indict me because my son was already dead."

Today, Linares is convinced that "everybody should have the right to a grand jury" because "it's not just one person deciding your fate. It's a bunch of people, and they can argue amongst themselves and have a lot of opinions, and from all the opinions then they can come out with the fair one, [better] than a judge."

The grand jury's action illustrates the power of community participation in the criminal justice system. The Framers, in providing the right to a grand jury and a trial by jury, realized that the jurors would be able to provide "play in the joints" of what could otherwise become a rigid and formalistic process. In Linares's case, the grand jurors' decision does not necessarily mean they felt that Rudy was right to take his son's life. A "no true bill" means only that the grand jury did not find sufficient evidence to prosecute Rudy for first-degree murder. Scott Nelson offers his own explanation: "They didn't only consider the letter of the law, but what the purpose of the law is. It's something we shouldn't encourage, because the law as written is supposed to be fair. . . . But every once in a while [a grand jury] draws the line the way they choose to; it's both a defect and a power of the grand jury. They have that authority, they understood it, they chose to do what they did."

Rudy Linares pleaded guilty to a misdemeanor charge of unlawful use of a weapon. He was sentenced to one-year conditional discharge (meaning he will serve no time in jail) and ordered to obtain counseling. At the hearing the judge said, "As far as punishment is concerned, I think you have suffered enough."

May 10, 1955

Mr. Everett D. Green
200 19th Street. S. E.
Washington, D. C.

Dear Mr. Green:

It now appears that your trial upon that
part of the original indictment charging murder in the
first degree will begin on Monday, May 16.

The District Attorney has informally advised
me that the Government would be content with a plea
of manslaughter in your case. I want you to clearly
understand that if this matter proceeds to trial and
results in a conviction, the Court will have no alternative but to impose the death penalty under the law.

I am enclosing a copy of this letter. If
you do not wish to change your mind, but insist upon
going to trial on the charge of first degree murder,
would you please so indicate at the bottom of the enclosed copy.

Sincerely yours,

George Blow

ec

Encl.

I wish to Plead Not Guilty

/s/ Everett D. Green

*L*etter in which Everett Green indicated his decision to risk a
second trial and the death penalty
REPRINTED BY PERMISSION OF GEORGE BLOW, ESQ.

Double Jeopardy:
Green v. United States

"Nor shall any person be subject for the same offence to be twice put in jeopardy of life or limb."

Ιν 1953, EVERETT GREEN WAS IN his early sixties. "He never did much in his life, but he was always trying," says George Blow, Green's attorney. White-haired, slightly paunchy, and extremely mild-mannered, Green was an unlikely candidate for a murder conviction. "He was a very simple man, a very likable fellow," says Blow. If Green's uneventful life was notable for anything, it was his devotion to Bettie Brown, a lifelong friend twenty years his senior.

Green had divorced in 1930 and moved to the District of Columbia, down the street from Brown. One night Green visited his friend during a snowstorm and fell ill. He ended up staying a month while Bettie Brown nursed him through pneumonia. For the next twenty-three years they rented rooms in the same house on the 1500 block of Massachusetts Avenue in Washington, D.C. As Bettie Brown's health began to fail, Green looked after her, fixing up the house, cooking meals, running errands, and keeping her company.

On Tuesday, May 26, 1953, at 7:40 A.M., firefighters responded to an alarm at the home of Bettie Brown and Everett Green. Finding the house locked tight, they broke in through the front windows, back door, and a skylight. They found Bettie Brown in bed in her first-floor room, dead. In the basement they found Green face down in two inches of bloody water in a bathtub. He had several superficial stab wounds in his chest and neck and was suffering from smoke inhalation. Firefighters carried Green to the yard and revived him.

At the hospital, Green told police sergeant Lionel Couture that he had awakened at approximately 7:00 A.M. and, smelling smoke, went to the basement to investigate. There, he said, a "tall, bald-headed colored man" attacked him, stabbing him several times with a "long dagger." Green said he lost consciousness briefly, then dragged himself to the bathtub before losing consciousness again.

Later that day, after talking with fire investigators, Sergeant Couture returned to the hospital. He asked Green why there appeared to be five separate fires throughout the house. Green responded that the intruder must have set them. And how did the intruder get out of a completely locked house, Couture wanted to know. Green said he had no explanation. Finally, Couture told Green that pencils and an open box of stationery were found on the kitchen table. Had he been writing letters? Green said no.

The next day, an acquaintance of Green's gave the police a letter she had just received. The envelope was postmarked Washington, D.C., May 26—12:30 P.M.—1953. The letter was from Everett Green.

> Tuesday A.M. Please notify W. T. Thompson, Fredericksburg, Virginia, of Miss Bettie Brown's death. A fine and good lady, a true friend to me. We both want it this way. Good-bye my friend, Everett. Please have my ashes thrown on the Chesapeake Bay.

At the bottom of the page was the word *Over.* Then on the other side: "The inclosed [sic] is for flowers for her." In the envelope were two twenty-dollar bills.

When confronted with the evidence, Green admitted that he wrote the letter. He explained that he had gone to check on Bettie Brown around midnight the night before the fire and found she had died in her sleep. He said he became so despondent that he contemplated suicide, wrote the letter, and posted it right away. Green insisted, however, that by morning he had changed his mind. He stuck to his story of being awakened by the smell of smoke and then attacked by the strange intruder.

Green was charged with arson and the first-degree murder of Bettie Brown. At his trial, a doctor testified without contradiction that Bettie Brown had died of smoke inhalation and could not have been dead seven hours before the fire, as Green claimed. Green took the stand in his own defense. Upon cross-examination, he conceded that he and Bettie Brown had been threatened with eviction several times, including the day before the fire, and that they both feared being institutionalized. Still, he did not budge from his account of the intruder.

The judge submitted the case to the jury on two counts, arson and murder. On the second count, he instructed the jury it could find Green guilty of murder in either the first or the second degree. The jury returned a verdict of guilty of arson and second-degree murder. The verdict said nothing about the first-degree charge. The judge sentenced Green to one to three years' imprisonment for arson and five to twenty years' imprisonment for murder in the second degree.

George Blow was assigned to handle Green's appeal. It was his first big criminal case. He searched meticulously through Green's trial record looking for what every appellate attorney hopes to find: an error in trial procedure requiring reversal. Blow found what he believed to be such an error, but the consequences of raising it were frightening.

The trial judge had made a mistake when he instructed the jury that it could convict Green of *either* first- *or* second-degree murder. The District of Columbia Criminal Code required that killing in the course of arson be classified as murder in the first degree. The guilty verdict showed that the jury was convinced Green had committed arson, and the evidence at trial tended to show that Bettie Brown died as a result of the fire. Therefore, under the D.C. statute, there was no evidence of second-degree murder. The judge should have instructed the jury that Green was either guilty of first-degree murder or he was not guilty.

Raising the error, Blow explained carefully to Green, meant taking a fearful risk. If Green succeeded in getting his second-degree murder conviction reversed, the state would surely try him again for first-degree murder. That crime carried an automatic death sentence. Green could either take the five to twenty years he already had, or risk a new trial and the death penalty. To Blow, it was an enormous decision.

But Green reminded his young attorney that he was sixty-four years old. Even the second-degree murder sentence meant he might spend the rest of his life in jail. He said simply that he would rather die. Green told his attorney to take the risk.

As Blow expected, the U.S. Court of Appeals for the D.C. Circuit agreed that the jury instruction was erroneous. But the court was clearly concerned about Green's gamble. "In seeking a new trial at which . . . the jury will have no choice except to find him guilty of first-degree murder or acquit him, Green is manifestly taking a desperate chance. He may suffer the death penalty," the court wrote. "We inquired of his counsel whether Green clearly understood the possible consequences of success on this appeal, and were told . . . he prefers death to spending the rest of his life in prison. He is entitled to a new trial."

Before that second trial, Blow raised what was his own "desperate chance" for Green. He argued that when the first jury found Green guilty of second-degree murder, it was *implicitly acquitting* him of the first-degree charge. Therefore, Blow asserted, to try Green again for first-degree murder was a violation of his Fifth Amendment right not to be subject to double jeopardy.

Under the double jeopardy clause, if a defendant appeals his conviction and the conviction is reversed because of an error at trial, under most circumstances the state may retry him for the same offense. If, however, the defendant is acquitted—that is, found not guilty—the state may not retry him for the same offense. George Blow argued that the verdict in the first trial was the same as if the jury had expressly found Green "not guilty of first-degree murder," and therefore he could claim double jeopardy.

Blow, however, was completely candid with Green: there was little hope for his argument. No court had yet held that the Fifth Amendment supported this novel claim. In fact, a 1905 Supreme Court case, *Trono v. United States,* rejected a similar claim brought under a double jeopardy statute in the Philippines. In *Trono,* the defendants had been charged with murder but were acquitted by the trial court, which instead found them guilty of assault only. They appealed the assault conviction to the Philippine Supreme Court. That court, acting under unusual local procedure, set aside the acquittal, found the defendants guilty of murder, and increased their sentences. A sharply divided U.S. Supreme Court let the ruling stand. *"Trono* was the major obstacle," says Blow. If that case was read to set forth the law under the Fifth Amendment double jeopardy clause, Green's claim would fail.

The judge for Green's second trial took one look at *Trono*, promptly rejected the double jeopardy claim, and ordered that the trial proceed. Blow enlisted the aid of Charles Ford, a renowned D.C. criminal trial attorney, and George Rublee II, a friend and associate, to put on a defense. But the facts, evidence, and witnesses had not changed from the first trial. The only real difference this time was that the judge submitted the case to the jury solely on the charge of murder in the first degree.

Green was convicted of the first-degree murder of his friend Bettie Brown. The judge imposed the mandatory death sentence and set a date for execution.

Green's attorneys appealed to the U.S. Court of Appeals for the D.C. Circuit, again arguing that the second trial violated Green's rights under the double jeopardy clause. In June 1956, the court decided that *Trono* was controlling and rejected Green's double jeopardy claim. The opinion noted that Green had been warned of the risk he was taking. He had gambled and lost.

Blow and Rublee took the only next step they could, appealing to the court of last resort. To their surprise, the U.S. Supreme Court took Everett Green's case. In April 1957, Blow argued to the Court that *Trono* should be confined to its unique context under a Philippine statute and that it did not, and should not, set forth the law of the land under the Fifth Amendment double jeopardy clause. The Fifth Amendment, Blow argued, protected a man like Green, who had essentially been acquitted of first-degree murder.

On June 24, the last day of the Court's term, Blow sat in the marble courtroom waiting for the final decision. He was stunned to hear that there would be no opinion in the matter of Everett Green that day. The case had been restored to the calendar for reargument the next term. The justices could not decide. It was extraordinary.

Blow reargued Green's double jeopardy claim yet again in October and finally, two months later, just before Christmas 1957, the Court issued its opinion. It wrote, "We do not believe that *Trono* should be extended beyond its peculiar factual setting to control the present case."

The Court continued, "Green was in direct peril of being convicted and punished for first-degree murder at his first trial. He was forced to run the gantlet once on that charge and the jury refused to convict him." It was precisely this "gantlet" of a criminal trial that the Framers had in mind when they drafted the double jeopardy clause.

"The underlying idea [of the clause]," the Court declared, "is that the State with all its resources and power should not be allowed to make repeated attempts to convict an individual for an alleged offense, thereby subjecting him to embarrassment, expense, and ordeal, and compelling him to live in a continuing state of anxiety and insecurity, as well as enhancing the possibility that even though innocent he may be found guilty."

Noting the "desperate chance" Green was forced to take after his first trial, the Court said, "The law should not, and in our judgment does not, place the defendant in such an incredible dilemma." By a vote of five to four, Green was spared the death penalty. The Court ordered his first-degree murder conviction reversed. The trial judge who carried out the Supreme Court's order told Green, "You are a lucky man. You are a free man."

At the time of Green's case, the District of Columbia provided released felons with free, one-way Greyhound bus tickets. "I think the District thought that would encourage them to leave town," George Blow says. He and Rublee saw their client off at the bus depot. Green had served briefly in World War I, so Rublee, an ex-marine, arranged for him to stay at a veteran's home in Virginia. He lived there until his death in 1961. As a veteran, Green was buried in Arlington National Cemetery.

Since *Green*, the double jeopardy clause has become a tangle of technical questions: When does "jeopardy" begin for the accused?

What exactly is meant by the "same offense"? What is to be done with a mistrial or hung jury? But each of these questions begins with the premise, set forth in the case of Everett Green: for the accused, a criminal trial is a risk, an embarrassment, an ordeal, and the state, with all its resources and power, cannot force an individual to run the gantlet over and over again.

J*acqueline Bouknight in the Baltimore City Jail, 1989*
CAROLINE KENNEDY

Right Against Self-incrimination:
Baltimore City Department of Social Services v. Bouknight

"No person shall be compelled in any criminal case
to be a witness against himself."

O<small>N JANUARY</small> 23, 1987, <small>THREE-</small>
month-old Maurice M. was admitted to Francis Scott Key Medical Center in Baltimore with a fracture of his right thighbone. X
rays showed old fractures of his upper arm and shoulder. He was
placed in a SPICA cast (a figure-eight bandage around his arm
and shoulder), in traction. His mother, twenty-year-old Jackie
Bouknight, said that a drug-addicted friend had pushed her during an argument and she fell on Maurice's leg. But hospital personnel, who had seen Jackie shake Maurice and throw him into
his crib while in the cast, suspected child abuse. The hospital's
assistant chief of orthopedics wrote, "I am concerned that this
child may suffer serious or fatal injuries if the conditions leading
to this form of abuse are not corrected."

Maurice was put under the supervision of the Baltimore Department of Social Services and, for a few months, Jackie cooperated
with the social workers. Then, one day, Maurice disappeared. Fearing that the child was endangered, or perhaps dead, a judge demanded that Jackie either produce Maurice or tell where he was.
Jackie Bouknight refused, claiming her Fifth Amendment right
against self-incrimination.

*   *   *

"I am not willing to answer . . . any more of these questions because I see you go about this examination to ensnare me: for seeing the things for which I am imprisoned can not be proved against me, you will get other matter out of my examination." So spoke John Lilburne, a twenty-three-year-old clothier's apprentice imprisoned for shipping seditious books into England in 1637. When called before the Star Chamber, Lilburne's refusal to take its oath began his twenty-year battle for liberty against the tyrannies of the king, Parliament, and Cromwell's military dictatorship. His struggle culminated in the recognition of the right against self-incrimination and in 1641 the abolition of the Star Chamber and its ecclesiastical counterpart, the High Commission.

The Star Chamber's oath required the accused to swear on the Bible that he would truthfully answer all questions without knowing why they were asked and without knowing the charges against him. After 1611, if anyone refused to take the oath he could be found in contempt of court and sent to prison until he agreed to swear the oath and answer questions. Even if he did not take the oath, under another rule the judge was allowed to convict the accused anyway, as if he had confessed to the crimes. Ever since Henry VIII had made himself head of the church as well as the state one hundred years earlier, the crime of heresy had merged with treason, and religious persecution had steadily increased. Hundreds of Catholics, Puritans, and Quakers had been tortured, imprisoned, burned, or executed for refusing to swear the oath and accuse themselves of crimes against the state. They drew inspiration from the trial of Jesus, who, when brought before Pontius Pilate and interrogated, refused to answer.

> And Jesus stood before the governor and the governor asked him, saying Art thou the King of the Jews? And Jesus said unto him, Thou sayest.
> And when he was accused of the chief priests and elders, he answered nothing.
> Then said Pilate unto him, Hearest thou not how many things they witness against thee?
> And he answered him to never a word; insomuch as the governor marvelled greatly.

Being forced to answer questions under oath violated not only the sanctity of conscience and the teachings of Jesus, but it also presented persons who took the oath with an excruciating choice. If they lied about their religious beliefs, they faced eternal damnation; if they told the truth, they faced execution.

When Lilburne was brought before the Star Chamber a second time, he again refused to swear the oath. He was found guilty of contempt and sentenced to a five-hundred-pound fine, whipping, punishment in the pillory, and imprisonment until he agreed to take the oath. "I was condemned," he later wrote, "because I would not accuse myself."

By the time Jackie Bouknight asserted her right to remain silent, the right had long been recognized as "one of the great landmarks in man's struggle to make himself civilized." It was transformed by the Framers from a mere rule of evidence, as it had been in England, into a constitutional principle and protected in the Fifth Amendment: "nor shall [any person] be compelled in any criminal case to be a witness against himself." Perhaps the only constitutional guarantee known by number to the general public, invoking the right to remain silent rather than incriminate oneself has come to be called "taking the Fifth."

Although it is one of the best known of the rights in the first ten amendments the right against self-incrimination is also one of the least popular. It is often perceived as a shield for the guilty rather than a shelter for the innocent, the argument being that those who are innocent have nothing to hide and no reason to remain silent. On the other hand, the Fifth Amendment may protect innocent persons who find themselves in incriminating circumstances, such as those called "Fifth Amendment Communists" by Senator Joseph McCarthy.

Furthermore, the U.S. system of justice is based on accusation, not inquisition. In an accusatory system, a person is innocent until proven guilty beyond a reasonable doubt. The state must investigate and present evidence to a jury to prove its case even though interrogating and torturing the suspect would clearly be more efficient. As one nineteenth-century English legal commentator put it, "It is far pleasanter to sit comfortably in the shade rubbing red pepper into a poor devil's eyes than to go about in the sun hunting up evidence."

Two central objections to the use of inquisitional tactics to obtain confessions emerged during the struggle for the right against self-incrimination. First, confessions obtained by torture or psychological pressure were thought to offend the dignity of man, the integrity of government, and the inviolability of conscience. The second, more practical reason is that over the centuries those who practiced criminal law came to believe that compelled confessions were often untrustworthy. Such confessions led to the conviction of innocent people, could not be relied on to support a guilty verdict, and ultimately undermined public confidence in the justice system.

As Chief Justice Earl Warren wrote in the Supreme Court's most famous Fifth Amendment decision, *Miranda v. Arizona*, "The privilege against self-incrimination—the essential mainstay of our adversary system—is founded on a complex of values. All these policies point to one overriding thought: the constitutional foundation underlying the privilege is the respect a government must accord to the dignity and integrity of its citizens. To maintain a 'fair state—individual balance,' to require the government 'to shoulder the entire load,' to respect the inviolability of the human personality, our accusatory system of criminal justice demands that the government seeking to punish an individual produce the evidence against him by its own independent labors, rather than by the cruel, simple expedient of compelling it from his own mouth."

Jackie Bouknight is a somewhat awkward young woman. Diagnosed as mildly retarded, she appears withdrawn and fearful of strangers. She grew up in Baltimore, the third of five children. As best as Jackie remembers, when she was about four, her mother took her and her brothers and sisters to the Department of Social Services and left them there. Jackie was placed in foster care, in at least six different homes, where she was mistreated and neglected. To Jackie, all but one of her foster parents were only in it for the money.

When Jackie's own child was released from the hospital in February 1987, he was placed in the same foster care system that had raised her. After a finding by the juvenile court that Jackie was incapable of providing "ordinary and proper care" for Maurice, he was declared a Child in Need of Assistance (CINA). Jackie was told that under the CINA program she could regain custody of Maurice if she agreed to cooperate with the Department of Social

Services. She signed a consent order, agreeing to attend parenting classes, meet weekly with a parent aide provided by the department, and refrain from physically punishing Maurice. Jackie complied, and her baby was returned to her on July 17, 1987.

At the time that the department agreed to return Maurice to Jackie, it did not know that the psychologist who evaluated her had recommended that she not be given custody. He found Jackie to be of borderline intelligence with an I.Q. of 74, functioning at the level of an eight- to ten-year-old rather than a twenty-one-year-old. The neglect and abuse that she had experienced in a series of foster homes contributed to her "lack of capacity for establishment of empathetic relationships with others and a need to rely upon [her]self for basic survival." The psychologist's summary included the following description of her relationship with Maurice: "She is not now able to relate constructively to her child, since her child is seen as fulfilling her needs rather than the reverse. She becomes totally frustrated and enraged to find herself unable to gain from her child what she wishes as a replacement for what she lacks [*sic*] in her own childhood. When her frustration mounts, she is likely to act out toward the child and see the child as abusive to her rather than herself as abusive to the child."

Shortly after Maurice was returned to Jackie, the Baltimore City Department of Social Services lost sight of him. Department social workers continued almost weekly efforts to make contact: sometimes they saw Jackie, who said the baby was with an aunt; sometimes Jackie said she would not be home when the worker wanted to schedule a visit; and sometimes Jackie was just not there. It was not until April 1988, seven months after anyone from the department or the hospital had seen Maurice, that social workers suspected something had happened to the child. They went to juvenile court for help.

A juvenile court judge ordered Jackie to produce her child or risk being held in contempt of court. Jackie told the authorities that her son was with her sister, Barbara, in Texas. But a check by the Dallas police failed to locate him. In fact, Barbara Bouknight said she had never seen Maurice. A week later, on April 27, Jackie was arrested.

According to Robin Parsons, Jackie's lawyer at the time, "They found her under a bed hiding in her foster father's home. They actually dragged her out of there and hauled her into court in handcuffs and the whole works. She came in wild, incoherent, her hair was all wild, she was just hysterical about going to jail. She herself had been a foster child and had been abused and she was just terrified of having her child in foster care." Maurice's father had been killed a month before in a drug-related shooting and Jackie had not regained her equilibrium since. She refused to say anything about Maurice.

The juvenile court judge ordered that Jackie be jailed for contempt. A person may be held in civil contempt of court for refusing to comply with a court order. Civil contempt is punished by a fine or by imprisonment, the purpose of which is to obtain compliance. The punishment is lifted as soon as the person performs the acts directed by the court. In Jackie's case, she could purge the contempt order by producing Maurice, revealing to the court his whereabouts, or providing information about Maurice to the police, her social worker, or the judge.

At hearings in May, Jackie took the Fifth. Her lawyers claimed that the contempt order was unconstitutional. They said that the order violated Jackie's Fifth Amendment right against self-incrimination if, in order to purge herself of contempt, she might have to say something, expressly or implicitly, that would link her to a crime. Her lawyers emphasized that detectives from the Homicide Division of the Baltimore City Police Department were already investigating the case and that Jackie was the prime suspect. Whether or not anything had happened to Maurice, her lawyers argued, Jackie's fear of incrimination was reasonable, substantial, and within the Fifth Amendment.

Robin Parsons says she believed the baby was all right and the real reason Jackie did not want to produce him was her fear that he would be taken from her. But, she adds, "I don't know to this day what lengths she would go to avoid foster care." The judge wanted to see the nineteen-month-old baby to satisfy himself that Maurice was in good health. He upheld the contempt order. But rather than produce her child, Jackie went to jail.

Her lawyers appealed the contempt order. Because of the importance of the issue and the fear for Maurice's well-being, Maryland's highest court, the Court of Appeals, took the case immediately without waiting for a decision by the intermediate court. The case raised two important questions: first, whether producing Maurice was protected by the Fifth Amendment at all, and if so, could the public interest in Maurice's welfare ever outweigh Jackie's right against self-incrimination?

The central issue in the case was whether the act of producing Maurice would violate Jackie's Fifth Amendment right. Interpreting the words of the Fifth Amendment, "no person . . . shall be compelled . . . to be a witness against himself," the Supreme Court has held that the Fifth Amendment protects only those incriminating communications that are both "compelled" and "testimonial."

For example, if a suspect waives his right to remain silent and makes a voluntary confession, it is not compelled and can be used against him. According to the Supreme Court, "It is the extortion of information from the accused himself that offends our sense of justice." In Jackie Bouknight's case there was no question that the contempt order constituted compulsion.

The second requirement for asserting the right to silence is that the communication being compelled must be "testimonial." At its most basic level, the Fifth Amendment protects suspects from giving testimony or answering questions that may incriminate them. But the Supreme Court has also held that in some instances the *act of producing* physical or tangible evidence can be testimonial. If the act of producing the evidence reveals to the government that the evidence in fact exists, that the accused possesses or controls it, or that the evidence produced is in fact the authentic item the government is requesting, then it is testimonial. But there is an exception. If the existence, possession, and authenticity are already known to the state or can be verified independently, then turning over the evidence is *not* testimonial.

The state argued that producing Maurice was not testimonial because his existence was known; Jackie had been awarded custody (possession); and he could be identified independently by X rays of his fractures (authenticity). As Ralph Tyler, assistant attorney general for the state of Maryland, put it, "The question [under the Fifth Amendment] is, are you telling us something we don't know? Are you adding to the sum total of the government's knowledge about possession, custody, control? And we argue the answer to that is no."

The state also argued that Jackie Bouknight fit into another exception to the Fifth Amendment rule regarding production of evidence. The Supreme Court has ruled that the Fifth Amendment cannot be invoked to avoid complying with basic state regulations that are designed to protect the public welfare. For example, if the government requires a regulated business to keep certain records, it may demand those records be produced without violating the Fifth Amendment.

Jackie's attorneys argued that exceptions for business records and regulatory schemes should not be extended to cover a case like Bouknight's. To them, the case turned on the fact that Jackie was suspected of homicide. In general, it is clear that a court cannot compel a murder suspect, under threat of contempt, to tell where he or she buried the body, or hid the murder weapon, without violating the right against self-incrimination. Similarly, Jackie's lawyers asserted, producing Maurice might require her to implicate herself in a crime, or provide a link in a chain of evidence connecting her with a crime. Either way, they said, it was a violation of the Fifth Amendment.

The state then made its final argument: even if requiring Jackie to produce Maurice was testimonial communication, protected by the Fifth Amendment, the state's interest in Maurice's safety outweighed Jackie's constitutional right against self-incrimination. "I don't think there is any way to look at this case other than you're talking about a child," says Ralph Tyler. "It seems to me it doesn't take a whole lot of imagination or law to recognize that children are different. And whatever else they are at nineteen months, they are entirely dependent." Therefore, the state claimed, in order to discharge its responsibility for Maurice's welfare, it must be able to compel his mother to produce him.

At the time of this case, there were over twenty-five hundred children in foster care in Baltimore alone, with about five hundred new children placed in shelter care each year. The parents of these children had all, like Jackie Bouknight, been found incapable of providing "ordinary and proper care" for their kids. Some say the state is not capable of much better. In 1984, the Legal Aid Bureau in Baltimore filed suit against the state and city for failing to adequately supervise and operate the foster care program. The Legal Aid Bureau's complaint cited numerous cases of physical and sexual abuse, including beatings, rapes, filthy conditions, alcoholic foster parents, parents who forced their foster children to eat their own vomit as punishment for being sick, parents who kept their foster children out of school to work for them, and one case of blindness caused by the parent's failure to seek medical attention for her foster child.

Following the Legal Aid Bureau's lawsuit, the state agreed to abide by a consent decree designed to improve the system. In Bouknight's case, the state contended that although the system was indeed in crisis, one of the few weapons it possessed to battle these tragic conditions was the power of the juvenile court to compel parents to bring their children in for evaluation. Direct observation of the children by social workers is absolutely critical in cases of suspected child abuse. Therefore, the state contended, in Bouknight's case a "public safety" exception to the Fifth Amendment was justified because its interest was in protecting children like Maurice, not in prosecuting Jackie for a crime.

"We're talking about trying to save a child," says Tyler. "If the rule really is that we as a people can do nothing, we're in big trouble. I don't think that is what the Fifth Amendment requires. The juvenile court has got to have the power to bring [the child] in front of the court. If you take that power away from the court, the inescapable result is that you are going to increase risk to children."

Jackie's lawyers argued that if the state was really interested in protection, not prosecution, it could offer Jackie a deal: immunity from prosecution in exchange for information about her child. This option was not available under Maryland law when Jackie was first held in contempt and put in jail. But by the summer of 1989, the law had changed. Prosecutors could offer Jackie immunity in exchange for information about Maurice, but they refused to do so. Jackie's lawyers asserted that this was proof that the state was more interested in convicting Jackie of a crime than in safeguarding Maurice.

Furthermore, they argued, the state always has a compelling need for information in its pursuit of justice, whether it is to solve a crime, punish an offender, protect a community, intercept a drug smuggler, or ferret out spies. But if none of these interests has justified suspending the Fifth Amendment, why should solving the problem in Jackie's case be any different? In any particular case, if one considers only society's interest, or even if one balances it against the Fifth Amendment, society's interest will often seem more important and more deserving. But as Justice Brandeis once wrote, "Experience should teach us to be most on our guard to protect liberty when the government's purposes are beneficent." For that is when it is the most difficult to remember the values behind the right to remain silent, and its bloody yet noble history, Jackie's attorneys said. And it is even more difficult to remember that society may have a greater interest in preserving this controversial right than it does in punishing each unpopular person who asserts it.

"If you look at the juvenile courts in this country and how they operate, they probably operate more closely . . . to the sort of ecclesiastical Court of High Commission from which the Fifth Amendment generated," says José Anderson, one of Jackie's attorneys. "They have great powers of inquiry over the total subject matter before them. If we make a decision in this country that in the interest of children we are going to permit a suspension of the Bill of Rights . . . then I think there will be an equally [difficult] problem whenever we get an [equally compelling] rationale. Tomorrow it may be the drug war, the next day it will be older citizens. It then becomes very easy for the government . . . to override any constitutional protection."

Placing Jackie as a direct descendant of John Lilburne in her silence, her lawyers urged the court not to make an exception to the Fifth Amendment. "It's not an easy case for your gut or for your head," says another of Jackie's lawyers, George Burns. "If you strip away from it the emotions and ask yourself how do we draw the line, there's no easy answer. But there is a correct one, and that is, 'There is no way we can permit that kind of balancing of individual rights.'"

The Maryland Court of Appeals agreed. It refused to find that the public's right to protect children outweighed Jackie's constitutional right against self-incrimination. The court held that the state, in forcing Jackie either to disclose Maurice's whereabouts or produce him, was compelling testimonial communication from her in violation of the Fifth Amendment. The court vacated the contempt order in its entirety and ordered Jackie released from jail.

But Maryland appealed the decision to the U.S. Supreme Court. Child welfare organizations across the country filed briefs as friends of the court supporting the state, as did the U.S. Conference of Mayors and the attorney general of Massachusetts on behalf of his state and twenty-five others. Not one supporting brief was filed on Jackie's behalf.

On February 20, 1990, the Supreme Court, by a vote of seven to two, reversed the Maryland court's decision. The Supreme Court acknowledged that producing Maurice or revealing his whereabouts did have "testimonial aspects" under the Fifth Amendment. The Court, however, held that Jackie Bouknight could not invoke the Fifth Amendment to avoid complying with the court order, because the order was part of a noncriminal regulatory scheme and Jackie had consented to state supervision.

The Child in Need of Assistance, or CINA, program was not aimed at criminal suspects, the Court explained. It was set up to protect children, not prosecute parents. Furthermore, Jackie had assumed the obligations of the CINA program, including the obligation to produce her child for inspection. Like businesspersons who enter a regulated industry in which the state requires them to maintain certain records and keep them available for government review, Jackie Bouknight could be required to produce Maurice.

The Court did not address the question of what would happen if a child disappeared and a parent suspected of abuse invoked the Fifth in a purely criminal context, apart from any regulatory scheme such as the CINA program. Consequently, the Court did not have to answer the question of whether the constitutional right against self-incrimination, which has long protected the accused in the face of public criticism, would have to give way in the interest of children.

Finally, the Court said that although the Fifth Amendment does not protect Jackie from the state's demand that she either produce Maurice or tell where he is, the Fifth Amendment may still protect her from prosecution. "In a broad range of contexts, the Fifth Amendment limits prosecutors' ability to use testimony that has been compelled," the Court wrote. It indicated that Jackie's case may well be one of those contexts. If so, prosecutors will not be able to use against Jackie information about Maurice obtained through legal compulsion.

As of the summer of 1990, Jackie Bouknight is still silent and still in prison, where she has been for the past two years, longer than anyone in Maryland's history jailed for contempt. The state has not offered immunity and Jackie is fighting her incarceration on other grounds, unrelated to her right against self-incrimination. Maurice has not been found.

Form 342 Order—For seizure prior to hearing and order to show cause—Property in imminent danger of destruction or serious damage

On reading the verified complaint and affidavit of plaintiff on file herein in which plaintiff requests that he be granted the immediate possession of ....1.......... [*describe property*], and after hearing and considering the evidence and testimony of plaintiff and ....2.......... [*specify other witnesses*], the court finds that plaintiff has shown ....3.......... [probable cause *or* reasonable probability] to believe:

1. ....4.......... [*Insert one of the findings set forth below.*]

That said ....5.......... [*property*] is perishable, and that said property will perish before any noticed hearing can be had herein.

That said ....6.......... [*property*] is in immediate danger of ....7.......... [destruction *or* serious harm *or* concealment] and that defendant threatens to ....8.......... [destroy *or* harm *or* damage *or* conceal] said property.

....9.......... [*Specify other grounds on which repossession prior to prejudgment hearing may be authorized.*]

2. That the property is located at ....10.......... [*address*], City of ....11.......... , County of ....12.......... , State of ....13.......... .

3. That plaintiff is ....14.......... [the owner of and] entitled to the possession of said property.

The Court, from the foregoing findings, concludes that this is an appropriate case in which possession of said property should be taken from defendant and delivered to plaintiff prior to a hearing. It is, therefore,

Ordered:

1. That on plaintiff's filing with this court a written undertaking, executed by two or more sufficient sureties, approved by this court, to the effect that they are bound to defendant in the amount of $....15.... for the return of ....16.......... [*property*] to defendant, if return thereof is ordered by the court, and for the payment to defendant of any sum as may from any cause be recovered against plaintiff, ...17.......... [a writ of possession *or* a writ of replevin *or* an order] ....18.......... [issue *or* be entered] directing the ....19.......... [Sheriff] of the County of ....20.......... , State of ....21.......... , to take into his possession said ....22.......... [*property*] pursuant to ....23.......... [*cite statute*] and deliver said property to plaintiff.

2. That ....24.......... , the above-named defendant, appear before this court in the courtroom of ....25.......... [*specify department, name and number, judge, etc.*] at ....26.......... [*address*], in the City of ....27.......... , County of ....28.......... , State of ....29.......... , on ....30.......... , 19..31.. , at the hour of ....32.......... , and then and there show cause, if any he has, why ....33.......... [*property*] should not have been taken from him and delivered to plaintiff, and why said property should not remain in plaintiff's possession pending the final determination of this action.

3. That service of this order, together with a copy of plaintiff's complaint and affidavit, on defendant shall be made ....34.......... [within ....35.......... days after the date of this order *or* on or before ....36.......... , 19..37..].

4. That the service of this order, together with a copy of plaintiff's complaint and affidavit, on defendant shall be made ....38.......... [by personal service *or* in accordance with ....39.......... (*cite statute*) *or specify service in such manner as the judge may determine to be reasonably calculated to afford notice thereof to defendant under the circumstances appearing from the complaint and affidavit*].

Dated ....40.......... , 19..41.. .

[*Signature of judge*]

A typical Writ of Replevin, used to repossess property, 1972
AMERICAN JURISPRUDENCE, PLEADING AND PRACTICE AND FORMS, *VOL. 21, NEW YORK: LAWYERS COOPERATIVE PUBLISHING COMPANY, 1972*

Due Process of Law:
Fuentes v. Shevin

"Nor shall any person be deprived of life, liberty, or property, without due process of law."

I<small>N</small> J<small>UNE</small> 1967, M<small>ARGARITA</small> Fuentes of Miami bought a Firestone gas stove and service contract on an installment plan. In November, she bought a stereo. All together, she owed Firestone about $600: the stove and stereo were worth $500, and there was an extra $100 financing charge. Mrs. Fuentes made her payments for more than a year, until the stove stopped working. When she could not get anyone to come fix it, Mrs. Fuentes stopped paying. At the time, she owed $204.05. On September 15, 1969, a Firestone representative went to small claims court, filled out a form known as a writ of replevin, and got it stamped by the court clerk. The writ of replevin authorized the sheriff to seize the stove and stereo from Mrs. Fuentes's house. It did not require that Mrs. Fuentes be notified.

Margarita Fuentes understood little English and spoke none. When the deputy sheriff appeared at her door later that day, she did not understand what was happening. She sent for her son-in-law, who refused to surrender the stove and stereo on the advice of his lawyer. After the sheriff explained the writ again, the son-in-law let him in, along with two men from Firestone who had been waiting outside in a truck. They took the property, leaving a bewildered Margarita Fuentes out $400, with no stove, no stereo, and no idea what to do next.

Pennsylvania law authorized a similar procedure. Paul and Ellen Parham purchased a Harmony House table, four stools, and a bed from Sears, Roebuck in February 1969. The property was worth $250. When Paul fell behind on the payments, Sears notified the Parhams that their account was overdue. On September 11, 1970, Sears posted a bond for double the value of the property and obtained a writ of replevin. Four days later, much to the Parhams' surprise, the sheriff arrived at their door and carted their furniture away.

Mitchell Epps of Philadelphia had defaulted on his payments, too. But he never thought he would lose his wedding ring, along with his stereo, watch, and a TV roof antenna.

Finally, Rosa Bell Andrews Washington, a Georgia native who had recently moved to Philadelphia, was in the midst of a custody battle for her son and daughter. She had no idea how Pennsylvania law operated. But her ex-husband, Lewis Washington, was a local deputy sheriff familiar with the replevin procedure. He obtained a writ authorizing the seizure of all their son's belongings from Rosa's house. "He had the law come in and just take stuff," says Rosa. "I was real upset." The sheriff removed the boy's bike, lamp, toys, and clothes.

Under Florida law, after Firestone seized Margarita Fuentes's stove and stereo, it was obliged to sue her in court to make the repossession of the property final. Thus, she had an opportunity to challenge the removal of her property, but only after it had been taken. In Pennsylvania, there was no such procedure. If the Parhams, Epps, or Rosa Washington wanted their property back, they had to hire a lawyer and file suit themselves. In addition, nothing under Pennsylvania law required that they even be told such a remedy was available. Both Florida and Pennsylvania required that the sheriff keep repossessed property for three days, during which time individuals could get their property back if they posted a bond for double its value. After three days, it was gone for good.

Fuentes in Miami, and Washington, Parham, and Epps in Philadelphia, challenged the replevin procedure as a violation of the constitutional command that no person shall be deprived of life, liberty, or property "without due process of law." The first question was whether such everyday items were "property" covered by the Constitution at all. If they were, the next question was: What process was due? What procedure did the state have to follow before the sheriff could come and take someone's property away? The plaintiffs argued that they were at least entitled to a hearing *before* the property was repossessed.

Because the replevin procedures were authorized by state law, the suit was brought under the Fourteenth Amendment's due process clause, which restricts state action. The Fourteenth Amendment clause is based on the due process clause of the Fifth Amendment, which applies to the federal government. The clauses parallel each other, with one protecting people against unfair deprivation by the states and the other by the federal government.

The essential purpose of the due process clause is to prevent government from acting arbitrarily. The focus is on the *procedure* itself, unlike other freedoms protected in the Bill of Rights, where the concern is with the substance and scope of the protection. The right to due process of law exists in both the criminal and civil justice systems. When "life" is at stake, procedures ensuring a fair trial and appeals process are required by due process as well as by the Sixth Amendment. "Liberty" as protected by due process has been defined to include many different interests, ranging from those of a prisoner facing actual deprivation of bodily freedom to the liberty to enter a contract, pursue a career, marry, and raise a family. The willingness of the Supreme Court to review regulations restricting these fundamental nonprocedural rights has become known as substantive due process.

But at the time the Fifth Amendment was drafted, the focus was on procedure. The origins of the due process clause can be traced back to chapter 39 of the Magna Charta, written in 1215, which provided: "No free man shall be captured or imprisoned . . . or outlawed or exiled or in any way destroyed except by the lawful judgment of his peers and by the *law of the land.*"

The concept of providing procedural safeguards came to America with the first colonists and appears as early as 1639 in Maryland's Act for the Liberties of the People. The act essentially paraphrased the Magna Charta (using the words "laws of this province"). The first American use of the term "due process of law" was first used in the amendments to the Constitution of 1787 proposed by New York State. It was then picked up by Madison and became part of the Fifth Amendment. This simple change from "law of the land" to "due process of law" has been called a "constitutional quantum leap forward." For the words "due process" have a built-in flexibility (some argue too much flexibility) that has allowed courts to adapt the Bill of Rights to changing social conditions for two hundred years.

Nonetheless, in 1970 and 1971, district courts in both Florida and Pennsylvania ruled against Fuentes, Epps, the Parhams, and Rosa Washington. It seemed the Constitution did not protect property on the order of a stove, a stereo, and a television antenna. The plaintiffs appealed to the U.S. Supreme Court. Their cases were combined and became known as *Fuentes v. Shevin.* (Robert Shevin was sued in his capacity as attorney general of Florida.)

The plaintiffs based their Supreme Court arguments on two recently decided cases. The first, decided three years earlier, held it unconstitutional for creditors to garnish the wages of someone who owed them money (that is, have the wages paid directly to the creditors) without notice and a prior hearing. Calling the practice "most inhuman," the Court recognized that the family of someone whose wages were garnished often went hungry or without heat, and frequently the wage earner lost his or her job altogether. The second case held that the state could not cut off a person's welfare benefits without a prior hearing. To do so violated the due process clause.

The lawyers for Sears, Firestone, Florida, and Pennsylvania argued that the "property" at issue in those cases was far different from that in *Fuentes*. Wages and welfare benefits were "absolute necessities of life," they said; the stove and stereo were not. But the Supreme Court refused to find a constitutional difference between wages and benefits on the one hand, and consumer goods on the other. "The household goods for which the appellants contracted and paid substantial sums, are deserving of . . . protection," the Court wrote. "A stove or a bed may be . . . essential to provide a minimally decent environment for human beings in their day-to-day lives. It is, after all, such consumer goods that people work and earn a livelihood in order to acquire."

The Court refused to get into the business of judging the relative value of the plaintiffs' selection of consumer goods. It declared, "The [due process clause] speaks of property generally. And under our free enterprise system, an individual's choices in the marketplace are respected, however unwise they may seem to someone else."

The states also argued that a hearing was pointless—after all, most of the plaintiffs had defaulted on their payments and admitted doing so. Holding a hearing for every person who defaulted on an installment plan would place a large and expensive burden on the state. And the end result would often be the same. The only difference would be that Sears and Firestone would repossess the property after the hearing instead of before.

But the plaintiffs maintained that there were cases in which buyers had legitimate claims or grievances against a company, or were being deprived of property unfairly, or even by mistake. If buyers could prevail at a prior hearing, the inconvenience and suffering caused by the removal of their property would be avoided.

The Supreme Court recognized that a prior hearing would impose an additional burden and expense on the state. But it also recognized that the Bill of Rights was not written to ensure the most efficient, cost-effective system of government. It was written to protect the individual. The due process clause in particular was intended to prevent the government from arbitrarily depriving persons of their most basic rights—to life, liberty, and property—and to ensure that if such a deprivation occurred, the government be required to act according to fundamental notions of justice and fairness.

"The Constitution recognizes higher values than speed and efficiency," the Court explained. "Indeed, one might fairly say of the Bill of Rights in general, and the Due Process Clause in particular, that they were designed to protect the fragile values of a vulnerable citizenry from the overbearing concern for efficiency and efficacy that may characterize praiseworthy government officials." The Court did recognize that there existed emergency situations (such as wartime or danger to the public health from contaminated food) when the public interest would be so high that property could be seized without a prior hearing.

And the Court did not specify precisely what type of hearing would be required in the case of individuals like Fuentes. Instead,

it indicated that variations in form would be acceptable in order
to minimize the burden on the state. For example, depending on
the individual and governmental interests at stake, persons may
be entitled to a full-blown adversarial proceeding in which both
sides are represented by lawyers and allowed to call witnesses,
while at other times, individuals may have only the right to appear before an administrative official and present their own case.
But no matter what form the hearing takes, the due process
clause requires that it be a real and meaningful test, and when
the individual interests are high, it must take place *before* a person can be deprived of life, liberty, or property. Some also believe
that there was more to the decision than just the timing of the
hearing. By coming down on the side of relatively powerless individuals against large corporate interests, the Court was expressing its distaste for the type of economic oppression and unfair
bargaining power represented by the writs of replevin.

By the time the Supreme Court decided *Fuentes* in June 1972,
Margarita Fuentes had gotten a new stove. A highway was being
built near the back of her house and she liked to cook lunch for
her fellow Cubans on the road crew. This time she bought one
that would hold up to heavy-duty use. The Parhams and Mitchell
Epps moved on. Rosa Bell Andrews Washington lost the battle
over her son, but was awarded custody of her daughter. She did
not attend the Supreme Court argument and twenty years later
had no idea that her case is still considered a landmark constitutional victory for ordinary Americans. Of having won, she says
simply, "It feels good."

J*osephine Jakubowski's arrest in Detroit, 1981*
PHOTOGRAPH BY TARO YAMASAKI; REPRINTED BY PERMISSION OF THE
DETROIT FREE PRESS

"Takings":
Poletown Neighborhood Council v. Detroit

"Nor shall private property be taken for public use, without just compensation."

I<small>N</small> 1980, THE BUMPER STICKERS in Detroit read, "Will the last one to leave please turn out the lights?" Since the industrial boom of World War II ended, 40 percent of the city population had fled. The once cohesive city had been sliced by six new freeways, which fractured neighborhoods and pulled the population toward the sprawl of split-level homes and shopping malls in the suburbs. Factories shut down, unemployment and crime rose, racial tensions erupted into the riots of the late 1960s, and in the 1970s, even the auto industry, Detroit's economic bedrock since the early part of the century, was crumbling. Then, in the spring of 1980, General Motors announced it was closing two more plants.

This time, however, the auto giant planned to build a replacement plant, a huge state-of-the-art factory that would provide some six thousand jobs. Although every state with ready-to-use "green fields" was clamoring for it, the leaders of GM were willing to put their prize within the city of Detroit. They were willing, that is, provided a "suitable" site could be found.

Within two months the city found a suitable site. The working-class neighborhood the city found was known as Poletown because of the area's rich Polish history. And some thirty-five hundred people happened to live there.

Of the area's thirty-five hundred residents, there were only about three hundred who would not strike a deal with the city. They would not deal because they could not put a price on what the city wanted to buy: their homes and their church. They were mostly elderly, mostly Polish first-generation Americans. They had lived in Poletown for nearly three-quarters of a century. Their mothers and fathers had lived and died there and these residents fully intended to do the same. So they pulled on their sensible shoes and, for the first time in their lives, picked up picket signs and went out to fight.

Eminent domain, the power of the government to take private property for public use, is something of a sleeping giant in the law. On the one hand, the power means that the government may "take"—that is, force you to sell—your place of business, your school, your land, your *home*. With this power the government has carved out highway systems, built hospitals and dams, and preserved wilderness areas as national parks. On the other hand, "eminent domain" is hardly a well-known phrase. Even though its impact is immediate and often enormous, the government's exercise of its power to condemn has not generated much popular debate. It is even somewhat hidden in the Bill of Rights. Tacked on to the end of the Fifth Amendment, after a series of rights protecting criminal suspects, is a clause that reads, "Nor shall private property be taken for public use without just compensation."

The takings clause, as it is called, was incorporated against the states in 1896. Most states also have a takings clause written into their own constitutions, with language that basically tracks the federal provision. For example, the Michigan Constitution states, "Private property shall not be taken for public use without just compensation therefor being first made or secured in a manner prescribed by law."

Much of the controversy surrounding the takings clause concerns the question of how much compensation is "just." This issue is largely fact-specific, presenting difficult but localized questions about how much one's home or business is worth.

Sometimes, however, the other half of the takings clause—"taken for public use"—is tested. Then the question becomes whether the government may take the property at all.

In the Poletown case, this issue was further highlighted by an unusual local law. In 1980, Michigan enacted a "quick-take" statute, which separated the two issues in a condemnation proceeding. Under the statute, courts could first decide the issue of whether the taking was constitutional, leaving for later the question of how much money each property owner would receive. As a result, the government was able to condemn an area in a matter of months rather than years.

The city of Detroit took advantage of the quick-take statute in the Poletown case, thus isolating the question: Does giving the land to General Motors constitute a "public use"? The city claimed that it was taking land and homes to alleviate an economic crisis. It argued that the benefit to a private corporation (General Motors) was only incidental. The residents claimed that most business activity benefits the public, so interpreting "public use" to include general economic stimulation would mean there is no limit to the use of eminent domain to help private corporations.

It was a new issue in the law of eminent domain and one that could affect homeowners in every state. The way things had been going in Detroit, it was inevitable that the question would be raised there. In effect, Mayor Coleman Young had asked for it.

Coleman Young, smart, aggressive, and outspoken, grew up on Detroit's depressed east side and then fought his way up the Michigan political system. In 1974, he became one of the first black mayors of a major U.S. city and, by all accounts, he had inherited a city in crisis. Though unemployment was a nationwide problem, in Detroit it had reached, as one Michigan judge put it, "calamitous proportions." By 1980, unemployment in the state of Michigan was at 14.2 percent. In the city of Detroit it was at 18 percent, and in the black community it was at nearly 30 percent. The major automobile manufacturers had reported their largest financial losses ever, and Chrysler Corporation, in particular, was surviving by the grace of millions of dollars in federally insured loans.

Mayor Young testified that if General Motors moved its new

plant to another state, Detroit would lose another six thousand jobs. The city would also lose thousands of auto-related businesses and millions of dollars in real estate and income tax revenue. As labor leader, state senator, and mayor, Coleman Young had seen it happen before. In the last decade, entire neighborhoods within the city limits had become ghost towns.

"I'm not prepared for, and I don't think the country should be prepared for, a throwaway city," Mayor Young declared. "You can't walk away from a city." Indeed, the auto industry and politicians elsewhere in Michigan had been denounced for doing just that. An automobile plant would close and a whole town go into decline as a result. Local leaders were accused of giving up on their communities.

Coleman Young, on the other hand, was fighting back. "I'm attempting to do something that has not happened anywhere in this country, to rebuild an industrial city within the boundaries." To accomplish that, the mayor knew he had to act rather than react. Before the Poletown controversy arose, Mayor Young says, "I had requested from Ford, General Motors, [and] Chrysler . . . that if they had any plans to expand or build new plants, the city of Detroit be given the first opportunity."

So in May 1980, when General Motors decided to create a state-of-the-art assembly plant, GM's chairman of the board, Tom Murphy, went to see Coleman Young first. The plant would be in Detroit, the chairman said, if—and only if—the city could meet GM's requirements. GM wanted four to five hundred acres cleared within the city limits. They wanted this man-made "green field" to be rectangular in shape and have access to the expressways and railroads. And they wanted it within a year.

"He came right into this office and indicated that my year was starting to run that day." Mayor Young smiles. "I don't think that he thought I could do it."

By July, the Detroit Economic Development Corporation, headed by Emmett Moten, had chosen the Poletown area and named it the Central Industrial Park. By October 31, the city had held a public hearing, issued a five-hundred-page Environmental Impact Statement, and gotten the requisite approval from the Detroit Common Council by a vote of five to one. Three days later, on November 3, 1981, a scant five months after Tom Murphy's visit to Young's office, the mayor signed a resolution condemning Poletown and authorizing it to be turned over to General Motors.

*   *   *

Walter and Josephine Jakubowski, a couple in their seventies, had lived in Poletown all their lives. In the early 1900s the area was predominantly Polish. It was a working-class neighborhood with neat frame houses on small rectangles of grass standing side by side in tight rows. The pride of the neighborhood was its churches, which the residents had built with their own hands, using materials they had bought with their own money. Built in 1919, the Church of the Immaculate Conception was one of the neighborhood's grandest, with a white marble altar rising to a high ceiling of mosaic renderings of the Blessed Mother. Walter was in the first graduating class of the Immaculate Conception grade school, right down the street from his parents' house on Cantor Road. Josephine had been born a few blocks away.

In 1929, Walter met Josephine at her cousin's candy store, next door to Walter's house. Josephine worked for three dollars a week as a nursemaid and Walter was trying to put himself through college. It was the Depression and entertainment was scarce. For twenty-five cents you got not only a movie at the local theater but also a dinner plate—one a week until you had a whole set. Otherwise, you sat on the porch and talked with people walking by. Everybody knew everybody else; they had all grown up together.

When Walter and Josephine married in 1934, they moved in with Walter's parents. It was a two-story white frame house, five rooms up and five down, with a closed-in porch that was used as an extra room as the extended family moved in and out. Over the next nearly half century, the events of Walter and Josephine's lives were mapped out along the single block between their home and their church. Walter's father, mother, and brother died in the house on Cantor, and it was there that Josephine gave birth to their four children. The children were baptized at Immaculate Conception and, like their father, attended school and were eventually married there. It was this house and this church that the city said had to make way for the new factory's parking lot.

In 1980, however, many disputed how much, if any, of this Rockwellian way of life was left in the Poletown area. "When I made a determination to take down houses," Mayor Young explains, "it was not as if it was a neighborhood where people lived cheek to jowl. The neighborhoods had deteriorated and were still deteriorating."

Even Walter admits that the pattern of life he and Josephine

cherished had long since disappeared from Poletown. The Edsel
Ford Expressway had split the area in half (only the neighborhood north of the expressway was slated for demolition). As
the neighborhood developed, people became more isolated and
the communal spirit began to disappear.

"In the old days, the mother or father died, the kids stayed in
their home," Walter says. "After a time, some people got scared
and others, you know, they called it upward mobility. The kids
moved out before the folks even died. Then the mother was probably widowed or left there with the home and the kids didn't
want it and there were no buyers. So the sharpies came in and
bought them for a song. Within a year, it was a mess. I mean,
they were left a shambles."

The row upon row of neat frame houses in Poletown slowly
gave way to a well-tended house standing defiantly between two
poor relations gone to pot.

Still, the residents argued, they were fighting to save not only
the carcass of the neighborhood, but also its soul. "Ethnicity" became their battle cry. In discussing the controversy, residents
talked as much about their heritage as they did about their
homes. And even though the neighborhood was really a melting
pot of Armenians, Albanians, Yugoslavs, Hispanics, and blacks, as
well as Poles, the name Poletown became one of the holdouts'
best weapons.

Those on the city's side were more than skeptical. They
claimed that before the GM project was announced the area was
not even called Poletown. Emmett Moten and his staff made a
point of refusing to use the nickname. Instead, they insisted on
calling the area Central Industrial Park. Mayor Young allowed
that there might have been an area known as Poletown but said,
"It's moved considerably north [into the area to be condemned]
since we started talking about a General Motors plant." And asserting that the area was at least half black as well as Polish,
Mayor Young stated, "It could more accurately be described as
Afro-Poletown."

While the holdouts undoubtedly realized that their cries of ethnicity played well to the public, their sentiments were just as undoubtedly sincere. For the handful of residents who had hung on
to their homes had likewise clung to the way of life their homes
represented. The fierce attachment to the local church also re-

mained. Michael Krowleski, a local social worker, says that upon introduction Poles from the area, like most people, take stock of one another. But instead of the usual conversation beginning with "Where do you live?" the exchange would go something like this: "What parish do you belong to?" "Saint Francis of Assisi." "Oh, yeah? I'm from Saint Andrews." To people like Walter and Josephine, the church was their identity and their anchor.

Walter says, "When I retired [in 1963] I had about a half acre out there in the western suburbs. I thought I wanted to move there. But Josephine was so attached to the church and we were involved with the church so much we wouldn't move for all the money in the world."

"Oh, we never planned on moving," Josephine says firmly.

It was the church that kept people in the neighborhood and it was around the church that they finally rallied. When the city first announced its plan, community leaders called a meeting and formed the Poletown Neighborhood Council. The council hired a local attorney, Ron Reosti, to challenge the taking in court. They also called members of Ralph Nader's litigation team from Washington. The "Nader boys," as the residents called them, set up a makeshift office in the basement of Immaculate Conception and brought with them professional organizational skills and media savvy. Still, they were outsiders.

Mayor Young called the Nader boys "carpetbaggers" and said they should mind their own business. "This man [Nader] has a phobia. Whenever GM is mentioned he froths at the mouth. I don't know why the people of Detroit should be punished because of his phobia."

So the longtime residents, those who would be affected most by the plan, did what came naturally. They turned to their local church. More specifically, they turned to the priest at the Immaculate Conception, to Father Joseph Karacevich, known to all as Father Joe.

Father Joe was a most unlikely candidate to take on the archdiocese, General Motors, and the city of Detroit. At fifty-eight, he was one of the older priests in the neighborhood. Pale and lean, with close-cropped hair and small wire spectacles, he was a good and a hardworking priest, but not an activist priest.

"He was a rather quiet man," says Father Frank Skalski, pastor of nearby Saint Hyacinth's. "He was never known for anything, for being outgoing or going out of the way to create attention to himself."

Indeed, Walter Jakubowski thinks the archdiocese was counting on Father Joe's mild-mannered personality. "I think it was all prearranged to put him in there, you know, figure that he was an elderly priest, timid soul . . . that he would go out like a meek lamb and there wouldn't be any problem. But he fooled them."

Actually, if the archdiocese was surprised at Father Joe's reaction, the priest himself may have been just as surprised. Before the controversy, according to Father Skalski, Father Joe "didn't care too much about meetings. He would come to meetings, say the opening prayer, and then say 'I have something to do' or 'Can I be excused?' . . . He just would leave. When we had the initial meeting [about the Poletown case], there was no response from him."

But as the threat to the neighborhood grew, it seemed everyone was turning to Father Joe. The parishioners naturally looked to him for guidance. The Nader boys moved their operation into Immaculate Conception, physically placing the controversy there. Then, predictably, the media sought out Father Joe. "The media would come to me," says Father Skalski, "and I'd say, look, he's the pastor, talk to him. We were pushing everything towards him." Thus as everything was pushed his way, Father Joe was faced with a choice.

"You have to remember that he was a priest. The church hurt him. But it hurt him to attack the archdiocese," Father Skalski says. "I'm sure within himself he had a struggle—do I serve the archdiocese or serve the cause of my people? And if he went on the side of the archdiocese he probably would have been rewarded for it, for being faithful to them. But he turned his back on the archdiocese and took the side of the people."

Father Joe never talked of his decision or of his feelings about his role in the Poletown case. Nonetheless, having taken the side of his parishioners, he fought for them with an audacity that some say bordered on foolhardiness. For he criticized not only General Motors and the city of Detroit, but also the archdiocese, an act for which he would eventually pay a price.

In the meantime, though, Father Joe became the "Iron Priest of Poletown." He assailed the taking of Poletown as a "criminal act" and the quick-take statute as an "evil law." He declared the parish to be a "symbol of the people's faith" and a "symbol of a basic fight for people's rights."

Now, *here* was something around which people like Josephine Jakubowski could rally. And as Josephine and the other "mothers of Poletown" began to protest, the media discovered them. Suddenly, the residents' greatest weakness—their position as senior citizens without connections or political clout—became their greatest strength.

They were white-haired and bespectacled, standing in the rain in their plastic kerchiefs, carrying hand-lettered signs that said things like "Saint Peter will want to know *why*." Josephine, a born nurturer, welcomed strangers, whether friend or foe in the controversy, with hot coffee and luncheon meat. When the water was shut off at Immaculate Conception, she walked down the street with a steaming teapot to serve the volunteers. She was not afraid to stand up to authority, even the bishops of her beloved church ("I was a Catholic before you were born") and if she did not get her way, she threatened to cry. The media loved Josephine Jakubowski.

When the mothers of Poletown picked flowers from their gardens, it was Josephine who weaved them into a funeral wreath and on Mother's Day led a procession of residents with a bulldozer to the home of Roger Smith, the new chairman of General Motors. "Happy Mother's Day, Mrs. Smith," they said. "Talk to Roger." When Ralph Nader came to town to lend support, it was Josephine who cooked him dinner, then asked for a hug. And the image that came to symbolize the Poletown case was a photograph of Josephine, in pink housecoat and powder-blue cardigan, leaning out of the back of a paddy wagon.

Mayor Young, on the other hand, was hurt and angered by his portrayal as something of a grandmother-basher. He railed against the press coverage, not only with the savvy of a seasoned politician who felt he was doing what was most politically and economically expedient, but also with the conviction of a man who felt absolutely certain that he was right.

"I'm familiar with urban renewal," Mayor Young says. "Only we called it black removal. My old neighborhood on the east side was literally bulldozed. But there were no humane [taking] laws such as we have now."

Mayor Young felt that under the Poletown plan, the residents were receiving generous sums for their homes, which would enable them to improve their standard of living. Furthermore, before he made the decision to take Poletown, Mayor Young made sure he had the support of his constituents. Archbishop Cardinal Dearden, spiritual leader of the 1.2 million Roman Catholics in the Detroit area, supported the plan, as did a majority of the Detroit population, including all but a handful from the area to be condemned.

Thus, Mayor Young says, the decision to trade the Poletown homes for jobs "was not a hard decision to make." The hard part, it would seem, would be to accomplish within only one year the largest urban condemnation proceeding in history. But Detroit was so desperate, and Coleman Young so determined, that within months the mayor and his staff had devised a plan to buy and bulldoze 16 churches, 2 schools, 1 hospital, 114 small businesses, 1,300 houses, and to relocate 3,500 people in the process. It was, as one Michigan judge who eventually heard the case noted, "a most impressive display of government efficiency."

That same judge, however, went on to say, "Behind the frenzy of official activity was the unmistakable guiding and sustaining, indeed controlling hand of the General Motors Corporation." It was this issue that Ron Reosti, on behalf of the Poletown Neighborhood Council, brought to court.

A Michigan statute authorized a municipality to condemn land if "necessary," for the purpose of creating commercial and industrial sites. The trial judge limited the issue to whether the city had complied with the statute. He decided that it had and ruled that the condemnation could proceed. "General Motors held no gun to the head of the city of Detroit," the judge said.

Ron Reosti decided he could not plod through the usual appeal process; buildings were being razed. So just before Christmas, he made a special appeal to the Michigan Supreme Court, asking permission to bypass the intermediate level. On January 29, 1981, the state's highest court granted the special appeal and ordered any further demolition in Poletown be halted pending a decision.

With a reprieve from the court, the Poletown residents intensified their efforts to save the neighborhood. Four of the Nader boys set up a round-the-clock work schedule from their headquarters in the basement of Immaculate Conception. A few weeks later, the church was literally sold out from under them. The court had enjoined demolition but not deal making in Poletown. Cardinal Dearden signed an agreement with the city of Detroit to sell Immaculate Conception for a reported $1.2 million, and to sell another area church, Saint John the Evangelist, for a reported $120,000.

"It's killing the spirit of the people," Father Joe declared. "We go down to a very basic definition of stealing. . . . This property was taken away from the people against their will." And the people of Poletown, their faith in one institution shaken, turned to another institution, the judiciary, for help.

In the Supreme Court of Michigan, the case did not rest on whether the city of Detroit had complied with the state statute, but on whether the statute was constitutional in the first place. Did the Poletown plan qualify as one for "public use"? On March 14, 1981, the court, by a vote of five to two, decided that it did.

"The power of eminent domain is to be used in this instance primarily to accomplish the essential public purposes of alleviating unemployment and revitalizing the economic base of the community," the court concluded. "The benefit to a private corporation is merely incidental."

In answer to the plaintiffs' protest that such a decision would give the city unlimited power to trade their homes for jobs, the court expressly limited its holding to the facts of the case before it. The general concept behind the Poletown taking had been approved, but that did not mean that every proposed condemnation would be approved "simply because it may provide some jobs or add to the industrial or commercial base." The public benefit must be "clear and significant," a standard the court felt had been met in this case.

In upholding the Poletown plan, the court wrote, "The most important consideration in the case of eminent domain is the necessity of accomplishing some public good which is otherwise impracticable. . . . The abstract right [of an individual] to make use of his own property in his own way is compelled to yield to the general comfort and protection of community." In effect, the court was saying, the law of eminent domain is a microcosm of the democratic principle of majority rule. Here, the parishioners of the Church of the Immaculate Conception were the minority who had to give way.

Or as Mayor Young put it, "We did what we had to do. If you

want to make an omelette, you got to crack some eggs—or you starve."

Two members of the court disagreed. One of the dissenters, Justice Ryan, wrote, "The reverberating clang of [this case's] economic, sociological, political, and jurisprudential impact is likely to be heard and felt for generations." He denounced the majority's "clear and significant public benefit" standard as far too ambiguous. "The state taking clause has now been placed on a spectrum that admits of no principles and therefore no limits," he wrote.

At the very least, Justice Ryan said, the government must retain some control over the enterprise that receives the condemned property in order to ensure that the public benefit continues. Here, the city of Detroit retained no such control. "General Motors will be accountable not to the public, but to its stockholders," he wrote. "Who knows what the automotive industry will look like in 20 years, or even in 10? For that matter, who knows what cars will look like then? For all that can be known now . . . the plant could be fully automated in 10 years." Justice Ryan concluded that the majority handed down an opinion that "seriously jeopardize[s] the security of all private property ownership."

By the time of the ruling, almost a third of the Poletown residents in the condemned area had moved out. Many had taken their money and left, willingly and happily, months ago. Others reluctantly picked up a profit on the sale of their homes, giving in to what seemed like the inevitable. Still, Walter, Josephine, Father Joe, and a handful of others were not close to admitting defeat.

"Oh, I always had hope," Josephine says without hesitation. "I always had faith."

The Jakubowskis and their neighbors had become something of a nationwide cause célèbre, participants in a modern-day David and Goliath struggle. Outside of Michigan at least, it seemed everyone was rooting for David. So General Motors, stung by the adverse publicity, came up with the idea of moving Immaculate Conception to another location, outside of the condemned area. It would no longer be the "neighborhood" church, but neither would it be one of the new-fangled suburban churches, or "gymchurches" as Father Skalski calls them, in which people like Walter and Josephine could find little comfort. Cardinal Dearden refused. The church would be deconsecrated by the end of April.

"Totally unacceptable," Father Joe declared. But the archdiocese informed Father Joe that his last mass would be Mother's Day, May 10.

"The church was full that night," Josephine recalls. "And he come out and he said to make no fuss. He says, 'I just have to leave quietly.' And everybody of course cried because it was so pitiful."

Poletown now resembled a war zone. Heaps of rubble from demolished buildings marked the streets. Homes abandoned but not yet bulldozed were left for scavengers, who made off with clapboard, roofing tiles, plumbing, and electric wiring. Arsonists worked the neighborhood and sirens wailed. The residents, too, were developing a battle mentality. When Josephine went off to meetings or protests, Walter stayed home to guard the house. Then, in June, the holdouts decided to move into Immaculate Conception. They wanted the church to be occupied by its parishioners if and when anyone tried to knock it down.

Josephine, new to this kind of protest, was somewhat baffled as to how to proceed. "I brought my pillow," she announces. "I figured I, well, I *couldn't* sleep on anybody else's pillow, so I brought my own." Others brought mattresses, blankets, gas stoves, and a supply of water, because the plumbing and electricity had already been shut off. Small white candles from the church were used for light. The parishioners, including Josephine, took turns spending the night to ensure that there would always be four or five people occupying the condemned church. Father Joe remained their leader, even though he was not allowed to enter the church or even the church grounds.

"We had to come out from the basement to see him," says Josephine. "Every day he would come. Every day."

Father Joe would arrive early and stand in the street, waiting to lend support to his former parishioners. "The minute he'd come around," says Walter, "we'd all gather around him, the shepherd. He always prayed with us."

Then, on July 14, Josephine got a call in the middle of the night. "That night was not my night to sleep at the church," she says. "Here I'm sleeping so peaceful and so nice and my husband

said, 'Hey, there's a call, you better go.' Well, my pillow was there
so I didn't even dress. You see, there was so many times they
were saying, 'They're coming in.'"

This time, though, a sympathetic member of the Detroit police
had tipped off the residents. The church bells rang out and
Josephine, along with a dozen other supporters, huddled in the
basement of Immaculate Conception, singing hymns and saying
the rosary. At dawn, the police broke through a makeshift barri-
cade the parishioners had set up at the door to their basement
bunker.

"They were nice," Josephine says. "We were praying and then
we sang and they didn't say nothing to us, so we got through. And
then they said, 'Are you through praying?' and I said yes."

The parishioners were arrested and led outside. A picture of
Josephine, framed by the blue-uniformed arm of a Detroit police
officer and the wire mesh door of a paddy wagon, made all of the
front pages the next day. As it turned out, the local prosecutor
declined to press charges and the group was detained only a few
hours. Walter picked up Josephine at the jail and the two went
home rather than return to the church.

"I couldn't get myself to go and watch it," Walter says. "It was
like tearing pieces of my flesh piecemeal. I had no stomach for
watching it." Even Josephine, who had stayed with her church
until almost the last moment, could not bring herself to be there
as the wrecking ball was moved into place. "Even if I wanted to, I
just couldn't do that," she says.

But Father Joe was there. Beyond the barricades, surrounded
by his former parishioners, Father Joe, weeping, knelt in prayer.
The church was demolished that afternoon.

Today, a sprawling, seventy-acre state-of-the-art factory sits on
hundreds of acres of parking lot where the old Poletown neighborhood used to be. The plant provides around three thousand
rather than six thousand jobs.

Walter and Josephine moved to a modern ranch house in the
suburbs and say they are happy enough. "But this is a house,"
Walter says. "That was a home." Father Joe moved in with Father Skalski at Saint Hyacinth's to await a new assignment, but
in less than a year was dead of heart failure at the age of fifty-

nine. And Mayor Coleman Young, in a fifth term, is still rebuild-ing his city. Plans are under way to take another neighborhood. This time the land is to be given to the Chrysler Corporation and this time no one is yelling that it is not for a "public use." The state's highest court has held that in this city, at this time, and under these circumstances, at least, such a taking is legal.

SIXTH AMENDMENT

"In all criminal prosecutions, the accused shall enjoy the right to a speedy and public trial, by an impartial jury of the State and district wherein the crime shall have been committed, which district shall have been previously ascertained by law, and to be informed of the nature and cause of the accusation; to be confronted with the witnesses against him; to have compulsory process for obtaining Witnesses in his favor, and to have the Assistance of Counsel for his defence."

Rebecca Machetti on death row in the Georgia Women's
Correctional Institution, 1979
DOUG MAGEE

Right to an Impartial Jury:
Machetti v. Linahan

"In all criminal prosecutions, the accused shall enjoy the right to a speedy and public trial by an impartial jury of the State and district wherein the crime shall have been committed."

"**I** WOULD SAY I'M SOMEBODY who, like Helen Reddy's song 'I Am Woman,' I am woman and damn proud of it. Sixteen years into this penitentiary and I'm still not a homosexual," says Rebecca Machetti. "I believe in equal rights, I believe in women having a just and respectable part in society and not just the part that we've had. In other words, we've come a long way baby, so why not say we're going further."

On Saturday of Labor Day weekend in 1974, a young Pan Am pilot home for the weekend in Macon, Georgia, decided to rent a small plane and take his fiancée and her sisters up for a spin. They wanted to look at a pool a friend of theirs had built, to see what it looked like from the air. As they were flying over a wooded area near a new subdivision, one of them spotted a deer. They flew down low to have a closer look. They passed over a white car parked at the edge of a dead-end, deserted road. Right next to the car they saw the body of a man lying on the pavement with blood running a long way down the street. They turned back to the airport and called the police. It was about 7:30 P.M.

The same evening, a young couple from the local high school was out driving around. They turned down the deserted road and saw the dead man. They also saw a woman, covered with blood, lying across the front seat of the car. They drove to the closest house and also called the police.

As it turned out, Bobby McElroy, who lived on a nearby street, had seen the white car drive down to the remote area around 5:00 P.M. that afternoon. He had seen a green Gremlin with Florida plates turn down the same street a short time later. He remembered because he used to own a Gremlin himself. He heard shots but thought nothing of it, since people used to hunt and shoot in those woods from time to time. He then saw the green car leaving with two men in it. Mrs. McElroy, who also saw them, remembered that the driver covered his face with his hand, though she got a pretty good look.

The dead man was Ronnie Akins, a forty-year-old employee of the Southern Natural Gas Company who installed TV antennas on the side. He was found with twenty-two dollars in his pocket and directions to the place where he died. The woman was his new wife, Juanita, twenty-eight, a schoolteacher. They had been married for less than three weeks. She would be buried in her wedding dress.

The police came out, sealed off the area, and took the bodies away. They figured Ronnie Akins had been told to stand facing the car with his hands on the roof, then had been shot through the back and in the head. His bloody handprint slid down the side of the car. Juanita had been hit several times with a pipe but had still been able to crawl into the car, to try to use the two-way radio to call for help. She had put her hands up to cover her face, but both had been practically shot off. The hole in her face was about four or five inches wide, big enough to put a hand through. In addition to Ronnie and Juanita's fingerprints, there was one other set of prints on the car, but police could not immediately identify them.

Ronnie Akins had three daughters, Vicki, Valerie, and Vanessa, from a previous marriage. They were living in North Miami Beach, Florida, with their mother, Rebecca. The next morning, when police went to notify the next of kin of the death in the family, Rebecca and her new husband, Tony Machetti, were at mass.

Later, when Ray Wilke, chief deputy sheriff of Bibb County, Georgia, called Rebecca to see if she knew who might have a motive for murdering her ex-husband, she told him Ronnie had been a drug dealer and a homosexual, and was probably murdered by another dealer. The sheriff asked the Florida police to interview Rebecca and her husband in person. Rebecca said she had been in Miami all weekend with her daughters. Valerie's boyfriend had been visiting. Tony said he had been on a fishing trip with a family friend, John Maree.

A month later, police interviewed Maree and took his fingerprints. They matched the unidentified prints on Ronnie Akins's car. Mrs. McElroy later identified Maree as the driver of the car she had seen leaving the crime scene in August. On October 16, 1974, Rebecca Machetti, Tony Machetti, and John Maree were all arrested. On November 6, they were taken to Georgia. The next day John Maree confessed. The evidence against him was the strongest; he was the only one of the three who could be placed at the crime scene. He agreed to testify against the Machettis in the hope of avoiding the death penalty.

Rebecca's divorce decree had become final on February 18, 1974, only six months before the murders. No longer satisfied with a middle-class, ordinary life-style, Rebecca wanted something more. "She looks like anybody you would see at the grocery store, but I think she always wanted renown of whatever type she could get," says Susan Boleyn, an assistant attorney general of Georgia, who grew up in Athens, Georgia, the same town as Rebecca Machetti. After the divorce came through, Rebecca had taken her three teenage daughters to Miami in search of a different life. She went to the racetrack, hung out at bars, and somehow got the notion that a Mafia connection would bring her the glamor she wanted.

On the night of June 1, Rebecca met a man named John Eldon Smith in a bar. A balding, bespectacled, mild-mannered insurance salesman from New Jersey, Smith was on an extended vacation in Miami recovering from the breakup of his own marriage. He fell hard for Rebecca. "I get the sense he was bedazzled or bewitched or whatever . . . I mean literally charmed into being something that he hadn't been before," says Jack Boger, Smith's attorney, "[though] there may have been a thread there that she picked up on. Kind of a loose sense that 'I want something dif-

ferent or more from my life.' And to some extent, he went on a
kind of crazy mission for her and was caught in it and stayed
initially loyal to her. I mean the way a courtier might stay loyal
to a damsel, or whatever, and [only] gradually woke up and realized, 'This is the craziest thing I've ever done in my life.'"

Together Rebecca and John Eldon converted to Catholicism
and decided to marry. They also decided that Smith would
change his name to something more exciting, and they chose An-
thony Israldo Machetti. They liked it because it sounded like a
machete knife, and it sounded Italian, Mafia-like. Rebecca became known as Becky Machetti.

The night after she met John Eldon Smith, Becky met John
Maree. Maree had been in the hauling business in New Jersey
before he got divorced and moved to Miami. "He's real tall, and
he's big, and he's your typical con artist fast talker. You know,
he's got the gift of gab. He's the real smooth-operator-type person," says Susan Boleyn. Though Becky was dating Smith, Maree
moved in with her and her daughters. He began having an affair
with the eldest who was then seventeen. They discussed marriage, and he promised to buy a farm when they got some money.
The money was to come from the proceeds of Ronnie Akins's life
insurance policy.

According to Maree's confession, Rebecca Machetti had masterminded the murders. She stood to gain financially from Ronnie Akins's death. Her divorce settlement provided that Ronnie
would keep a life insurance policy of twenty thousand dollars in
effect for his daughters, payable on his death. Maree said Rebecca
had offered him one thousand dollars to drive with Tony to
Georgia. Knowing that Ronnie installed TV antennas on the side,
it was her idea that they lure him to a remote area with an in-
stallation request. She had acquired drugs and a hypodermic sy-
ringe. Being a nurse, she showed them how to inject the drugs
into a vein in the arm. The original plan was to knock Ronnie out
and then inject him with the drugs, to make it look as if he had
overdosed. But when Juanita Akins started screaming, the plan
had changed, and Tony had gotten his shotgun out of the car and
blown the Akinses away.

Tony and Rebecca were tried separately in January and February 1975. In their legal proceedings they were known as John Eldon Smith and Rebecca Machetti. They were each convicted of

two counts of murder and sentenced to two consecutive death sentences. Maree pleaded guilty, testified at Tony's and Rebecca's trials, and got life.

At the time, Rebecca Machetti was the only woman on Georgia's death row. Maryann Oakley, two years out of law school and practicing employment discrimination law, became Rebecca's lawyer. She had never worked on a capital case, but her relationship with Becky "became literally, until death or reversal do us part." The NAACP Legal Defense and Educational Fund, which had waged a ten-year battle against the death penalty, agreed to help with Oakley's expenses. They were representing John Eldon Smith.

In a sense, Georgia has been the Supreme Court's laboratory for death penalty law. In a 1972 case, *Furman v. Georgia*, the Supreme Court held that the arbitrary, random, and capricious way the death penalty was administered at the time violated the Eighth Amendment's prohibition against "cruel and unusual punishment," and many death sentences across the country were vacated. State legislatures responded by passing new statutes designed to address the problems identified by the Supreme Court. Georgia was one of those states. Its new law was upheld in the 1976 case *Gregg v. Georgia*, which held that if "fairly" administered, the death penalty was a constitutional punishment. John Eldon Smith and Rebecca Machetti were among the first people to be sentenced to death under the new statute, and lawyers who believed the statute still operated unfairly were determined to fight for them.

The NAACP Legal Defense Fund had developed a checklist of possible constitutional violations that were common in the trials of people who received death sentences. But in what has now become standard operating procedure for lawyers whose clients are sentenced to death, Maryann Oakley and two young legal interns decided to dig deeper into the unique local aspects of Rebecca Machetti's trial.

They discovered some surprising statistics. It turned out that both blacks and women were underrepresented in the jury selection process that led to the convictions of Rebecca Machetti and John Eldon Smith. The 1970 census showed that black people comprised 34 percent of Bibb County's population, but at the time of Rebecca's trial only 19 percent of those on the list from which the trial juries were selected were black. The grand jury list was 27 percent black. The disparity for women was worse. Though the population of Bibb County was 54 percent female, only 18 percent of those on the trial jury list were women, a 36 percent disparity, and only 12 percent of the list of grand jurors were women, a 42 percent disparity.

Some effort had been made by the six male jury commissioners to correct the racial disparity, but no effort had been made to increase the number of women serving on Bibb County juries. Maryann Oakley was convinced that the disparity resulted from the Georgia jury selection law in effect at the time, which allowed women to "opt out" of jury service if they desired, no questions asked. She believed that this law deprived Rebecca Machetti of her Sixth Amendment right to an impartial jury.

On January 21, 1975, six days before John Eldon Smith's trial, and one month before Rebecca Machetti's, the Supreme Court decided *Taylor v. Louisiana*. In that case, a defendant challenged a law that excluded women from jury duty unless they *requested* to serve (an "opt-in" statute). The Court held that the law was unconstitutional, violating the right to an impartial jury. According to the Supreme Court, the Sixth Amendment guarantees that a trial jury must be selected from a representative cross-section of the community. It does not guarantee that the jury itself will mirror the composition of the community, only that the list or pool from which the jury is chosen must not exclude large or distinctive groups of the population. Oakley believed that by severely underrepresenting blacks and women, the Bibb County jury list did just that. The disparity was carried through to the jury that convicted Rebecca Machetti; it was composed of eleven men and only one woman.

In *Taylor*, the Supreme Court held that the fair cross-section requirement of the Sixth Amendment was violated by the systematic exclusion of women, who accounted for 53 percent of the eligible citizens of the community. "The thought is that the factors which tend to influence the action of women are the same as those which influence the action of men—personality, background, economic status—and not sex. . . . But, if the shoe were on the other foot, who would claim that a jury was truly representative of the community if all men were intentionally and systematically excluded from the panel? The truth is that the two sexes are not [interchangeable]; a community made up exclusively of one is different from a community composed of both; the subtle interplay of influence one on the other is among the imponderables. To insulate the courtroom from either may not in a given case make an iota of difference. Yet a flavor, a distinct quality, is lost if either sex is excluded."

In *Taylor*, the state of Louisiana had argued that the system of jury selection that excluded women served the state's interest in maintaining stable family life. But the Supreme Court, citing statistics compiled by the Department of Labor, concluded that this state interest no longer reflected contemporary society. In 1974, 54.2 percent of women between the ages of eighteen and sixty-four were in the labor force, 45.7 percent of women with children under eighteen were working, 67.3 percent of single mothers were working, as were 51.2 percent of mothers whose husbands were present in the household. "If at one time it could be held that Sixth Amendment juries must be drawn from a fair cross section of the community but that this requirement permitted the almost total exclusion of women, this is not the case today," wrote the Supreme Court.

Oakley decided to petition the Georgia courts for a writ of habeas corpus, which allows prisoners to challenge the legality of their detention (not their guilt or innocence). She claimed that the jury that convicted and sentenced Rebecca Machetti was unconstitutionally selected, and Machetti's conviction was therefore invalid. Georgia's opt-out statute, though different from the opt-in statute declared unconstitutional in *Taylor*, functioned the same way. If the principles enunciated by the Court in *Taylor* held true, Oakley reasoned, then Georgia's opt-out statute must also be unconstitutional.

The Framers considered trial by jury in criminal cases so important that it alone among all of the rights ultimately guaranteed by the Bill of Rights in 1791 was first protected in the Constitution of 1787. But even though the Constitution guaranteed the right to a jury in a criminal trial, many believed the protection was not strong enough. The Sixth Amendment reinforced the right by specifying that the trial must be speedy and public (not secret), and that the jurors must be impartial and from the district, not just the state, where the crime was committed. This last requirement grew out of the belief that members of the local community were best qualified to reach a just verdict. The Framers also objected to the English practice of taking colonists back to England to stand trial in front of a jury that knew nothing about life in America, and whose passions and prejudices against the colonists could easily be aroused by the Crown's prosecutor.

Although today the historical role of the jury as a check on the oppressive power of government is perhaps not as vital as it was in the days of the royal prerogative, the jury's other virtues are now recognized by the Supreme Court as equally important. By encouraging citizens to participate in government, it is hoped that they will gain respect for the rule of law. The men and women who sit on a criminal jury hold the fate and freedom of the accused in their hands, because they decide whether the state has proved its case beyond a reasonable doubt. This role is particularly important when a person's life is at stake, as it was in Rebecca Machetti's case. And in order to perform it, to truly sit in judgment, the jury must be impartial, as the Constitution says. To ensure that a jury is impartial, lawyers from both sides conduct what is known as "voir dire." They question all prospective jurors before trial to uncover any bias or prejudice that may affect their ability to be impartial.

In addition, history has shown that the jury as a group can reach a balanced result only if it reflects the different beliefs and attitudes of the community. As Justice Thurgood Marshall once wrote, "When any large and identifiable segment of the community is excluded from jury service, the effect is to remove from the jury room qualities of human nature and varieties of human experience, the range of which is unknown and perhaps unknowable." It is thought that the different experiences of blacks and whites, men and women, may allow them to evaluate more accurately which witnesses are telling the truth and which are not. Ultimately, this diversity is designed to contribute to the jury's understanding of what really happened and allow its members to piece together the truth. As Smith's lawyer, Jack Boger, says, "To systematically deprive the jury of the input [of a group] is like a person losing one of his senses. You may still have four senses, but you don't have five. You may still be able to hear, but you can't see."

According to Rebecca Machetti, "If [only] there had been some

women on [the jury] who could have related to me and would
have related to the truth . . . but nobody knew who I was. I had a
reputation as a Mafia queen. I had never even seen a gangster,
but they took the Roman Catholicism, they took the fully stocked
bar, they took the Catholic name, they took the fact that I had
married a man from New Jersey, they took the fact that I go to
the horse track, and I'm good, they took all these things together.
When the D.A. got through with me, the woman was looking
down her nose at me and the eleven men wanted to fix me for
having killed a good old Georgia boy. . . . Perhaps if there had
been more women, from a different mentality or a different strata
of society, perhaps it would have been different, but this particular bitch I got on the jury was just that."

In addition to the opt-out statute's exclusion of women, Oakley
challenged the jury's impartiality on other grounds. First, Legal
Defense Fund statistics show that blacks and women are less
likely than white men to vote for the death penalty. Therefore,
Oakley argued, their underrepresentation made Rebecca's jury
not impartial, but unconstitutionally likely to vote for death upon
conviction. Second, two jurors, one of whom was a woman, had
been disqualified because they expressed opposition to the death
penalty when questioned at voir dire. Because their point of view
would be missing from the deliberations in the jury room, Oakley
contended that the result would be a jury that was not drawn
from a representative cross section of the community, but one
that was skewed toward the death penalty.

The state rebutted Oakley's arguments one by one, but it could
not dispute her jury statistics. Instead it claimed that under
Georgia law, any objection to the composition of the jury should
have been raised at the time of trial, so Rebecca Machetti had
missed her chance. Machetti had not even raised the claim when
she appealed her conviction directly, but only in her state habeas
corpus petition, which was filed on January 9, 1978, after her conviction became final.

The judge sat on the case for almost a year and a half; Machetti
sat on death row. On May 9, 1979, he denied all her claims and
the Georgia Supreme Court affirmed. But on January 9, 1979,
while the judge was still considering the case, the U.S. Supreme
Court had declared unconstitutional a Missouri statute that allowed women to automatically opt out of jury service. It was ex-

actly like Georgia's law. The Supreme Court made it clear that the decision applied retroactively to all juries sworn since the date *Taylor* had been decided, January 21, 1975, a month before Machetti's trial.

The new case gave Oakley one more chance: federal court. She filed a petition for habeas corpus in federal district court. But the district court ruled that Machetti had challenged the jury too late. Oakley appealed to the Court of Appeals for the Eleventh Circuit. It reversed the lower court, found Georgia's opt-out statute unconstitutional, and awarded Rebecca Machetti a new trial.

Rebecca's new lawyers interviewed prospective jurors for a week in Bibb County. But due to the publicity surrounding the case, most people had their minds made up. The lawyers convinced the judge that going ahead would result in another violation of Rebecca's right to be tried by an impartial jury. The judge agreed to move the trial to another county. Gwinnett County is part of suburban Atlanta and has a more affluent, professional population. Unlike Bibb County, it is in north Georgia, above the "gnat line," below which it is so hot and humid that there are gnats all summer and, coincidentally, the death penalty is frequently imposed.

The judge who presided at Becky's first trial, Cloud Morgan, also presided at her second trial. John Maree testified against her again, as did two of her three daughters. Rebecca's main defense was that she was not involved in the murders, that she had been duped by Smith and Maree, who were down in Miami, taking advantage of women they supposed to be rich. At the second trial, Rebecca's lawyers presented more evidence on her side: character witnesses who had known her all her life, in Miami, and in prison; her troubled early life (her father and younger brother were found shot dead in an apparent suicide-murder when she was seventeen); and the fact that she had no prior criminal record. Her lawyers also argued that since Rebecca was six hundred miles away when Ronnie and Juanita Akins were murdered, if she participated at all, her responsibility was greatly reduced.

This time there were five women on the jury. "This jury was different because for the first time men and women sat in a box and listened to me," says Rebecca. "These women that were on that jury were my kind of people. They were open-eyed, they didn't hide their heads, they smiled at me, they stayed interested, they didn't look forward, they didn't yawn, they didn't go to sleep. They acted like they really and sincerely came to serve both justice and their call to be a jury person. They also acted like they gave a damn about me as a member of the human race. . . . I do believe that because those women were on the jury I had a group of people willing to sit down and say, 'OK, let's hear, and let's see if we can help you,' and in their own way I think they tried. Sure they found me guilty, but they could have done a lot worse." Rebecca Machetti received two consecutive life sentences at her second trial, but was spared the death penalty.

John Eldon Smith was also appealing his conviction during this period. The process moved faster for him, however, and by the time he challenged the exclusion of women from the jury that convicted him, he was in his *second* habeas proceeding. The state and federal courts ruled that he failed to show a reason for not raising the claim earlier, and refused to grant him a new trial. Though his jury was selected in the same unconstitutional manner as Rebecca's, John Eldon Smith died in the electric chair on December 15, 1983.

John Maree, the only one of the three who could be placed at the crime scene, was released from prison on December 23, 1987.

The Framers realized that the right to be tried by an impartial jury, like other rights protected in the Bill of Rights, can mean the difference between life and death. Rebecca Machetti's nine-year string of appeals, not uncommon for those convicted of serious crimes, demonstrates the tenacity with which criminal defendants cling to those rights. Her story and that of John Eldon Smith show how the deprivation of one right may affect the assertion of others, and how difficult it sometimes is for the system to arrive at a just result. As the only judge who dissented from the Eleventh Circuit's decision not to grant John Eldon Smith a new trial wrote:

> This case again illustrates the difficulty, if not the impossibility, of imposing the death penalty in a fair and impartial manner. It is a classic example of how arbitrarily this penalty is imposed. Maree . . . will live because the evidence against him was overwhelming and the prosecutor needed his testimony to convict Smith and Machetti.
>
> Machetti, the mastermind in this murder, has had her convic-

tion overturned, has had a new trial and has received a life sentence. This court overturned her first conviction because in the
county where her trial was held, women were unconstitutionally
underrepresented in the jury pool. Her lawyers timely raised this
constitutional objection. They won; she lives.

John Eldon Smith was tried in the same county by a jury drawn
from the same unconstitutionally composed jury pool, but because
his lawyers did not timely raise the unconstitutionality of the jury
pool, he [will die] by electrocution. . . .The fairness promised [by
the Supreme Court] in *Furman v. Georgia*, has long been forgotten.

But from the vantage point of Susan Boleyn and the state of
Georgia, John Eldon Smith's execution after eight years on death
row and two trips through the habeas process was not unjust.
Says Boleyn, "The injustice of it is that Rebecca *didn't* get the

S*tate's Exhibit #16 in* Coy v. Iowa, *1985: the backyard tent where*
the assault took place
REPRINTED BY PERMISSION

Right to Confront:
Coy v. Iowa

"In all criminal prosecutions, the accused shall enjoy
the right to be confronted with the witnesses against
him."

THIRTEEN-YEAR-OLD KATHY
Brown dragged a Ping-Pong table across her small backyard in
Clinton, Iowa.* She carefully pulled it into place, end to end with
another Ping-Pong table standing a few feet from the back patio.
She then threw several old blankets, sheets, and a tablecloth
across the tables so they hung over the sides, touching the ground
and completely enclosing the crawl space beneath. It was August
2, 1985, a cool, clear summer evening, and Kathy was building a
tent. She had just called her friend Linda Thompson to come and
sleep over.

Linda arrived about 9:00 that night with her sleeping bag
and pillow. She and Kathy brought out to the makeshift tent
everything they needed for a backyard camp-out: their sleeping
bags, pillows, a flashlight, an electronic game called Simon, a
Tupperware container of cookies, two plastic cups, and some
cola. The two girls spread out their sleeping bags, ate some cook-

---

*The names of both girls in this story, and the names of their families, have been
changed to protect their identities.

ies, played Simon a little, and talked a lot, mostly about starting eighth grade. They fell asleep sometime between 10:30 and 11:00 P.M.

In the middle of the night, Kathy, only half asleep, saw a hand pull back one of the blankets draped over the tables. A man she assumed was her father crawled into the tent carrying a small white bag, which he placed on the ground. Kathy first realized the man was not her father when he grabbed her by the throat.

The intruder knelt between Kathy and Linda and took Linda by the throat too. He told the girls, "If you scream, I'll knock you out." They did not scream. The intruder said, "I thought there would only be one of you." He asked them how old they were, and they replied, "Thirteen."

The man then sat back and ordered Kathy and Linda out of their sleeping bags. He told them to take off all of their clothes, except their underwear. The girls complied: Kathy removed her sweat pants and sweat shirt, Linda her sweat shirt and shorts. The man again warned them not to scream. He said, "I won't kill, but I'll just hurt you."

The man ordered the girls to lie back down. He kissed them and fondled their breasts. "If you scream," he said putting his hands to their breasts, "that's how fast I can react." He asked Kathy and Linda if they were virgins. They did not respond because neither knew what a virgin was.

The man then ordered the girls to remove their underwear and to lie back down. He put their underwear in the white bag and began kissing and fondling the girls again, first one, then the other, and sometimes at the same time. Then the man stopped and told the girls to kiss each other. Kathy and Linda complied briefly. The man ordered them to "keep doing it" and "act like you like it."

The man then took off his pants. He made the girls fondle his penis and put it in their mouths. He asked the girls to urinate on his face but they told him they could not. They then heard him urinating into one of the plastic cups.

The assault lasted about an hour and a half. Neither Kathy nor Linda said a word except to answer, very softly, yes or no to the assailant's questions. Sometimes Linda would say "sir." Once or twice the man lifted the side of the tent to see if anyone was nearby and the girls could tell that it was getting light.

The man ordered the girls to lie naked on their stomachs atop their sleeping bags. He lay down between them and began discussing how he would get away. He thought out loud about getting some rope and tying them up. He continued to stroke the girls and tell them how sweet they were. He warned them if they told anyone, they would go through a terrible ordeal with a lot of people, including the police.

Finally, the intruder tied Kathy's arms behind her back with her sweatshirt and did the same to Linda. He gathered up the white bag with the girls' panties in it, the black-and-red flashlight Kathy had brought to the tent, and the yellow plastic cup with the white interior that he had used. Then he leaned over to the girls, who were trembling, bound and naked, on the bedding, and told them not to move because he would be back in two minutes.

Kathy and Linda lay still for fifteen to twenty minutes, fearing the man would come back. When he did not reappear, they freed themselves and pulled back the blankets covering the tent. It was light by now, 6:00 A.M. They went into the house, where Kathy's parents were just waking up.

Clinton is in the middle of the eastern border of Iowa, right on the Mississippi River. The townspeople are mostly blue-collar workers and farmers, hit hard by the agricultural depression of the 1970s and 1980s. There are four elementary schools, one high school, and a center of town. On the east is the Mississippi. Drive out of town in any other direction and all you see is cornfields and sky.

The Browns' home is on the northernmost edge of town. The neighborhood is literally a swatch of suburbia cut into a cornfield. The Browns' street, like others in the area, rolls along with new ranch and split-level houses on either side, and then comes up short where the fields begin. The neighborhood is mostly made up of young, middle-income families like the Browns and Thompsons. A crime like the one that occurred in the Browns' backyard is always enormous for the people involved. In a town like Clinton, it is enormous for the community as well.

At 7:00 A.M. police officer Lyle Smith arrived at the Brown

residence to "secure" the area. He photographed the crime scene, marked items for evidence, and, along with some of the Browns' neighbors, began searching the area for clues. Police officer Larry Speakman went to the hospital to interview Kathy and Linda.

The girls described a man of medium height, or medium to tall. They said he had "goldish brown" hair with a skinny, braided ponytail, maybe a few inches long, sticking out at the back of his head. They remembered either dark blue pants or shorts, athletic-type, with white piping down the sides. Neither could remember if the man wore any shirt or shoes. Kathy thought he had worn a strange dark green mask made of socklike material knotted together with holes for the eyes, nose, and mouth. She thought the man had white makeup slashed on the lower part of his face under the mask. Linda did not remember any mask, but described the same odd white makeup.

Both girls said the man wore his watch in a peculiar manner, way up on his forearm, almost to the elbow, with the face turned in. Kathy said the watch face had numbers on it and was upside down. And both Kathy and Linda heard a motorcycle start up and roar off just after the man left the tent.

It soon became apparent, though, that neither Kathy nor Linda could describe the assailant's features. It had been dark in the tent and the girls were terrified. The man had warned them not to look at his face and if they did look up, he shined the flashlight in their eyes. Neither of the girls would ever be able to identify the man for the police.

Mr. Brown, however, was convinced he knew who the assailant was. He told the police to question John Avery Coy, the man who had taken up residence next door in the Bingham house. Karen Bingham, a teacher at a local community college, had recently divorced. Her young son had moved out with his father, and Karen and her eleven-year-old daughter kept the house. Karen met John Coy, thirty-four, in January while he was taking courses at the community college. He moved in with Karen and her daughter in April. As far as anyone in the neighborhood was concerned, John Coy was an able-bodied man without a job, who played music too loud and too late at night and who was rumored to have an alcohol problem. He had made no friends on the block. As the officer who took Mr. Brown's statement put it, "He really had nothing good to say about Mr. Coy."

Brown had seen Coy in a lounge chair in the Bingham backyard the day before. The Browns' backyard has a tall wooden fence along the back end of the yard and up the far side. But in between the Browns' yard and the Bingham yard, there is a chain-link fence instead. Because of the house and wooden fence, the makeshift tent could not have been visible from the street or even from the house directly behind the Browns'. According to Brown, however, John Coy had a clear view of the backyard through the chain-link fence, and on August 2, had watched while Kathy built her tent.

Around 10:00 A.M., the morning after the crime, Brown saw Coy heading down the street with what appeared to be a suitcase. Brown called out to Officer Speakman in the backyard. Speakman radioed for assistance and a routine computer check on John Avery Coy. Then he caught up with Coy a few blocks away.

Coy was carrying a knapsack and a black, hard plastic case that turned out to contain a videocassette recorder and videotapes that he was returning to the store. He stood a broad six foot three inches tall. He had a round, pudgy, clean-shaven face and light brown hair cut short. But he was wearing his watch in a peculiar manner, way up on his forearm, almost to the elbow, with the face turned in.

Coy told Speakman he had been asleep all night and knew nothing of the crime. While they were talking, the computer check turned up an outstanding warrant on Coy from Cedar Rapids for operating a vehicle while under the influence of alcohol (OWI). Coy was arrested on the outstanding traffic warrant, but there was not enough evidence to arrest him in connection with the assault.

When Kathy's father heard this news, he started across his lawn toward the Bingham home. "I felt I knew who the guilty one was," says Brown, "so I was looking for some evidence." A neighbor followed Brown because he feared there would be trouble.

The two men knocked on the Binghams' door. When they got no answer, they walked through an unlocked back door into the downstairs of the Binghams' split-level home. They looked through every room: the living room, den, laundry room, bathrooms, and three bedrooms. Finally, in the kitchen by the back door, they saw a yellow plastic cup with a white interior, slightly torn, lying atop the trash. The cup had a putrid smell.

Brown immediately told Officer Speakman, who obtained a search warrant for the Bingham home. There, the police found the cup in the kitchen trash, a flashlight and batteries similar to the one taken from the tent on a shelf in the garage, and a white cloth bag in the backyard. They arrested John Coy on two counts of lascivious acts with a child.

From jail, Coy called the only local attorney he knew, Jack Wolfe. From 1980 to 1982, Wolfe had been Clinton's first and last public defender. When the short-lived public defender program was shut down, Wolfe began taking court appointments to represent indigent defendants and thus developed a practice in criminal defense. He had represented Coy some months earlier on an OWI charge in Clinton (unrelated to the outstanding OWI charge in Cedar Rapids, which led to Coy's arrest). The court appointed Wolfe to represent Coy on the new charge. Wolfe discussed plea bargaining with Coy, but Coy refused. He insisted that he was not guilty.

Gary Rolfes, a local attorney, had a general practice and worked part-time for the Clinton County Attorney's Office. Clinton was quiet enough that a part-time prosecutor could handle all of the felony cases in town. Thus Rolfes was assigned the Coy case. He says, "I'm convinced he, Coy, was the only individual who could have committed that crime."

There was, however, only circumstantial evidence against Coy and, in fact, parts of the girls' description seemed to indicate that Coy was not the assailant. In addition, there was not, nor would there ever be, a positive identification of the assailant. Because Kathy and Linda were the only witnesses to the crime, their testimony became crucial. Their testimony was, of course, needed to establish the facts of the crime. More important, the testimony would have an enormous emotional impact on the jury.

"When we started out, the parents said that these children could not talk about this," says Rolfes. "They wouldn't really open up and say what had happened to them, but you knew that something more than what they were letting on had happened.

You just could tell. They just didn't . . . God, they just didn't talk about such things."

As with many victims of sexual abuse, Kathy and Linda were talking about it in other ways. Both girls wanted the lights on at night and it would be four years before either could sleep with the window open, even in the summer swelter. Linda wanted extra locks everywhere. "Our house was like Fort Knox," her mother says.

Eventually, Mrs. Thompson says, Linda did begin talking to her parents. "She would look at me and we would hug each other and cry." Kathy, on the other hand, was becoming more withdrawn, unable to discuss the crime with her parents, let alone a lawyer. According to her mother, "Kathy had a real hard time talking about it. One night I was going to work and I said, 'Kathy, why don't you just write it all down?' It got pretty scribbly in places because she couldn't say the words. But we gave it to Gary and it helped a lot." The girls began meeting with Rolfes after school and came to trust him and tell their story.

But there was another problem. "They wouldn't come near the courthouse," Rolfes says. "They were just horrified at the idea." So to ease the girls' fear, he began taking Kathy and Linda to the courthouse at 9:00 at night, after everyone had gone home.

The main courtroom of the Clinton County Courthouse is a large open room with high ceilings and tall windows along two walls. The raised bench for the presiding judge stands at the front of the courtroom between an American flag and the Iowa state flag. Behind the bench is a WPA mural portraying Justice holding her scales. To the left of the bench is the witness box, also raised, with a chair and microphone. To the left of the witness box is the jury box—two rows of dark wood swivel chairs enclosed by a wooden railing. In front of the bench are the two long, rectangular counsel tables. Then come the wooden railing with its little swinging door and the rows of wooden pews for spectators. It looks like a model for the American county courtroom.

At night "we'd have the whole courthouse to ourselves," Rolfes says. "I'd turn on the microphones, let them sit in the box, hear their voices." Three or four times the girls went with their parents and lawyer to the courthouse. But, Rolfes says, "As we got closer to the trial [the girls' fear] would intensify more."

"We sat down with the girls," Kathy's mother says, "and they said, 'You know, we are not going to do it,' and we said, 'You gotta do it. That's the law.'" Rolfes suggested they might be able to use some sort of special arrangement to shield Kathy and Linda from the defendant, or remove them from the courtroom altogether. Just four months previously, the Iowa Assembly had passed a statute allowing a child witness (one under fourteen years of age) to testify via closed-circuit television or "behind a screen or mirror." The girls and their parents told Rolfes that a device like that would make it easier on all of them.

On November 7, 1985, at a pretrial hearing, Gary Rolfes requested that the child witnesses be allowed to testify via closed-circuit television in a room adjacent to the courtroom. Rolfes proposed that the judge, attorneys, witnesses, and Coy be in the adjacent room, with a screen placed between the witness and Coy. The girls' testimony would then be wired back into the courtroom, where the jury would watch it on a monitor.

Jack Wolfe was on his feet. He objected to the procedure on the grounds that it would give the overwhelming impression that Coy was guilty, thus eroding his constitutional right to the presumption of innocence. Wolfe also strongly objected that the procedure violated Coy's Sixth Amendment right "to be confronted with the witnesses against him." In addition, he argued, such protective devices made no sense in Coy's case because the girls could not identify him as the assailant. They would simply be testifying about what happened to them. They would not, indeed could not, make any personal connection between the events and Coy.

The judge overruled Wolfe's objections. He decided that the girls should testify in the courtroom using only the screen. That way, the judge reasoned, the jury would get a firsthand look at both Coy and the witnesses during the testimony. Coy would be able to see the girls through the screen, but they would not be able to see him. Wolfe continued to object that even the screen violated Coy's right to confront, but the judge overruled him and ordered the screen.

Actually there was no screen at the time. The statute was so new, no device had ever been built. So the courthouse janitor put together a frame on a stand about six feet tall and four feet across, painted it white, and installed a pane of one-way glass donated by a local glass company. When the screen was tested before trial, it functioned more like a window than a one-way mirror. So four spotlights were focused on the glass from the defendant's side, ensuring he could not be seen from the witness chair.

The trial began on November 14, 1985. The first two witnesses were Linda Brown and Kathy Thompson. The screen was pushed into place on a diagonal so it stood between the witness and John Coy, who sat at the counsel table catercorner to the witness box. The venetian blinds were drawn and the lights dimmed. The spotlights were turned on the screen. "It was weird," Jack Wolfe says. "It was like theater."

The girls entered through a back door of the courtroom. Linda testified first.

A: A guy came in our tent and grabbed our throats.
Q: Did he say anything?
A: "Don't scream."
Q: Anything else?
A: He was surprised that there were two of us.
Q: What did he say with regard to that?
A: He goes, "I thought there would only be one of you."
Q: And what happened next?
A: He told us to get out of our sleeping bags.
Q: Did you do that?
A: Yes.
Q: Did you take off all your clothes?
A: No, not our underwear.
Q: How come?
A: Because he told us not to.
Q: And then what happened?
A: He started feeling us around.
Q: Where did he touch you?
A: Our breasts and our vaginas.
Q: Did he say anything during this time?
A: I don't remember.

And so it went for several hours. Each girl sat nervously in the witness chair, answering in three- or four-word sentences as Gary Rolfes guided them through the details of the attack. The girls spoke softly, but through the microphone their voices filled the courtroom. They looked at their hands or at Rolfes. To this day, Linda has never seen John Coy.

Jack Wolfe's cross-examination was brief. He did not try to

deny the assault took place, nor did he try to discredit the girls' account. Instead, he emphasized that neither girl could identify John Coy as the assailant.

The screen was then removed and the lights turned back up for the rest of the trial, another two and a half days. One expert for the prosecution testified that three fingerprints on the flashlight found in the Bingham garage were positively identified as Coy's. He said no fingerprints could be identified on the batteries or cup. Another expert witness testified that the dried liquid in the cup found in the Bingham home was urine. He also testified that he had analyzed several hairs taken from the bedding in the tent and one hair taken from Linda's shorts. Three of the hairs from the bedding were pubic hairs similar to those of John Coy and dissimilar to those of the girls. The hair from Linda's shorts was a head hair similar to those of John Coy and dissimilar to those of the girls.

Upon cross-examination, however, the expert explained that, unlike fingerprints, hairs could not positively be identified as belonging to a specific person. He could say positively if a hair did *not* belong to an individual—that is, the three pubic hairs definitely did not come from Kathy or Linda. But the most the expert could state on the other side was that the hairs were *similar* to those of a particular individual, that the hairs *could* have come from John Coy. The expert could not estimate how many other people might also have matching hairs, and he admitted he could not even determine whether the hairs were from a man or a woman. Finally, the expert testified on cross-examination that the hairs found to be dissimilar from Coy's were not tested against Kathy and Linda. Therefore no one could say whether those hairs came from the girls or yet another unknown individual.

Kathy's father, Mr. Brown, took the stand next. He testified that on August 2 he gave his daughter a flashlight to take into the tent. He described it as black with a red top, a special industrial flashlight issued to him at work. Mr. Brown also testified that before giving the flashlight to Kathy, he took out the old blue batteries and put in two new red industrial D-cell batteries. Gary Rolfes held up the black-and-red industrial flashlight and the two red industrial batteries found in the Bingham garage. Brown said they were just like his own. He could not, however, state positively that they were *in fact* the flashlight and batteries from the tent.

Officers Speakman and Smith each took the stand and re-counted finding the flashlight and batteries, the yellow cup with the white interior, and the white bag. Upon cross-examination, the officers admitted that a thorough search of the Bingham house and the surrounding area never turned up any blue pants or shorts with white piping, any green mask or masklike mate-rial, any white makeup, or the girls' panties. Nor did they find any sign of a motorcycle.

The defense presented three witnesses. A friend of Coy's testi-fied that during the time she had known him, which included the time of the crime, Coy's hair had never been anywhere near long enough for a ponytail. She said she had never known Coy to own or ride a motorcycle. Finally she testified that John Coy always wore a digital watch. Kathy had testified that the assailant's watch, worn in the peculiar manner, had a traditional round watch face with numbers.

Karen Bingham took the stand next. She testified that on the night of August 2 she was in New York with her two children visiting her parents. Coy was to fly out the next day, the day of his arrest, to meet Karen and her family and discuss wedding plans. They were then going to Pennsylvania so Karen could meet Coy's parents. Coy, of course, never showed up. Karen also testi-fied that Coy had never worn a ponytail, never owned or rode a motorcycle, and always wore a digital watch. She was quite sure about the watch because shortly before the crime, sometime in July, Karen had bought Coy a new watch. She was certain she had bought the same kind of K-Mart digital watch he always wore.

The last witness for the defense was John Coy. Dressed in a jacket and tie, Coy sat composed in the witness chair and an-swered his lawyer's questions in a calm, clear voice. Coy said he had been sitting in the Bingham backyard in the late afternoon of August 2. He said he noticed something going on in the Browns' backyard, but did not really pay any attention and did not recall seeing Kathy there. In answer to the question "Did you in any way molest or have any contact with two thirteen-year-old girls that evening?" Coy answered, "No, sir, I did not."

Coy testified that he went to sleep about 10:00 that night and awoke about 9:00 the next morning. He said he went outside to collect the mail and noticed some debris in the driveway.

Q: Could you explain to the jury what that was?
A: The plastic cup that's been shown as evidence here was in my driveway, and also, there was a flashlight on the corner of the driveway just outside of the garage door.
Q: Was there any other garbage that you picked up when you went out there?
A: It was like a cupcake wrapper, a plastic wrapper. There was something else. I don't recall if it was a stick or what it was, but something else that I did pick up.
Q: Do you recall what you did with that junk?
A: The flashlight was just outside of the garage door, as I stated, and there were tools on the floor not three feet away from there that were inside the garage. It appeared that the flashlight had been kicked out, and I wondered if maybe the batteries had corroded. I didn't know how long it had been out there. I took the top off of the flashlight and removed the batteries. . . . I set the flashlight on the shelf just inside the door and, to the best of my knowledge, I thought I threw the cup in the garbage there, but apparently I had taken the stuff upstairs and threw it in the garbage.
Q: Now, did you know whose flashlight it was?
A: I suspected it was Karen's. I knew it wasn't mine.
Q: Was it on the lawn or somewhat obscured?
A: It wasn't obscured. There was a tree on the corner of the garage. It was partially under the tree in plain sight.
Q: Were you able to determine how it ended up getting out there?
A: I really didn't think about it at the time. I just picked it up.

The state recalled Officer Smith to the stand. Smith testified that he and several others thoroughly searched the area around the Brown and Bingham house between 8:00 and 10:00 A.M. He said if there had been a flashlight on the lawn or a plastic cup on the driveway, he certainly would have noticed it. He also said there was no wind blowing that morning.

The jurors deliberated for less than five hours. On November 19, 1985, they returned a verdict of guilty of two counts of lascivious acts with a child. The judge imposed the harshest sentence allowed by Iowa law. He sentenced Coy to the maximum prison term for each count—five years—and ordered that they be served consecutively.

Coy appealed to the Iowa Supreme Court. The Sixth Amendment guaranteed him a right to "confront the witnesses against him." Wasn't a physical barrier between the witnesses and the accused a plain violation of this right? The Iowa Supreme Court said no.

The confrontation clause, it seemed, was not so simple. For some time, the clause had been wrapped up in two other areas of criminal litigation: hearsay and cross-examination. First, it had long been accepted that the confrontation clause guaranteed the defendant that trial witnesses would testify under oath and be subject to cross-examination, and that the judge and jury would be able to observe the witnesses in order to assess their credibility. These are the same fundamental principles underlying the complicated rules of hearsay.

Hearsay is basically a statement made by a person who is not testifying on the stand, as when a witness says, "X told me . . ." Whatever X said, it was not said under oath or subject to cross-examination, and the jury certainly could not see X when X said it. The general rule is that such out-of-court statements, or hearsay, are not to be admitted at trial to prove the truth of their content.

As with almost any rule, though, there are exceptions to the rule against hearsay. What if X is dead? What if X is an undercover informer who does not want to be identified? What if X is charged with the crime as well? The cases spin out endless scenarios, each one measured against the confrontation clause.

Even if the witness is in court (so there is no hearsay), the right to cross-examine may still be frustrated. Cross-examination—"the greatest legal engine ever invented for the discovery of truth"—has long been recognized as an essential element of the right to confront. Therefore, attempts to limit cross-examination, like attempts to admit hearsay, must comport with the constitutional right to confront. What if cross-examination is stymied by the witness invoking a privilege not to testify, such as the doctor-patient privilege? What if the witness has a sudden memory lapse? One landmark Supreme Court case spent fifty pages discussing the right to confront and cross-examine in the context of a young man who, despite two previous statements to police, took the stand and claimed he could not remember a thing because he was high on acid at the time of the crime.

The confrontation clause became a thicket of technical hearsay

rules overlapping bizarre instances of limitations on the right to
cross-examine. So when John Coy claimed that a physical barrier
between the accused and his accusers violated his fundamental
right to confront, the Supreme Court of Iowa said he was wrong.
The state court saw no problems in the Coy case with hearsay or
cross-examination and thus no violation of the confrontation
clause.

In 1988, the U.S. Supreme Court, by a vote of six to two, reversed. "Most of this Court's encounters with the Confrontation
Clause have involved either the admissibility of out-of-court
statements . . . or restrictions on the scope of cross-examination,"
the Court wrote. "The reason for that is not, as the State suggests,
that these elements are the essence of the Clause's protection—
but rather, quite to the contrary, that there is at least some room
for doubt (and hence litigation) as to the extent to which the
Clause includes those elements, whereas . . . 'simply as a matter
of English' it confers at least 'a right to meet face to face all those
who appear and give evidence at trial.'"

The language of the confrontation clause, the Court stated,
"comes to us on faded parchment." Citing the Roman governor
Festus's treatment of his prisoner Paul, the Court stated that the
right to confrontation has a "lineage that traces back to the be-
ginnings of Western legal culture."

Then, in an unconventional move, the Court went on to cite
literature and popular culture as well. "Shakespeare was thus describing the root meaning of confrontation when he had Richard
the Second say: 'Then call them to our presence—face to face,
and frowning brow to brow, ourselves will hear the accuser and
the accused freely speak . . .' *Richard II*, Act I, sc. 1." Bringing us
up-to-date, the Court stated, "What was true of old is no less true
in modern times," and offered President Eisenhower's views on
face-to-face confrontation in his hometown of Abilene, Kansas:
"It was necessary to meet anyone face to face with whom you
disagree. You could not sneak up on him from behind, or do any
damage to him, without suffering the penalty of an outraged citizenry. . . . In this country, if someone dislikes you, or accuses you,
he must come up in front. He cannot hide behind the shadow."
The Court even cited the cliché "Look me in the eye and say
that."

This judicial foray into literature and anecdote was offbeat but by design. The Court wanted to make a plain and poignant point: "There is something deep in human nature that regards face-to-face confrontation between accused and accuser as 'essential to a fair trial in a criminal prosecution.'" The rights secured by the confrontation clause, indeed by the Bill of Rights, are founded not only on legal precedent, but also on human experience and things "deep in human nature."

The Court acknowledged that the face-to-face encounter may well "upset" the truthful rape victim or abused child. "But by the same token it may confound and undo the false accuser, or reveal the child coached by a malevolent adult," the Court said. "It is a truism that constitutional protections have costs."

Turning to the actual screen used in the case of John Avery Coy, the Court wrote, "It is difficult to imagine a more obvious or damaging violation of the defendant's right to a face-to-face encounter." The Court noted that the confrontation clause may not be absolute and may, in some circumstances, give way to other important interests. The Court, however, concluded that if exceptions do exist, they were not to be found in the case of John Coy.

The Iowa statute had created a "legislatively imposed presumption of trauma" for *all* child witnesses. In the *Coy* case, the trial court had made no individualized finding that these particular witnesses under these circumstances needed this kind of special protection. The statute allowed the judge to impair the right to confront without a showing that it was necessary in a specific case. Something more, the Supreme Court held, was needed to override the fundamental promise of the Sixth Amendment.

Justice O'Connor wrote an important concurring opinion to make clear that she thought there could be cases in which the right to confront would have to give way to the interest of protecting a child witness. She agreed that more than a generalized legislative finding of necessity, such as that in the Iowa statute, would be required before any protective arrangement could be used to frustrate the constitutional right. But Justice O'Connor noted that at the time of the case, thirty-three states had statutes authorizing some kind of protective device for child witnesses. "[I] wish to make clear that nothing in today's decision necessarily dooms such efforts by state legislatures to protect child witnesses." She thus specifically left open the possibility that a statute could be fashioned that would be in accord with the right to confront.

The Supreme Court sent Coy's case back to the Iowa court, which ordered a new trial. By that time Kathy and Linda were seventeen, finishing high school, and beginning to put the assault behind them. The local papers had obeyed the court's request and never published the girls' names—only a few kids in the neighborhood knew. In fact, one girl in Linda's English class wrote an essay on the crime not knowing that one of the victims was sitting next to her. When the retrial was suggested, the Browns and Thompsons left it up to the girls. Kathy and Linda did not need to discuss it with their parents or even each other. They absolutely refused to go through another trial.

"We could have just subpoenaed the girls and forced them to testify," says Bruce Ingham, the new Clinton prosecutor. "But our attitude is pretty much victim oriented here in that if the victim doesn't want to go forward, neither do we." On the day the new trial was scheduled to start, Ingham dropped the case.

Kathy and Linda, their families, and Gary Rolfes remain convinced that John Avery Coy is the man who crawled into the tent that night. Kathy and Linda say if they had known Coy would simply go free, they would have testified at the original trial without the screen or any other device. They say they would have just kept their eyes on their lawyer no matter what.

"When we went through the original trial, we figured the law's the law and we'll just do what the law says," Kathy's mother says now. "Well, we did. And we didn't really care for what the law came up with."

John Avery Coy married Karen Bingham and moved with her and her daughter to Pennsylvania.

*   *   *

N.B. In June 1990, *Maryland v. Craig* reached the Supreme Court. In *Craig*, a six-year-old child had accused a kindergarten teacher of sexual abuse. Pursuant to a Maryland statute, the trial judge determined that the specific child witness would suffer "serious emotional distress" if required to testify in the courtroom. In such circumstances, the statute allowed the child, prosecutor, and defense counsel to go to a separate room. The judge, jury, and defendant remained in the courtroom and watched the child's testimony and cross-examination on a closed-circuit television monitor. The defendant never physically confronted the child face to face. Because the judge in *Craig* made specific findings of trauma regarding the particular child, the Maryland case squarely raised the question unanswered in *Coy:* Does the confrontation clause ever permit a child witness to testify against a defendant without looking the defendant in the eye?

By a vote of five to four, the Supreme Court answered yes. The Court held that the right to a face-to-face confrontation with a witness is not absolute. Justice O'Connor wrote for the Court, "The Confrontation Clause reflects a *preference* for face-to-face confrontation at trial . . . a preference that must occasionally give way to considerations of public policy and the necessities of the case." The Court pointed out that hearsay is often admitted under one of many exceptions to the hearsay rule. Given such long acceptance of the admission of hearsay, the Court argued, the confrontation clause could not be interpreted as absolute.

The Court also found that the Maryland procedure preserved the central purpose of the right to confront—ensuring reliability of evidence—as well as the other elements of the right (the witness testifies under oath: the judge, jury, and defendant observe— albeit via a monitor—the witness's demeanor; and the witness is subject to full cross-examination). Thus, the Court held that if a protective device is found to be necessary in the particular case for the particular child, and if that child's testimony is subject to rigorous adversarial testing to ensure reliability, then to further the important state interest of protecting the child, the state may employ a closed-circuit television procedure.

Justice Scalia, who had strongly objected to the use of the screen in *Coy*, objected just as strongly to the use of closed-circuit television in *Craig*. "Seldom has this Court failed so conspicuously to sustain a categorical guarantee of the Constitution against the tide of prevailing current opinion."

Because of *Craig*, Justice Scalia wrote, "the following scene can be played out in an American courtroom for the first time in two centuries: A father whose young daughter has been given over to the exclusive custody of his estranged wife . . . is sentenced to prison for sexual abuse on the basis of testimony by a child the parent has not seen or spoken to for many months; and the guilty verdict is rendered without giving the parent so much as the opportunity to sit in the presence of the child, and to ask, personally or through counsel, 'it is really not true, is it, that I—your father (or mother) whom you see before you—did these terrible things?' Perhaps this is a procedure today's society desires; perhaps (though I doubt it) it is even a fair procedure; but it is assuredly not a procedure permitted by the Constitution." Justice Scalia did not, however, convince a majority of the Court.

Testimony by Dr. X in 1966 About Curare A Key Factor of New Inquiry Into Deaths

By M. A. FARBER

Special to The New York Times

HACKENSACK, N. J., Jan. 7 —Between Sept. 21, 1965, and Sept. 28, 1966, Dr. X bought 24 vials of purified curare from a surgical supply company in northern New Jersey, according to records in the original investigation into the "unusual or unexplained" deaths at Riverdell Hospital in Oradell.

On Nov. 1, 1966, 18 vials of curare—most of them nearly empty—were found in Dr. X's locker at Riverdell after it was opened by Dr. Stanley Harris, another surgeon, who had come to suspect Dr. X of killing patients at the hospital.

Why Dr. X bought the curare, and why he kept many vials of the respiratory depressant in his locker, were key questions asked during the investigation in November 1966 conducted by Guy W. Calissi, who was the Bergen County Prosecutor.

In his testimony, Dr. X denied any wrongdoing and explained that he was using the curare in his research on dogs.

Curare is sometimes administered to relax muscles during surgery, but it can be lethal if improperly used.

This is the second of two articles concerning an investigation into the possibility that nine or more patients were murdered over a 10-month period at Riverdell Hospital in Oradell, N.J. nearly a decade ago.

The first article disclosed that Joseph C. Woodcock Jr., the Bergen County Prosecutor, had reopened an official inquiry into the deaths as a result of an investigation by The New York Times.

Mr. Woodcock has obtained a court order for the exhumation of three bodies whose tissues will be examined for curare. A 1966 investigation centered on whether a Riverdell surgeon had used curare to kill his colleagues' patients. That inquiry began when 18 vials of the drug were found in the surgeon's locker at the hospital.

Because the surgeon, who no longer practices at Riverdell, was not charged with a crime, his name is being withheld by The Times and he is being referred to as Dr. X.

In 1962 Dr. X joined the faculty of a medical school in New Jersey as a part-time, unsalaried lecturer. Within a year he had received a $500 grant to develop a medical instrument and $300 of that grant was used to purchase 12 dogs for the project. Dr. X told Mr. Calissi that curare was not involved in the research, that the experiments were done under the auspices of the medical school, and that the project ended in 1964.

But, Dr. X testified, he wanted to do additional research on dogs in 1965-66, including a posterior liver biopsy test that, he said, would require the use of curare. And although he testified that he earned $50,000 at Riverdell alone in the year preceding the investigation, he said he could not afford to buy dogs for these experiments. So after his grant expired in 1964, he said he began to buy curare and to obtain dogs in an "unofficial" way at the medical school.

Detectives assigned to the investigation in November 1966 found that the 24 vials of purified curare bought by Dr. X

Continued on Page 22, Column 1

*F*ront-page article by Myron Farber, New York Times, *January 8, 1976*

Right to Compulsory Process:
In re Myron Farber

"In all criminal prosecutions, the accused shall enjoy
the right to have compulsory process for obtaining
witnesses in his favor."

O<small>N</small> M<small>ARCH</small> 19, 1966, F<small>OUR</small>-year-old Nancy Savino of Bergen County, New Jersey, woke up
complaining of a stomachache. The doctor thought it might be
acute appendicitis and told Mrs. Savino to take Nancy to Riverdell Hospital for observation. After observing Nancy throughout
the night, Dr. Stanley Harris, a new surgeon at Riverdell, decided
to operate. He found that instead of appendicitis, Nancy had mes-
enteric cysts that were pressing against her small intestine. After
surgery Nancy was recovering well; the next day she was coloring
and making cutouts in bed. But on March 21 at 8 A.M., when a lab
technician came by to draw some blood, Nancy did not move.
The technician called for help. Dr. Mario Jascalevich, the senior
surgeon at the hospital, came from a nearby room but was unable
to revive the little girl. He pronounced her dead at 8:15 A.M. The
autopsy report stated that "an anatomical, pathological cause of
death is not evident. There was no warning and no reason to an-
ticipate the sudden death."

Five months later, on August 20, 1966, Frank Biggs, a fifty-
nine-year-old accountant, entered Riverdell Hospital to have part

of his stomach removed as treatment for his bleeding ulcer. His surgery went smoothly and he too was recovering well, until eight days later, at 9:10 P.M., when he began having trouble breathing and started turning blue. The nurse on duty requested help. Dr. Jascalevich happened to be in the hospital, which was unusual at that hour, and he gave Biggs a stimulant and some adrenaline. But by 9:30 P.M. Biggs was dead. The autopsy report attributed Biggs's death to ventricular fibrillation—an excessively rapid heartbeat, possibly caused by a large amount of urine in his bladder. But Biggs's own doctor, among others, was not convinced.

Carl Rohrbeck was scheduled for elective hernia surgery on December 13, 1965. Around 7:30 A.M. Dr. Jascalevich visited Rohrbeck. He told a nurse who was present to cancel surgery and get an IV started. She did so, and then left the room, leaving Dr. Jascalevich with the patient. She saw Dr. Jascalevich leave Rohrbeck's room, then return five minutes later to the nurse's station, where he informed her that Rohrbeck was dead. Dr. Jascalevich told Rohrbeck's doctor that he had a "premonition" about operating on the patient. The medical examiner who prepared the autopsy report thought it odd that Rohrbeck died *before* his operation, yet had reported no complaints while in the hospital. On his report, the medical examiner attributed Rohrbeck's death to heart failure.

Within a year, there were ten other mysterious deaths at Riverdell Hospital. By late October, Dr. Stanley Harris had become alarmed. When he reviewed the circumstances of the deaths, he found that all the patients who died had been on an intravenous tube, several of the deaths had occurred around 8:00 A.M., and most had been caused by respiratory failure. He suspected that the patients had been injected with poison. Another element the deaths had in common was the presence of the hospital's senior surgeon, Dr. Mario Jascalevich.

On October 31, 1966, Dr. Harris got the number and combination of Dr. Jascalevich's hospital locker. Later that day when no one was around, he opened it. What he saw confirmed his worst fears: eighteen nearly empty vials of curare and a number of syringes and needles.

Originally extracted from plants of the Amazon jungle, curare, and its modern alkaloid, d-turbocurarine, can be a deadly poison when injected into the body. In proper doses, it is used during surgery to regulate breathing because it relaxes the breathing muscles completely. An excessive dose can paralyze these muscles, causing respiratory arrest and death.

Alerted by Riverdell's doctors and directors, the Bergen County, New Jersey, prosecutor's office began an investigation into the deaths. Dr. Jascalevich vehemently denied any involvement. He claimed he was using curare to conduct experiments on dogs in an effort to learn more about its effects during surgery. Dr. Jascalevich pointed out that none of his own patients had died. He claimed that the other doctors were motivated to attack him by professional jealousy and internal hospital power struggles. The prosecutor dropped the investigation after a few weeks due to lack of evidence, and because a reliable means of testing for the presence of curare in the tissue of bodies already embalmed and buried did not exist at the time. Dr. Jascalevich resigned from Riverdell Hospital in February 1967.

Eight years later, in August 1975, an article appeared in the *New York Times* about an unrelated series of deaths in a Veterans Administration Hospital in Michigan. According to the article, investigators suspected a muscle relaxant was involved, possibly curare, because patients had experienced breathing failure and cardiac arrest. When Myron Farber, an investigative reporter at the *Times*, read the article, he was reminded of an anonymous letter that, by coincidence, had come to the *Times* earlier that summer. Though the letter did not mention any doctor or hospital by name, it charged that the chief surgeon of a hospital had murdered thirty to forty patients ten years earlier.

Farber went to work. He found out the name of the hospital— Riverdell—went to the Bergen County prosecutor's office, and obtained permission to inspect the file of the earlier investigation. He made copies of those documents and located a deposition given by Dr. Jascalevich in 1966 that was missing from the original file. Farber interviewed everyone he could find: prosecutors who conducted the original investigation, doctors, nurses, and technicians at Riverdell, and the families of patients who had died mysteriously in 1966. He tracked down people connected with the investigation, now dispersed all over the country. He even visited a man living in South Carolina whom he convinced to send a statement to the prosecutor's office regarding Dr. Jascalevich's dog experiments. Farber also spoke with several pathologists, including Dr. Michael Baden, deputy chief medical examiner of New York City, who had been consulted in the 1966 investigation. The results of Farber's investigations were published in two *New York Times* articles in January 1976.

Also, in January 1976, Sybil Moses, the Bergen County assistant prosecutor, informed Judge Theodore Trautwein of the Bergen County Superior Court that her office had reopened its investigation into the deaths at Riverdell Hospital. She also consulted Dr. Baden and filed a sworn affidavit from him. The affidavit stated, "In my professional opinion, the majority of the cases reviewed are not explainable on the basis of natural causes and are consistent with having been caused by a respiratory depressant." It went on to state that "recent technological advances [in testing] would now permit the detection of very minute amounts of d-tubocurarine in tissues from dead bodies," which had not been possible at the time of the 1966 investigation.

Dr. Baden recommended that the bodies of the patients who had died inexplicably ten years earlier be exhumed and autopsied again. Moses requested the court's authorization to dig up the bodies of Nancy Savino, Carl Rohrbeck, Frank Biggs, and two others. The day after Judge Trautwein signed the order authorizing exhumation of the five bodies, the first of a series of articles on the investigation by Myron Farber appeared in the *New York Times*. Dr. Jascalevich was not mentioned by name. The article referred to him only as "Dr. X."

The first body to be exhumed was that of little Nancy Savino. It turned out to be in remarkably good condition considering that she had been buried for nearly ten years. Dr. Baden conducted the autopsy himself under strict security procedures. Nancy's remaining organs were removed and tissue samples taken. These were sent to research laboratories to be tested by a variety of the sophisticated, newly developed procedures: radioimmunoassay, thin-layer chromatography, and mass spectrometry.

One by one the tests came back positive, showing the presence of curare in the tissues of Nancy Savino, and later in Frank Biggs and Carl Rohrbeck. The tests were inconclusive in the two other bodies. On May 18, the grand jury handed up an indictment charging Mario E. Jascalevich with five counts of murder.

His jury trial began in March 1978, before Judge William Arnold, another superior court judge. It would last until the end of October, becoming the longest trial of a single criminal defendant in U.S. history until that time. On May 23, Myron Farber was served with a subpoena that created a constitutional crisis and a trial within a trial.

The subpoena demanded that Farber appear as a witness and turn over to Dr. Jascalevich's defense lawyers "all statements, pictures, memoranda, recordings and notes of interviews of witnesses for the defense and prosecution." According to Farber, "It was like asking for my desk."

Dr. Jascalevich asserted, as he had in the 1966 investigation, that he was the innocent victim of a conspiracy among other Riverdell doctors to frame him for murder. His lawyers argued that a second conspiracy existed, between Myron Farber and the prosecutor's office, and that the two were interwoven.

The second conspiracy theory was based on the fact that it was not until Myron Farber showed up in Hackensack, got permission from the prosecutor's office to comb through the investigation files, and interviewed everyone remotely connected with the deaths that Dr. Jascalevich, who had been quietly pursuing his practice, was again the subject of a murder investigation. Dr. Jascalevich's lawyers, Ray Brown and Henry Furst, claimed that only by knowing what Farber knew, and what he had been told by others, could they successfully defend their client.

Dr. Jascalevich's lawyers claimed that Farber had a number of items relevant to their defense. They wanted records of his conversations with Dr. Baden and Dr. Harris, as well as three other witnesses who were now unavailable. One witness had died, one refused to speak with the defense lawyers, and the third, Lee Henderson, the South Carolina man, had given a statement to Farber that was important for Dr. Jascalevich's alibi. More important than these specific items, the defense claimed that they needed the rest of Farber's research because there might be something in it that could furnish a lead in the case, the importance of which Farber himself might not be aware.

Farber refused to comply with the subpoena. He argued that the defense could interview most of the same people he had interviewed, including Dr. Baden and Dr. Harris. He rejected the defense assertion that he had been working with the prosecution or functioning as an investigator. He maintained that he had been doing his job as a reporter for the *New York Times*, independently and on his own. The results of his efforts appeared in his articles, which were available to both sides.

If he had had information that would have acquitted or convicted Dr. Jascalevich, Farber says, he would have found a way to publish it. He would have gone back to his source for permission to at least reveal the nature of the information, if not the identity of the source, in his articles. "No reporter in his right mind keeps material sealed away in his drawer of such consequence as to set a man free from a murder charge, or even to convict him," he says. "The whole drive at the paper is to print whatever good stuff you have about anything." Farber also claims he would have considered a subpoena that was narrow in scope and requested specific items the defense had been unable to get elsewhere. He does not say he would have complied with it, however.

The central reason for Farber's refusal to turn over his material was that he had gathered it in confidence. Farber believed that turning it over would not only compromise some of the people he had spoken with, but would make them, and others, less likely to trust him or other reporters in the future. "Not only from a practical point of view, but from a personal, ethical point of view, you can't just sit in a car in a dark lane with a young woman or an older man and spend *days* convincing them, 'This is not for publication' [but I] need some guidance,' and then get a subpoena and willy-nilly turn it over," says Farber. "Who wants to be a whore? Who wants to be smiling when you promise someone something and not be faithful if it doesn't work out?"

To an investigative reporter like Farber, the importance of confidential sources cannot be overestimated. People are often reluctant to speak to a reporter because it could cost them a job or a friendship, but they nevertheless feel an obligation to come forward. Often they will do so only on the condition that their name not be revealed. Sometimes an investigative reporter may have to talk to dozens of sources, each of whom contributes a link in a chain, each of which is necessary in order to piece together a full story.

In addition to his personal objections to revealing confidential sources and information, Farber's refusal to turn over his material was based on his belief that the First Amendment's protection of freedom of the press includes a reporter's privilege to protect sources. "In sensitive matter after sensitive matter, dealing not only with high crimes and misdemeanors, but with corruption, with civic mismanagement, with subjects that have a direct bearing on how people live, and what kind of decisions need to be made for them to live better, the quality of what is written [at the *New York Times*], what I have written, has been enhanced immeasurably and the public has been better enlightened as a result of our ability to speak to people in confidence," Farber says. "There will never be a way to get around that. That is what I would argue ought to be be the construction flowing from the First Amendment—there is a real public service performed here."

But no matter how close a connection Farber saw between a free press and the protection of confidential sources, the courts had not yet recognized it. In fact, in the 1972 case of *Branzburg v. Hayes*, the Supreme Court rejected a reporter's claim that the First Amendment provided him with a privilege to refuse to divulge confidential information to a grand jury. In *Branzburg*, a reporter had been allowed to watch two men synthesizing hashish from marijuana on the condition that he not reveal their identities. When subpoenaed by the grand jury he refused to identify the individuals. The Supreme Court found that the public interest in law enforcement outweighed the uncertain burden that would be placed on news gathering by requiring the reporter to testify. "From the beginning of our country," the Court wrote, "the press has operated without constitutional protection for press informants, and the press has flourished."

Farber's lawyers believed his case differed from *Branzburg* because Farber's sources were not engaged in criminal acts, Farber was not being called before a grand jury, and Dr. Jascalevich had access to the same material through other channels. Therefore, they felt that although the Court had ruled against the press in *Branzburg*, the First Amendment might still protect Farber. In addition, although the Supreme Court had declined to create a reporter's privilege based on the First Amendment to the *federal* Constitution, the Court had specifically stated that the states were free to recognize a reporter's privilege based on their own *state* constitutions or state laws. New Jersey was one of the states that did so shortly after the *Branzburg* decision came down.

In creating this statutory privilege, called a "shield law," the

New Jersey legislature went beyond the requirements of the federal Constitution to provide reporters with additional protection. Under the shield law, reporters were to be considered like lawyers, doctors, and priests, who had long been privileged to refuse to disclose information told to them in confidence by their clients, patients, and penitents.

Each time the law recognizes a "testimonial privilege," it represents a determination that society values certain relationships based on trust more than it values the search for litigated truth in a particular case, and it accepts the fact that certain information, no matter how relevant, will not be available. Floyd Abrams, a well-known First Amendment lawyer who represented Myron Farber and the *New York Times*, puts it this way: "There is a price tag on a privilege—the price tag is that some information won't come out and that the information which won't come out might have been useful."

In the midst of Dr. Jascalevich's murder trial, Judge Arnold scheduled a hearing on the controversy over Farber's research. Knowing he faced a difficult battle, and determined not to reveal his sources, Farber put all his material into storage. He divided up his files and distributed them to various locations where they could not be traced. At the court hearing on June 22, 1978, Farber's lawyers argued that he had a testimonial privilege to withhold the information based on the First Amendment and the New Jersey shield law. There were three aspects of the subpoena that they found objectionable: first, it requested disclosure of confidential sources and information; second, it was overbroad, sweeping in scope, asking for everything Farber had; and third, it did not specify why or how the material was relevant to the defense.

Dr. Jascalevich's lawyers replied that to say Farber's files were not relevant was "an absurdity" and refused to narrow the subpoena. Defense lawyer Ray Brown announced, "I want it all." In a criminal trial, where the prosecution must prove its case beyond a reasonable doubt, evidence can be used for purposes other than to convict or acquit the defendant (for example, to attack the credibility of a witness). Also, many pieces of evidence are necessary to build a defense, especially when the case involves complicated scientific information and hundreds of witnesses. Not knowing exactly what Farber did or did not have, and what links his information might provide in building a defense strategy, the defense lawyers claimed they were entitled to see the material and then decide.

Defense lawyer Henry Furst explains why Farber's claim that he would have revealed anything that could be important to the defense was not satisfactory: "I don't want my client's rights to rest on the good faith of *any* reporter. . . . I hope that they wouldn't sit on evidence, but just because a reporter carries a First Amendment press card doesn't mean that as a class they are better or worse than any other group of people." Even Farber's lawyer, Floyd Abrams, agrees in principle. "We can't have liberties dependent on people behaving well. The legal system proceeds, the Bill of Rights in particular proceeds, without that sort of trust. The Bill of Rights assumes a government that will misbehave without specific limitations on its behavior. . . . The legal answer has to come from certain neutral legal principles."

Dr. Jascalevich's defense team based its demand for the material squarely on one of those principles: the compulsory process clause of the Sixth Amendment. In its enumeration of the trial rights of a defendant, the Sixth Amendment provides: "In all criminal prosecutions the accused shall enjoy the right to have compulsory process for obtaining witnesses in his favor." The New Jersey Constitution provides the same right in the same language. Compulsory process includes the legal mechanisms to require people to give depositions and be present in court to testify at trial or pretrial hearings. It also includes the right to compel the production of documents. These rights are enforced primarily by the use of a subpoena, like the one served on Myron Farber, which notifies persons that they must appear or that documents in their possession must be produced.

The right of compulsory process and its companion, the confrontation clause, directly provide defendants with their most basic right: the right to present a defense. As Chief Justice Earl Warren wrote for the Supreme Court, "The right to offer the testimony of witnesses, and to compel their attendance, if necessary, is in plain terms the right to present a defense, the right to present the defendant's version of the facts as well as the prosecution's to the jury so it may decide where the truth lies." The struggle over Farber's files thus pitted the First Amendment against the Sixth—Farber's claim of a First Amendment reporter's privilege against Dr. Jascalevich's Sixth Amendment right to defend himself.

To Dr. Jascalevich's lawyer, Henry Furst, "the Sixth Amendment is the paramount amendment. It guarantees all our other rights, including our First Amendment rights, because it provides for a fair trail. It prevents the press and the courts from being taken over, as they are in a totalitarian country. It guarantees that First Amendment liberties [including freedom of the press] will be as uninhibited as possible, and that includes the right to investigate crimes," which Myron Farber enjoyed.

On June 30, 1978, Judge Arnold, who had been presiding over Dr. Jascalevich's murder trial since it began in March, denied Myron Farber's motion to quash the subpoena. He ordered Farber to turn the material over for an *in camera* inspection by the court, or risk being held in contempt. In an *in camera* inspection the judge reads the material in private and then decides what, if any, material can be released. Farber and his lawyers believed that Farber was entitled to a hearing to determine the relevance of the material *before*, not after, *in camera* inspection. But Judge Arnold refused to provide such a hearing until after he himself had reviewed the files. The judge felt that without seeing Farber's files he was being "asked to make a decision in a vacuum."

In camera review is an attempt to compromise between two conflicting interests: one side's request to use the material in open court and the other side's interest in preserving confidentiality. In perhaps the most famous compulsory process case of all, *in camera* inspection was upheld as a compromise solution over the objections of President Nixon, who claimed executive privilege to withhold tapes of his conversations from a special prosecutor.

Farber refused to turn the material over to Judge Arnold, so a contempt hearing was scheduled before Judge Trautwein, who had signed the exhumation order. On July 24, Judge Trautwein found Myron Farber and the *New York Times* guilty of contempt. Before Farber was sentenced, he made a statement in which he attempted to explain his actions. First, he pointed out that he had already testified as a witness at Dr. Jascalevich's murder trial, where he answered as many questions as he felt he could and declined to answer only those that he felt would reveal confidential sources or information. He went on to say of Judge Arnold's order to turn over all his material relating to the case:

In effect, [it] commands me to violate confidences that I received in my effort to learn, and report the truth about this case. And this I cannot do.

I deeply appreciate how much our civilization, and civility, depends on order and the rule of law. I am not a fanatic or an absolutist and, like all men who daily submit to reason, I have been torn by doubt on many matters. But not on this matter. I believe the First Amendment means what it says about freedom of the press and that it was annexed to the Constitution with full knowledge that an unfettered but responsible press was crucial to our nation. The benefit was to the public, not to the press. . . . The inevitable result of my compliance with this Order would be my conversion into an investigative agent for the parties to this case. This is not what Madison and his contemporaries had in mind for the press, nor is it what the legislatures of New Jersey, New York, and other states intended when they passed statutes protecting newsmen's confidential materials.

But in refusing to comply with the subpoena, Farber was denying a request for evidence from a man accused of murder. The defendant's need for the evidence seemed to overwhelm Farber's own, both in human terms and as a matter of fundamental constitutional rights. If the right to present a defense is perhaps the most basic right criminal defendants have, how can courts deny them, without ever seeing it, the evidence that they claim is critical to the exercise of that right?

After Farber finished his statement, Judge Trautwein addressed him from the bench: "You are saying . . . you shall be the judge as to whether this violates your privilege . . . but it seems to me that somewhere within the whole fabric of constitutional protection and statutory newsman's privilege, there has to be some person, or body or tribunal, that can say, 'Mr. Farber, we don't suspect your integrity at all, but let's take a little peek at [the material] to see whether or not what you say is the truth . . . in this instance, a case that is being tried where a man is charged with murder, whose liberty for the rest of his life is at stake, you say, 'Myron Farber shall be the sole judge.'" Judge Trautwein pointed out that if Dr. Jascalevich was eventually convicted of murder, the conviction might be overturned on appeal because he was denied evidence needed to present his defense, and "because of the recalcitrance of [Myron Farber] and *The New York Times*."

Judge Trautwein then imposed the maximum sentence: a two-thousand-dollar fine to be paid within twenty-four hours and confinement in the county jail until Farber complied with Judge Arnold's order to produce the material. After compliance, Farber was to serve an additional six-month jail term. The *New York Times* was fined five thousand dollars per day until it turned over its files to Judge Arnold. The newspaper was also ordered to pay an additional fine of one hundred thousand dollars as a criminal penalty. Farber was taken into custody by the sheriff that same afternoon.

Three days later, the prosecution in Dr. Jascalevich's murder trial rested its case. Judge Arnold threw out two of the five counts of murder for insufficient evidence. The three murder charges that remained were those of Nancy Savino, Frank Biggs, and Carl Rohrbeck.

Farber was released from jail pending his appeal to the Supreme Court of New Jersey and the U.S. Supreme Court. On August 4, the Supreme Court declined to hear his case, finding his appeal to be premature. Farber was sent back to jail.

A week later Farber had a habeas corpus hearing (to challenge the legality of his incarceration) in federal district court. At the hearing, testimony focused on a contract Farber had signed to write a book about the case before he himself became a figure in it, and on a movie contract he had turned down. Dr. Jascalevich's lawyers claimed that Farber was saving his confidential material for the book, and the judge accused him of "standing on an altar of greed." Farber withdrew his habeas petition rather than disclose the whereabouts of his manuscript and returned to jail.

On August 30, after nearly a month in jail and no sign of compliance by Farber, the New Jersey Supreme Court agreed to review Farber's case and he was released from jail pending the court's decision. The arguments were essentially the same as before. Farber claimed a First Amendment and statutory privilege to refuse to turn over his material without a hearing. Dr. Jascalevich claimed that Farber's refusal violated his Sixth Amendment right to compulsory process and a fair trial. While waiting for the court's decision, Farber again took the stand in Dr. Jascalevich's murder trial. For three days he answered questions about his relationship with the prosecutor's office at the time he began investigating the Riverdell deaths, about his relationship with Dr. Baden's office, and about his book and movie contracts. He answered the questions until Dr. Jascalevich's lawyers demanded his files, then things were back to where they had always been.

On September 21, 1978, the Supreme Court of New Jersey voted five to two to uphold Farber's contempt conviction. It rejected his claim of First Amendment protection.

Without the existence of a constitutional privilege, Myron Farber's argument came to rest wholly on the New Jersey shield law, while Dr. Jascalevich's claim remained based on the Sixth Amendment. In the hierarchy of the law, the federal Constitution is supreme. In case of a conflict, it outweighs state constitutions and federal or state statutes. No matter how strongly the New Jersey legislature had worded the statute protecting reporters, the court agreed with the doctor and "the elementary but entirely sound proposition that where Constitution and statute collide, the latter must yield."

In deference to the First Amendment, the New Jersey legislature, and its shield law, the court did set forth a procedure for resolving future cases: the defense must satisfy the judge that there exists a reasonable probability that the information sought by the subpoena is relevant to the defense, that it cannot be obtained in a less intrusive manner, and that the defendant has a legitimate need to see and use it. The judge is to make a preliminary determination on these factors before ordering any material to be produced for *in camera* inspection. This was much like what Farber had requested. The Supreme Court of New Jersey, however, upheld Judge Arnold's decision to order an *in camera* inspection without specifically finding these conditions to have been met, because Judge Arnold was so thoroughly familiar with the case by the time he issued the order, and because Farber's "close working relationship" with the prosecutor's office weakened his claim.

Farber appealed to the U.S. Supreme Court, but it turned him down. On October 12, Farber again refused to turn over his files and was sent back to jail, raising a difficult question of enforcement. Floyd Abrams, who represents many members of the press, says, "Those of us who have advocated qualified [reporter's] privileges on occasion aren't promising that our clients are going to obey. All we're saying is as a First Amendment matter, you shouldn't force our client to answer this question, to disclose this source, unless you put the plaintiff through some serious hoops. That doesn't mean that if he goes through the hoops we are necessarily going to abide by the court order. . . . Our only defense is that we think what we're doing is important enough that we are going to do it and pay the punishment."

Eleven days later, on the afternoon of October 23, 1978, Dr. Jascalevich's murder trial was over. The case went to the jury. Myron Farber had never turned over his files. The next morning, Judge Trautwein, recognizing that the outcome was out of the hands of the New Jersey courts, released Farber from jail, where he had spent a total of thirty-nine days. Judge Trautwein also suspended Farber's six-month contempt sentence and ended the daily fines against the *New York Times*, which by then had paid $286,000.

That same morning, October 24, 1978, after deliberating for only two hours, the jury found Dr. Jascalevich not guilty of the murders of Nancy Savino, Frank Biggs, and Carl Rohrbeck.

In 1980, the New Jersey Board of Medical Examiners found Dr. Jascalevich guilty of gross malpractice for a series of incidents unrelated to his trial and revoked his medical license. In 1981, he moved back home to Argentina.

In 1982, Governor Brendan Byrne of New Jersey pardoned both Myron Farber and the *New York Times* of their criminal contempt convictions and ordered $101,000 refunded to the *Times*. The governor found that their purpose had been "to stand on a noble, if sometimes imperfect principle." He did not say that they were right.

Harrison Cronic in 1983, at the time his case was accepted by the United States Supreme Court

Right to Counsel:
United States v. Cronic

"In all criminal prosecutions, the accused shall enjoy the right to have the Assistance of Counsel for his defence."

MOST PEOPLE KNOW THAT THE Constitution guarantees the defendant in a criminal trial a lawyer, but how good does the lawyer have to be? In 1980, the government indicted Harrison Cronic on thirteen counts of mail fraud, alleging that he had masterminded a complex check-kiting scheme between banks in Florida and Oklahoma. Postal investigators pieced together the case for nearly five years, producing thousands of documents. To represent Cronic, the court appointed a young real estate attorney who had never tried a case. . . and gave him twenty-five days to prepare. Cronic went to the U.S. Supreme Court claiming that his attorney was so ineffective at trial that it was a violation of his Sixth Amendment right to have "the Assistance of Counsel for his defence."

According to Harrison Cronic, "My family has been part of the American experience since September 19, 1749, when Valentin Cronic, arriving on the ship *Patience*, first set foot on American soil in Philadelphia, PA." Cronic himself is a soft-spoken, courteous man, sometimes given to grandiose pronouncements.

Pondering his predicament, he came to the conclusion that "the law in our constitutional system of government is the final arbiter of power which itself, like a cloud, is always visible, always fluid, intangible, yet indestructible." Cronic's detractors say he is simply a well-polished con man. His supporters say he is a decent man whose obsession with his case makes him appear arrogant.

In 1973, Harrison Cronic's father started Skyproof Manufacturing Company, a Tampa, Florida, business that made roof supports, or trusses, for mobile homes. Harrison, then in his early thirties, took over Skyproof in 1974. He hired a young woman, Carolyn Cummings, to do secretarial work. He also made Cummings the president and sole shareholder of Skyproof. According to Harrison, he wanted to remain anonymous in the new company because a previous business had gone bankrupt, leaving him with some bad publicity and an IRS claim.

In 1975, Cronic contacted Wylie Merritt, an accountant he knew in Norman, Oklahoma, and asked him to open a bank account for Skyproof there. From June through September, on an almost daily basis, hundreds of checks were exchanged between Skyproof's bank in Tampa, Florida, and the one in Norman. Cronic determined the amount and timing of each deposit, but all of the checks and bank records bore Carolyn Cummings' name. The government would later claim that the exchange of checks was a classic check-kiting scheme, the largest Oklahoma had ever seen at that time.

In a typical check-kiting scheme, the check-kiter opens an account at Bank A with a nominal deposit. He writes a check on that account for a large sum, say fifty thousand dollars. The check-kiter then opens an account at Bank B and deposits the fifty-thousand-dollar check from Bank A. At the time of deposit in Bank B, the check is not supported by sufficient funds in the account at Bank A. Bank B, however, unaware of this fact, gives the check-kiter immediate credit on his account at Bank B. During the several-day period that the check on Bank A is being processed for collection, the check-kiter writes a fifty-thousand-dollar check on his account at Bank B and deposits it into his account at Bank A. At the time of the deposit of that check, Bank A gives the check-kiter immediate credit on his account there, and on the basis of that grant of credit pays the original fifty-thousand-dollar check when it is presented for collection.

In effect, the check-kiter exploits the time it takes to process checks between different banks. The scheme artificially inflates the balances in the bank accounts when, in fact, the check-kiter is really just shuffling worthless paper back and forth, timed to stay one step ahead of any check bouncing due to insufficient funds. In the meantime, the check-kiter can use the credit given on an artificially inflated account as an interest-free loan for as long as the kite lasts.

In October 1975, four months after the exchange of checks began, an official at the Tampa bank reviewed Skyproof's account and concluded that the company was fronting for a kite. The Tampa bank immediately returned Skyproof's checks and refused to accept any more. When the checks started bouncing in Norman, officials of the Oklahoma bank called Wylie Merritt and accused him of check kiting.

Cronic immediately flew out to meet with the president and attorney for the Norman bank. He asked that they begin the meeting with a prayer. Then he said that if there were any problems with the Skyproof account, it was due to bookkeeping errors. The company had grown quickly and Cronic conceded he had never set up an adequate system of accounting. He assured the Norman officials that he had never intended to defraud anyone and promised that if there were any overdrafts on the account, he would make good. He gave them a letter, signed by Cummings as president of Skyproof, transferring all available funds to the Norman bank.

The next month, Cronic gave the bank a promissory note, or IOU, for nearly half a million dollars and secured the note with a mortgage on a Texas bottling plant that Skyproof owned. Again Cummings signed all of the documents. Less than two weeks later, before the note came due, the Norman bank took over the bottling plant. They operated the plant for two years without accounting for profit or loss.

The bank also tipped off U.S. postal inspectors. If there had indeed been a kite between Oklahoma and Florida, it was conducted through the U.S. mail and was therefore a violation of the federal mail fraud statute. Postal inspectors, with U.S. Attorney John E. Green, began the tedious task of tracking a paper trail of hundreds of checks and thousands of documents between two states.

Four and a half years later, in February 1980, Green's office indicted Harrison Cronic, Wylie Merritt, and Carolyn Cummings on thirteen counts of mail fraud. The indictment alleged that they had deposited in the Oklahoma bank $4,841,073.95 in checks drawn on the Tampa bank when they knew there were insufficient funds to cover the checks. Merritt and Cummings plea-bargained and agreed to cooperate with the prosecution. Both were to testify that they were merely puppets in the scheme of the mastermind, Harrison Cronic. Merritt was to testify that he knew nothing of any kite or intent to defraud. Cummings was to testify that she suspected a fraud in the strange flow of checks, but Harrison assured her that it was common practice, and she simply did what she was told. Harrison Cronic was to stand trial in federal district court in Oklahoma on all thirteen counts, facing sixty-five years in prison.

In June, Cronic's retained attorney, who was also representing Carolyn Cummings, withdrew because of the conflict of interest. There is also some suggestion that Cronic could not keep up with the lawyer's bills. Harrison Cronic told the court he could not afford an attorney and asked that one be appointed to defend him. In Oklahoma at the time, lawyers appointed to indigent defendants in federal court were chosen from an alphabetical list of all local attorneys. For Cronic, Judge Eubanks of the Western District Court of Oklahoma picked the name of Chris Colston.

Colston had been a real estate attorney for six years but had never tried a case. He was not versed in the rules of procedure and evidence that govern a trial, had never argued before a judge or jury, and had never worried about perfecting a trial record for appeal. The government gave Colston the keys to the storage room containing the dozens of cartons of evidence in Cronic's case. "When I first saw those records," he says, "I was just totally, totally shocked and frightened."

According to Colston, he told Judge Eubanks he was not qualified to handle a criminal case, especially one of this magnitude, but that the judge said, in effect, "I'm sure you'll do fine." Harrison Cronic was also somewhat alarmed by Colston's appointment and began to say so to the court. Judge Eubanks responded, "If you're getting around to saying you want to select your own lawyer, no way. You have got a good lawyer and if you want your own, go hire your own. This man was appointed under

our system. . . . He's qualified or I wouldn't have appointed him."
Judge Eubanks gave Colston twenty-five days to prepare for trial.

Colston asked Ryland Rivas, an associate in his office with
criminal trial experience, to help. Colston says that although he
was overwhelmed at first, once he reviewed the documents he
realized they were really the same thing over and over. He says
that he felt competent to handle the trial.

Colston and Cronic, however, did not have an easy relationship. Colston had sized Cronic up as "an excellent southern
gentleman con man." He goes on to clarify: "By con man, I mean
he could sell snake oil." Colston says all of Cronic's suggestions
for defense witnesses were fiascos—"The witnesses couldn't wait
to burn him"—and that his client was incapable of telling the
truth. As soon as they hit a snag in preparing the defense, Cronic
would simply change his story.

Whether con man or gentleman, Cronic was not a passive client. He was relentless in all respects—relentlessly polite, relentlessly upbeat ("Never once did I see him downcast," says
Colston, "no matter how bad things got"), and relentless about
pursuing and perfecting his defense. He blanketed the court and
his attorney with his own motions and briefs. He badgered Colston to find out what happened to the bottling plant and to conduct new audits on the bank's records. He insisted he had never
created a kite and that to the extent there was any overdraft, he
had completely covered it. When Cronic persisted in making suggestions and passing along stacks of notes at trial, Colston seated
Ryland Rivas between himself and Cronic to keep his client at
bay. Nonetheless, when at the end of the trial Judge Eubanks told
Cronic he thought Colston had "done a tremendous job," Cronic
agreed.

The defense Colston presented did not deny there was a kite,
nor did it deny the Norman bank lost any money. Colston's defense was to argue that it was all Carolyn Cummings's fault. After
all, Cummings was the president and sole shareholder of Skyproof and she signed every check and document. Cronic's name
and signature were nowhere to be found.

What Colston did not raise was the defense of good faith. In
many jurisdictions, including Oklahoma, passing a bad check or
even a series of bad checks *alone* is not enough to convict under
the mail fraud statute. The individual must have *intended* to de-

fraud. As one of Cronic's later attorneys explains, "If I bounce a check and immediately make good on it, that indicates my good faith and that I didn't intend to defraud." Cronic's actions— promptly promising to make good and transferring funds and then the bottling plant to the bank—would not erase the crime if the jury found that Cronic had intended to defraud the bank in the first place. On the other hand, the jury could take those actions as evidence of Cronic's good faith and the fact that he did not intend to defraud. The federal courts that cover Oklahoma recognized good faith as a complete defense to mail fraud.

Colston, however, did not raise the issue and the judge gave no instruction to the jury on the good faith defense. Several prosecution witnesses testified, without objection from Colston, that the Skyproof accounts were indeed a kite. Norman bank officials testified, also without objection, that the bank lost varying amounts ranging from four to five hundred thousand dollars. They said that although Cronic never signed on behalf of Skyproof, through telephone calls and meetings they had concluded he was in charge. Carolyn Cummings took the stand and, as expected, testified that she simply did "whatever Harry told me to do."

Colston did not call any witnesses or produce any evidence for the defense. But he repeatedly emphasized that there was no record of Cronic's involvement. If a crime was committed, he argued, responsibility lay with Carolyn Cummings.

The jury convicted Cronic of eleven of the thirteen counts. The judge sentenced him to twenty-five years in prison.

Colston dutifully filed an appeal claiming, among other things, that he had had inadequate time to prepare. Cronic, out on bail, began to investigate his case and prepare his own version of his appeal. For months it was his full-time job. He uncovered what he thought was proof that the Norman bank did not really lose money because the bottling plant he had given them more than covered any possible overdraft. And he discovered the constitutional claim, under the Sixth Amendment, of ineffective assistance of counsel.

Originally, in England, the right to counsel was upside down. A person charged with treason or a felony was denied counsel, but a person charged with a misdemeanor or the defendant in a civil suit was entitled to the full assistance of a lawyer. The rule was

"so outrageous and so obviously a perversion of all sense of proportion," it was constantly under attack in England. But as one
Supreme Court justice put it, "To the credit of her American colonies, let it be said that so oppressive a doctrine had never obtained a foothold there." Twelve of the original thirteen colonies
recognized the right to counsel in criminal cases, a few limiting it
to the most serious crimes.

Indeed, the Supreme Court has recognized, "Of all the rights
that an accused person has, the right to be represented by counsel
is by far the most pervasive for it affects his ability to assert any
other rights he may have." Although the words do not appear in
the Bill of Rights, it is often said that the Sixth Amendment,
which requires a speedy and public trial, an impartial jury, and
the right to confrontation and compulsory process, guarantees a
"fair trial." The first several clauses of the amendment promise
that an individual accused of a crime and facing the tremendous
power of the state will have certain guarantees of fairness; the
last clause of the Sixth Amendment provides the accused with a
lawyer to ensure that the promise is kept.

The foundation of a fair trial is something the Supreme Court
has called the "unique strength" of our criminal justice system;
the adversarial process. Under the U.S. Constitution, a criminal
trial is not inquisitorial, with one omnipotent judge or panel of
judges empowered to interrogate the accused and then determine
guilt or innocence. The process is instead an adversarial one. The
government and the accused—bound by the Constitution, state
law, and rules of evidence and procedure—each make the strongest possible argument for their side. According to the Supreme
Court, "The very premise of our adversary system of criminal justice is that partisan advocacy on both sides of a case will best
promote the ultimate objective that the guilty be convicted and
the innocent go free."

Without an attorney, however, the great adversarial process is
a mismatch. "Left without the aid of counsel [the accused] may
be put on trial without a proper charge and convicted upon improper evidence," the Supreme Court wrote. "He lacks both the
skill and knowledge to prepare his defense, even though he [may]
have a perfect one." Thus, in the landmark 1963 case *Gideon v.
Wainwright*, the Supreme Court held that the Sixth Amendment
guarantee of counsel is such a fundamental right it must apply to

the states as well as the federal government. "In our adversary system of criminal justice," the Court declared, "any person haled into court who is too poor to hire a lawyer, cannot be assured a fair trial unless counsel is provided for him."

Nine years later, the Court held that the *Gideon* rule applied to all criminal cases, whether classified as petty, misdemeanor, or felony, where the accused faces imprisonment. In the same case, the Court noted the practical problem of who would be providing all of this defense. And a year later in an address to a law school, Chief Justice Burger worried that "we are more casual about qualifying the people we allow to act as advocates in the courtrooms than we are about licensing our electricians."

The legal community was well aware of egregious examples of poor representation by defense attorneys. For example, one conviction was reversed because the defendant's court-appointed lawyer repeatedly admitted his client's guilt to the jury, and another because the defendant's trial counsel testified for the prosecution. Other cases, such as Cronic's, were less extreme and raised a difficult question: when does a poor performance by counsel rise to the level of a constitutional violation? As one court put it, "While a criminal trial is not a game in which the participants are expected to enter the ring with a near match in skills, neither is it a sacrifice of unarmed prisoners to gladiators."

The Supreme Court has long recognized that the right to counsel is the right to "effective" assistance of counsel. At the time of Cronic's case, however, the Court had not articulated a standard by which "effectiveness" should be judged. In general, the lower courts had evolved from asking whether the trial was simply a "farce and mockery" (and therefore a violation of the right to counsel) to asking whether counsel's performance was "reasonable." The Tenth Circuit, where Cronic's appeal would be heard, was of the view that ineffective representation could be *inferred* by looking to certain factors, such as counsel's experience and preparation time, without any specific proof that the defendant had *actually* been prejudiced by his or her lawyer's performance.

Cronic was given a new court-appointed attorney for his appeal, in which he raised the ineffectiveness claim. Cronic acknowledged that he had previously praised Colston in the presence of Judge Eubanks. He explained that he was so distressed by his trial and by counsel's performance that he consulted a therapist, who told him that Colston needed positive reinforcement. The therapist advised Cronic to compliment his attorney and, Cronic explained, he simply complied.

Cronic claims that he also had problems with his appellate lawyer, but that this time he did not try to be accommodating. "I spent as much time writing my own briefs as I did battling my attorney . . . it was absolutely exasperating," he says. Nonetheless, Cronic won. In 1982, the Tenth Circuit held that Cronic had been denied effective assistance of counsel in violation of the Sixth Amendment.

The government immediately appealed to the Supreme Court and the Court took the case. It was time to set a uniform standard for the right to effective assistance of counsel. For this argument, Cronic did not wait for a new court-appointed attorney. Through a relative, he wrote to Steven Duke, a criminal law professor at Yale Law School. Duke agreed to take the case and the Court approved his appointment. Cronic finally had an attorney who satisfied him. "Steven Duke was most kind in allowing me to assist in my case in the Supreme Court," he says.

The Supreme Court, however, rejected the Tenth Circuit's decision, which "inferred" ineffectiveness without finding any specific error by counsel. The Court said that the disparate preparation time allotted to each side did not necessarily mean Cronic's attorney could not provide an effective defense. Furthermore, the Court did not find Colston's youth or inexperience dispositive. "Every experienced criminal defense attorney once tried his first criminal case," the Court wrote. Cronic's case was remanded for an evaluation of counsel's performance under the new standard set forth in its companion case, *Strickland v. Washington*.

In *Strickland*, the Court declared that the purpose of the Sixth Amendment right to counsel is to guarantee a fair trial. Therefore, "the benchmark for judging any claim of ineffectiveness must be whether counsel's conduct so undermined the proper functioning of the adversarial process that the trial cannot be relied on as having produced a just result." The Court set out a two-part test for making such a judgment. First, the defendant must identify specific acts or omissions by counsel that were outside of the wide range of professionally competent assistance. Second, the defendant must show that counsel's errors prejudiced the defense to the point where he was denied a fair trial.

Cronic's case was sent back to Judge Eubanks for a hearing under the new *Strickland* standard. Judge Eubanks, however, had apparently had it with Harrison Cronic. At one point in the proceedings before the hearing, Cronic said, "Thank you." The judge replied, "Well, you're not welcome. I think you're a swindler and a cheat and you wouldn't see the light of day if I had any choice." He gave Cronic's new appointed counsel, David Booth, nine days to prepare for the hearing. Then, at the hearing, when David Booth asked to confer with his client, Judge Eubanks said, "Yes. I believe you should, because he'll sure as fire claim you're incompetent and sue you if you don't confer with him."

Under questioning by Booth, Colston testified that he still believed that, under the circumstances, the defense he presented was competent. He also said that by the end of the trial he was sure he had had enough time to prepare. Colston explained that he had claimed to the contrary in Cronic's first appeal simply because it was his job to represent his client. "I had an obligation to throw it in there whether I felt that way or not," he said.

After the hearing, Judge Eubanks concluded that new evidence showed that the bank lost closer to $135,000, as opposed to the nearly $500,000 accepted as the loss at trial. The judge also concluded that Harrison Cronic had received effective assistance of counsel. "You just can't make a silk purse out of a sow's ear," he said.

Steven Duke flew back across the country to appeal Judge Eubanks's decision. In a scant three-page opinion, the Tenth Circuit finally, in 1988, answered the question of whether Colston's performance had violated Cronic's Sixth Amendment rights. Following the *Strickland* command, the Court found Colston's failure to raise or investigate the good faith defense to be a specific error under prevailing professional standards. Noting that Colston's explanation for his defense was that he was seeking to "cloud the issues," the court wrote, "This cannot be a satisfactory explanation under *Strickland* or any authority for a selection of a 'defense.'"

In addition, the Tenth Circuit pointed to Colston's failure to investigate the bank's records or challenge bank officials' repeated and erroneous statements at trial that nothing was paid on the overdraft on Skyproof's account. The question of how much money, if any, the bank lost would not erase the crime if

Cronic intended to defraud. But, the court explained, the wide variation in the amount of the bank's alleged loss "must cast some doubt" on the bank's position.

Because Cronic's counsel did not raise what could have been a complete defense and did not investigate whether the bank actually lost money, the court concluded that Cronic had been prejudiced under the *Strickland* standard. The court also said that the judge "demonstrated a degree of hostility toward the defendant which prevented an impartial conclusion." The Tenth Circuit ordered another trial.

Nearly a decade after he was first charged and almost fifteen years after the alleged kite, Harrison Cronic got a new trial before a new judge. He also got a new court-appointed lawyer, Gary Peterson, to defend him. Peterson was given just three weeks to prepare for trial. Peterson, however, was a seasoned criminal attorney. In addition to murder, kidnapping, and robbery cases, he had tried white-collar criminal cases with vast paper trails and had argued many times before both judge and jury. Most important, as Peterson points out, it was the second trial. He already knew the government's case and what the witnesses would say.

On November 1, 1988, a jury again found Cronic guilty of mail fraud. Peterson had raised the good faith defense but says "the jury was just not convinced." This time, however, Cronic was sentenced to ten, not twenty-five, years in prison. Cronic thinks that his attempts to make good and the question as to the bank's actual loss, both brought out at the second trial, helped to lessen his sentence.

Chris Colston and U.S. Attorney Green think Harrison Cronic took the state for a long and expensive ride. "[He] was really playing games with the court," Green says. According to Colston, "Harrison manipulated the system, that was his goal in life."

On the other hand, Steven Duke argues, "Under any standard, Cronic did not have effective assistance of counsel." To Duke, Cronic's case is emblematic of the problems inherent in a system of criminal defense by appointment. "It permits society to proclaim all these wonderful rights without having to pay up," Duke says. "Society does not want to pay the costs of an effective system of defense representation. These people are for the most part guilty. . . . [People] say, 'Why should we not only pay for the police, the court system, and the prosecutors, but also pay for the defense and experts for the defense?'

"One answer," says Duke, "is the Constitution requires it. Another is that a lot of innocent people can get convicted under a system that doesn't guarantee adequate representation . . . and that could be you."

For his part, Harrison Cronic remains relentlessly upbeat, relentlessly polite. He insists he has no animosity toward those involved in his case. Wylie Merritt and Carolyn Cummings, he says, simply did what they had to do when they turned on him. Chris Colston was well intentioned but in over his head. U.S. Attorney Green was just doing his job. Judge Eubanks, Cronic allows, "put Mr. Colston in an untenable position and should have recognized the problem." Still, he philosophizes, "This is not a perfect system and life is not always fair."

Harrison Cronic has begun serving his ten-year sentence at a prison in Texas. "It's a camp," he says. "We live in dormitories. I live with an architect. My executive banker just left."

*   *   *

N.B. On April 11, 1990, the Tenth Circuit issued its decision on Harrison Cronic's appeal from his second conviction. The court was apparently convinced that Cronic had deliberately created a kite. But Gary Peterson found a technical error in the jury instructions and argued that it required reversal. The Tenth Circuit wrote, "We reluctantly agree." The court reversed Cronic's conviction and, because of the nature of the error, he cannot be tried again. Harrison Cronic is currently working on a landscaping crew in Georgia.

SEVENTH AMENDMENT

"In Suits at common law, where the value in controversy shall exceed twenty dollars, the right of trial
by jury shall be preserved, and no fact tried by a
jury, shall be otherwise re-examined in any Court of
the United States, than according to the rules of the
common law."

[3]

ARTICLE the ELEVENTH.

No appeal to the Supreme Court of the United States, shall be allowed, where the value in controversy shall not amount to one thousand dollars, nor shall any fact, triable by a Jury according to the course of the common law, be otherwise re-examinable, than according to the rules of common law.

ARTICLE the TWELFTH.

In suits at common law, the right of trial by Jury shall be preserved.

ARTICLE the THIRTEENTH.

Excessive bail shall not be required, nor excessive fines imposed, nor cruel and unusual punishments inflicted.

ARTICLE the FOURTEENTH.

No State shall infringe the right of trial by Jury in criminal cases, nor the rights of conscience, nor the freedom of speech, or of the press.

ARTICLE the FIFTEENTH.

The enumeration in the Constitution of certain rights, shall not be construed to deny or disparage others retained by the people.

ARTICLE the SIXTEENTH.

The powers delegated by the Constitution to the government of the United States, shall be exercised as therein appropriated, so that the Legislative shall never exercise the powers vested in the Executive or Judicial; nor the Executive the powers vested in the Legislative or Judicial; nor the Judicial the powers vested in the Legislative or Executive.

ARTICLE the SEVENTEENTH.

The powers not delegated by the Constitution, nor prohibited by it, to the States, are reserved to the States respectively.

Teste,

JOHN BECKLEY, CLERK.

In SENATE, *August* 25, 1789.

Read and ordered to be printed for the consideration of the Senate.

Attest, SAMUEL A. OTIS, SECRETARY.

NEW-YORK, PRINTED BY T. GREENLEAF, near the Coffee-House.

A*n early draft of the Seventh Amendment, appearing here as*
ARTICLE THE TWELFTH

Right to a Civil Jury: "Complexity"

THE SEVENTH AMENDMENT MAY be the one most likely to directly affect, and disrupt, an average citizen's life. Americans can go through a whole lifetime without being searched by police or accused of a crime, without asserting their right to free speech in a controversial manner, or without having a soldier quartered in their home. But few escape a call to jury duty. And in the latter half of the twentieth century, as civil lawsuits become longer and more complex, service on a civil jury has become an increasingly hair-raising prospect.

In California, several housewives sat for five months pondering the concepts of cross-elasticity of supply and demand and product interface manipulation in the computer industry. The jurors had to answer, among many other questions, "Was it appropriate, given the economic determinants of a market, such as demand and supply substitutability and barriers to entry, to treat IBM-compatible disk drives as a separate market, considering the functions performed by the drives, the alternatives actually or potentially available for performing those functions, and the price/performance characteristics of those alternatives?"

In New York, an estimated eleven hundred composers and lyricists filed a lawsuit for copyright violations. The trial was expected to last four months and the plaintiffs, all eleven hundred of them, each had to prove his or her own individual injury and damages. And in another courtroom, a judge was preparing for jury selection in a case that was scheduled to last *two years*. They were all taking part in one of the "fundamental guarantee[s] of the rights and liberties of the people"—the civil jury.

The Seventh Amendment guarantees the right to a jury in a civil—as opposed to criminal—trial. Like the criminal jury, the civil jury was designed to act as a check on the arbitrary power of the state. But as the gigantic civil trial becomes more commonplace, some courts and commentators argue that the civil jury has itself become an instrument of arbitrary power, because jurors are deciding cases they cannot possibly understand. Thus, some experts argue for the creation of a "complexity exception" to the Seventh Amendment. They say the exception would save time and expense for the judiciary, ensure a fairer result, and, presumably, spare the hapless civil juror.

Historically, the right to a civil jury has been one of the most prized and accepted of all those in the Bill of Rights. It was included in the original Jamestown charter of 1607, and by 1776 all thirteen colonies protected the right in some form. In fact, the biggest commotion caused by the right to a civil jury occurred when it was left out of the new Constitution. Alexander Hamilton, though defending the omission, wrote, "The objection to the [Constitution], which has met with the most success . . . is that relative to the want of a constitutional provision for the trial by jury in civil cases."

Once the right was secured in 1791, it generated little of the public debate and controversy that surrounds many of the other amendments in the Bill of Rights. The Supreme Court has repeatedly recognized that the right to a civil jury has "so firm a place in our history" and is "so fundamental and sacred to the citizen" that it must be "jealousy guarded by the courts."

To much of the American public there is indeed something almost sacred in the concept of a "jury of one's peers." In fact, the jury is sometimes seen as a safety valve in highly controversial cases (for example, those that involve political or racial issues), or cases that require drawing fine lines between certain kinds of behavior (for example, negligence suits). When judges decide such cases, their rulings may appear arbitrary or be vulnerable to charges of corruption or bias. It is thought that a jury lends the appearance of fairness and legitimacy to such difficult cases and therefore bolsters public confidence in the judicial system.

Of course, the jury is thought to actually ensure fairness as well. The Seventh Amendment places a high value on the collective "wisdom of the community," which is in some ways considered superior to that of a single judge. In addition, the jury can dispense what is known as "black box" justice. Unlike a judge, it issues a verdict without an opinion to explain or justify its decision. Where a judge would have to apply the law strictly, the jury is free to modify harsh results to conform to perceived community values. Thus, the end result of the lay person's participation in the judicial process, it is said, is both the appearance and the actuality of a fair system of justice.

Nonetheless, as long as the civil jury has existed, it has had its detractors. The Federalists, pushing for ratification of the Constitution, were constantly defending the document's lack of a civil jury guarantee. Alexander Hamilton devoted all of *Federalist Paper* No. 83 to the subject. In a section that foreshadowed the modern "complexity" debate, he wrote, "The circumstances that constitute cases proper for courts of equity are in many instances so nice and intricate that they are incompatible with the genius of trials by jury. They require often such long, deliberate, and critical investigation as would be impracticable to men called from their occupations, and obliged to decide before they were permitted to return to them."

Some scholars and practitioners have argued that a jury is, at worst, an irrational instrument and, at best, an extremely odd method of determining facts and resolving disputes. "Trial by jury," one historian wrote, "[is] inherently absurd—so much so that no lawyer, judge, scholar, prescription-clerk, cook, or mechanic in a garage would ever think for a moment of employing that method for determining the facts in any situation that concerned him."

And from a juror's point of view, the Seventh Amendment often casts him or her in some fairly unconventional roles. The civil jury system may inject complete strangers into intimate family disputes, as in will contests. Civil juries also referee neighborhood spats about hedge heights, mete out the blame in fender-benders, and, on occasion, make enormous statements of public policy. When Alabama Ku Klux Klansmen murdered a young black man at random, an all-white civil jury held not only the individuals but the organization itself responsible. The jury's $7 million verdict essentially put the local Klan chapter out of business.

Civil jurors are also asked to make difficult, or even seemingly impossible, decisions. Jurors in negligence suits, for example, often must put a price tag on a life or limb that was lost. One New York jury had to decide how much to award a couple in their late sixties after the husband lapsed into an irreversible coma as the result of a bee sting at a country club. (The jury ordered the club to pay the husband $1.4 million for his injury and his wife $250,000 for "loss of services.")

Those who argue for a complexity exception to the Seventh Amendment say that in massive civil cases, the problems for jurors have reached new, intolerable levels. They say these cases are "difficult" not in the sense that they are disturbing or unusual, but because they are beyond the juror's comprehension. The right to a civil jury in these cases, they argue, is nothing more than the "right to an irrational verdict."

The Seventh Amendment states, "In Suits at common law . . . trial by jury shall be preserved." Because the amendment speaks of "preserving" a right to a jury, its meaning is explicitly rooted in history. Originally in England, and then in the United States, there were two principle kinds of courts: common law and equity. Depending on the type of lawsuit and the remedy sought, a case had to be brought in *either* one court or the other. Those brought "at law" were entitled to be heard by a jury. Those brought "in equity" were decided by a judge.

In the United States, in 1938, law and equity were merged. There became only one court—a civil court—in which all non-criminal cases would be heard. But because of the Seventh Amendment, whether a party could ask for a jury depended on whether the nature of the case, viewed historically, would have been heard at common law or equity. Most of the suits that are the focus of the complexity issue have been held to be analogous to cases heard "at law" and therefore are entitled to a jury.

Nevertheless, some proponents of the complexity exception believe the Supreme Court opened the door for them in a 1970 case. The case itself did not present the complexity question. But in footnote 10, the Court set forth three of the factors that determine whether a civil case will be tried to a jury: historical custom, the remedy sought, and "the practical abilities and limitations of juries." In 1976, a Washington district court decided that the third sentence of the footnote was of "constitutional dimension" and denied the right to a jury in a complicated securities fraud case. Four years later, the footnote was famous. Large corporations that wanted no part of a jury argued the footnote in court, judges considered it, and scholars wrote long articles about it. Some rejected the footnote argument altogether, some thought it left room for doubt, but most concluded it was not the definitive answer to the complexity issue. Part three of footnote 10, they said, was an unusual place for the High Court to announce a major constitutional decision.

Proponents of the complexity exception turned with more success to the due process clause of the Fifth Amendment. If the jury did not have a reasonable understanding of the law and facts, they argued, the trial could not be considered "fair" under traditional concepts of due process. They maintained that, in these circumstances, the Fifth Amendment right should "outweigh" the Seventh Amendment right. Furthermore, they argued that in the highly complex case the Seventh Amendment jury was no longer performing its proper function anyway. The jury could hardly reflect the "wisdom of the community" if its members did not know what was going on.

Indeed, some argue that in a particularly drawn out case, the jury is no longer even representative of the community. One judge sat through a giant antitrust case, then had to declare a mistrial because the overwhelmed jurors could not reach a decision. In denying the right to a jury for the new trial, he wrote, "The eleven jurors to whom this case was submitted probably represented a random cross-section of people in the community who could afford to spend ten months serving on a jury, but it is open to question whether they were a true cross-section of the community." The New York judge faced with eleven hundred plaintiffs and an estimated four-month trial asked, "Must litigants be left with a panel consisting solely of retired people, the idle rich, those on welfare, and housewives whose children are grown?"

As these comments indicate, any controversy over juries inevitably focuses on some basic assumptions about the people who sit on them—that is, ordinary Americans. Some courts have become indignant on behalf of the nation's populace. In rejecting the complexity exception, one judge wrote, "This argument unnecessarily and improperly demeans the intelligence of the citizens of this Nation." Others take a different tack and acknowledge the difficulties civil jurors may have, but wonder whether a judge could do any better. The massive litigation following the breakup of AT&T prompted one judge to write, "[The jury] includes an engineer, a hearing system designer, an accountant, a purchasing agent, an aircraft mechanic, a chemist, a bank loan officer, a secretary, a housewife, a clerk, and a college employee. . . . It is at least doubtful that the experiential background of any judge could match that of this particular jury." One commentator suggested that if there is to be a complexity exception, it must encompass judges as well.

Many courts have simply skirted the issue by saying whether or not an exception exists, the case before it is simply not "complex enough." Only two federal appellate courts, those at the level just below the Supreme Court, have decided the issue. They came out on opposite sides.

The Third Circuit, which covers Pennsylvania, New Jersey, Delaware, and the Virgin Islands, was faced with an antitrust suit charging a thirty-year conspiracy involving almost a hundred firms around the world. It required an understanding of complex law, U.S. and Japanese market conditions and business practices, and thousands of transactions. The lower court refused to find a complexity exception to the Seventh Amendment and held that a jury could hear the case. On appeal, the Third Circuit reversed. The court accepted the Fifth Amendment due process argument. "There is a danger that jury verdicts will be erratic and completely unpredictable, which would be inconsistent with even-handed justice," the court wrote. It cautioned, however, that "Due Process should allow denials of jury trials only in exceptional cases."

On the other hand, the Ninth Circuit, which covers California and other western states, was faced with a case alleging massive securities violations and fraud. There were over a hundred thousand pages of documents, and it was estimated the trial would last two years. "Concern was also expressed," the court noted, "as to where a courtroom could be found to seat all the attorneys, let alone the parties to the case."

Nevertheless, the Ninth Circuit expressly rejected the proposed complexity exception to the Seventh Amendment. "Such practical considerations diminish in importance when they come in conflict with the constitutional right to a jury in civil cases," the court concluded. It also expressed great confidence in the abilities of the average American and said that, with the proper guidance, a jury could handle any case put before it, no matter how lengthy and complex. "Jurors, if properly instructed and treated with deserved respect," the court wrote, "bring collective intelligence, wisdom, and dedication to their tasks, which is rarely equalled in other areas of public service."

The U.S. Supreme Court has never decided the Seventh Amendment complexity issue. Except for a narrow ruling in one jurisdiction, the constitutional right to a civil jury enters its third century intact. It may be because there is a reason for the instinctive rallying for the right to trial by jury; maybe an engineer, accountant, secretary, and clerk, combined, do ensure a fair trial, even in the face of the new enormously complex civil case. Or it may be because, as one leading commentator on civil trials put it, "The jury is like rock music. Classical theory frowns; the masses applaud. And in a democracy the felt need of the masses has a claim upon the law."

EIGHTH
AMENDMENT

"Excessive bail shall not be required, nor excessive fines imposed, nor cruel and unusual punishments inflicted."

Ricky Tison (left) *and Raymond Tison on death row in the Arizona State Penitentiary, 1989*
CAROLINE KENNEDY

Cruel and Unusual Punishment: *Tison v. Arizona*

For as long as they could remember, their father had been in jail. The three Tison brothers, Donny, Ricky, and Raymond, grew up in the rural Arizona town of Casa Grande. The town was so small the boys can remember the day the sidewalks were put in. Ironically, for men destined to become the focus of the largest and fiercest manhunt in Arizona history, the Tison brothers recall their childhood as idyllic days of wide-open spaces, unlocked doors, fishing, and lots of family. The one thing missing was their incarcerated father, Gary.

The boys' mother, Dorothy, met Gary when she was in high school and he was in prison. He was serving seven to fifteen years for armed robberies committed with his brother, Joe. As soon as Gary was paroled and Dorothy graduated from high school, they were married. They had three sons in three years.

A year after that, Dorothy and Gary began a lifelong and deadly pattern: Gary committed more armed robberies, was arrested, escaped briefly (thereby compounding his sentence), and was sent back to prison. Dorothy packed up the young boys for weekly visits to their father and created for herself and her sons a wildly romanticized view of Gary Tison. To them, he became a heroic figure, misunderstood by authorities and unjustly treated by the system.

Within five years Gary was paroled. It was the only time the boys really spent with him as a "home father." He lived up to his mythic status, and more, spinning out fantastic tales of dangerous secret missions he had performed for an ungrateful government that had turned on him and caused all his problems.

Then it started again. Gary passed a bad check and got involved in a smuggling scheme that went sour. He was arrested and his parole revoked. As he was transported back to prison by a single guard, Gary somehow produced a gun, shot the guard dead, and escaped. He was quickly captured and his twenty-year sentence upped to life in prison. At first, Dorothy did not tell her sons about the murder, but for some reason the principal at the boys' school announced the crime to the students. After that, the Tison household would refer to the incident as the time the guard "died." Apparently, Dorothy Tison was unwilling or unable to do anything but encourage her sons to grow up in the thrall of their father.

Even from jail, Gary exercised considerable day-to-day influence over the boys. A prison official who worked with Gary on the inmates' newspaper says, "[Gary] would come in in the morning and talk about . . . kids' scores on spelling tests or one of the kids getting a new pair of shoes . . . just routine conversations that if I hadn't known better I would have thought he had gone home and talked it over at the dinner table." As they grew older, Gary Tison would order his sons to get haircuts or would take away their car privileges when they acted up. When they grew too old to be chauffeured by their mother to the prison each Sunday, the brothers continued the weekly visits on their own.

Although the three boys were each only eleven months apart, the two youngest, Ricky and Raymond, were closest. "Because of that," Ricky says, "Donny always had to go outside of us . . . make his own way." Whether forced by a sibling triangle or because he alone sensed that perhaps his father belonged in jail, Donny was the only son who showed signs of breaking the strange family bond. He had other friends, part-time work on his own, and for two years went off to the marines. Raymond and Ricky stayed home. They worked odd jobs together as car mechanics and roofers, but mostly just helped out in their grand-parents' gas station. They spent a lot of time with Dorothy. When either Raymond or Ricky was asked, "Who is your best friend?" each boy would answer, "My brother and my mother."

Unlike their father, neither Raymond nor Ricky had a criminal record. They were arrested one time for stealing a case of beer and sentenced to pick up trash along a six-mile stretch of high-way. Other than that, they never caused problems. Ever. "We tried to keep Mom happy," Raymond says.

By the time Donny returned from the marines, in 1978, Ray-mond and Ricky were wrapped up in Gary Tison's dreams of es-cape and Dorothy's desire to have her husband back. Gary had chalked up one more failed escape attempt seven years earlier and was desperate to try again. By all accounts, Gary was an "enthusiastic manipulator" not only of his family, but of the tan-gled prison bureaucracy. Somehow, the three-time escapee and killer of a prison guard managed to get himself transferred to the Trusty Annex, a medium-security facility across the street from the maximum-security compound. With the help of Gary's brother, Uncle Joe, the boys lined up a Lincoln Continental as a getaway car and began stockpiling an arsenal of guns.

On a Sunday visit at the end of July, Gary told his sons, ages eighteen, nineteen, and twenty, that the escape would be in one week. The plan was so far along, even Donny agreed. Gary said they would be taking another inmate, Randy Greenawalt, with them. As the captain's clerk, Randy was the only inmate allowed in the prison control room, where he typed up the next day's work roster. Randy's job was the key to Gary's plan. The brothers would later say they had never met Randy before and did not know he was convicted of one murder and suspected of several more. They would also later say that their father promised them no one would be hurt.

On the morning of July 30, 1978, Raymond walked into the entrance foyer of the visitor's area of the Trusty Annex. A glass partition separated the foyer from the guards' control room. The partition was much like a teller's window at a bank, with a slot at counter-top level to pass papers back and forth and a small con-versation hole slightly higher up. Under prison procedure, vis-itors registered at the window and a guard in the control room pressed a buzzer to open an electronically locked door between the foyer and a hallway. Visitors were then searched in the hall-way before walking into a small yard set up with picnic tables. Only after the visitors had arrived was the inmate brought to the yard. That morning, Raymond registered with a guard, Sergeant Hodo, then walked through the procedure, as he had done for most of his life, and met his father in the yard. Randy Greenawalt was typing in the control room.

A short time later, Donny and Ricky entered the foyer with a picnic basket. Like Raymond, they knew all the guards by name and were greeted warmly. One of the guards, Ed Barry, would later testify that he walked into the control room on the morning of the thirtieth and saw Randy Greenawalt picking up a two-way radio.

"Now, Randy," Ed Barry said, "put the radio back down on the counter."

Randy Greenawalt looked at Barry. "Just come quietly all the way into the room," he told the guard, "and you won't be hurt."

It was only then that Barry looked over toward the foyer. He says, "Ricky Tison had a shotgun pointing through the conversa-tion hole in the window at Sergeant Hodo's head."

The brothers' picnic basket was packed with guns. Donny passed a shotgun and a pistol through the slot to Randy Green-awalt. Randy opened the electronic door for Donny and Ricky, then walked down the short hallway to the door to the visitors' yard, where Gary and Raymond were waiting. Heavily armed, the Tisons and Greenawalt herded all of the guards and visitors into a storage room and locked the door. The five men then strolled out to the Tison family Ford in the parking lot, packed up the picnic basket full of guns, and drove away.

A short distance down the road, the fugitives switched to the Lincoln. They drove all day, sticking to back roads, then stopped for the night at an abandoned house, a shack really, far out in the desert, miles from anywhere. One of the tires on the Lincoln had developed a slow leak, so the boys took the only spare from the trunk and changed the tire. The next day they headed west, then turned north onto U.S. Route 95, a little-traveled link between the towns of Yuma and Quartzsite, again driving all day and into the night.

Outside Yuma, Arizona, a young marine, John Lyons, was packing for a trip. He was taking his wife, Donnelda, and twenty-two-month-old son, Christopher, for a visit home to Omaha,

Nebraska. His fifteen-year-old niece, Theresa Tyson (no relation to Gary Tison's family), had been staying with the Lyonses and they were going to drop her at home along the way. John and a friend packed the luggage into the Lyonses' orange Mazda. John also put two handguns in the car, a .38 air weight automatic revolver in the glove compartment and an old .45 in the back hatch. Around 11:00 P.M. (they wanted to escape the desert heat), the Lyons family and Theresa climbed into the Mazda and headed north on U.S. Route 95.

The Tisons and Randy Greenawalt were nearing Quartzsite when the right rear tire of the Lincoln blew. Gary Tison was furious, screaming and cursing at his sons. After a flawless escape, the fugitives were in the middle of the desert in the middle of the night with a flat tire and no spare. They tried to drive on but were soon riding on the tire's metal rim. They needed another car.

Gary decided Raymond looked the least threatening and elected him to flag down a passing motorist. Raymond stood alone by the disabled Lincoln while Ricky and Donny, armed with revolvers, hid off to the right side of the road. Gary and Randy, armed with shotguns, crossed the highway and waited in the darkness on the other side. One car passed Raymond without stopping. Another car passed, but the driver must have had second thoughts because the car slowed and made a U-turn. The orange Mazda slowly made its way back and parked behind the disabled Lincoln. John Lyons got out of the car.

"What's the problem?" he asked.

Donnelda Lyons also got out of the car and began walking toward the Lincoln to see if she could help. As Raymond took John Lyons around to the rear of the car to show him the flat, the other four men emerged with guns drawn. John Lyons froze. Donnelda Lyons, halfway between the two cars, turned and started back toward the Mazda. Gary Tison had crossed the highway and was approaching from the rear of the Mazda, his shotgun leveled at Donnelda. She kept going toward the car. The boys started to get nervous. The lady would not stop. Gary stood braced on the road looking at Donnelda through the sight of his shotgun, but she kept walking. She was going to get her baby from the car.

Gary let Donnelda take Christopher from the Mazda and Theresa Tyson followed all of them out onto the road.

John Lyons was trying to stay calm. "We don't want any trouble," he said. He told the Tisons about the guns in the Mazda. "We don't want any trouble," he kept saying over and over. "Hey, we stopped to help you." In the short time it took to usher the Lyons family up the highway and force them into the back of the Lincoln, no car or truck passed by.

Raymond took the wheel of the Lincoln and Donny sat in the passenger seat covering the Lyons family in the back. Gary, Ricky, and Randy followed in the Mazda. The two cars turned around and headed back down the highway, turned left onto the dirt road the Tisons had just come up, then right onto an even smaller dirt road, or gas line road, set up to mark the gas pipes underneath.

About a mile down the gas line road the cars stopped. The group was in the middle of the desert. If a car passed by on the highway, none of them would hear it. There was almost no moon. The cars' headlights provided the only illumination.

The two cars were parked trunk to trunk. The Lyons family was forced in front of the headlights of the Lincoln while Raymond, Ricky, and Randy switched belongings from car to car. Gary was pacing back and forth between the two cars, pushing the boys to move faster. Raymond and Randy were packing the trunks while Ricky was combing through the interior of the Mazda. Gary became impatient, screaming at Ricky to just heap the Lyonses' things together. Ricky scooped everything into Donnelda's satchel and put it in the trunk. Gary went back to help Donny guard the Lyons family huddled together in the beam of the headlight. There really was no need; there was absolutely no place for the captives to go.

Gary told Raymond to back the Lincoln farther off the dirt road, up by some brush, and he followed behind on foot. After parking the car, Raymond got out and began walking back to the group. Suddenly he jumped. Gary Tison was firing into the radiator and headlights of the Lincoln. He shot off several rounds, then leaned his shotgun across his forearm and walked back toward the others trembling by the Mazda. "Lincolns are hard to kill," he muttered to Raymond as he walked by.

John, Donnelda, Christopher, and Theresa were herded up to

the Lincoln and again ordered into the backseat. John Lyons was pleading for their lives. "Jesus, don't kill us," he said. "You all just tell us what you want us to do, and we will sit out here till midafternoon." John Lyons was looking back and forth, turning around, trying to appeal to each of the captors because he didn't know who would listen. "Give us some water," he said. "That's all we ask for, just leave us out here and you all go home."

The boys looked at Gary. They would say later that he appeared to be in conflict with himself. He stayed silent for a long time. Then Gary ordered Donny back to the Mazda to get the water jug. But the small car was packed so full Donny could not get to the jug. Gary became impatient again, yelling at Donny to hurry up, demanding the water. So Ricky and Raymond walked back to the Mazda to help. What happened next is unclear.

Ricky says they retrieved the water jug and took it back to their father. Raymond says they were still back at the Mazda looking for the water. In any event, both boys heard blasts and looked up to see the steady flashes from a shotgun on either side of the Lincoln.

The doors to the Lincoln were closed and the Lyons family crammed inside. Randy Greenawalt was on the left side of the car and Gary Tison on the right. Both were firing point-blank into the Lincoln. Gary and Randy stopped once or twice to reload and then continued shooting. The three Tison boys stood stunned, watching.

When Randy's shells were spent, he lowered his shotgun and walked back to the Mazda and the boys. Gary stayed at the Lincoln for a few moments waiting, perhaps looking for signs of movement. He walked around to the other side, fired another round or two into the car, and then walked back to the Mazda. Gary ordered his sons into the backseat and Randy took the wheel. The five men squeezed in around all of their belongings and drove back toward the highway. Nobody said a word about the killings, or about anything else.

The left rear door of the shattered Lincoln opened slowly and John Lyons staggered out. He fell, face up and arms askew, about twenty-five feet behind the car, where he died. He had shotgun blasts, all at close range, to the left shoulder, right abdomen, right and left chest, and left rear of the skull. His wrists had been shot off when he raised his arms in an instinctive but futile attempt to fend off the barrage.

Donnelda Lyons lay dead, slumped in the backseat, her hair and clothes littered with shotgun shells. She had a shotgun blast in the left rear skull and the left and right chest. When the shooting started, Donnelda had apparently wrapped her body around her child. Christopher lay between her legs, still in her arms, killed by a single blast which shattered his skull.

Theresa Tyson, miraculously, had been hit only once in the right hip. She made her way out of the car and crawled away from the carnage. Her body was not found until more than a week later, several hundred feet away, so badly decomposed the exact cause of death could not be determined. The coroner says Theresa probably bled to death. She was apparently trying to reach the highway when she died.

The five fugitives bumped along in the small Mazda. They stopped briefly to pick up some spray paint and the boys transformed the Lyonses' car from orange to silver-gray. But it was just a matter of time before the Lyons family was discovered and the Mazda became the focus of the manhunt. The Tisons needed a new car.

On August 2, 1978, around 9:00 at night, in a sparsely populated neighborhood outside of Flagstaff, Arizona, Kathleen Ermentraut walked outside to see why her dog was barking. She thought she saw a small car in the next driveway but could not see any people. She started back toward the house when she heard a voice say, "Kathy."

"I stopped dead in my tracks," she says. "It was very dark. . . . The voice came again. I said, 'Randy, is that you?'"

Kathy Ermentraut supported her three grandchildren with a newspaper route. She had met the twenty-five-year-old Randy Greenawalt five years earlier when her son was in prison with him. For about a year she wrote to Randy as a mother. "And then it just got deeper and deeper," she says. "I guess I would be what you call in love with him."

Randy convinced Kathy to take out a loan to buy them another car. The next day, he returned to Kathy's house with Donny Tison. Randy stayed home with two of the grandchildren while Kathy, Donny, and a third grandchild went into town. Donny picked out a used dark blue 1970 Chevy pickup truck, and waited with Kathy's grandchild while she went to the bank to arrange financing. She then went home to deliver her newspapers.

Later that night Kathy drove down Slayton Road with a cache of ammunition in her car. By prearrangement, she began to slow when she saw the headlights of a car blink three times. Just as her car rolled to a stop, Randy stepped out of the darkness. Kathy handed him the ammunition. Then, Kathy recalls, "Somebody said, 'Randy, it's time to go.' Another voice said, 'Don't tell anybody or we will get you.'" Randy walked out of sight.

Sometime in the next week, probably after August 8, the fugitives switched vehicles again. August 8 is the day a young Texas couple, James and Margene Judge, disappeared. James and Margene had just been married on Saturday, August 5, and left in their blue-and-silver van for a honeymoon camping trip in Colorado. Margene's father gave her a one-hundred-dollar bill as a gift right before she left. On August 8, Margene called her parents from South Fork, Colorado, and told them that she and James would spend a few days fishing there. A clerk at the Foothill supermarket in South Fork remembered having a conversation with Margene that day. Later the same day Randy Greenawalt and Raymond and Ricky Tison entered the same store. The clerk remembered them because Randy looked especially bedraggled and none of the men bought anything.

On August 9 Randy, Ricky, and Raymond entered the Bayfield Sure Value supermarket, a few miles down the highway from South Fork. They bought three cartons of cigarettes with a one-hundred-dollar bill. The bodies of Margene and James Judge were found four months later just outside of Bayfield, each killed by a single gunshot to the head at close range. The Tisons and Randy Greenawalt were never charged with the murder of the newlyweds, but when law enforcement officials finally caught up with the fugitives they were in James and Margene's van.

At an intersection south of Casa Grande, Arizona, around 1:00 A.M., police sergeant Valenzuela and deputy sheriffs Wade Williams, Steve Grebb, and William Jewell spread their patrol cars across the road. The police had gotten a tip that the Tisons and Greenawalt might be headed south across the border. The four officers saw headlights and could make out a blue-and-silver van, but were not concerned. They were looking for a Mazda. As the van slowed, Jewell approached on the driver's side and Valenzuela on the passenger side.

Donny was driving with Ricky next to him in the front seat. Raymond was asleep in the back of the van when he heard Donny call out that patrol cars were up ahead. Gary told Donny to slow down as if he was going to stop, and then to ram the roadblock. Donny slowed and the officers approached.

"Run it!" Gary Tison yelled.

Donny hesitated. There did not really seem to be any point anymore.

"Run it!" Gary screamed again and Donny jammed his foot down on the accelerator. Gary grabbed a rifle and Randy a .257 Magnum. They knocked out the back window and started shooting.

When the van ran through the roadblock, the officers dove for cover. William Jewell was first into his car and sped off in pursuit. Wade Williams jumped into his car, with Steve Grebb loading his rifle in the passenger seat. Valenzuela radioed for help. Jewell, with both hands gripped to the steering wheel and speeding along at nearly a hundred miles per hour, caught up with the van but could not return fire. In the car behind him, Steve Grebb was leaning out of the passenger window, rifle in hand.

Williams flew past Jewell, and Grebb opened fire. The high-speed gun battle lasted for several miles. Then, when the van passed the crest of a hill and Grebb could not see the road ahead, he pulled back. He knew there was a second roadblock. As the van barreled down the slope on the other side of the hill, four officers stood in the road, legs braced in a firing position, squeezing off rounds point-blank into the van.

Randy and Gary were still shooting out of the back window. Raymond lay on the floor of the van and Ricky, in the front passenger seat, lunged for cover. Somehow Donny, blinded by headlights and ducking a barrage of bullets, drove the van in between the patrol cars on the road and cleared the roadblock. Then the van swerved suddenly to the right. It skidded to a stop in a swirl of gravel and dust. Donny had been shot several times in the head. He fell forward onto the steering wheel and then sideways onto his brother. Ricky, splattered with Donny's blood, struggled to get up. Although he was by far the oldest and slowest of the five, Gary Tison was the first out of the van. Without looking back, he shouted, "Every man for himself!" and vanished into the desert.

When the van went off the road, Wade Williams slammed on his brakes and the patrol car skidded sideways. As the headlights swerved to the right across the desert, they caught the outline of a figure running. Steve Grebb leaned out of the window and fired a single shot. The figure fell to the ground.

Donny Tison lay unconscious but still breathing in the front seat of the van. Wade Williams cuffed him while William Jewell pulled out his wallet. Only then did the officers realize they had caught up with the "Tison gang."

The police turned their alley lights, those atop the patrol car, onto the area around the van. A police helicopter swept in, scanning the desert with its spotlight. The beam from the helicopter caught the outlines of three men lying prone. Ricky and Raymond lay side by side a few yards from the van. Randy was alone a little farther out.

Through bullhorns, the police ordered the man lying nearest to come in with hands above his head. Ricky Tison, shirtless and covered with blood, obeyed. The officers cuffed Ricky and asked him if he was hurt. "I'm okay," he said. "That's my brother's blood. He needs help."

Raymond came in next. As they were cuffing him, he told the police he was armed. An officer pulled John Lyons's .38 revolver from inside Raymond's shirt. Neither of the Tisons resisted. In fact, the police said later, they seemed scared. Two officers went out and brought Randy in. They took two guns from him and found two more where Ricky and Raymond had been lying. None of the three was hurt; they had simply dropped to the ground when Steve Grebb fired.

Raymond, Ricky, and Randy were separated, stripped naked, cuffed at the wrists and ankles, and interrogated for five hours. Paramedics came around 2:00 A.M., but they were not allowed to go to Donny until daybreak, by which time he was dead. Gary Tison remained at large for more than a week. He was finally found in the desert, dead of exposure and dehydration. A sock full of dried-out cactus berries and John Lyons's .45 lay beside his body.

Raymond, Ricky, and Randy Greenawalt were tried together for the escape and the shootout at the roadblock. They were convicted and sentenced to thirty years to life for assault with a deadly weapon. They also got four to five years on each of several lesser charges.

The three were tried separately for the murder of the Lyons family. Randy stood trial as the actual triggerman. Raymond and Ricky were to be tried under the old but still widely used "felony-murder" doctrine.

Under the law of felony-murder, a person who commits a felony is liable for *any* death that occurs during the felony, regardless of whether that person actually did the killing. Each state has its own rules regarding felony-murder. For example, some states charge the felony-murderer with a lesser degree of murder than the actual triggerman. Other states vary the charges depending on what kind of felony is involved. In Arizona, all participants in a kidnapping or robbery are held legally responsible for the acts of their accomplices. Thus Raymond and Ricky, as participants in the felonies of kidnapping and armed robbery, could be just as liable as Randy Greenawalt for the murder of the Lyons family. In addition, Arizona allows the death penalty for felony-murder.

Faced with the likelihood of a death sentence, Raymond and Ricky agreed to a plea bargain. They would testify against Randy Greenawalt in exchange for a life sentence. They gave detailed statements to the prosecutor and to Randy's attorney regarding the murder of the Lyons family. The boys thought their testimony would be limited to that incident, but unexpectedly the prosecutor began asking Raymond questions about the prison break and how it was planned. Raymond refused to answer.

"I had no idea you were going to be asking about other people involved, about the escape," he said. "I thought it was just going to be [the murder]. But that's it, I'm not involving nobody else." He refused to say any more.

Although the brothers had not told their attorneys, Dorothy had helped plan the prison break. With their father and brother already dead, the boys now refused to implicate their mother. The plea bargain was withdrawn.

Raymond's and Ricky's trials were swift. Gary's brother, Joe, took the stand in each and testified against his nephews. He identified himself as a marijuana salesman and explained how he obtained the getaway car for the escape. Several prison guards and police officers testified about the breakout and violent capture. A stream of experts outlined the details of the Lyonses' deaths and described the Tisons' enormous arsenal. The prosecutor emphasized that the boys fled the murder scene and remained with the killers for ten days. No one could tie Raymond or Ricky to the actual act of killing, but the Arizona felony-murder law was explained very carefully to the jury. Raymond and Ricky were found guilty of felony-murder and sentenced to death.

The death penalty was not, as is commonly expressed, "abolished" by the Supreme Court in 1972 and "reinstated" in 1976. A majority of the Supreme Court has never held that the death penalty is "cruel and unusual punishment" per se under the Eighth Amendment. Rather, in a 1972 case, *Furman v. Georgia*, a majority of the Court held that capital punishment, *as it was then administered*, violated the Eighth Amendment.

In *Furman*, Justices Brennan and Marshall concluded that all capital punishment was unconstitutional. Three concurring justices focused on the arbitrary way in which the death penalty was imposed. They pointed out that in most states there were no guidelines for the sentencer to follow. Judges and juries had unlimited discretion in deciding when to impose a sentence of death. "People live or die, dependent on the whim of one man or of twelve," Justice Douglas wrote. The result, according to these justices, was that the death penalty was meted out unfairly; there was no meaningful distinction between those who were spared and those who were sentenced to die. As Justice Stewart wrote: "These death sentences are cruel and unusual in the same way that being struck by lightning is cruel and unusual . . . the [Eighth Amendment] cannot tolerate the infliction of a sentence of death under legal systems that permit this unique penalty to be so wantonly and freakishly imposed."

In response to *Furman*, thirty-five states passed new death penalty statutes designed to comply with the new constitutional ruling. One of these revamped statutes reached the Supreme Court in the 1976 case *Gregg v. Georgia*. Troy Gregg had been convicted on two counts of armed robbery and murder and sentenced to death. The Supreme Court, by a vote of seven to two, upheld the death sentence. The Court concluded that the new Georgia statute eliminated the arbitrary and capricious elements that the *Furman* decision had found unconstitutional. The new statute required the sentencing jury to make specific findings regarding the aggravating and mitigating circumstances of the crime, and provided an automatic appeal to the Georgia Supreme Court, which would compare the death sentence to the sentences imposed in other similar cases.

More important, the *Gregg* Court pointed out that *Furman* had not squarely answered the question of whether the death penalty is always "cruel and unusual punishment." "We now hold," the Court wrote, "that the punishment of death does not invariably violate the Constitution."

The Court then had to decide the standard by which the death penalty in a given situation was to be judged. When is it constitutional for the government to kill a man or woman? The answer was not limited to notions of "cruelty" existing at the time the Bill of Rights was drafted. Rather, the Court said, "The Amendment must draw its meaning from the evolving standards of decency that mark the progress of a maturing society."

To determine the standard of decency to which society had evolved, the Court looked for guidance to two institutions presumed to represent the will of the people: state legislatures and juries. Thirty-five new state death penalty statutes and countless death sentences from juries indicated to the Court "society's endorsement of the death penalty for murder."

The Court, however, declared that any punishment must also accord with the basic concept underlying the Eighth Amendment: "the dignity of man." A punishment cannot result merely in gratuitous suffering, but must serve a social purpose and be proportionate to the crime.

According to the Court, the death penalty serves two principal social goals: retribution and deterrence. The Court noted the bitter controversy over whether the death penalty acts to deter people from committing murder and decided to defer to the state legislatures in this area. As for retribution, the Court wrote, "In part, capital punishment is an expression of society's moral outrage at particularly offensive conduct. This function may be unappealing to many, but it is essential in an ordered society that asks its citizens to rely on legal proceedings rather than self-help to vindicate their wrongs."

Applying the standard of legislative and jury reaction and the twin objectives of deterrence and retribution, the Court found that the death penalty in the case of Troy Gregg did not violate the Eighth Amendment's prohibition against cruel and unusual punishment. A year later, the Supreme Court used the same standard to declare the death penalty a cruel and unusual punishment for the crime of rape when no life is taken. Then in 1982, in *Enmund v. Florida*, a case that would loom large in the *Tison* decision, the Court measured the ancient felony-murder rule against the still "evolving standards of decency."

Enmund v. Florida was a classic felony-murder case: Enmund was driving the getaway car. Earl Enmund and Sampson and Jeanette Armstrong set out to rob the Kerseys, an elderly couple given to bragging about how much cash they kept in their home. While Enmund waited in the car, the Armstrongs, both armed, went to the back door of the Kersey house. They asked for water for an overheated car. When Mr. Kersey came out of the house to help, Sampson Armstrong pulled his gun and demanded Kersey's money. Mr. Kersey screamed. His wife came out of the house, gun in hand, and opened fire, wounding Jeanette Armstrong. The Armstrongs then killed the Kerseys, took their money, and ran to Enmund waiting in the car. Enmund helped them flee and dispose of the murder weapons. He was sentenced to death under Florida's felony-murder statute.

What did the "evolving standards of decency" say about the death penalty for someone like Enmund? The Supreme Court canvassed state statutes across the country and found that no more than one-third of them would allow a death sentence "solely because the defendant somehow participated in a robbery in the course of which a murder was committed." Turning to the actions of juries, the Court stated that American juries had rejected the death penalty for defendants who did not actually kill. Since 1955, not a single person who was convicted of felony-murder—but did not kill, attempt to kill, or intend to kill—had been executed. Only three such people were then on death row. The Court also noted that "the doctrine of felony murder has been abolished in England and India, severely restricted in Canada and a number of other Commonwealth countries, and is unknown in continental Europe."

Deterrence did not seem to be served in Enmund's case because he did not intend to kill, and because death occurred so rarely in a crime like Enmund's. The Court noted that only about half of one percent of robberies resulted in homicide. Whether retribution was served, the Court stated, depended on Enmund's personal culpability.

Criminal culpability is measured not only by individuals' *actions*, but also their *mental state* at the time of the crime. Their actions determine the level of their personal responsibility. Their mental state helps determine their degree of moral guilt. For example, under the law of some states, one who carefully plans and intentionally carries out a cold-blooded murder is presumed more blameworthy than one who kills in the heat of passion. In Enmund's case, the Court concluded, "Putting Enmund to death to avenge two killings that he did not commit and had no intention of committing or causing does not measurably contribute to the retributive end of ensuring that the criminal gets his just deserts." Enmund's death sentence was vacated.

Many thought the *Enmund* decision prohibited a death sentence for one who did not intend to kill. So, on appeal, Ricky's and Raymond's attorneys argued that the Tison brothers were like Earl Enmund—they did not kill or intend to kill, so they could not be put to death. The Arizona Supreme Court disagreed and upheld the death sentences.

In 1985, the Tisons appealed to the U.S. Supreme Court. In an unusual move, the Court took the case even though the Tisons had not exhausted all of their appeals in the courts below. The case would be a benchmark in identifying society's evolving standards of decency, asking not only what type of *crime*, but also what type of *person* warranted the death penalty.

The Supreme Court accepted that Raymond and Ricky Tison did *not* intend to kill as that term is understood in criminal law. Thus, the Court focused on the hard question: Under the Eighth Amendment, and in light of *Enmund*, may the state execute a person who did not kill, attempt to kill, or intend to kill? By a vote of five to four, the Court answered yes.

Earl Enmund, the Supreme Court said, not only had no intention of killing, but had no "culpable mental state" at all. On the other hand, the Court concluded Raymond and Ricky may have had a culpable mental state—reckless indifference to the value of human life.

"Reckless indifference to the value of human life may be every bit as shocking to the moral sense as an 'intent to kill,'" the Court wrote. By way of example, the Court suggested "the person who tortures another not caring whether the victim lives or dies, or the robber who shoots someone in the course of the robbery, utterly indifferent to [whether the victim dies]." The Court found that a person who was "recklessly indifferent to the value of human life" could deserve the death penalty.

Although it would be up to the trial court to decide whether the Tison brothers, in fact, exhibited such "reckless indifference," the Court indicated that there might be evidence to support that finding. It noted that the brothers "brought an arsenal of lethal weapons into the Arizona State Prison, which [they] then handed over to two convicted murderers, one of whom [they] knew had killed a prison guard in the course of a previous escape attempt." The Court thought it clear that Raymond and Ricky could foresee that someone might be killed during the felonies. It also emphasized that neither of the Tisons tried to help the victims "before, during or after the shooting." As the Court put it, Raymond and Ricky "chose to aid those whom [they] had placed in a position to kill rather than their victims."

The Tisons' case could be further distinguished from *Enmund*, the Court continued, because Earl Enmund played a minor role in his crime. Raymond and Ricky, on the other hand, were major participants in every stage of the felonies of kidnapping and armed robbery. Until the moment of the murders, their participation was indistinguishable from that of Gary Tison or Randy Greenawalt. The Court declared that the *Tison* case raised the issue of a special class of felony-murderers: those who were major participants in the felony and who exhibited a reckless indifference to the value of human life.

The Court did not undertake the same rigorous analysis it had in other cases, including *Enmund*, but did briefly canvass state felony-murder statutes across the country. It concluded that there was a consensus allowing the death penalty in circumstances like the Tisons'. The Court then sent the case back to the Arizona courts to determine whether Raymond and Ricky met the new standard of "major participation plus reckless indifference to human life." If so, they could be put to death.

Justice Brennan, writing in dissent, challenged the majority's method of canvassing the state statutes. He argued that the result was distorted because the Court's survey excluded states that have abolished the death penalty or authorized it only in circumstances very different from the Tison case. "When these jurisdictions are included," he wrote, "one discovers that approximately three-fifths of American jurisdictions do not authorize the death penalty for a nontriggerman absent a finding that he intended to kill."

In addition, the dissent criticized the majority for not evaluating the full range of evidence. The dissent argued that the single most important statistic remained unchanged since *Enmund:* no individual convicted of felony-murder in the last twenty-five years who did not kill, attempt to kill, or intend to kill had been executed. To the dissent, the cases of Earl Enmund and Ricky and Raymond Tison were the same "in every respect that mattered."

The dissent also challenged the Court's analysis of the "reckless indifference" standard, at least as it related to Raymond and Ricky Tison. "The Court offers as examples 'the person *who tortures* another not caring whether the victim lives or dies, or the robber *who shoots* someone in the course of the robbery, utterly indifferent to [whether the victim dies],'" Justice Brennan stated. "But the constitutionality of the death penalty for those individuals is no more relevant to this case than it was to *Enmund*, because this case, like *Enmund*, involves accomplices *who did not kill*."

Finally, the dissent took issue with the Court's application of the standard to the facts of the case. "For example," the dissent wrote, "while the Court has found that [Raymond and Ricky] made no effort prior to the shooting to assist the victims, the uncontradicted statements of both are that just prior to the shootings they were attempting to find a jug of water to give to the family." The dissent argued that there was no evidence that the brothers anticipated the Lyons family would be killed, or that they could have done anything to prevent the murders or help the victims afterward. The dissent also criticized the Court for ignoring a psychologist's statement that the brothers' actions may have been the result of "conditioning" by their father and a statement by a probation officer who, after reviewing the Tisons' case, concluded they should not be put to death.

Justice Brennan then restated his personal belief that the death penalty is, in all cases, cruel and unusual punishment. He thought that the Court's disagreement about the "reckless indifference" standard and how it applied to the Tisons was proof that it is not possible to formulate and apply such standards fairly to each individual case of murder. Justice Brennan felt that Ricky and Raymond's case "illustrates the enduring truth . . . that the tasks of identifying 'those characteristics of criminal homicides and their perpetrators which call for the death penalty, and [of] express[ing] these characteristics in language which can be *fairly* understood and applied by the sentencing authority appear to be . . . beyond present human ability.'"

Arizona uses a gas chamber to execute its condemned prisoners. All eighty-six death row inmates are housed in the Arizona State Penitentiary in the dusty little town of Florence. Preceded by miles of a flat highway through barren desert, the prison first looms up out of the dust in the form of extremely high chain-link fences topped by scrolls of barbed wire. Inside the fences are more fences and several guardhouses. Large, sand-colored buildings make up the main compound, where most of the prisoners live. The buildings are arranged around a courtyard of burnt-out grass, crisscrossing sidewalks, and a flagpole.

At the back of the courtyard is a small, two-room, rectangular gray-brick building with a flat roof. The smaller of the concrete rooms contains two cells, really just metal bars stuck around a metal bunk and a small cracked and stained porcelain sink.

The larger room contains what looks like an antiquated diving capsule, or part of a submarine, bolted to the floor and ceiling. It is big enough to hold only a large, square metal chair. Below the chair is a cannister. For an execution, the cannister contains cyanide pellets suspended over an ammonia mixture. The seat faces the hatchlike door. Behind it, curving around the sides of the capsule are small windows. In contrast to the dank cells in the adjacent room, the death chamber has a fresh coat of bright sky-blue paint. On the windows of the capsule are little blue-and-white print curtains that match the walls. Next to the capsule is a black wall phone without a dial, a direct line from the governor's office.

Fourteen days before a scheduled execution, the condemned prisoner is moved from his regular cell to a special unit just off death row. There he is under round-the-clock observation and is allowed little contact with others.

Twenty-four hours before the execution, the prisoner is moved to a cell in the death house. He may request a last meal and give the warden names of those he would like to invite to watch through the little windows. The prisoner can meet with the prison chaplain, who is also available, upon request, to meet with the family, attend the execution, and assist in the burial plans.

Six hours before the execution, the prisoner is allowed one noncontact visit with a family member or friend. He must talk to them through the cage. For the next five hours he can receive visits from his attorney and the chaplain.

Fifteen minutes before the execution, the condemned prisoner is strip-searched and given a pair of shorts to wear. Women are given a shirt as well. The prisoner is then put in the capsule, strapped in at the wrists, arms, ankles, legs, and across the chest, and the hatch is closed and sealed.

If the black telephone does not ring, a designated prison official pulls a lever that drops the cyanide pellets into the ammonia mixture in the cannister under the chair. The combination of cyanide and ammonia produces a poisonous gas that fills the chamber. "They last as long as they can hold their breath," according to a deputy warden, who has witnessed several executions. "It takes longer to clean it up than it does to kill them."

There has not been an execution in Arizona since 1963. Like many jurisdictions, Arizona has undergone a long back-and-forth process between the legislature and the courts, trying to pull its death penalty statute and individual capital sentences within the constitutional command. Several prisoners at the Arizona penitentiary have been moved to the special cells to begin preparations to die, but they have all received reprieves from the court before their execution dates.

Ricky and Raymond Tison live in a building outside the main compound. More fences and barbed wire and a secured checkpoint precede a very ordinary looking hallway. Administrative offices are to the right, death row to the left. Coming just around the corner from a set of standard institutional offices where people come and go in the normal course of a workday, death row looks like some kind of bizarre human-scale laboratory experiment.

Through a locked door is a short, glass-walled hallway, the first section of cellblock 6, or death row. The hallway is eerily quiet. Behind the glass on either side are the "pods": two small levels with two cells on the top and two underneath. Each cell-front has the customary bars with a solid metal door, painted either bright orange or blue, in the center. The door has a horizontal slash for meal trays. The cell is six by ten feet with a bunk, toilet, sink, and desk. A metal plate with air holes is bolted over the single window in the cell. Raymond and Ricky Tison live, as they have for more than a decade, in the same pod in side-by-side cells.

Arizona death row is for the most part a lock-down facility—many inmates spend twenty-three and a half hours a day in their cells. There is no common area and no cafeteria. Guards bring meals to the prisoners in their cells. Three times a week the prisoners are allowed out, one at a time, into an exercise pen and then into a single stall for a fifteen-minute shower.

Raymond and Ricky spent several years on lock-down but gradually earned, through good behavior, the right to have a job. Raymond works in the law library keeping the inventory up to date. He is paid forty cents an hour. "But then," he says, "I have no overhead." Ricky works as a "pod porter" for ten cents an hour. But his is the better job because he is out of his cell as often as three times a day to clean the pod and pick up meal trays. Raymond and Ricky are rarely allowed out of their cells together, but when one is on his way to a shower or work, he stops to talk with his brother through the barred window.

Ricky is taller, huskier, and more gregarious than Raymond. He has a pronounced overbite, which caused a stir at his murder trial because his face seems fixed in a grin even when he does not think anything is funny. Raymond is smaller and more thoughtful, his fingers yellowed from cigarettes.

They look much younger than their thirty and thirty-one years. "The strange thing about prison, it has a preserving effect," says Raymond. "Externally," says Ricky, "we don't have the same kinds of anxieties or pressures that people have to deal with on the street . . . we're in a controlled system."

Many prisoners, of course, rebel against the "control" of a penitentiary, constantly battling with the guards and administration. In a way, the brothers seem to have adapted to incarceration with the same strange equanimity with which they adapted to their father's prison status growing up. It is the way they cope with the day-to-day reality of death row.

"You have people who just freak out," Raymond says. "If you want to bang your head against the wall, go ahead, it's not going to bring you any closer to what you want. . . . After a time you learn to choose your battles more carefully. . . . Use your intelligence to get what you need."

"The best thing to do," says Ricky, "is to accept the fact that they wear the uniforms and you don't."

When asked about living under a sentence of death, Ricky and Raymond quickly sit forward, both talking at once. They say they do not want the death sentence emphasized. Their family—everyone—makes too much of it. They want to push it aside. "We even have that problem with our attorneys," Ricky says. "We perceive the death sentence . . ."

The rush of words stops. Ricky pauses, then finally, emphatically, says, "We don't feel as though we're going over to that little gray building. We actually *believe* we're going to get off death row."

"That's not an irrational belief," Raymond adds. "It's a belief based on our case . . . you're willing to accept blame for that which you deserve blame, but not for that which you don't."

Both brothers say it took them several years, but they have now "made peace with the past." Ricky sits silent, staring, while Raymond tries to explain. "You have to deal with having directly or indirectly caused so much harm in so many people's lives. That's what you think of when you're spending all this time. You ask why. If you've had faith in God you tend to lose faith in God.

"You know this is going to be your constant companion for the rest of your life, so you come to terms with it. You make your own peace and hope that at some point those others you've hurt will be able to forgive you. They're under no obligation whatsoever, and I will understand quite well. They are going to hate us probably for the rest of their lives and we can't blame them for that. They have a right to that.

"There's only one person who could answer the question of

why any of that had to happen and he's dead," Raymond continues. When his lawyer counsels him not to get into specific aspects of their crime, Raymond cuts him off, angry for the first time. "I'm not going to talk about the facts of the case, but I want to say this, just in reference to Dad.

"I have a lot of anger towards him. You know, I've come to realize who he was and what he was all about. And that . . ." Raymond looks for words and then for a long time blinks back tears. Finally, he asks if he can talk about something else.

Raymond and Ricky say what keeps them going every day is "the will to survive and Sunday-morning visits." Dorothy Tison visits her sons for two hours each week. Raymond and Ricky sit in side-by-side visitor's booths, phones in hand. Dorothy sits on the other side of the glass partition, across from her sons, balancing two phones. It is the same prison that used to house Gary Tison and from which his sons helped him to make his fatal escape. Each Sunday, Dorothy Tison continues her trips to visit her incarcerated family, second generation.

When the *Tison* case was remanded to the Arizona court for resentencing under the new "major participation and reckless indifference to human life" standard, the original trial judge simply applied the new standard to the old record and imposed the death penalty again. The Tisons appealed to the Arizona Supreme Court. In 1988, it held that the brothers were entitled to a new, full evidentiary hearing to determine whether their actions and mental state at the time of the crime met the Supreme Court standard set forth in their case.

By many accounts, Raymond and Ricky appear to have been "major participants" in the felonies of kidnapping and armed robbery. But whether the new judge who resentences the brothers decides they also exhibited a "reckless indifference to the value of human life" will depend in part on how he chooses to view the facts: two young men who broke a known killer out of prison, armed him and another convicted murderer with an arsenal of weapons, willingly aided the escapees in the abduction of a family, and made no effort to stop the killings or help the victims afterward; or two young men, boys really, blinded by loyalty to their father, who not only did not kill, attempt to kill, or intend to kill, but participated in the felonies with the understanding that no one would be hurt, and then got caught up in events beyond their control.

TABLE 1

DEATH PENALTY DISPOSITIONS SINCE JANUARY 1, 1973*

Executions	115
Suicides	27
Commutations	51
Died of natural causes or killed while on death row	44
Sentences vacated under unconstitutional statutes	559
Convictions/sentences reversed on other grounds	935

*The year after *Furman v. Georgia.*
SOURCE: NAACP Legal Defense and Educational Fund, Inc. (as of July 1989).

TABLE 2

State	Method of Execution	Number of Death Row Inmates
Alabama	Electrocution	93
Arizona	Gas chamber	86
Arkansas	Lethal injection or electrocution*	31
California	Gas chamber	247
Colorado	Lethal injection	3
Connecticut	Electrocution	1
Delaware	Lethal injection or hanging†	7
Florida	Electrocution	294
Georgia	Electrocution	102
Idaho	Lethal injection or firing squad	16
Illinois	Lethal injection	120
Indiana	Electrocution	50
Kentucky	Electrocution	28
Louisiana	Electrocution	39
Maryland	Gas chamber	19
Mississippi	Gas chamber	45
Missouri	Lethal injection	73
Montana	Hanging or lethal injection	10
Nebraska	Electrocution	13
Nevada	Lethal injection	45
New Jersey	Lethal injection	25
New Mexico	Lethal injection	2
North Carolina	Gas chamber or lethal injection	81

*Choice for those sentenced before March 4, 1983.
†Choice for those sentenced before June 13, 1986.

Ohio	Electrocution	92
Oklahoma	Lethal injection	98
Oregon	Lethal injection	15
Penn-sylvania	Electrocution	115
South Carolina	Electrocution	46
Tennessee	Electrocution	69
Texas	Lethal injection	283
Utah	Firing squad or lethal injection	8
Virginia	Electrocution	40
Washington	Lethal injection	7
Wyoming	Lethal injection	2
Federal jurisdictions (U.S. military)	Lethal injection	5
TOTAL		2210

NINTH AMENDMENT

"The enumeration in the Constitution, of certain rights, shall not be construed to deny or disparage others retained by the people."

10ᵗʰ and 11ᵗʰ incorporated.

ARTICLE the ELEVENTH.

No appeal to the Supreme Court of the United States, shall be allowed, where the value in controversy shall not amount to one thousand dollars, nor shall any fact, triable by a jury according to the course of the common law, be otherwise re-examinable, than *in any Courts of the U.S.* according to the rules of common law. *a*

ARTICLE the TWELFTH.

where the Value in controversy shall exceed twenty dollars

In suits at common law, the right of trial by jury shall be preserved. *a*

ARTICLE the THIRTEENTH.

Excessive bail shall not be required, nor excessive fines imposed, nor cruel and unusual punishments inflicted. *a*

ARTICLE the FOURTEENTH.

No State shall infringe the right of trial by jury in criminal cases, nor the right of conscience, nor the freedom of speech, or of the press. *dele*

ARTICLE the FIFTEENTH.

The enumeration in the Constitution of certain rights, shall not be construed to deny or disparage others retained by the people. *a*

ARTICLE the SIXTEENTH.

The powers delegated by the Constitution to the government of the United States, shall be exercised as therein appropriated, so that the Legislative shall never exercise the powers vested in the Executive or Judicial; nor the Executive the powers vested in the Legislative or Judicial; nor the Judicial the powers vested in the Legislative or Executive. *dele* *not a*

ARTICLE the SEVENTEENTH.

to the U.S.

The powers not delegated by the Constitution, nor prohibited by it, to the States, are reserved to the States respectively, *or to the People* *a*

Teste,

J O H N   B E C K L E Y, Clerk.

In Senate, *August* 25, 1789.

Read and ordered to be printed for the consideration of the Senate.

Attest,   SAMUEL A. OTIS, Secretary.

*A*n early draft of the Ninth Amendment, appearing here as
ARTICLE THE FIFTEENTH

Rights Retained by the People: Privacy

THE BILL OF RIGHTS, WHICH Franklin D. Roosevelt called "the great American charter of personal liberty and human dignity," is less than four hundred words long. It is clear that the Founders recognized no single document could include all of the rights of the American people and so, after creating the list of specific rights in the first eight amendments, they drafted the Ninth. It is not at all clear, however, what the Ninth Amendment means.

It declares, "The enumeration in the Constitution, of certain rights, shall not be construed to deny or disparage others retained by the people." Because it speaks of "other" rights, the Ninth Amendment necessarily raises the questions: what exactly are these other rights and, more important, who decides? For example, many Americans believe they have a "right to privacy" against the government. But the word *privacy* never appears in the Constitution. Can a right that is not specifically named in that document be constitutionally protected? Though it may seem an abstract question, the answer implicates crucial issues involving the government's role in a woman's decision to have a baby or an abortion, or a man's decision to engage in homosexual activity in the bedroom of his home. Curiously, the Ninth Amendment, which by its very language raises the question of "unenumerated rights," as they are called, has remained largely on the sidelines in a fierce controversy played out in other parts of the Constitution.

To protect fundamental rights not specifically mentioned in the Constitution, courts have long looked to the Fifth and Fourteenth amendments, which declare that an American may not be deprived of "life, liberty, or property, without due process of law." Originally, the focus under the clause was on the *procedure* used to deprive one of life, liberty, or property. But in the early twentieth century, courts began to give the word *liberty* substantive content. By the 1950s the due process clause had been interpreted to protect many unenumerated rights—from a student's right to study a foreign language, to a criminal suspect's right to refuse to allow the police to pump his stomach for evidence. Giving substance to the right of "liberty" in this way is known as substantive due process (as opposed to "procedural" due process). It is said to cover rights that are "deeply rooted in this Nation's history and tradition" and "implicit in the concept of ordered liberty such that neither liberty nor justice would exist if [they] were sacrificed."

Critics argue that because substantive due process is not bound to a specific constitutional provision other than the open-ended concept of "liberty," it gives judges license to impose their personal beliefs on the Constitution, creating and striking down laws at will. As Justice Holmes wrote when the debate was just beginning, "I see hardly any limit but the sky to the invalidating of [state laws] if they happen to strike a majority of this Court as for any reason undesirable." A fundamental principle in the structure of U.S. government is that legislatures, elected by the people and therefore presumably most directly accountable to them, are empowered by the Constitution to create law. Thus, some argue that if the judicial branch instead assumes the power to create rights in the name of "liberty," it is acting like the legislature, thereby upsetting the balance of power so carefully created by the Framers. For example, why should nine justices, rather than state legislatures, decide what is or is not covered by the ambiguous notion of privacy? According to Chief Justice Rehnquist, "It is basically unhealthy to have so much authority concentrated in a small group of lawyers who have been appointed to the Supreme Court and enjoy virtual life tenure."

In all the hullabaloo over rights not specifically listed in the Constitution, the Ninth Amendment was largely ignored. In fact, it became something of a joke. (During the confirmation hearings on Justice Rehnquist's nomination to be Chief Justice of the United States, one senator began a question on "unenumerated rights" by saying, "Do not smile when I refer to the Ninth Amendment.") But in 1965, in a case called *Griswold v. Connecticut*, a Supreme Court justice relied on the Ninth Amendment (albeit in a concurring opinion) to strike down a state statute dealing with contraceptive devices. *Griswold* soon became a landmark decision, staking out the arguments that would be batted about for the next twenty-five years in the highly charged debate over the existence of a constitutional right to privacy.

A Connecticut law made it a crime for any person to use a drug or instrument for the purpose of preventing conception, and for any person to assist or counsel another to do so. The law applied to married and unmarried persons alike. Anyone convicted under the law faced a fine of not less than fifty dollars or imprisonment for not less than sixty days, or both. In 1961, a member of the Planned Parenthood League of Connecticut and a New Haven physician were arrested for giving *married couples* information about contraceptive devices. They were fined one hundred dollars each.

Two concurring Supreme Court justices, Harlan and White, relied on the standards of substantive due process to strike down the Connecticut law. They argued that the right "to be free of regulation of the intimacies of the marriage relationship" was at least as compelling as rights previously protected under the due process clause, and that the state had shown no rational reason for its law. Justice Harlan was not troubled by the fear of unlimited judicial power in interpreting the due process clause. "'Specific' provisions of the Constitution, no less than 'due process,' lend themselves as readily to 'personal' interpretations by judges," he wrote. After all, the Court regularly answered equally difficult questions such as which searches were "unreasonable" under the Fourth Amendment or which punishments "cruel and unusual" under the Eighth.

The majority opinion, written by Justice Douglas, did not rely on the thorny substantive due process cases, but instead relied on a new theory that became, if possible, even more controversial. Justice Douglas pointed out that many rights that are not specifically mentioned in the Constitution, but are *derived* from specific provisions, have long been protected by the Court. For example, the right to associate with whomever one pleases and the right to educate a child in a school of a parent's choice are not mentioned anywhere in the Constitution. Yet the Court has construed the First Amendment to protect those rights.

Thus, Justice Douglas concluded in a famous line, "Specific guarantees in the Bill of Rights have penumbras, formed by emanations from those guarantees that help give them life and substance." In other words, there exist certain buffer zones around each constitutional provision that prohibit the government from doing something not in itself prohibited by a specific provision of the Constitution. Justice Douglas wrote that although the right to privacy is not specifically mentioned, several of the first ten amendments create buffer zones of privacy: the right to free association derived from the First Amendment; the Third Amendment's prohibition on quartering troops in the home; the Fourth Amendment's declaration that the people shall be "secure in their persons, houses, papers and effects"; the Fifth Amendment's self-incrimination clause; and the Ninth Amendment's enigmatic reference to retained rights. Indeed, the overall scheme of the Bill of Rights could be viewed as affirming a fundamental right to privacy for the American people.

"We deal with a right of privacy older than the Bill of Rights," Justice Douglas concluded. He then raised the alarming image of actual enforcement of the Connecticut law. "Would we allow the police to search the sacred precincts of marital bedrooms for telltale signs of the use of contraceptives?" he asked.

Finally, Justice Arthur Goldberg (joined by Chief Justice Warren and Justice Brennan) wrote a separate opinion to explain, for the first time by a Supreme Court justice, the special role the Ninth Amendment must play. He began with the amendment's history. There is scant legislative history on the Ninth Amendment because it passed the House and Senate with little debate. But it had been generally accepted that the Ninth was Madison's answer to the charge that a Bill of Rights could never be comprehensive enough to protect all fundamental rights. Many who opposed the idea of a Bill of Rights did so not because they thought the specified rights should not be protected, but because they feared that a list of specific rights would be interpreted to mean other rights that were not mentioned were therefore *not* protected. Alexander Hamilton went so far as to write, "Bills of rights . . . are not only unnecessary in the proposed constitution, but would even be dangerous."

So in presenting the Ninth Amendment to Congress, Madison said: "It has been objected also against a bill of rights, that, by enumerating particular exceptions to the grant of power . . . it might follow by implication, that those rights which were not singled out, were intended to be assigned into the hands of the General Government, and were consequently insecure. This is one of the most plausible arguments I have ever heard urged against the admission of a bill of rights into this system; but I conceive, that it may be guarded against. I have attempted it, as gentlemen may see by turning to the last clause of the fourth resolution [the Ninth Amendment]."

Thus, Justice Goldberg argued, to hold that a "right of privacy in marriage" is not protected by the Constitution simply because it is not listed in the first eight amendments is to ignore the Ninth. He was careful to say that the Ninth Amendment is not, as some commentators feared, a "bottomless well" in which judges could simply "find" rights. Rather, it is a guide to interpreting the Constitution, which lent support to the argument that the due process clause and "penumbras" from the other amendments in the Bill of Rights protected a right to privacy.

Not to find such a right, Justice Goldberg argued, would allow the government to regulate family size without constitutional challenge. "Surely the Government . . . could not decree that all husbands and wives must be sterilized after two children have been born to them," he wrote. Justice Goldberg acknowledged that some may be "shocked" by the Court's holding that the Constitution protects marital privacy, but said, "It is far more shocking to believe that the personal liberty guaranteed by the Constitution does not include protection against such totalitarian limitation of family size." He declared the right of privacy in the marital relation to be one of the rights "retained by the people" under the Ninth Amendment.

The two dissenting justices, Black and Stewart, attacked the very concept of unenumerated constitutional rights, whether found in the penumbras of amendments, the due process clause, the Ninth Amendment, or some combination of those theories and provisions. With respect to Justice Goldberg's unprecedented reliance on the Ninth Amendment, the dissent merely found it to be substantive due process in different garb.

The two dissenting justices also disagreed with Justice Goldberg's historical interpretation of the Ninth Amendment. "To say that the Ninth Amendment has anything to do with this case is to turn somersaults with history," they wrote. They agreed with the general proposition that the Ninth Amendment was meant to address concerns about a limited list of rights. It was the next step in the analysis that they disagreed with. The dissenting justices pointed to the identical Madison passage used by Justice Goldberg to reach a very different conclusion. They argued that the Ninth Amendment was never intended to give judges the power to construe the Constitution so as to find unenumerated rights protected there. Instead, the Ninth Amendment was simply to make clear that by listing certain exceptions to the grant of power to the federal government, the Framers did not intend that unspecified rights "be assigned into the hands of the General Government [the United States]." The Ninth Amendment was not a grant of power to judges, but a restatement of the basic tenet that the power of the federal government be limited.

Justice Stewart summed up the dissent's position on the anti-contraception statute at issue in *Griswold:* "I think this is an uncommonly silly law. . . . But we are not asked in this case to say whether we think this law is unwise, or even asinine. We are asked to hold that it violates the United States Constitution. And that I cannot do."

After *Griswold*, the Ninth Amendment flourished for the first time. It was invoked by schoolboys who wanted to wear long hair, fundamentalists who wanted to challenge school textbooks, felons seeking to avoid imprisonment in the maximum security section of a penitentiary, and groups who claimed a right to a healthful environment. Courts for the first time wrote of "Ninth Amendment rights."

Commentators and scholars, abruptly confronted with courts actually putting the Ninth Amendment to use, were forced to take note. Some concluded that the "rights retained by the people" under the Ninth were not a mysterious, unspecified group to be discovered, one by one, by judges. Instead, "retained rights" were simply those specifically set out in places other than the Constitution—that is, in state statutes, state constitutions, and the common law. One scholar wrote, "Surely, if a mandate to judges had been intended, matters could have been put more clearly. James Madison . . . could easily have drafted an amendment that said something like 'The courts shall determine what rights, in addition to those enumerated here, are retained by the people.'" To some, the Ninth Amendment stood for no more than the unremarkable proposition that rights not listed in the Constitution had not been handed over to the government.

In contrast, other commentators argued that it should not be presumed that an entire provision in the Bill of Rights had almost no meaning. Some picked up on Justice Goldberg's view of the Ninth Amendment as a rule of construction. One scholar pointed out that "only the Ninth Amendment is directly and avowedly addressed to the very subject of how the Constitution is to be construed." Thus, the Amendment lends strong support to the proposition that there are individual rights that may be derived from "liberty" or the structure of the Bill of Rights, and that such rights should be protected by the Constitution. There was no reason to believe that judges would be any less responsible in this area of constitutional interpretation than in any other. The fact that there were bona fide disputes about exactly which rights were constitutionally protected "shows only that constitutional interpretation (unsurprisingly) leaves room for argument."

Despite the flurry of Ninth Amendment activity in the lower courts and legal literature, the Supreme Court did not resolve the disputes, nor even shed much light on them. After *Griswold*, the Ninth Amendment began to fade from Supreme Court jurisprudence. The right to privacy continued to unsettle the courts and the public more than any other "unenumerated right," but the Ninth Amendment (and the penumbra theory) were eclipsed by the due process clause.

In 1970, in *Roe v. Wade*, a Texas district court, relying in part on *Griswold*, struck down a state statute prohibiting abortions unless necessary to save the mother's life. The district court even wrote of a "Ninth Amendment right to have an abortion." By a vote of seven to two, the Supreme Court upheld the lower court decision. It did not, however, accept this invitation to dramatically increase the Ninth Amendment's reach.

Instead, the Court relied on the due process clause. "This right of privacy," the Court wrote, "whether it be founded in the Fourteenth Amendment's concept of personal liberty and restrictions upon state action, *as we feel it is*, or, as the District Court determined, in the Ninth Amendment's reservation of rights to the people, is broad enough to encompass a woman's decision whether or not to terminate her pregnancy" (emphasis added). The Ninth Amendment had gone from prominence in a concurring opinion to a "hedge" in less than ten years.

In the next important Supreme Court test of the right to privacy, the Ninth Amendment nearly vanished. In August 1982, an Atlanta police officer arrested Michael Hardwick for engaging in sodomy with a consenting male adult in the bedroom of his own home. Hardwick claimed that the constitutional right to privacy protected private sexual activity and that the Georgia law criminalizing sodomy (whether between homosexual, heterosexual, married, or unmarried persons) was therefore unconstitutional. The district court agreed. Relying in large part on *Griswold* and another case, *Stanley v. Georgia*, in which the Supreme Court held that the state could not make it a crime to possess obscene material in the privacy of one's own home, it struck down the sodomy law.

The Supreme Court, by a vote of five to four, reversed. The manner in which the majority and dissent each characterized the case showed just how far apart they were in this area. The majority declared, "The issue presented is whether the Federal Constitution confers a fundamental right upon homosexuals to engage in sodomy." The dissent countered, "This case is no more about a 'fundamental right to engage in homosexual sodomy' . . . than *Stanley v. Georgia* was about a fundamental right to watch obscene movies. . . . Rather, this case is about 'the most comprehensive of rights and the right most valued by civilized men,' namely, 'the right to be let alone.'"

The majority conceded that "the cases are legion" in which the due process clause was given substantive content, including the right to privacy. But the Court restated the standard to be applied and wrote, "To claim that a right to engage in [homosexual sodomy] is 'deeply rooted in this Nation's history and tradition' or 'implicit in the concept of ordered liberty' is, at best, facetious." The Ninth Amendment did not appear at all in the majority opinion. The dissent mentioned it in a passing reference to *Griswold.*

In 1989, an angry and bitterly divided Supreme Court decided *Webster v. Reproductive Health Services.* By a vote of five to four, the Court upheld a Missouri statute that placed restrictions on abortion, including a requirement that before performing an abortion on a woman twenty or more weeks pregnant, a doctor must first determine whether the fetus is "viable." The opinions focused on *Roe* and on due process and the right to privacy in general. The Ninth Amendment, however, had vanished.

In the wake of *Webster,* the future of the constitutional "right to privacy" is uncertain. And it appears that, for the moment at least, the Ninth Amendment has no role to play. The Court has moved away from any kind of consensus on the right to privacy, and even farther away from any resolution about the meaning of the Ninth Amendment. Still, a shadow from *Griswold* and lower-court opinions remains. Thus, Chief Justice Rehnquist's statement at the outset of the privacy debate, nearly two decades ago when the Ninth Amendment was still in the fray, remains apt for not only the privacy controversy, but also for the peculiar plight of the Ninth Amendment. The Court, Chief Justice Rehnquist wrote, has accomplished "the seemingly impossible feat of leaving this area of the law more confused than it found it."

TENTH AMENDMENT

"The powers not delegated to the United States by the Constitution, nor prohibited by it to the States, are reserved to the States respectively, or to the people."

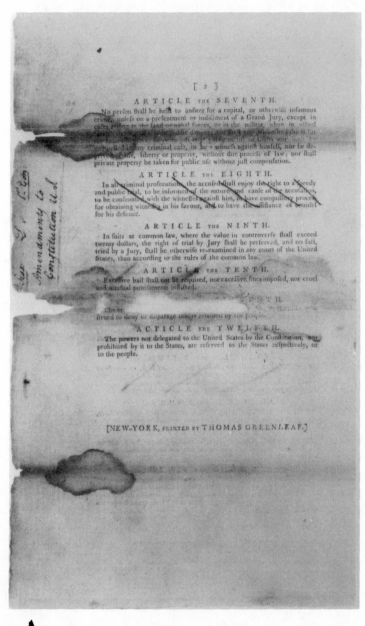

[2]

ARTICLE the SEVENTH.

No person shall be held to answer for a capital, or otherwise infamous crime, unless on a presentment or indictment of a Grand Jury, except in cases arising in the land or naval forces, or in the militia, when in actual service in time of war or public danger; nor shall any person be subject for the same offence to be twice put in jeopardy of life or limb; nor shall be compelled in any criminal case, to be a witness against himself, nor be deprived of life, liberty or property, without due process of law; nor shall private property be taken for public use without just compensation.

ARTICLE the EIGHTH.

In all criminal prosecutions, the accused shall enjoy the right to a speedy and public trial, to be informed of the nature and cause of the accusation, to be confronted with the witnesses against him, to have compulsory process for obtaining witnesses in his favour, and to have the assistance of counsel for his defence.

ARTICLE the NINTH.

In suits at common law, where the value in controversy shall exceed twenty dollars, the right of trial by Jury shall be preserved, and no fact tried by a Jury, shall be otherwise re-examined in any court of the United States, than according to the rules of the common law.

ARTICLE the TENTH.

Excessive bail shall not be required, nor excessive fines imposed, nor cruel and unusual punishments inflicted.

ARTICLE the ELEVENTH.

The enumeration in the Constitution, of certain rights, shall not be construed to deny or disparage others retained by the people.

ARTICLE the TWELFTH.

The powers not delegated to the United States by the Constitution, nor prohibited by it to the States, are reserved to the States respectively, or to the people.

[NEW-YORK, PRINTED BY THOMAS GREENLEAF.]

*A*n early draft of the Tenth Amendment, appearing here as
ARTICLE THE TWELFTH

Powers Reserved to the States: Minimum Wage

Some consider the Tenth Amendment to be a companion to the Ninth, stating a principle rather than providing a right. Others believe the Framers would not have included the Tenth Amendment if it merely expressed the "unremarkable" notion that the states should not be wholly devoured by the federal government. Instead, proponents of a strong Tenth Amendment claim it is a source of one of the most powerful forces in our nation's history: states' rights.

Although the principle of states' rights has been used for destructive purposes, it can also have a benevolent aspect. State governments represent the people more directly than the federal government. At times, they have acted first and gone farther to protect the individual, while at other times the federal government has defended the people against the states. For example, around the turn of the century, states enacted laws to improve the horrendous working conditions of the time, only to have them struck down by the Supreme Court. Later, in the 1960s, the federal government, supported by the Supreme Court, took the lead in civil rights and social welfare legislation against strong state resistance, particularly in the effort to desegregrate the nation's schools. In some respects, the pendulum swung again twenty years later in the "Reagan Revolution" of the 1980s, when the federal government cut back its scope, and the Supreme Court limited certain individual rights. In response, some states looked to their own legislatures and constitutions as sources of greater protection than the federal government was willing to provide.

This system of government by both federal and state authority is called federalism. Each center of power prevents the other from becoming too strong, and individual freedom is thereby preserved. The structure of federalism is detailed not in the Tenth Amendment, but in article I of the Constitution, which lists the powers delegated to Congress and those prohibited to the states. One of Congress's Article I powers is the power to regulate "Commerce . . . among the several States." The question for the Tenth Amendment is whether, on behalf of the states, it can actively block Congress's exercise of this power, or whether the amendment is only a powerless parchment barrier.

James Madison, the "father of the Bill of Rights," described federalism as follows: "The powers delegated by the proposed Constitution to the Federal Government are few and defined. Those which are to remain in the State Governments are numerous and indefinite. The former will be exercised principally on external objects, as war, peace, negotiation and foreign commerce; . . . the powers reserved to the several States will extend to all the objects, which, in the ordinary course of affairs, concern the lives, liberties and prosperities of the people."

Today it is often difficult to perceive the federal government's powers as "few and defined," because when it acts within an area of delegated power, federal authority is complete—that is, until it collides with a state power, or individual right, protected by another part of the Constitution. The struggle between the commerce clause and the Tenth Amendment is one of these collisions. On the Supreme Court it has turned into a full-fledged battle. And while the structure of federalism may seem remote from the daily lives of most Americans, the battle has been fought where it often hits hardest, in our paychecks.

In the late nineteenth century, the Industrial Revolution sucked thousands of the impoverished and the new immigrants into brutal and dangerous working conditions in mines, mills, railroads, and factories. Twelve-hour workdays, six-day work-weeks, occupational injuries, and illness were common. So was child labor. In 1916, under its power to regulate interstate commerce, Congress passed a law prohibiting the transportation across state lines of goods manufactured in any mill, cannery, shop, or factory that employed children under fourteen, or children between fourteen and sixteen who worked more than eight hours a day, more than six days a week, or who worked night shifts. The law was challenged by a father and his two minor sons who risked losing their jobs in a North Carolina cotton mill.

Lawyers for the federal government argued that under the commerce clause, Congress had the power to ban child labor. "The evil effects on the child's physical well-being [are] not confined to the so-called dangerous occupations. Night work and excessive hours of labor indoors in factories . . . stunt the physique and decrease the resistance to disease. The child worker becomes dwarfed in body and mind, and the State is deprived of that vigorous citizenship on which the success of democracy must depend."

The federal government also argued that states that allowed child labor could charge lower prices for their goods, and thereby enjoyed an unfair economic advantage. Because a state that prohibited child labor could not determine which products from other states were made by children and forbid them to enter its territory, the federal government claimed that the only way to solve the problem was for Congress to prescribe a uniform national rule.

Opponents waved the banner of state sovereignty. They objected to federal interference. They argued that Congress's power to regulate "Commerce *among* the several States" extended only to *interstate* commerce. Any attempt to regulate conditions of manufacture *within* state boundaries was an abuse of that power.

In *Hammer v. Dagenhart*, decided in 1918, the Supreme Court agreed. It struck down the Child Labor Law, calling it "repugnant to the Constitution." The Court did not address the social policy behind the law, or the conditions that prompted its passage, but instead analyzed its effect on the structure of government. "This court has no more important function than . . . to preserve inviolate the constitutional limitations upon the exercise of authority, federal and state." The Court justified its action with an ominous warning about the danger of such legislation. "If Congress can thus regulate matters entrusted to local authority all freedom of commerce will be at an end, the power of the States over local matters may be eliminated, and thus our system of government may be practically destroyed."

Twenty years later, Congress again attempted to regulate labor conditions. By this time another massive economic transformation had occurred; and the Supreme Court was presented with another opportunity to define the evolving relationship between the federal government and the states. The Great Depression had thrown millions out of work, off their land, and onto relief. Franklin D. Roosevelt and the Democratic majority in Congress believed that the only way to remedy the national economic disaster was through a national economic recovery program. When Roosevelt and his fellow New Dealers looked to the Constitution for federal authority for their comprehensive program of economic legislation, they drew upon the commerce clause. But the Supreme Court read the Constitution differently. It struck down one after another of Roosevelt's laws, declaring them to be beyond the scope of Congress's commerce power and in violation of the Tenth Amendment. Roosevelt's frustration culminated in the court-packing plan of 1937. He proposed increasing the number of justices from nine to fifteen, thereby assuring a majority who would uphold his legislation. This constitutional crisis was narrowly averted by congressional rejection of the plan and by the retirement of one justice, allowing Roosevelt to form a new majority who upheld the important National Labor Relations Act.

In 1938, Congress passed the Fair Labor Standards Act, which mandated a minimum wage of twenty-five cents an hour and a higher overtime rate after forty-four hours of work. Since congressional authority once again stemmed from the commerce clause, the act actually prohibited the shipment in interstate commerce of goods manufactured by employees who received a subminimum wage. By prohibiting their shipment, Congress effectively outlawed their production as well, because goods that could only be sold in their home state were relatively useless.

A Georgia lumber manufacturer charged with numerous violations of the act objected that federal power over interstate commerce did not extend to the conditions of wholly local manufacture. Even if the goods were to be shipped out of state eventually, only the states could regulate working conditions within their own boundaries, he claimed. He argued that the power to regulate local employment was not within one of the federal government's enumerated powers, but was reserved to the states by the Tenth Amendment.

In 1941, in *United States v. Darby*, the Supreme Court disagreed. It overruled *Hammer v. Dagenhart* and stated, "The power of Congress over interstate commerce is complete in itself, may be exercised to its utmost extent, and acknowledges no limitations other than are prescribed in the Constitution." In response to the argument that the Tenth Amendment was such a limitation, the Court wrote, "The Amendment states but a truism that all is retained which has not been surrendered. There is nothing in the history of its adoption to suggest that it was more than declaratory of the relationship between the national and state governments as it had been established by the Constitution before the amendment." Many people assumed that after *Darby*, the Tenth Amendment was essentially dead, no longer capable of limiting congressional regulation of interstate commerce.

Both *Hammer* and *Darby* involved the regulation of private employers. But inevitably the Supreme Court was faced with the tougher question of whether the commerce clause allowed the federal government to regulate the states themselves (in the form of state governments).

In 1970, the country faced runaway inflation, President Nixon feared an economic disaster, and Congress authorized temporary wage and price controls. At the time, the minimum wage was sixty cents an hour. Increases in salaries, rents, dividends, and interest were to be limited to 5.5 percent. But the state of Ohio, claiming its Tenth Amendment right to act as a sovereign state, authorized salary increases of 10.6 percent for sixty-five thousand state employees.

In *Fry v. United States*, the Supreme Court struck down these increases. It held the wage controls to be a valid exercise of the federal commerce power. Ohio had to comply.

The Tenth Amendment was mentioned only in a footnote. The Court accepted the interpretation set forth in *Darby* that the Tenth Amendment was a truism. But the footnote continued, "It is not without significance. The Amendment expressly declares the constitutional policy that Congress may not exercise power in a fashion that impairs the States' integrity or their ability to function effectively in a federal system."

But what did that mean? Did it reinvigorate the Tenth Amendment, empowering it once again to take on the federal government? Or was it yet another truism? The answer came in 1976, in *National League of Cities v. Usery.* Or did it?

In a five to four decision in *National League of Cities,* the Supreme Court struck down an Act of Congress extending the federal minimum wage to almost all state employees. It was the first successful challenge to the commerce clause on federalism grounds since 1936. The Court wrote, "We have repeatedly recognized that there are attributes of sovereignty attaching to every state government which may not be impaired by Congress, not because Congress may lack an affirmative grant of legislative authority to reach the matter, but because the Constitution [in the Tenth Amendment] prohibits it."

The Court continued: "One undoubted attribute of state sovereignty is the States' power to determine the wages which shall be paid to those whom they employ in order to carry out their governmental functions." In other words, although it is within Congress's power to set a national minimum wage that private businesses must pay their workers, when Congress attempts to force state governments to pay their employees the same wage, it is prevented from doing so by the Tenth Amendment. Employees in areas of "traditional government functions," such as fire fighters, police officers, sanitation workers, and public health personnel, were to remain within the state's control. This was so even though it meant that a state highway patrol officer, for example, could be paid less than a high school student working at MacDonald's for the summer. (The minimum wage was then two dollars an hour.)

Justice Brennan, writing for three of the dissenting justices, strongly objected. The dissent argued that regulating the minimum wage and requiring the states to pay it was clearly within the federal commerce power. "There is no restraint based on state sovereignty . . . anywhere expressed in the Constitution; our decisions over the last century and a half have explicitly rejected the existence of any such restraint on the commerce power." Reserving areas of "traditional government function" to the states was an "abstraction without substance, founded neither in the words of the Constitution nor on precedent." Justice Brennan cited a string of cases rejecting the Tenth Amendment as a limit on Congress's powers, quoted *Darby* ("The Amendment states but a truism"), compared the majority opinion to the discredited decisions that precipitated Roosevelt's court-packing plan, and accused the majority of committing the ultimate judicial sin of injecting their own beliefs into the law. He concluded by calling the Court's decision a "catastrophic body blow to Congress' power under the Commerce Clause."

The battle lines were drawn. Both sides perceived the struggle over the structure of government to be crucial.

It is unusual for the Supreme Court to overrule itself, and it is extremely unusual for the Court to overrule a recent decision, but only nine years later, the Supreme Court did just that. Justice Brennan's view prevailed. Or more accurately, it had persuaded one justice, Harry Blackmun, who had written a lukewarm concurring opinion in *National League of Cities*, to change his mind. In *Garcia v. San Antonio Metropolitan Transit Authority*, the Court again divided five to four, but this time it went the other way. State employees were entitled to receive the federal minimum wage after all. By this time, it had risen to $3.35 an hour.

The difficulty of differentiating traditional government functions from nontraditional ones persuaded the Court to reject that standard for determining areas of state sovereignty, calling it "inconsistent with established principles of federalism." In the eight years between *National League of Cities* and *Garcia*, lower federal courts had held that licensing automobile drivers, operating a municipal airport, and operating a highway authority were traditional government functions, while regulating traffic on public roads, regulating air transportation, and operating a mental health facility were not. The Court called it "difficult if not impossible" to identify an organizing principle distinguishing one set of functions from the other. In *Garcia*, the Court held that it did not matter. Whether workers in San Antonio's mass transit system were performing a traditional government function or not, under the commerce clause they were to be paid the federal minimum wage.

Although the lawyers for both sides had been directed to answer the question "Whether or not the principles of the Tenth

Amendment as set forth in *National League of Cities v. Usery* should be reconsidered" the Court did not include the Tenth Amendment in its discussion of the issues. Instead it looked to article I of the Constitution to support its broad conception of the federal commerce power. First the Court analyzed the enormous powers exercised by Congress, including the power to regulate commerce, regulate currency, declare war, and raise an army. Next, the Court looked at the powers withdrawn from the states. For example, the states are forbidden to enter treaties, lay import or export taxes, or keep troops without the consent of Congress. Finally, the states did not need the Tenth Amendment to protect them. According to the Court, state interests were well provided for by their representatives and senators. Given the great benefit the states derived from their participation in the federal system, the Court found state sovereignty was well protected, and the burden of paying minimum wage to state employees did not destroy it.

The four dissenting justices in *Garcia* were as passionate as their opponents had been in *National League of Cities*, and they made similar accusations. Justice Lewis Powell, now in dissent, accused the new majority of injecting *its* views into the law: "I note that it does not seem to have occurred to the Court that *it*— an unelected majority of five Justices—today rejects almost 200 years of the understanding of the constitutional status of federalism." According to Justice Powell, the Court's opinion "emasculated" the states' power, paid "lip service" to their role, relegated them to the "trivial role that opponents of the Constitution feared they would occupy," and finally, reflected a "serious misunderstanding, if not an outright rejection, of the history of our country and the intention of the Framers of the Constitution."

Justices Rehnquist and O'Connor each wrote their own dissenting opinions. Justice Rehnquist was brief, declining to "spell out the fine points of a principle that will I am confident, in time again command the support of a majority of this Court."

Justice O'Connor also stood her ground. "The Court today surveys the battle scene of federalism and sounds a retreat," she wrote. "Like Justice Powell I would prefer to hold the field, and at the very least, render a little aid to the wounded [states]." She too saw dire consequences in the majority's decision. "There is now a real risk that Congress will gradually erase the diffusion of power between State and Nation on which the Framers based their faith in the efficiency and vitality of our Republic." Like Justice Rehnquist, she refused to accept defeat and concluded her dissent, "I share [the] belief that this Court will in time again assume its constitutional responsibility."

So the struggle over the meaning of the last amendment in the Bill of Rights will continue. At the moment, it appears to be a truism once again. But the Supreme Court may decide it represents instead a reservoir of power waiting to be exercised by the states. Either way, the Tenth Amendment, along with the other nine, will continue to preserve the freedoms of the Bill of Rights for the ultimate sovereign of our constitutional framework: "We the People."

Epilogue

During the time we were working on this book, the Bill of Rights hit the front pages in the flag burning controversy. Gregory Johnson, demonstrating outside the 1984 Republican Convention, set fire to an American flag while chanting "America, the Red, White and Blue, We Spit on You!" The United States Supreme Court voted five to four that the First Amendment protected burning the flag in political protest. The close decision and resulting uproar reflected a deep national split between those who found flag burning abhorrent but believed freedom of expression more important, and those who did not believe that freedom of speech meant the government was powerless to protect our national symbol.

People on both sides reacted emotionally, patriotically, and with absolute conviction. Legislation to protect the flag was introduced in Congress. The President not satisfied, called for a constitutional amendment. If passed, the flag-burning amendment would have limited the Bill of Rights for the first time in its two-hundred-year history. The amendment was narrowly defeated.

Like the Ku Klux Klan story from Kansas City, the flag burning case implicates one of the most fundamental—and controversial—elements of the First Amendment. Just how much unpopular conduct must society tolerate in the name of "free speech"? In the flag burning decision, the Supreme Court looked to an earlier, also controversial, case in which the Court held that forcing schoolchildren to recite the Pledge of Allegiance, an oath fundamentally at odds with their religious beliefs, violated the students' First Amendment rights. The Court wrote in that case: "Freedom to differ is not limited to things that do not matter much. That would be a mere shadow of freedom. The test of its substance is the right to differ as to things that touch the heart of the existing order."

To us, the flag burning case illustrates another aspect of the Bill of Rights—it protects people who have done distasteful, even dreadful, things. On the one hand, it is easy to celebrate people like Margarita Fuentes or Julius and Tina Hobson, who, in the face of formidable government power and corporate bureaucracy, fought hard for the rights of the individual. On the other hand, many of our most important rights have been won by people who were something less than heroic. Furthermore, good people can be hurt in the process, for example, the two young girls in a backyard tent in Iowa. The Supreme Court wrote in that case, "It is a truism that Constitutional protections have costs."

It is also a truism that constitutional principles that are easily supported in the abstract can become troublesome in the unforeseeable predicaments of modern life. To some, the glorious phrase "freedom of the press" takes on difficult dimensions in the context of thermonuclear war. And other principles, difficult in themselves, can become even more so, as when Jacqueline Bouknight, a disturbed young woman suspected of child abuse, refuses to answer when authorities ask, "Where is your child?"

We have included these cases on purpose, because they "touch the heart of the existing order" and because things really happen this way.

Justice Holmes observed of the Constitution, "It is an experiment, as all life is an experiment." The tool we have been given to manage this grand experiment is a few hundred words written two centuries ago. The instrument is necessarily imprecise. What specific rights are protected by the concept of "liberty"? We are still finding out.

But a tool is effective only if people know how to use it. We have tried in this book to show how disparate people have used the Bill of Rights in their—and our—defense. We have focused on the stories of the people, because our great rights truly cannot be found by "rummaging among old parchments, but are written, as with a sunbeam, in the whole volume of human nature." As important as the words inked on parchment is an understanding of how, two hundred years after the Framers have gone, we as Americans are still moving to the measure of their thought.

Appendix
The Constitution of the United States of America

We the People of the United States, in Order to form a more perfect Union, establish Justice, insure domestic Tranquility, provide for the common defence, promote the general Welfare, and secure the Blessings of Liberty to ourselves to our Posterity, do ordain and establish this Constitution for the United States of America.

ARTICLE I

Section 1. All legislative Powers herein granted shall be vested in a Congress of the United States, which shall consist of a Senate and House of Representatives.

Section 2. [1] The House of Representatives shall be composed of Members chosen every second Year by the People of the several States, and the Electors in each State shall have the Qualifications requisite for Electors of the most numerous Branch of the State Legislature.

[2] No Person shall be a Representative who shall not have attained to the Age of twenty five Years, and been seven Years a Citizen of the United States, and who shall not, when elected, be an Inhabitant of that State in which he shall be chosen.

[3] Representatives and direct Taxes shall be apportioned among the several States which may be included within this Union, according to their respective Numbers, which shall be determined by adding to the whole Number of free Persons, including those bound to Service for a Term of Years, and excluding Indians not taxed, three fifths of all other

Persons. The actual Enumeration shall be made within three Years after the first Meeting of the Congress of the United States, and within every subsequent Term of ten Years, in such a Manner as they shall by Law direct. The Number of Representatives shall not exceed one for every thirty Thousand, but each State shall have at Least one Representative; and until such enumeration shall be made, the State of New Hampshire shall be entitled to chuse three, Massachusetts eight, Rhode Island and Providence Plantations one, Connecticut five, New York six, New Jersey four, Pennsylvania eight, Delaware one, Maryland six, Virginia ten, North Carolina five, South Carolina five, and Georgia three.

[4] When vacancies happen in the Representation from any State, the Executive Authority thereof shall issue Writs of Election to fill such Vacancies.

[5] The House of Representatives shall chuse their Speaker and other Officers; and shall have the sole Power of Impeachment.

Section 3. [1] The Senate of the United States shall be composed of two Senators from each State, chosen by the Legislature thereof, for six Years; and each Senator shall have one Vote.

[2] Immediately after they shall be assembled in Consequence of the first Election, they shall be divided as equally as may be into three Classes. The Seats of the Senators of the first Class shall be vacated at the Expiration of the Second Year, of the second Class at the Expiration of the fourth Year, and of the third Class at the Expiration of the sixth Year, so that one third may be chosen every second Year; and if Vacancies happen by Resignation, or otherwise, during the Recess of the Legislature of any State, the Executive thereof may make temporary Appointments until the next Meeting of the Legislature, which shall then fill such Vacancies.

[3] No Person shall be a Senator who shall not have attained to the Age of thirty Years, and been nine Years a Citizen of the United States, and who shall not, when elected, be an Inhabitant of that State for which he shall be chosen.

[4] The Vice President of the United States shall be President of the Senate, but shall have no Vote, unless they be equally divided.

[5] The Senate shall chuse their other Officers, and also a President pro tempore, in the Absence of the Vice President, or when he shall exercise the Office of President of the United States.

[6] The Senate shall have the sole Power to try all Impeachments. When sitting for that Purpose, they shall be on Oath or Affirmation. When the President of the United States is tried, the Chief Justice shall preside: And no Person shall be convicted without the Concurrence of two thirds of the Members present.

[7] Judgment in Cases of Impeachment shall not extend further than to removal from Office, and disqualification to hold and enjoy any Office of honor, Trust, or Profit under the United States: but the Party convicted shall nevertheless be liable and subject to Indictment, Trial, Judgment, and Punishment, according to Law.

Section 4. [1] The Times, Places and Manner of holding Elections for Senators and Representatives, shall be prescribed in each State by the Legislature thereof; but the Congress may at any time by Law make or alter such Regulations, except as to the Places of chusing Senators.

[2] The Congress shall assemble at least once in every Year, and such

Meeting shall be on the first Monday in December, unless they shall by Law appoint a different Day.

Section 5. [1] Each House shall be the Judge of the Elections, Returns, and Qualifications of its own Members, and a Majority of each shall constitute a Quorum to do Business; but a smaller Number may adjourn from day to day, and may be authorized to compel the Attendance of absent Members, in such Manner, and under such Penalties as each House may provide.

[2] Each House may determine the Rules of its Proceedings, punish its Members for disorderly Behaviour, and, with the Concurrence of two thirds, expel a Member.

[3] Each House shall keep a journal of its Proceedings, and from time to time publish the same, excepting such Parts as may in their Judgment require Secrecy; and the Yeas and Nays of the Members of either House on any question shall, at the Desire of one fifth of those Present, be entered on the Journal.

[4] Neither House, during the Session of Congress, shall, without the Consent of the other, adjourn for more than three days, nor to any other Place than that in which the two Houses shall be sitting.

Section 6. [1] The Senators and Representatives shall receive a Compensation for their Services, to be ascertained by Law, and paid out of the Treasury of the United States. They shall in all Cases, except Treason, Felony and Breach of the Peace, be privileged from Arrest during their Attendance at the Session of their respective Houses, and in going to and returning from the same; and for any Speech or Debate in either House, they shall not be questioned in any other Place.

[2] No Senator or Representative shall, during the Time for which he was elected, be appointed to any civil Office under the Authority of the United States, which shall have been created, or the Emoluments whereof shall have been encreased during such time; and no Person holding any Office under the United States, shall be a Member of either House during his Continuance in Office.

Section 7. [1] All Bills for raising Revenue shall originate in the House of Representatives; but the Senate may propose or concur with Amendments as on other Bills.

[2] Every Bill which shall have passed the House of Representatives and the Senate, shall, before it become a Law, be presented to the President of the United States; If he approves he shall sign it, but if not he shall return it, with his Objections to that House in which it shall have originated, who shall enter the Objections at large on their Journal, and proceed to reconsider it. If after such Reconsideration two thirds of that House shall agree to pass the Bill, it shall be sent together with the Objections, to the other House, by which it shall likewise be reconsidered, and if approved by two thirds of that House, it shall become a Law. But in all such Cases the Votes of both Houses shall be determined by yeas and Nays, and the Names of the Persons voting for and against the Bill shall be entered on the Journal of each House respectively. If any Bill shall not be returned by the President within ten Days (Sundays excepted) after it shall have been presented to him, the Same shall be a Law, in like Manner as if he had signed it, unless the Congress by their Adjournment prevent its Return in which Case it shall not be a Law.

[3] Every Order, Resolution, or Vote, to Which the Concurrence of the

Senate and House of Representatives may be necessary (except on a question of Adjournment) shall be presented to the President of the United States; and before the Same shall take Effect, shall be approved by him, or being disapproved by him, shall be repassed by two thirds of the Senate and House of Representatives, according to the Rules and Limitations prescribed in the Case of a Bill.

Section 8. [1] The Congress shall have Power To lay and collect Taxes, Duties, Imposts and Excises, to pay the Debts and provide for the common Defence and general Welfare of the United States; but all Duties, Imposts and Excises shall be uniform throughout the United States;

[2] To borrow Money on the credit of the United States;

[3] To regulate Commerce with foreign Nations, and among the several States, and with the Indian Tribes;

[4] To establish an uniform Rule of Naturalization, and uniform Laws on the subject of Bankruptcies throughout the United States;

[5] To coin Money, regulate the Value thereof, and of foreign Coin, and fix the Standard of Weights and Measures;

[6] To provide for the Punishment of counterfeiting the Securities and current Coin of the United States;

[7] To Establish Post Offices and Post Roads;

[8] To promote the Progress of Science and useful Arts, by securing for limited Times to Authors and Inventors the exclusive Right to their respective Writings and Discoveries;

[9] To constitute Tribunals inferior to the supreme Court;

[10] To define and punish Piracies and Felonies committed on the high Seas, and Offences against the Law of Nations;

[11] To declare War, grant Letters of Marque and Reprisal, and make Rules concerning Captures on Land and Water;

[12] To raise and support Armies, but no Appropriation of Money to that Use shall be for a longer Term than two Years;

[13] To provide and maintain a Navy;

[14] To make Rules for the Government and Regulation of the land and naval Forces;

[15] To provide for calling forth the Militia to execute the Laws of the Union, suppress Insurrections and repel Invasions;

[16] To provide for organizing, arming, and disciplining, the Militia, and for governing such Part of them as may be employed in the Service of the United States, reserving to the States respectively, the Appointment of the Officers, and the Authority of training the Militia according to the discipline prescribed by Congress;

[17] To exercise exclusive Legislation in all Cases whatsoever, over such District (not exceeding ten Miles square) as may, by Cession of particular States, and the Acceptance of Congress, become the Seat of the Government of the United States, and to exercise like Authority over all Places purchased by the Consent of the Legislature of the State in which the Same shall be, for the Erection of Forts, Magazines, Arsenals, dock-Yards, and other needful Buildings;—And

[18] To make all Laws which shall be necessary and proper for carrying into Execution the foregoing Powers, and all other Powers vested by this Constitution in the Government of the United States, or in any Department or Officer thereof.

Section 9. [1] The Migration or Importation of Such Persons as any of

the States now existing shall think proper to admit, shall not be prohibited by the Congress prior to the Year one thousand eight hundred
and eight, but a Tax or duty may be imposed on such Importation, not
exceeding ten dollars for each Person.

[2] The Privilege of the Writ of Habeas Corpus shall not be suspended,
unless when in Cases of Rebellion or Invasion the public Safety may require it.

[3] No Bill of Attainder or ex post facto Law shall be passed.

[4] No Capitation, or other direct, Tax shall be laid, unless in Proportion to the Census or Enumeration herein before directed to be taken.

[5] No Tax or Duty shall be laid on Articles exported from any State.

[6] No Preference shall be given by any Regulation of Commerce or
Revenue to the Ports of one State over those of another: nor shall Vessels
bound to, or from, one State be obliged to enter, clear, or pay Duties in
another.

[7] No Money shall be drawn from the Treasury, but in Consequence
of Appropriations made by Law; and a regular Statement and Account of
the Receipts and Expenditures of all public Money shall be published
from time to time.

[8] No Title of Nobility shall be granted by the United States: And no
Person holding any Office of Profit or Trust under them, shall, without
the Consent of the Congress, accept of any present, Emolument, Office, or
Title, of any kind whatever, from any King, Prince, or foreign State.

Section 10. [1] No State shall enter into any Treaty, Alliance, or Confederation; grant Letters of Marque and Reprisal; coin Money; emit Bills
of Credit; make any Thing but gold and silver Coin a Tender in Payment
of Debts; pass any Bill of Attainder, ex post facto Law, or Law impairing
the Obligation of Contracts, or grant any Title of Nobility.

[2] No State shall, without the Consent of the Congress, lay any Imposts or Duties on Imports or Exports, except what may be absolutely
necessary for executing its inspection Laws: and the net Produce of all
Duties and Imposts, laid by any State on Imports or Exports, shall be for
the Use of the Treasury of the United States; and all such Laws shall be
subject to the Revision and Controul of the Congress.

[3] No State shall, without the Consent of Congress, lay any Duty of
Tonnage, keep Troops, or Ships of War in time of Peace, enter into any
Agreement or Compact with another State, or with a foreign Power, or
engage in War, unless actually invaded, or in such imminent Danger as
will not admit of delay.

ARTICLE II

Section 1. [1] The executive Power shall be vested in a President of the
United States of America. He shall hold his Office during the Term of
four Years, and, together with the Vice President, chosen for the same
Term, be elected, as follows:

[2] Each State shall appoint, in such Manner as the Legislature
thereof may direct, a Number of Electors, equal to the whole Number of
Senators and Representatives to which the State may be entitled in the
Congress; but no Senator or Representative, or Person holding an Office
of Trust or Profit under the United States, shall be appointed an Elector.

[3] The Electors shall meet in their respective States, and vote by

Ballot for two Persons, of whom one at least shall not be an Inhabitant of the same State with themselves. And they shall make a List of all the Persons voted for, and of the Number of Votes for each; which List they shall sign and certify, and transmit sealed to the Seat of the Government of the United States, directed to the President of the Senate. The President of the Senate shall, in the Presence of the Senate and House of Representatives, open all the Certificates, and the Votes shall then be counted. The Person having the greatest Number of Votes shall be the President, if such Number be a Majority of the whole Number of Electors appointed; and if there be more than one who have such Majority, and have an equal Number of Votes, then the House of Representatives shall immediately chuse by Ballot one of them for President; and if no Person have a Majority, then from the five highest on the List the said House shall in like Manner chuse the President. But in chusing the President, the Votes shall be taken by States, the Representation from each State having one Vote; A quorum for this Purpose shall consist of a Member or Members from two thirds of the States, and a Majority of all the States shall be necessary to a Choice. In every Case, after the Choice of the President, the Person having the greater Number of Votes of the Electors shall be the Vice President. But if there should remain two or more who have equal Votes, the Senate shall chuse from them by Ballot the Vice President.

[4] The Congress may determine the Time of chusing the Electors, and the Day on which they shall give their Votes; which Day shall be the same throughout the United States.

[5] No person except a natural born Citizen, or a Citizen of the United States, at the time of the Adoption of this Constitution, shall be eligible to the Office of President; neither shall any Person be eligible to that Office who shall not have attained to the Age of thirty five Years, and been fourteen Years a Resident within the United States.

[6] In case of the removal of the President from Office, or of his Death, Resignation or Inability to discharge the Powers and Duties of the said Office, the Same shall devolve on the Vice President, and the Congress may by Law provide for the Case of Removal, Death, Resignation or Inability, both of the President and Vice President, declaring what Officer shall then act as President, and such Officer shall act accordingly, until the Disability be removed, or a President shall be elected.

[7] The President shall, at stated Times, receive for his Services, a Compensation, which shall neither be encreased nor diminished during the Period for which he shall have been elected, and he shall not receive within that Period any other Emolument from the United States, or any of them.

[8] Before he enter on the Execution of his Office, he shall take the following Oath or Affirmation: "I do solemnly swear (or affirm) that I will faithfully execute the Office of President of the United States, and will to the best of my Ability, preserve, protect and defend the Constitution of the United States."

Section 2. [1] The President shall be Commander in Chief of the Army and Navy of the United States, and of the militia of the several States, when called into the actual Service of the United States; he may require the Opinion, in writing, of the principal Officer in each of the executive Departments, upon any Subject relating to the Duties of their respective

Offices, and he shall have Power to grant Reprieves and Pardons for Offenses against the United States, except in Cases of Impeachment.

[2] He shall have Power, by and with the Advice and Consent of the Senate, to make Treaties, provided two thirds of the Senators present concur; and he shall nominate, and by and with the Advice and Consent of the Senate, shall appoint Ambassadors, other public Ministers and Consuls, Judges of the supreme Court, and all other Officers of the United States, whose Appointments are not herein otherwise provided for, and which shall be established by Law; but the Congress may by Law vest the Appointment of such inferior Officers, as they think proper, in the President alone, in the Courts of Law, or in the Heads of Departments.

[3] The President shall have Power to fill up all Vacancies that may happen during the Recess of the Senate, by granting Commissions which shall expire at the End of their next Session.

Section 3. He shall from time to time give to the Congress Information of the State of the Union, and recommend to their Consideration such Measures as he shall judge necessary and expedient; he may, on extraordinary Occasions, convene both Houses, or either of them, and in Case of Disagreement between them, with Respect to the Time of Adjournment, he may adjourn them to such Time as he shall think proper; he shall receive Ambassadors and other public Ministers; he shall take Care that the Laws be faithfully executed, and shall Commission all the Officers of the United States.

Section 4. The President, Vice President and all civil Officers of the United States, shall be removed from Office on Impeachment for, and Conviction of, Treason, Bribery, or other high Crimes and Misdemeanors.

ARTICLE III

Section 1. The judicial Power of the United States, shall be vested in one supreme Court, and in such inferior Courts as the Congress may from time to time ordain and establish. The Judges, both of the supreme and inferior Courts, shall hold their Offices during good Behaviour, and shall, at stated Times, receive for their Services a Compensation, which shall not be diminished during their Continuance in Office.

Section 2. [1] The judicial Power shall extend to all Cases, in Law and Equity, arising under this Constitution, the Laws of the United States, and Treaties made, or which shall be made, under their Authority;—to all Cases affecting Ambassadors, other public Ministers and Consuls;—to all Cases of admiralty and maritime Jurisdiction;—to Controversies to which the United States shall be a Party;—to Controversies between two or more States;—between a State and Citizens of another State;—between Citizens of different States;—between Citizens of the same State claiming Lands under the Grants of different States, and between a State, or the Citizens thereof, and foreign States, Citizens or Subjects.

[2] In all Cases affecting Ambassadors, other public Ministers and Consuls, and those in which a State shall be a Party, the supreme Court shall have original Jurisdiction. In all the other Cases before mentioned, the supreme Court shall have appellate Jurisdiction, both as to Law and Fact, with such Exceptions, and under such Regulations as the Congress shall make.

[3] The trial of all Crimes, except in Cases of Impeachment, shall be

by Jury; and such Trial shall be held in the State where the said Crimes shall have been committed; but when not committed within any State, the Trial shall be at such Place or Places as the Congress may by Law have directed.

Section 3. [1] Treason against the United States, shall consist only in levying War against them, or, in adhering to their Enemies, giving them Aid and Comfort. No Person shall be convicted of Treason unless on the Testimony of two Witnesses to the same overt Act, or on Confession in open Court.

[2] The Congress shall have Power to declare the Punishment of Treason, but no Attainder of Treason shall work Corruption of Blood, or Forfeiture except during the Life of the Person attainted.

ARTICLE IV

Section 1. Full Faith and Credit shall be given in each State to the public Acts, Records, and judicial Proceedings of every other State. And the Congress may by general Laws prescribe the Manner in which such Acts, Records and Proceedings shall be proved, and the Effect thereof.

Section 2. [1] The Citizens of each State shall be entitled to all Privileges and Immunities of Citizens in the several States.

[2] A Person charged in any State with Treason, Felony, or other Crime, who shall flee from Justice, and be found in another State, shall on demand of the executive Authority of the State from which he fled, be delivered up, to be removed to the State having Jurisdiction of the Crime.

[3] No Person held to Service or Labour in one State, under the Laws thereof, escaping into another, shall, in Consequence of any Law or Regulation therein, be discharged from such Service or Labour, but shall be delivered up on Claim of the Party to whom such Service or Labour may be due.

Section 3. [1] New States may be admitted by the Congress into this Union; but no new State shall be formed or erected within the Jurisdiction of any other State; nor any State be formed by the Junction of two or more States, or Parts of States, without the Consent of the Legislatures of the States concerned as well as of the Congress.

[2] The Congress shall have Power to dispose of and make all needful Rules and Regulations respecting the Territory or other Property belonging to the United States; and nothing in this Constitution shall be so construed as to Prejudice any Claims of the United States, or of any particular State.

Section 4. The United States shall guarantee to every State in this Union a Republican Form of Government, and shall protect each of them against Invasion; and on Application of the Legislature, or of the Executive (when the Legislature cannot be convened) against domestic Violence.

ARTICLE V

The Congress, whenever two thirds of both Houses shall deem it necessary, shall propose Amendments to this Constitution, or, on the Application of the Legislatures of two thirds of the several States, shall call a Convention for proposing Amendments, which, in either Case, shall be valid to all Intents and Purposes, as part of this Constitution, when ratified by the Legislatures of three fourths of the several States, or by Conventions in three fourths thereof, as the one or the other Mode of Ratification may be proposed by the Congress; Provided that no Amendment which may be made prior to the Year One thousand eight hundred and eight shall in any Manner affect the first and fourth Clauses in the Ninth Section of the first Article; and that no State, without its Consent, shall be deprived of its equal Suffrage in the Senate.

ARTICLE VI

[1] All Debts contracted and Engagements entered into, before the Adoption of this Constitution, shall be as valid against the United States under this Constitution, as under the Confederation.

[2] This Constitution, and the Laws of the United States which shall be made in Pursuance thereof; and all Treaties made, or which shall be made, under the Authority of the United States, shall be the supreme Law of the Land; and the Judges in every State shall be bound thereby, any Thing in the Constitution or Laws of any State to the Contrary notwithstanding.

[3] The Senators and Representatives before mentioned, and the Members of the several State Legislatures, and all executive and judicial Officers, both of the United States and of the several States, shall be bound by Oath or Affirmation, to support this Constitution; but no religious Test shall ever be required as a Qualification to any Office or public Trust under the United States.

ARTICLE VII

The Ratification of the Conventions of nine States shall be sufficient for the Establishment of this Constitution between the States so ratifying the Same.

ARTICLES IN ADDITION TO, AND AMENDMENT OF, THE CONSTITUTION OF THE UNITED STATES OF AMERICA, PROPOSED BY CONGRESS, AND RATIFIED BY THE LEGISLATURES OF THE SEVERAL STATES PURSUANT TO THE FIFTH ARTICLE OF THE ORIGINAL CONSTITUTION.

AMENDMENT I [1791]

Congress shall make no law respecting an establishment of religion, or prohibiting the free exercise thereof; or abridging the freedom of speech, or of the press; or the right of the people peaceably to assemble, and to petition the Government for a redress of grievances.

AMENDMENT II [1791]

A well regulated Militia, being necessary to the security of a free State, the right of the people to keep and bear Arms, shall not be infringed.

AMENDMENT III [1791]

No Soldier shall, in time of peace be quartered in any house, without the consent of the Owner, nor in time of war, but in a manner to be prescribed by law.

Amendment IV [1791]

The right of the people to be secure in their persons, houses, papers, and effects, against unreasonable searches and seizures, shall not be violated, and no Warrants shall issue, but upon probable cause, supported by Oath or affirmation, and particularly describing the place to be searched, and the persons or things to be seized.

Amendment V [1791]

No person shall be held to answer for a capital, or otherwise infamous crime, unless on a presentment or indictment of a Grand Jury, except in cases arising in the land or naval forces, or in the Militia, when in actual service in time of War or public danger; nor shall any person be subject for the same offence to be twice put in jeopardy of life or limb; nor shall be compelled in any criminal case to be a witness against himself, nor be deprived of life, liberty, or property, without due process of law; nor shall private property be taken for public use, without just compensation.

Amendment VI [1791]

In all criminal prosecutions, the accused shall enjoy the right to a speedy and public trial, by an impartial jury of the State and district wherein the crime shall have been committed, which district shall have been previously ascertained by law, and to be informed of the nature and cause of the accusation; to be confronted with the witnesses against him; to have compulsory process for obtaining witnesses in his favor, and to have the Assistance of Counsel for his defence.

Amendment VII [1791]

In Suits at common law, where the value in controversy shall exceed twenty dollars, the right of trial by jury shall be preserved, and no fact tried by jury, shall be otherwise re-examined in any Court of the United States, than according to the rules of the common law.

Amendment VIII [1791]

Excessive bail shall not be required, nor excessive fines imposed, nor cruel and unusual punishments inflicted.

Amendment IX [1791]

The enumeration in the Constitution, of certain rights, shall not be construed to deny or disparage others retained by the people.

Amendment X [1791]

The powers not delegated to the United States by the Constitution, nor prohibited by it to the States, are reserved to the States respectively, or to the people.

AMENDMENT XI [1798]

The Judicial power of the United States shall not be construed to extend to any suit in law or equity, commenced or prosecuted against one of the United States by Citizens of another State, or by Citizens or Subjects of any Foreign State.

AMENDMENT XII [1804]

The Electors shall meet in their respective states and vote by ballot for President and Vice-President, one of whom, at least, shall not be an inhabitant of the same state with themselves; they shall name in their ballots the person voted for as President, and in distinct ballots the person voted for as Vice-President, and they shall make distinct lists of all persons voted for as President, and of all persons voted for as Vice-President, and of the number of votes for each, which lists they shall sign and certify, and transmit sealed to the seat of the government of the United States, directed to the President of the Senate;—The President of the Senate shall, in the presence of the Senate and House of Representatives, open all the certificates and the votes shall then be counted;—The person having the greatest number of votes for President, shall be the President, if such number be a majority of the whole number of Electors appointed; and if no person have such majority, then from the persons having the highest numbers not exceeding three on the list of those voted for as President, the House of Representatives shall choose immediately, by ballot, the President. But in choosing the President, the votes shall be taken by states, the representation from each state having one vote; a quorum for this purpose shall consist of a member or members from two-thirds of the states, and a majority of all the states shall be necessary to a choice. And if the House of Representatives shall not choose a President whenever the right of choice shall devolve upon them before the fourth day of March next following, then the Vice-President shall act as President, as in the case of the death or other constitutional disability of the President.—The person having the greatest number of votes as Vice-President, shall be the Vice-President, if such number be a majority of the whole number of Electors appointed, and if no person have a majority, then from the two highest numbers on the list, the Senate shall choose the Vice-President; a quorum for the purpose shall consist of two-thirds of the whole number of Senators, and a majority of the whole number shall be necessary to a choice. But no person constitutionally ineligible to the office of President shall be eligible to that of Vice-President of the United States.

AMENDMENT XIII [1865]

Section 1. Neither slavery nor involuntary servitude, except as a punishment for crime whereof the party shall have been duly convicted, shall exist within the United States, or any place subject to their jurisdiction.

Section 2. Congress shall have power to enforce this article by appropriate legislation.

AMENDMENT XIV [1868]

Section 1. All persons born or naturalized in the United States, and subject to the jurisdiction thereof, are citizens of the United States and of the State wherein they reside. No State shall make or enforce any law which shall abridge the privileges or immunities of citizens of the United States; nor shall any State deprive any person of life, liberty, or property, without due process of law; nor deny to any person within its jurisdiction the equal protection of the laws.

Section 2. Representatives shall be apportioned among the several States according to their respective numbers, counting the whole number of persons in each State, excluding Indians not taxed. But when the right to vote at any election for the choice of electors for President and Vice President of the United States, Representatives in Congress, the Executive and Judicial officers of a State, or the members of the Legislature thereof, is denied to any of the male inhabitants of such State, being twenty-one years of age, and citizens of the United States, or in any way abridged, except for participation in rebellion, or other crime, the basis of representation therein shall be reduced in the proportion which the number of such male citizens shall bear to the whole number of male citizens twenty-one years of age in such State.

Section 3. No person shall be a Senator or Representative in Congress, or elector of President and Vice President, or hold any office, civil or military, under the United States, or under any State, who having previously taken an oath, as a member of Congress, or as an officer of the United States, or as a member of any State legislature, or as an executive or judicial officer of any State, to support the Constitution of the United States, shall have engaged in insurrection or rebellion against the same, or given aid or comfort to the enemies thereof. But Congress may by a vote of two-thirds of each House, remove such disability.

Section 4. The validity of the public debt of the United States, authorized by law, including debts incurred for payment of pensions and bounties for services in suppressing insurrection or rebellion, shall not be questioned. But neither the United States nor any State shall assume or pay any debt or obligation incurred in aid of insurrection or rebellion against the United States, or any claim for the loss or emancipation of any slave; but all such debts, obligations and claims shall be held illegal and void.

Section 5. The Congress shall have power to enforce, by appropriate legislation, the provisions of this article.

AMENDMENT XV [1870]

Section 1. The right of citizens of the United States to vote shall not be denied or abridged by the United States or by any State on account of race, color, or previous condition of servitude.

Section 2. The Congress shall have power to enforce this article by appropriate legislation.

AMENDMENT XVI [1913]

The Congress shall have power to lay and collect taxes on incomes, from whatever source derived, without apportionment among the several States, and without regard to any census or enumeration.

AMENDMENT XVII [1913]

[1] The Senate of the United States shall be composed of two Senators from each State, elected by the people thereof, for six years; and each Senator shall have one vote. The electors in each State shall have the qualifications requisite for electors of the most numerous branch of the State legislatures.

[2] When vacancies happen in the representation of any State in the Senate, the executive authority of such State shall issue writs of election to fill such vacancies: *Provided*, That the legislature of any State may empower the executive thereof to make temporary appointments until the people fill the vacancies by election as the legislature may direct.

[3] This amendment shall not be so construed as to affect the election or term of any Senator chosen before it becomes valid as part of the Constitution.

AMENDMENT XVIII [1919]

Section 1. After one year from the ratification of this article the manufacture, sale, or transportation of intoxicating liquors within, the importation thereof into, or the exportation thereof from the United States and all territory subject to the jurisdiction thereof for beverage purposes is hereby prohibited.

Section 2. The Congress and the several States shall have concurrent power to enforce this article by appropriate legislation.

Section 3. This article shall be inoperative unless it shall have been ratified as an amendment to the Constitution by the legislatures of the several States, as provided in the Constitution, within seven years from the date of the submission hereof to the States by the Congress.

AMENDMENT XIX [1920]

[1] The right of citizens of the United States to vote shall not be denied or abridged by the United States or by any State on account of sex.

[2] Congress shall have the power to enforce this article by appropriate legislation.

AMENDMENT XX [1933]

Section 1. The terms of the President and Vice President shall end at noon on the 20th day of January, and the terms of Senators and Representatives at noon on the 3d day of January, of the years in which such terms would have ended if this article had not been ratified; and the terms of their successors shall then begin.

Section 2. The Congress shall assemble at least once in every year, and such meeting shall begin at noon on the 3d day of January, unless they shall be law appoint a different day.

Section 3. If, at the time fixed for the beginning of the term of the President, the President elect shall have died, the Vice President elect shall become President. If the President shall not have been chosen before the time fixed for the beginning of his term, or if the President elect shall have failed to qualify, then the Vice President elect shall act as President until a President shall have qualified; and the Congress may by law provide for the case wherein neither a President elect nor a Vice

President elect shall have qualified, declaring who shall then act as President, or the manner in which one who is to act shall be selected, and such person shall act accordingly until a President or Vice President shall have qualified.

Section 4. The Congress may by law provide for the case of the death of any of the persons from whom the House of Representatives may choose a President whenever the right of choice shall have devolved upon them, and for the case of the death of any of the persons from whom the Senate may choose a Vice President whenever the right of choice shall have devolved upon them.

Section 5. Sections 1 and 2 shall take effect on the 15th day of October following the ratification of this article.

Section 6. This article shall be inoperative unless it shall have been ratified as an amendment to the Constitution by the legislatures of three-fourths of the several States within seven years from the date of its submission.

Amendment XXI [1933]

Section 1. The eighteenth article of amendment to the Constitution of the United States is hereby repealed.

Section 2. The transportation or importation into any State, Territory, or possession of the United States for delivery or use therein of intoxicating liquors, in violation of the laws thereof, is hereby prohibited.

Section 3. This article shall be inoperative unless it shall have been ratified as an amendment to the Constitution by conventions in the several States, as provided in the Constitution, within seven years from the date of the submission hereof to the States by the Congress.

Amendment XXII [1951]

Section 1. No person shall be elected to the office of the President more than twice, and no person who has held the office of President, or acted as President, for more than two years of a term to which some other person was elected President shall be elected to the office of President more than once. But this Article shall not apply to any person holding the office of President when this Article was proposed by the Congress, and shall not prevent any person who may be holding the office of President, or acting as President, during the term within which this Article becomes operative from holding the office of President or acting as President during the remainder of such term.

Section 2. This article shall be inoperative unless it shall have been ratified as an amendment to the Constitution by the legislatures of three-fourths of the several States within seven years from the date of its submission to the States by the Congress.

Amendment XXIII [1961]

Section 1. The District constituting the seat of Government of the United States shall appoint in such manner as the Congress may direct:

A number of electors of President and Vice President equal to the whole number of Senators and Representatives in Congress to which the District would be entitled if it were a State, but in no event more than the least populous state; they shall be in addition to those appointed by the states, but they shall be considered, for the purposes of the election of President and Vice President, to be electors appointed by a state; and they shall meet in the District and perform such duties as provided by the twelfth article of amendment.

Section 2. The Congress shall have power to enforce this article by appropriate legislation.

AMENDMENT XXIV [1964]

Section 1. The right of citizens of the United States to vote in any primary or other election for President or Vice President, for electors for President or Vice President, or for Senator or Representative in Congress, shall not be denied or abridged by the United States or any State by reason of failure to pay any poll tax or other tax.

Section 2. The Congress shall have power to enforce this article by appropriate legislation.

AMENDMENT XXV [1967]

Section 1. In case of the removal of the President from office or of his death or resignation, the Vice President shall become President.

Section 2. Whenever there is a vacancy in the office of the Vice President, the President shall nominate a Vice President who shall take office upon confirmation by a majority vote of both Houses of Congress.

Section 3. Whenever the President transmits to the President pro tempore of the Senate and the Speaker of the House of Representatives his written declaration that he is unable to discharge the powers and duties of his office, and until he transmits to them a written declaration to the contrary, such powers and duties shall be discharged by the Vice President as Acting President.

Section 4. Whenever the Vice President and a majority of either the principal officers of the executive departments or of such other body as Congress may by law provide, transmit to the President pro tempore of the Senate and the Speaker of the House of Representatives their written declaration that the President is unable to discharge the powers and duties of his office, the Vice President shall immediately assume the powers and duties of the office as Acting President.

Thereafter, when the President transmits to the President pro tempore of the Senate and the Speaker of the House of Representatives his written declaration that no inability exists, he shall resume the powers and duties of his office unless the Vice President and a majority of either the principal officers of the executive department or of such other body as Congress may by law provide, transmit within four days to the President pro tempore of the Senate and the Speaker of the House of Representatives their written declaration that the President is unable to discharge the powers and duties of his office. Thereupon Congress shall decide the issue, assembling within forty-eight hours for that purpose if not in session. If the Congress, within twenty-one days after receipt of the latter written declaration, or, if Congress is not in session, within twenty-one days after Congress is required to assemble, determines by two-thirds vote of both Houses that the President is unable to discharge the powers and duties of his office, the Vice President shall continue to discharge the same as Acting President; otherwise, the President shall resume the powers and duties of his office.

AMENDMENT XXVI [1971]

Section 1. The right of citizens of the United States, who are eighteen years of age or older, to vote shall not be denied or abridged by the United States or by any State on account of age.

Section 2. The Congress shall have power to enforce this article by appropriate legislation.

Endnotes

The clauses in the Bill of Rights that are not illustrated by a story are the First Amendment establishment of religion clause, the Sixth Amendment speedy and public trial clauses, and the Eighth Amendment excessive bail and fines clauses.

Unless otherwise noted below, all quotations in the text are drawn from interviews with the authors.

Epigraph: The quotation from Alexander Hamilton can be found in *The Papers of Alexander Hamilton, Volume 1: 1768–1778,* ed. Harold C. Syrett (New York: Columbia University Press, 1961), p. 122.

AUTHORS' NOTE

14 The quotation from Justice Frankfurter is from *U.S. v. Rabinowitz,* 339 U.S. 56, 69 (1950) (Frankfurter, J., dissenting).

FIRST AMENDMENT

Freedom of Speech:
Missouri Knights of the Ku Klux Klan v. Kansas City

27 In an article discussing the Eighth Circuit decision regarding desegregation in Kansas City schools, it was reported that the

Kansas City school district proper is 74 percent minority students. Lynn Byczynski, "8th Circuit: Suburbs Can Drop Out of Desegregation Plan," *National Law Journal*, December 29, 1986, p. 6.

28 The case upholding the conviction of Eugene Debs is *Debs v. United States*, 249 U.S. 211 (1919).

29 The comparison between Debs and George McGovern can be found in Kalven, "Ernst Freund and the First Amendment Tradition," *University of Chicago Law Review* 40 (1973): 237, quoted in Lockhart, Kamisar, Choper, and Shiffrin, eds., *Constitutional Rights and Liberties*, p. 300n. a.

29 The case upholding the convictions of Communist leaders involved in a highly organized conspiracy is *Dennis v. United States*, 341 U.S. 494 (1951).

29 The case striking down the convictions of fourteen second-string party officials advocating Communist teachings is *Yates v. U.S.*, 354 U.S. 298 (1957).

29 The case in which the Supreme Court reformulated the "clear and present danger" test is *Brandenburg v. Ohio*, 395 U.S. 444 (1969).

30 Further to the discussion of First Amendment protection of leafletting: the importance of leafletting was underscored by the Supreme Court in *Lovell v. City of Griffin*, 303 U.S. 444, 452 (1938), where it said that "the liberty of the press is not confined to newspapers and periodicals. It necessarily embraces pamphlets and leaflets. These indeed have been historic weapons in the defense of liberty."

Thus in *Schneider v. State (Town of Irvington)*, 308 U.S. 147 (1939), an ordinance was held to be void as applied where it required someone who distributed literature door to door to obtain a license.

The right to leaflet is not, however, absolute. A municipality can prohibit "throwing literature broadcast in the streets" or pass other content-neutral restrictions. *Schneider*, pp. 160–61; see also *Heffron v. International Society for Krishna Consciousness*, 452 U.S. 640 (1981), upholding a state rule confining distribution of printed literature at a state fair to specific fixed booth locations.

30 Further to the discussion of First Amendment protection of symbolic expression: it is not clear at what point certain "conduct" harbors enough "speech" so that it is protected under the First Amendment. See Tribe, *American Constitutional Law*, p. 827. One way to look at the issue is to perceive symbolic speech as a combination of speech and conduct—that is, speech plus. It is the "plus" in this combination that can be regulated by the states. See, e.g., *Cox v. Louisiana*, 379 U.S. 559, 563–64 (1965). To what extent such regulation can be imposed depends on the historical relation between speech and the kind of conduct, the setting in which it takes place, and the general relation between the conduct and what

the speaker is trying to convey. See, e.g., *Adderley v. Florida*, 385 U.S. 39 (1966) (demonstration on premises of county jail not protected); *Brown v. Louisiana*, 383 U.S. 131 (1966) (silent protest on public library premises protected).

30   The case involving black armbands worn in school to protest the Vietnam War is *Tinker v. Des Moines Independent Community School District*, 303 U.S. 503 (1969).

30   The case involving the Nazis' request to march in Skokie is *Collin v. Smith*, 578 F.2d 1197 (7th Cir. 1978), quoting *Street v. New York*, 394 U.S. 576, 592 (1969).

30   The description of a public forum is from *Hague v. CIO*, 307 U.S. 496, 515 (1939) (Opinion of Roberts, J.).

31   In fact, Reverend Cleaver and Councilman John Sharp first proposed a resolution deleting the public access channel and substituting a community programming channel in its place. In cable TV terms, the difference between a public access channel and a community programming channel is control. Unlike a public access channel, a community programming channel is the cable company's property; it can exercise its own First Amendment rights like a newspaper publisher. The company decides what programs will air on the community programming channel and bears responsibility for their content. The company is also free to refuse any program it does not wish to air.

When this resolution failed to pass, Sharp and Cleaver then decided to propose the resolution at issue in this case, a resolution that would eliminate the public access channel altogether.

32   Milton, "Aeropagitica, a Speech for the Liberty of Unlicensed Printing" (1644), reprinted in *The Portable Milton*, ed. Douglas Bush (London: Penguin Books, 1977), p. 199.

32   The quotation from Justice Holmes about the marketplace of ideas is from his dissenting opinion in *Abrams v. United States*, 250 U.S. 616 (1919).

32   Justice Brandeis's defense of free speech is quoted from his dissenting opinion in *Whitney v. California*, 274 U.S. 357 (1927).

34   The lawsuit filed by the Klan is *Missouri Knights of the Ku Klux Klan v. Kansas City*, 723 F. Supp. 1347, 1348 (W.D. Mo. 1989). The Klan sued the city, which authorized the elimination of the public access channel, rather than the cable company. Only by suing the city could the First Amendment be implicated, since generally speaking, the Bill of Rights does not restrict private parties, but only the government.

The Ku Klux Klan argued that the active role played by local government in establishing a cable franchise brought the First Amendment into play. For example, in order to install a cable system, the company must tear up the streets to lay the cables, or string up wires on existing telephone lines, a process that inconveniences the public and must be approved by local authorities. Perhaps most important, in awarding a cable franchise, local government grants the company a profitable monopoly, in return for which the government may require certain services, like a public access channel. Once the First Amendment was implicated, any further government action, such as the elimination of the channel, also had to meet First Amendment requirements of being content-neutral and nondiscriminatory.

Sometimes, however, action by a private party can be treated as if it is action by the state—that is, "state action"— to which constitutional restrictions apply. But as Justice Rehnquist put it: "The question whether particular conduct is 'private' on the one hand, or 'state action' on the other, frequently admits of no easy answer." *Jackson v. Metropolitan Edison Co.*, 419 U.S. 345, 349–50 (1974). The question to be asked is "whether there is a sufficiently close nexus between the State and the challenged action of the [private party] so that the action of the latter may be fairly treated as that of the State itself." *Jackson*, p. 351.

35   The case that held flag burning to be protected by the First Amendment is *Texas v. Johnson*, 109 S. Ct. 2533 (1989). Johnson, a political demonstrator, was handed a flag during demonstrations at the 1984 Republican National Convention in Dallas. When the demonstration arrived in front of City Hall, Johnson doused the flag with kerosene and set it on fire, accompanied by chants of "America, the red, white, and blue, we spit on you!" Johnson was then prosecuted for violating a Texas criminal statute that made it a crime to "desecrate" the flag in a way "the actor knows will seriously offend" onlookers. Texas Penal Code Ann. 42.09(a)(3) (1989).

The Supreme Court overturned Johnson's conviction holding that Johnson's burning of the American flag was expressive conduct protected by the First Amendment. The Court wrote: "If there is a bedrock principle underlying the First Amendment, it is that the Government may not prohibit the expression of an idea simply because society finds the idea itself offensive or disagreeable." *Johnson*, p. 2544. A political outcry resulted. On July 18, 1989, the Flag Protection Act of 1989 was introduced in the U.S. Senate. It was intended to prohibit flag desecration in a content-neutral way. The actor was no longer punished for flag burning only if he knew it would "seriously offend" onlookers. The Flag Protection Act of 1989 became law, prohibiting flag desecration and punishing anyone who "knowingly mutilates, defaces, physically defiles, burns, maintains on the floor or ground or tramples" on the flag. 19 U.S.C. 700(a)(1) (1989). The president in the meantime called for a constitutional amendment. Instead of putting an end to the controversy, the Flag Protection Act itself became the focus of protests. Flags were burned in several places, including the steps of the U.S. Capitol. Prosecutions were brought against the flag burners.

Two district courts held the new statute to be unconstitutional under the First Amendment and ruled in favor of the defendants.

The Flag Protection Act of 1989, however, provided for a direct appeal to the U.S. Supreme Court.

On June 11, 1990, in the consolidated cases of *U.S. v. Eichman* and *U.S. v. Haggerty*, 110 S. Ct. 2404 (1990), the Supreme Court found that the statute violated the First Amendment. The Court held that the new act suffered from the same fundamental flaw as the Texas statute in *Johnson:* "It suppresses expression out of concern for its likely communicative impact" (p. 2409). The Court declined the government's invitation to reassess its conclusion in light of a recent "national consensus" favoring the punishment of flag burners. "Even assuming such a consensus exists," the Court wrote, "any suggestion that the Government's interest in suppressing speech becomes more weighty as popular opposition to that speech grows is foreign to the First Amendment" (Ibid.). The process for amending the Constitution is set forth in article V.

That same month, the proposed constitutional amendment failed to gain the necessary votes in the House of Representatives, and for the moment, the controversy has subsided.

35   In the Dial-a-Porn case, the Supreme Court upheld a statute prohibiting interstate transmission of obscene commercial telephone messages, saying that "obscenity" is not protected by the First Amendment. At the same time it held that a total ban on "indecent" telephone calls went too far. *Sable Communications of California, Inc. v. FCC*, 109 S. Ct. 2829 (1989). While it may seem that Dial-a-Porn is a marginal issue, the numbers indicate otherwise. A service in New York City received 6 to 7 million calls in six months. *Carlin Communications, Inc. v. FCC*, 787 F.2d. 846, 848 (2d Cir. 1986). Also, phone sex has been the subject of various serious commentators. See, e.g., Comment, "Telephones, Sex, and the First Amendment," *UCLA Law Review* 33 (1986): 1221.

Freedom of the Press:
United States v. The Progressive

39   The quoted passage is from Morland, "The H-Bomb Secret: To Know How Is to Ask Why," *Progressive* (November 1979): 3.

41   The Griffin Bell quotations are from Griffin B. Bell and Ronald Ostrow, *Taking Care of the Law* (New York: William Morrow, 1982), p. 131.

The Erwin Knoll quotation about having the government "licked" is from Knoll, "Wrestling with Leviathan: The Progressive Knew It Would Win," *Progressive* (November 1979): p. 13.

An affidavit is a written declaration or statement of fact, made voluntarily and confirmed by an oath or affirmation of the party making the statement or declaration. The oath or affirmation can be administered by any person with authority to do so, usually a notary public.

41   The Howard Morland quotation is from Morland, "The H-Bomb Secret—Learning It Is Easy, Once You Know the Handshake," *Progressive* (May 1979): p. 26.

41–42   The Howard Morland quotation about eastern Tennessee is from ibid., p. 24.

The Howard Morland quotations about Vietnam and the H-bomb are from H. Morland, *The Secret That Exploded* (New York: Random House, 1979), p. 24.

The quotation about Howard Morland's personality is from Richard Cohen, "The Road to Censorship, a Double-Edged Sword?" *Washington Post*, May 10, 1979, sec. B, p. 1.

The letter from Howard Morland to the *Progressive* is reprinted in Knoll, "Born Secret: The Story Behind the H-Bomb Article We're Not Allowed to Print," *Progressive* (May 1979): pp. 13–14.

44   The Howard Morland article on the H-bomb that was the subject of the lawsuit was printed in the November 1979 issue of the *Progressive*, pp. 3–12. The quoted passage about the "key" to the H-bomb secret appears on page 3. The other quoted passages are from page 12.

45   Memorandum to the president from Griffin B. Bell, attorney general, dated March 24, 1979.

45   Milton, "Areopagitica, a Speech for the Liberty of Unlicensed Printing" (1644), reprinted in Bush, ed., *The Portable Milton*, pp. 151–205.

One of the colonists' major complaints against the Crown was the English common law crime of seditious libel—laws prohibiting speech critical of and aimed at overthrowing the government. See *Bridges v. California*, 314 U.S. 252, 264 (1941), citing Schofield, "Freedom of the Press in the United States," *Publications American Sociol. Soc.* 9 (1914): 67, 76. Some scholars argue that the First Amendment was largely intended to prohibit repression by way of seditious libel prosecutions. See Zechariah Chaffee, Jr., *Free Speech in the United States* (Cambridge: Harvard University Press, 1942), p. 21. Others have challenged this notion. They point out that while opinions differed widely in colonial America as a whole, there was often a large degree of homogeneity within a particular community. In this view, it was the intolerance of the various communities, governors, and local councils that was the instrument of oppression, rather than the courts. See, e.g., Levy, *Emergence of a Free Press* (New York: Oxford University Press, 1985), pp. 16–61.

45   *Near v. Minnesota*, 283 U.S. 697, 713 (1931).

46   The Supreme Court quote about debate being "uninhibited, robust and wide-open" is from *New York Times Co. v. Sullivan*, 376 U.S. 254, 270 (1964).

The Thomas Jefferson quotation is from Zechariah Chafee, Jr., *Freedom of Speech and Press* (New York: Carrie Chapman Catt Memorial Inc., 1955), p. 48.

47 Justice Black's quotation is from the Pentagon Papers case: *New York Times Co. v. United States*, 403 U.S. 713, 716–17 (1971).

The Supreme Court passage setting out the national security exception to the prior restraint doctrine is in *Near*, p. 716.

47 Justice Stewart's quotation about national security and the press is from *New York Times Co. v. United States*, 403 U.S. 713, 728 (1971).

48 Chief Justice Burger's quotation about the Pentagon Papers case is from ibid., p. 751.

The rule about "direct and immediate" harm is from ibid., pp. 726–27.

The grave consequences that were at stake, and the strong feelings involved in the Pentagon Papers case are aptly illustrated by the closing paragraph of Justice Blackmun's dissent: "I hope that damage has not already been done . . . if . . . these newspapers proceed to publish . . . and there results therefrom 'the death of soldiers, the destruction of alliances . . .' to which list I might add . . . the prolongation of the war and further delay in the freeing of United States prisoners, then the nation's people will know where the responsibility for these sad consequences rests." Ibid., p. 763 (Blackmun, J., dissenting).

48 The allegation of "potential destruction in a nuclear holocaust" is from *United States v. The Progressive, Inc.*, United States District Court for the Western District of Wisconsin, Plaintiff's Statement of Points and Authorities in Support of Application for a Temporary Restraining Order and Motion for Preliminary Injunction, p. 15.

49 Letter from Albert Einstein to the Emergency Committee of Atomic Scientists, dated January 22, 1947, is reprinted in *The Progressive* (November 1979): p. 6.

49 The quotation from the government affidavits is from William C. Grayson, Jr., "A Brief History of *The Progressive* Case," prepared for Office of Classification, U.S. Department of Energy, Washington D.C., December 1987.

Atomic Energy Act of 1954, 42 U.S.C. 2280 (1982 Supp. V 1987).

51 The quotation about Dr. Teller's article is from Michael McDonald Mooney, "Right Conduct for a Free Press," *Harper's* 260 (March 1980): p. 42.

Erwin Knoll's quotation about censorship is from Douglas E. Kneeland, "Affidavits Censored in Bomb Article Case," *New York Times*, March 21, 1979, p. 16.

The *Progressive* case in district court is *United States v. The Progressive, Inc.*, 467 F. Supp. 990 (W.D. Wis. 1979).

51   The best way to understand the overbreadth doctrine is to
     think first of the literal meaning of the word *overbroad*—that
     is, is the statute worded in such a way that it reaches speech
     that is constitutionally protected? For example, a statute that
     says "speaking is prohibited in all crowded theaters" is over-
     broad. Surely one is free to say "something," even though one
     cannot falsely scream "fire" in a crowded theater. Thus, the
     statute reaches both protected speech and unprotected
     speech.
         When courts look at whether a statute is overbroad, they
     do so in two ways: one is called the "as applied" method of
     judicial review; the other method is to look at whether the
     statute is unconstitutional "on its face." Assume *X* is standing
     trial because he falsely screamed "fire" in a crowded theater
     and thus violated the statute. As a defense, *X* says that the
     statute is unconstitutional because it is overbroad.
         A court that uses the "as applied" method looks at the stat-
     ute's application to the case before it—*X*'s situation. If the
     court finds that what *X* said is not constitutionally protected
     speech, it will uphold the statute. But if the court finds that
     X's speech is protected under the First Amendment, it will
     hold only this particular application of the statute uncon-
     stitutional. The statute stays on the books, but is truncated
     by the court's ruling that it cannot be applied to these facts.
         A court that declares a statute void "on its face" can do so
     even if *X*'s conduct (falsely screaming "fire") is not protected
     under the First Amendment. This is so because the court will
     look at all applications of the statute, not only *X*'s case. If in a
     substantial number of possible situations, the statute would
     prohibit protected speech (even if *X*'s speech is not pro-
     tected), the court will hold the statute to be "void on its
     face," thus effectively sending it back to the legislature for
     redrafting. See, e.g., *Gooding v. Wilson* 405 U.S. 518 (1972).
         One of the reasons to use the "void on its face" method of
     judicial review in First Amendment cases is that the statute
     may have a "chilling effect." Although a particular
     application is constitutionally sound (e.g., to *X* falsely scream-
     ing "fire" in the crowded theater), leaving an overbroad stat-
     ute on the books may deter others from speaking out of fear
     of being prosecuted as well. See Note, "The Chilling Effect in
     Constitutional Law," *Columbia Law Review* 69 (1969): 808.
     For further discussion, see Henry M. Hart, *Hart and
     Wechsler's The Federal Courts and the Federal System*, 3rd ed.
     by Paul M. Bator et al. (Westbury, N.Y.: Foundation Press,
     1988); see also Note, "The First Amendment Overbreadth
     Doctrine," *Harvard Law Review* 83 (1970): 844–46.
         Vagueness is a doctrine closely related to overbreadth. The
     Supreme Court stated the underlying principle as follows:
     "no man shall be held criminally responsible for conduct
     which he could not reasonably understand to be proscribed."
     United States v. Harris, 347 U.S. 612, 617 (1954).

52   The quotation from Griffin Bell is from Bell and Ostrow, *Taking Care of the Law*, p. 133.

52   Friedman, "The United States v. The Progressive," *Columbia Journalism Review* (July/August 1979): 22.

53   The quotation from Griffin Bell is from Bell and Ostrow, *Taking Care of the Law*, p. 135.
      The case was dismissed on appeal. *United States v. The Progressive, Inc.*, 610 F.2d 819 (7th Cir. 1979).
      The injunction by the district court was issued *pendente lite*—that is, while the case lasts.

53   Erwin Knoll's introductory comment is from Knoll, "The Secret Revealed," *Progressive* (November 1979): 2.

Freedom of Religion:
Lyng v. Northwest Indian Cemetery Protective Association

57–60 Additional information regarding Indian religious beliefs and practices can be found in an excerpt from a report by Dorothea Theodoratus, reprinted in the Joint Appendix to the Briefs for Petitioners and Respondents, *Lyng v. Northwest Indian Cemetery Protective Association*, 106 S. Ct. 1319 (1988) (No. 86-1013), pp. 110–97.

61   Testimony of Sam Jones, Trial Transcript, *Northwest Indian Cemetery Protective Association v. Peterson*, C-82–4909 vol. 2, March 15, 1983 (hereafter Trial Transcript), p. 239

61   The Indians also filed a number of statutory claims against the road, alleging government violations of: the American Indian Religious Freedom Act of 1978; reserved fishing and water rights of the Indians; the federal government's trust responsibility to the Indians; the National Historic Preservation Act and Executive Order 11593; the National Environmental Policy Act; the National Forest Management Act of 1976; the Federal Water Pollution Control Act; the Porter-Cologne Water Quality Control Act; the Multiple Use, Sustained Yield Act; and the Administrative Procedure Act. Only the constitutional issue reached the Supreme Court.

61–63 Historical information is drawn largely from Thomas Curry, *The First Freedoms: Church and State in America to the Passage of the First Amendment* (New York: Oxford University Press, 1986). See also Mark DeWolfe Howe, *The Garden and the Wilderness: Religion and Government in American Constitutional History* (Chicago: University of Chicago Press, 1965); Michael McConnell, "The Origins and Historical Understanding of Free Exercise of Religion," *Harvard Law Review* 103: 1416 (May 1990); *Everson v. Board of Education*, 330 U.S. 1 (1947); *Abington School District v. Schempp*, 374 U.S. 203 (1963).

62   The Church of England was established in Virginia, South Carolina, North Carolina, Maryland, Georgia, and New York. Massachusetts and Connecticut recognized Congregationalism as their official religion. Delaware, New Jersey,

Pennsylvania, and Rhode Island did not establish an official religion. New Hampshire's system of local control was so decentralized that it did not amount to an establishment. See Curry, *First Freedoms*, pp. 105–6.

62   Patrick Henry's bill provided that all should be taxed for the support of the Christian denomination of their choice. Funds not designated to a particular denomination would be allocated to education. For further information on the battle over the assessment bill, see Curry, *First Freedoms*, pp. 140–46.

62   Madison's "Memorial and Remonstrance Against Religious Assessments" is reprinted in *Everson*, as an appendix to the dissenting opinion of Justice Rutledge.

62   Thomas Jefferson's "Bill for Establishing Religious Freedom" is reprinted in Thomas Jefferson, *Writings* (New York: Library of America, Literary Classics of the United States, 1984), pp. 346–48.

63   Madison's original draft of the religion clauses is reprinted in Curry, *First Freedoms*, p. 199. Madison's other models for the religion clauses of the First Amendment were the Revolutionary era state constitutions and Bills of Rights. The free exercise of religion was protected in all except Connecticut's, whose Declaration of Rights was less elaborate than those of the other states. It was the only right so universally guaranteed. Bernard Schwartz, *The Great Rights of Mankind: A History of the American Bill of Rights* (New York: Oxford University Press, 1977), pp. 86–90.

63   The quotation describing the meaning of the establishment clause is from *Everson*, pp. 15–16.
     Over the years, the Supreme Court has identified three tests for determining whether a statute violates the establishment clause: "First, the statute must have a secular purpose; second, its principal or primary effect must be one that neither advances nor inhibits religion. . . ; finally, the statute must not foster 'an excessive government entanglement with religion.'" *Lemon v. Kurtzman*, 403 U.S. 602, 612–13 (1971).
     The court has also recently expressed some approval of a simpler version of the test, proposed by Justice O'Connor, which would reduce its three "prongs" to two: one focusing on institutional entanglement, the other on the question of "'whether the government intends to convey a message of endorsement or disapproval of religion.'" *Wallace v. Jaffree*, 472 U.S. 38, 61 (1985), citing *Lynch v. Donnelly*, 465 U.S. 668, 690–91 (1984) (O'Connor, J., concurring).

63   The basic test for determining whether the free exercise clause has been violated is set forth in *Sherbert v. Verner*, 374 U.S. 398 (1963). The free exercise clause was incorporated against the states in *Cantwell v. Connecticut*, 310 U.S. 296 (1940). The establishment clause was incorporated in *Everson* in 1947.
     Since then a number of approaches have been suggested to reconcile the doctrinal tension between the two religion

clauses. One approach is embodied in the Jeffersonian "strict separation" theory. The government both prevents establishment of religion and protects its exercise when it erects a "wall of separation" between it and the church.

Another approach has been to say that, taken together, the two clauses mean that the government simply may not "aid" religion. The "no-aid" formulation, however, runs into the problem of defining what the term *aid* should be taken to mean.

A third approach has been to posit "neutrality" as the guidepost—the government must remain "strictly neutral" with respect to religion. The Court, however, has never embraced the concept of strict neutrality, which would limit any government attempts either to confer benefits or to impose burdens on religion. Such an approach would seem incongruent in a modern society. The exceptions the Court has allowed to the neutrality approach, in any case, suggest to some commentators that the Court has in fact carved out "zones" of both required and permissible "accommodation" with respect to issues touching on religion. See Laurence H. Tribe, *American Constitutional Law*, 2d ed. (Mineola, New York: Foundation Press, 1988), sec. 14-4.

63 The case involving the Seventh-Day Adventist is *Sherbert*. The case involving the Jehovah's Witness is *Thomas v. Review Board, Indiana Employment Security Division*, 450 U.S. 707 (1981).

64 The district court's decision in the Indians' case is *Northwest Indian Cemetery Protective Association v. Peterson*, 565 F. Supp. 586 (1983) (N.D. California).

64 The California Wilderness Act is Pub. L. No. 98-425, 98 Stat. 1619 (1984).

64 The Ninth Circuit Court of Appeals' decision is *Northwest Indian Cemetery Protective Association v. Peterson*, 795 F. 2d 688 (1986).

64 The case involving the Amish is *Wisconsin v. Yoder*, 406 U.S. 205 (1972).

65 Justice Douglas's description of the free exercise clause is from his concurring opinion in *Sherbert*.

66 Chief Justice John Marshall's description of a constitution can be found in Beveridge, *The Life of John Marshall* (1919), p. 343, quoted in William B. Lockhart, Yale Kamisar, Jesse H. Choper, and Steven H. Shiffrin, eds., *Constitutional Rights and Liberties*, 6th ed. (St. Paul, Minn.: West, 1986), p. 30.

66 The Supreme Court opinion in the Indians' case is *Lyng v. Northwest Indian Cemetery Protective Association*, 106 S. Ct. 1319 (1988). The justices voted five to three in favor of the Forest Service. Justices Brennan, Marshall, and Blackmun dissented. Justice Kennedy did not participate in the decision. A tie vote would have affirmed the lower court's decision in favor of the Indians.

Freedom of Assembly:
Hobson v. Wilson

72–73　Testimony of Abe Bloom, Trial Transcript, *Hobson v. Wilson*, Civil Action no. 76-1326, vol. 260, November 24, 1981 (hereafter Trial Transcript), p. 123.

73–74　Memorandum to W. C. Sullivan from C. D. Brennan, May 9, 1968, re: COINTELPRO, Internal Security, Disruption of the New Left (Plaintiff's Exhibit 3).

74　Letter to SAC, Albany et al. from Director, FBI, May 10, 1968, re: COINTELPRO (Plaintiff's Exhibit 3).

74　Airtel to SAC, Albany et al. from Director, FBI, March 4, 1968, re: COINTELPRO, Black Nationalist—Hate Groups, Racial Intelligence (Plaintiff's Exhibit 2a).

75　Letter to SAC, Albany et al, May 10, 1968. (Plaintiff's Exhibit 3).

75　Airtel to SAC, Chicago et al. from Director, FBI, August 21, 1969, re: COINTELPRO–New Left (Plaintiff's Exhibit 18).

75　Airtel to Director, FBI from SAC, WFO, September 24, 1969, re: COINTELPRO Black Nationalist—Hate Groups Racial Matters (Black United Front) (Plaintiff's Exhibit 20).

75　Airtel to Director, FBI from SAC, WFO, October 1, 1969, re: COINTELPRO Black Nationalist—Hate Groups Racial Matters (Black United Front) (Plaintiff's Exhibit 21).

75,77　Memorandum to Director, FBI, from SAC, New York, October 10, 1969, re: COINTELPRO–New Left ('Bananas' Leaflet) (Plaintiff's Exhibit 23).

75–76　Letter to SAC, New York from Director, FBI, October 15, 1969, re: COINTELPRO–New Left (Plaintiff's Exhibit 24).

76　Testimony of Tina Hobson, Trial Transcript, vol. 260, November 24, 1981, p. 71.

78　Memorandum to Director, FBI, from SAC, New York, re: CO-INTELPRO–New Left, February 3, 1970 (Plaintiff's Exhibit 31).

78　Memorandum to C. D. Brennan from G. C. Moore, August 20, 1970, re: Counterintelligence Matters, New Left—Black Panther Party (Plaintiff's Exhibit 7).

78　Airtel to SAC, Baltimore et al. from Director, FBI, September 9, 1970, re: COINTELPRO, Black Nationalist—Hate Groups, Racial Intelligence—Black Panther Party; COINTELPRO–New Left—Security Matter. (Plaintiff's Exhibit 8).

78　Memorandum to W. C. Sullivan from C. D. Brennan, April 27, 1971, re: Counterintelligence Programs (COINTELPROS) Internal Security-Racial Matters (Plaintiff's Exhibit 36).

78　The lawsuit filed in the district court is *Hobson v. Wilson*, 556 F. Supp. 1157 (1982).

80　The federal civil rights conspiracy statute under which the case was brought reads, "If two or more persons in any State or Territory conspire to go in disguise on the highway or on the premises of another, for the purpose of depriving, either directly or indirectly, any person or class of persons of the equal protection of the laws, or of equal privileges and immunities under the laws [and] in any case of conspiracy set forth in this section, if one or more persons engaged therein do, or cause to be done, any act in furtherance of the object of such conspiracy, whereby another is injured in his person or property, or deprived of having and exercising any right or privilege of a citizen of the United States, the party so injured or deprived may have an action for the recovery of damages occasioned by such injury or deprivation, against any one or more of the conspirators." 42 U.S.C.A. 1985(3).

80 The case that held freedom of association to be incorporated against the states is *N.A.A.C.P. v. Alabama*, 357 U.S. 449 (1958).

80 Historically, the right of assembly is connected with the right of petition, which stretches back to the Magna Charta, written in 1215. In fact, the right of petition first enabled the legislature to assume the initiative: when the king summoned Parliament to supply funds for the support of the government, the House of Commons began to petition the Crown for a redress of grievances as a condition for voting the money.

    Through the centuries the right became recognized and in 1689, the English Bill of Rights provided that it was the "right of subjects to petition the King."

    In our own country, the rights of assembly and petition were asserted often in the colonial period and, in fact, are mentioned in the Declaration of Independence. "In every stage of these Oppressions We Have Petitioned for Redress in the most humble terms. Our repeated petitions have been answered only by repeated injury." After the Revolution, four of the newly independent states guaranteed the rights of assembly and petition in their state constitutions: North Carolina, Massachusetts, New Hampshire, and Pennsylvania.

    During the debates over the Bill of Rights in August 1789, one delegate proposed to delete the right of assembly from the clause guaranteeing the freedoms of speech and debate because it was too obvious. "If people freely converse together, they meet to assemble for that purpose; it is a self-evident inalienable right which the people possess; it certainly is a thing that would never be called into question." He compared it to listing the right to put on your hat and felt it was "derogatory to descend to such minutiae." Others disagreed and the provision passed. David Fellman, "Constitutional Rights of Association," *Sup. Ct. Rev.* (1961): 74.

80 The passage by Chief Justice Hughes is from *De Jonge v. Oregon*, 299 U.S. 353 (1937), the case that incorporated the right of peaceable assembly against the states.

81 Information concerning the history of COINTELPRO can be found in the Church Committee's report, "Select Committee to Study Governmental Operations with Respect to Intelligence Activities," Final Report S. Rep. No. 755, Book II (In-

telligence Activities and the Rights of Americans), 94th Cong., 20th Sess. (1976) (hereafter Senate Report).

83   Testimony of Charles Brennan, Trial Transcript, vol. 267, December 4, 1981, pp. 823, 827, 828.

83   Memorandum to W. C. Sullivan from C. D. Brennan, April 30, 1968, re: Program for Apprehension and Detention of Persons Considered Potentially Dangerous to the National Defense and Public Safety of the United States (DETPRO) (Plaintiff's Exhibit 80).

84   The quotation from Harlan Fiske Stone can be found in Senate Report, p. 3.

84   The quotation from George Moore can be found in Senate Report, p. 11, n. 48.

85   The case enabling individuals to sue government officials personally is *Bivens v. Six Unknown Named Agents*, 403 U.S. 388 (1971).

85–86   As stated in the text, the judge instructed the trial jurors that they could find an FBI defendant immune only if they found the defendant sincerely and reasonably believed his conduct was lawful. Trial Transcript, vol. 275, December 17, 1981, p. 251.

In other words, "An official would not receive qualified immunity if he knew or reasonably should have known that the action he took within his sphere of official responsibility would violate the constitutional rights of the [plaintiff] or if [the official] took the action with the malicious intention to cause a deprivation of constitutional rights or other injury." *Hobson v. Wilson*, 737 F.2d 1, 24 (1984), quoting *Wood v. Strickland*, 420 U.S. 308 (1975). Thus, at the time of the trial the qualified immunity defense had both subjective and objective elements.

After the trial, in *Harlow v. Fitzgerald*, 457 U.S. 800 (1982), the Supreme Court redefined the qualified immunity defense to eliminate the subjective element, using instead only the objective "reasonable person" standard. Under the new standard, "government officials performing discretionary functions generally are shielded from liability for civil damages insofar as their conduct does not violate clearly established statutory or constitutional rights of which a reasonable person would have known." *Harlow*, p. 818.

The Court of Appeals agreed with the defendants that the *Harlow* standard governed the case, but found that even under the *Harlow* standard the defendants were not entitled to immunity. *Hobson*, p. 24. Under *Harlow*, if the law was "clearly established" at the time the conduct occurred, the government actor is presumed to have known the law governing his conduct.

The court concluded "that the acts defendants were alleged to have committed violated fundamental and well-established constitutional rights, and that defendants are entitled neither to immunity nor consequently, to reversal of the verdicts against them on this ground." *Hobson*, p. 25.

For more on qualified immunity, see discussions of Third and Fourth amendments.

86 The Court of Appeals' decision is *Hobson v. Wilson*, 737 F.2d 1 (D.C. Cir. 1984).

87 The distribution of damages is detailed in a memorandum by U.S. District Court Judge Louis Oberdorfer, dated October 22, 1986, *Hobson v. Brennan*, Civil Action no. 76-1326.

87–88 Testimony of Charles Brennan, Trial Transcript, vol. 271, December 10, 1981, p. 588.

SECOND AMENDMENT

Right to Keep and Bear Arms: *Quilici v. Morton Grove*

Victor Quilici and the trustees who voted against Morton Grove's ordinance refused to speak with the authors.

93 Unlike the ordinance banning the *possession* of handguns, local ordinances forbidding the *carriage* of concealed weapons have a long history. In 1838–39, for example, Alabama forbade any person from carrying "concealed about his person, any species of fire arms, or any Bowie knife, Arkansaw [*sic*] tooth pick, or any other knife of the like kind, dirk, or any other deadly weapon." *State v. Reid.* 1 Ala. 612, 614 (1840). *State v. Buzzard*, 4 Ark. 18 (1842); *Nunn v. Georgia*, 1 Ga. 243 (1846).

96 The Morton Grove ordinance is titled "An Ordinance Regulating the Possession of Firearms and Other Dangerous Weapons," Ordinance no. 81-11. It is reprinted in *Quilici v. Village of Morton Grove*, 532 F. Supp. 1169, 1185 (D.C. Ill. 1981).

97 In addition to the Second Amendment claims, Quilici argued that the ordinance violated the Illinois constitutional right to bear arms, a Ninth Amendment implied right to self-defense, and the Fifth Amendment's prohibition of taking private property.
   Two other lawsuits were filed, one with the support of the NRA and the other on behalf of the Second Amendment Foundation (another gun lobbying organization). The three were consolidated into one: *Quilici v. Village of Morton Grove*, 532 F. Supp. 1169 (D.C. Ill. 1981).
   Because a constitutional issue was at stake, Morton Grove removed the case to federal court. The process called "removal" works as follows: If a plaintiff brings an action in state court that involves issues of federal or U.S. constitutional law, the defendant may switch the case to federal court before the state court reaches a judgment. See 28 U.S.C. 144(a)(8).

97 For an example of the literature dealing with the peculiarities of the Second Amendment, see S. Levinson, "The Embarrassing Second Amendment," *Yale Law Journal* 99 (Dec. 1989):637.

98 In addition to the language of the Second Amendment the individual rights (or progun) advocates find support for their

position in the organization of the Bill of Rights. Madison originally proposed that the amendments be inserted into the text of the Constitution rather than added as amendments. The "right to keep and bear arms" was initially included with the other individual rights in article I, section 9, rather than as a limitation on the militia clause of article I, section 8. When Congress voted to add the Bill of Rights as amendments at the end of the Constitution instead, if the Second Amendment were intended as a limitation on the states, the argument goes, it should have been grouped with the Ninth and Tenth amendments. Since it was grouped between the other individual rights in the First and Fourth amendments, it must also have been intended to be one.

98   The Statute of Northampton, enacted in 1328, provided: "No man great or small [is] to go nor ride armed by night nor by day in fairs, markets, nor in the presence of the justices or other ministers nor elsewhere." Persons violating the statute were punished by forfeiture of "their armour to the King and their bodies to prison at the King's pleasure." Reprinted in Philip Kurland and Ralph Lerner, eds., *The Founders' Constitution* (Chicago: University of Chicago Press, 1987), 5:209.

Over the centuries, Parliament passed a number of statutes restricting the ownership or use of weapons. In 1541, for example, a statute limited ownership of crossbows and handguns to persons with incomes over one hundred pounds a year. Later, Parliament passed a series of game acts that restricted the use of weapons to those qualified to hunt. The Game Act of 1671 went further than its predecessors. By raising the property qualification for hunting from forty to one hundred pounds annual income from land, it disqualified all but large landholders. The qualification to hunt thus became *fifty* times that required to vote, and those not qualified were not allowed to keep any guns. Gamekeepers appointed by the landowners were permitted, with a warrant, to search for and confiscate weapons.

The Militia Act of 1662 had previously authorized officers in the militia to confiscate weapons. Charles II used the Militia Act and the royal proclamation to further restrict gun ownership.

Indeed, Charles II's firearms regulations resemble the United States' Gun Control Act of 1968, enacted three centuries later. Under Charles's provision, "Gunsmiths were ordered to produce a record of all weapons they had manufactured over the past six months together with a list of their purchasers. In the future they were commanded to report every Saturday night to the ordinance office the number of guns made and sold that week. Carriers throughout the kingdom were required to obtain a license if they wished to transport guns, and all importation of firearms was banned." J. L. Malcolm, "The Right of the People to Keep and Bear Arms: The Common Law Tradition," *Hastings Law Review Quarterly* 10 (1983):285.

Charles II, a Protestant, was succeeded by his brother

James, a Catholic, who continued Charles's policy of arms restrictions and confiscations, increasingly directing them against his Whig political opponents and Protestant subjects.

After James II was driven from England in 1688, his daughter Mary and her Protestant husband, William of Orange, assumed the throne in the Glorious Revolution. Parliament, determined to protect Englishmen from further abuses of royal power like those they endured under the arbitrary Stuarts, presented William and Mary with a Declaration of Rights. In 1689, William and Mary agreed to recognize these thirteen fundamental rights, which were then incorporated into the legislation recognizing William and Mary as king and queen. This document became known as the English Bill of Rights. One clause of this important ancestor of our own Bill of Rights provided "that the subjects which are protestants, may have arms for their defense suitable to their condition and as allowed by law." See Malcolm, "The Right of the People to Keep and Bear Arms," p. 285; D. Hardy, "Armed Citizens, Citizen Armies toward a Jurisprudence of the Second Amendment," *Harvard Journal of Law and Social Policy* 9:559. Excerpt from the English Bill of Rights reprinted in Kurland and Lerner, *The Founders' Constitution*, 5:210.

99   The information about the Articles of Confederation can be found in articles II, VI, and IX, "Articles of Confederation, November 15, 1777," reprinted in Michael Kammen, ed., *The Origins of the American Constitution: A Documentary History* (New York: Viking Penguin, 1986), p. 10.

99   Madison's original draft of the provision that eventually became the Second Amendment read: "The right of the people to keep and bear arms shall not be infringed; a well armed but well regulated militia being the best security of a free Country; but no person religiously scrupulous of bearing arms shall be compelled to render military service in person." The congressional debate focused almost entirely on the religious exemption, which was eventually voted down. After modifications by the Senate, the Second Amendment was rewritten into its final form by the House and included in the Bill of Rights. Portion of the House debate reprinted in Kurland and Lerner, *The Founders' Constitution*, 5:210–11.

99   Congress's militia power is set forth in the U.S. Constitution, article I, section 8.

100   The district court decision is reported as *Quilici v. Morton Grove*, 532 F. Supp. 1169 (N.D. Ill. 1981).

100   The case in which the Supreme Court declined to incorporate the Second Amendment against the states is *Presser v. Illinois*, 116 U.S. 252 (1886). For a general explanation of the incorporation doctrine, see the Historical Note.

100   *Quilici v. Morton Grove*, 695 F.2d 261 (7th Cir. 1982).

101   The debate in Morton Grove has spread nationally and cities such as San Francisco also enacted gun restrictions. At least one town, Keenesaw, Georgia, had the opposite reaction, going so far as to require its citizens to own firearms as an

outgrowth of the Second Amendment and calling Morton Grove "Moron Grove." J. Anderson, "A Reporter at Large: An Extraordinary People," *New Yorker* (November 12, 1984):163.

In *U.S. v. Miller,* the Court upheld a 1934 federal law that required registration of firearms with barrels less than eighteen inches in length, subject to criminal penalty. *Miller,* 307 U.S. 174 (1939). Congress prevented transport of these weapons based on its power to regulate interstate commerce, even if the activity was not directly commercial. *Heart of Atlanta Motel v. United States,* 379 U.S. 241, 276, n. 11 (1964). (For more on Congress's power to regulate interstate commerce, see discussion of Tenth Amendment.) The Supreme Court has not considered the Second Amendment limits on such statutes since the *Miller* case.

103   FBI Statistics for 1988 show the following:

Total number of homicides in 1988	17,260
Number attributed to handguns	7,557
Percentage all homicides handgun related	45%
Percentage homicides shotgun related	6%
Percentage homicides rifle related	4%
Percentage homicides other guns	5%
Total percentage of homicides related to all guns	60%

SOURCE: *Uniform Crime Reports for the United States,* Federal Bureau of Investigation, U.S. Dept. of Justice, Washington, D.C., p. 12.

THIRD AMENDMENT

Quartering Troops: *Engblom v. Carey*

107   The quotation about a Constitution approaching immortality is from Beveridge, *The Life of John Marshall* (1919), quoted in Lockhart, Kamisar, Choper, and Shiffrin, *Constitutional Rights and Liberties,* p. 30

107   Benjamin Franklin's quotation about the Quartering Act is from a letter to the *Gazeteer and New Daily Advertiser,* 2 May 1765, reprinted in Kurland and Lerner, *The Founders' Constitution,* 5:215.

108   The colonist's quotation on the Quartering Act is from a letter from Joseph Hawley to Elbridge Gerry, 18 February 1776, reprinted in ibid., p. 216.

108   Patrick Henry's remarks are from the debate in the Virginia Ratifying Convention, 16 June 1788, cited in ibid., p. 217.

108   The case involving securities and the Third Amendment is *Securities Investor Protection Corp. v. Executive Securities Corp.,* 433 F. Supp 470 (S.D.N.Y. 1977).

109   The case involving a veterans parade and the Third Amendment is *Jones v. United States Sec'y of Defense,* 346 F. Supp. 97 (D. Minn. 1972).

109   The case involving the 1947 Housing and Rent Act and the Third Amendment is *United States v. Valenzuela*, 95 F. Supp. 363, 366 (S.D. Cal. 1951).

109   The prison guards' case in district court is *Engblom v. Carey*, 522 F. Supp. 57, (S.D.N.Y. 1981).

   The plaintiffs also sued under the due process clause of the Fourteenth Amendment. The court found, however, that this deprivation of property was not "of constitutional dimension." As discussed under the Fifth Amendment, the courts will generally require more than the mere existence of a procedural framework to create a cognizable due process interest. Here, there was no showing of a "legitimate expectation based on mutual understanding concerning control of staff housing" in the event of a strike. *Engblom*, p. 68. The court pointed out the unique character of the housing in question, noting that plaintiffs "were employees of a very specialized institution who, in applying for and accepting on-grounds housing, must be charged with knowledge of the risks and the possible limitations on their 'rights' involved." Ibid. The court went on to remark that even if a constitutionally protected interest in the premises was found, the common law doctrine of "necessity" would be applied to the state's action, since its "taking" was "in the public interest to lessen the real danger of disorder" at the prison. Ibid., citing Restatement (Second) of Torts, secs. 196, 262; W. Prosser, *The Law of Torts*, 3d ed. (1971), sec. 24. The court also dismissed plaintiff's claim that delay of mail delivery stated a claim of constitutional proportions, holding that the "interference" was "unrelated to the government's censorship of an interest in the content of the mail," such that the First Amendment was not offended.

   On appeal, the Second Circuit was far less taken with the novelty of plaintiff's living arrangements—at least with regard to the Third Amendment claim. It analogized the Third Amendment with privacy interests protected by the Fourth Amendment, which extend to "one who owns or lawfully possesses or controls property." *Rakas v. Illinois*, 439 U.S. 128, 143–44 (1978). The court referred to provisions of the New York Real Property Actions and Proceedings Law and the Department of Corrections' Directive and Rules ("which repeatedly refer to the occupants as tenants") in coming to its conclusion that a finding on behalf of plaintiffs of "a substantial Tenancy interest in their staff housing [in which] they enjoyed significant privacy due to their right to exclude others from what were functionally their homes," was not precluded by the facts on the record. *Engblom*, p. 964. The court affirmed the lower court's dismissal of the due process claim on essentially the same grounds, citing the emergency situation and the necessity of quick action "as bearing on what process was due" the dispossessed striking guards. See *Mathews v. Eldridge*, 424 U.S. 319 (1976), in notes to the Fifth Amendment discussion.

Here, "the absence of pre-deprivation process did not violate [the plaintiffs'] Due Process rights." *Engblom*, p. 965.

110 Justice Douglas, in dissent in *Poe v. Ullman*, 367 U.S. 497, 522 (1961), wrote, "Can there be any doubt that a Bill of Rights that in time of peace bars soldiers from being quartered in a home 'without the consent of the Owner' should also bar the police from investigating the intimacies of the marriage relation?"

This position foreshadowed Justice Douglas's controversial opinion in *Griswold v. Connecticut*, 381 U.S. 479 (1968). In *Griswold*, Justice Douglas wrote that "emanations" from certain provisions in the Bill of Rights, including the First, Third, Fourth, Fifth, and Ninth Amendments, form "penumbras" of privacy that protect the right of married couples to use contraceptives.

The penumbra theory, however, has been rejected in other contexts. For more detail, see discussion of the Ninth Amendment.

Justice Story's explanation of the meaning of the Third Amendment is from Joseph Story, *Commentaries on the Constitution* (1833), sec. 1003, p. 709; reprinted in Kurland and Lerner, *The Founders' Constitution*, 5:218.

110 The district court's quotation about the guards' possessory interest is from *Engblom v. Carey*, 522 F. Supp. 57, 67–68 (S.D.N.Y. 1981).

111 The Second Circuit case reversing the lower court is *Engblom v. Carey*, 677 F.2d 957 (2d Cir. 1982).

111 The case that finally dismissed the guards' claim is *Engblom v. Carey*, 572 F. Supp. 44, 46 (S.D.N.Y. 1983), citing *Harlow v. Fitzgerald*, 457 U.S. 800 (1982).

FOURTH AMENDMENT

Unreasonable Search and Seizure: *McSurely v. McClellan*

117 Testimony of Alan McSurely, Trial Transcript, *McSurely v. McClellan*, Civil Action no. 516-169, U.S. District Court, District of Columbia, Judge Bryant (hereafter Trial Transcript), November 22, 1982, pp. 134–49.

119 Margaret McSurely's quotation is from Richard Harris, *Freedom Spent* (Boston: Little, Brown, 1976), p. 141.

122–123 Testimony of James Madison Compton, Trial Transcript, November 29, 1982, pp. 19–62.

124 Testimony of John J. Burke, Trial Transcript, December 3, 1982, pp. 98–100.

Kentucky's antisedition statute, now repealed, is reprinted in *McSurely v. Ratliff*, 282 F. Supp. 848, 849, n. 1 (E.D. Ky. 1967).

125–127 Alan McSurely's quotations about the search are from Testimony of Alan McSurely, Trial Transcript, November 23, 1982, pp. 148–58.

128 The note from Margaret McSurely to Drew Pearson is reprinted in Harris, *Freedom Spent*, p. 175.

The case declaring the Kentucky antisedition law unconstitutional is *McSurely v. Ratliff*, 282 F. Supp. 848 (E.D. Ky.
1967).

129 The "safekeeping order" is reprinted in *McSurely v. Mc-
Clellan*, 553 F.2d 1277, 1282, n. 9 (D.C. Cir. 1976) (en banc).

129 The information regarding Resolution 150 is from *Riots, Civil
and Criminal Disorders, 1969: Hearings Before the Permanent
Subcommittee on Investigations of the Committee on Government Operations*, 91st Cong., 1st Sess. 2950 (1969) (statement
of the chairman).

129–130 The "court records" cited are from *McSurely v. McClellan*, p.
1298, n. 74.

130 The passage about the *New York Times* article is from Testimony of Alan McSurely, Trial Transcript, November 23, 1982,
pp. 58–59.

131 Testimony of Alan McSurely, Trial Transcript, November 23,
1982, pp. 66–68.

131–132 The case ordering the return of the McSurelys' documents is
McSurely v. Ratliff, 398 F.2d 817 (6th Cir. 1968).

132–134 Testimony of Alan McSurely, Trial Transcript, November 22,
1982, pp. 104–12.

134 Testimony of Margaret McSurely, Trial Transcript, December
3, 1982, pp. 11–12.

134–136 Charles Francis Adams, ed., *The Works of John Adams*
(Boston: Little, Brown, 1856), 2:524.

136 Further to the background on Fourth Amendment law: Note
that in the case hypothesized, in order for the policeman to
search your pockets, he or she must first have also *seized* you.
As a leading treatise puts it, "In the overwhelming majority
of cases in which an objection is raised concerning the obtaining of incriminating evidence from a person, the central
issue is whether the antecedent 'seizure' of the person was in
compliance with the Fourth Amendment. This is because it is
not ordinarily possible to obtain such evidence without first
making a seizure, and because the determination of the seizure issue is likely to govern without regard to whether what
happened thereafter was or was not a search." Wayne R.
LaFave, *Search and Seizure: A Treatise on the Fourth Amendment* (St. Paul, Minn.: West Publishing, 1978), vol. 1, sec. 2.6.
In the case posed, the legality of the search will therefore
often depend on whether or not the initial seizure was made
pursuant to valid authority, such as a warrant or the existence of "probable cause" to arrest. Note that under certain
circumstances—in particular, where a substantial intrusion
into the body is involved—a search may be unconstitutional
notwithstanding a prior lawful custodial arrest. *Schmerber v.
California*, 384 U.S. 757 (1966).

136 Justice Brandeis's quote about the right to be let alone is
from *Olmstead v. United States*, 277 U.S. 438, 478 (1928)
(Brandeis, J., dissenting).
The full passage regarding a "reasonable expectation of

Endnotes

privacy" under the Fourth Amendment is in *Katz v. United States*, 389 U.S. 347, 360 (1967) (Harlan, J., concurring). The essence of *Katz* lay in rejecting the *Olmstead* court's narrow, propertylike reading of the Fourth Amendment, which had focused on the issue of deciding which sorts of *places* were and were not protected by its provisions. Holding that "the Fourth Amendment protects people, not places" (*Katz*, p. 351), the *Katz* court sought to transform the inquiry from one focusing on the physical act of intruding into a particular area, to one focusing on the reasonable expectations of privacy that the individual holds. It should be noted, however, that this expansive holding has been narrowed in certain instances over the years by the Supreme Court.

There are many exceptions to the Fourth Amendment's warrant requirement—a requirement the Supreme Court has described as a constitutional "preference." See, e.g., *United States v. Ventresca*, 380 U.S. 102, 107 (1965). If a warrantless search falls within one of these exceptions, it is not necessarily an "unreasonable search" within the meaning of the Fourth Amendment.

One major exception involves warrantless searches made incident to a lawful arrest. Under current law, an arresting officer may search without a warrant "the arrestee's person and the area 'within his immediate control'—construing that phrase to mean the area from which he might gain possession of a weapon or destructible evidence." LaFave, *Search and Seizure*, vol. 2, sec. 4.1(a), quoting *Chimel v. California*, 395 U.S. 752 (1969). Cf. *Maryland v. Buie*, 110 S. Ct. 1093 (1990), distinguishing *Chimel* on facts and allowing a limited protective sweep of entire house incident to arrest where police have reasonable belief that dangerous persons may be hidden inside. Another exception, relying on the so-called "exigent circumstances" doctrine, allows the police to conduct a warrantless search when there is a substantial risk that they will lose valuable evidence if they take the time to obtain a warrant from a magistrate. This covers the "hot pursuit" situation mentioned in the text. *Warden v. Hayden*, 387 U.S. 294 (1967) (police arriving several minutes after armed suspected felon entered house may conduct search without first obtaining warrant). A third major exception to the warrant requirement is search after consent has been obtained from the subject of the search. LaFave, *Search and Seizure*, vol. 2, sec. 4.1(a).

Some believe that these exceptions to the warrant requirement threaten to swallow the rule. "The fact of the matter is that a great majority of police . . . searches are made and upheld notwithstanding the absence of a warrant." Y. Kamisar, W. LaFave, and J. Israel, *Modern Criminal Procedure*, 6th ed. (St. Paul, Minn.: West Publishing, 1986), p. 297.

138   Further to the background on the exclusionary rule: Although initially formulated in 1914, in *Weeks v. United States*, 232

U.S. 383, and applied against the states in 1961, *Mapp v. Ohio*, 367 U.S. 643 (1961), the exclusionary rule remains the subject of controversy. Proponents of the rule cite both the *Mapp* court's straightforward rationale that denying use of the rule "is to grant the right but in reality to withhold the privilege and enjoyment" (p. 656) and Justice Brandeis's famous dissent in an earlier case: "Decency, security, and liberty alike demand that government officials shall be subjected to the same rules of conduct that are commands to the citizen. In a government of laws, existence of the government will be imperilled if it fails to observe the law scrupulously. . . . To declare that in the administration of the criminal law the end justifies the means—to declare that the government may commit crimes in order to secure the conviction of a private criminal—would bring terrible retribution." *Olmstead*, p. 485 (Brandeis, J., dissenting).

Those opposed to the rule argue, as did Justice Cardozo, that "the question is whether protection for the individual would not be gained at a disproportionate loss of protection for society," or, in short, whether it is proper for "the criminal . . . to go free because the constable has blundered." *People v. Defoe*, 242 N.Y. 13, 24, 21, 150 N.E. 585, 589, 587 (1926).

Indeed, the Supreme Court, while holding fast to the exclusionary rule, has imposed limitations on its use. The rule applies only to the individual whose Fourth Amendment rights have been violated; illegally seized evidence may be introduced against others. *Rakas v. Illinois*, 439 U.S. 128 (1978). Also, there are a variety of contexts in which the exclusionary remedy has been held not to apply. See, e.g., *United States v. Leon*, 468 U.S. 897 (1984) (rule inapplicable to bar use of evidence obtained on the basis of a search warrant ultimately ruled invalid); *Stone v. Powell*, 428 U.S. 465 (1976) (no habeas corpus relief on grounds that evidence obtained in an unconstitutional search was introduced at trial); and *United States v. Calandra*, 414 U.S. 338 (1974) (witness summoned to testify before grand jury may not refuse to answer questions on the ground that they are based on evidence obtained in an illegal search).

In an important recent decision, however, the Court drew in the reins, ruling that the exception to the exclusionary rule which allows introduction of evidence obtained in violation of the Fourth Amendment for the limited purpose of impeaching the defendant's testimony should *not* be further expanded to allow impeachment of all defense witnesses. *James v. Illinois*, 110 S. Ct. 648 (1990). "So long as we are committed to protecting the people from the disregard of their constitutional rights during the course of criminal investigations," the Court wrote, "inadmissibility of illegally obtained evidence must remain the rule, not the exception" (p. 655).

Further to the background on requirements of a Constitutional warrant: While the Supreme Court has used more than one definition of "probable cause" over the years, the central inquiry posed is whether a reasonable person would conclude, from the "totality of the circumstances," that a crime had occurred or that evidence of a crime was located in the place to be searched. See J. Hall, Jr., *Search and Seizure*, sec. 5.8 (1982 and Supp. 1988). See also *Illinois v. Gates*, 462 U.S. 213 (1983). The probable cause requirement applies *both* to warrantless searches, conducted usually on the basis of "exigent circumstances," and searches made pursuant to a warrant issued by a magistrate. LaFave, *Search and Seizure*, vol. 1, sec. 3.1(a). The primary purpose of the rule is to protect citizens from arbitrary police intrusions by requiring that the police act only on the basis of some articulable modicum of evidence.

The "particularity" requirement embedded in the Fourth Amendment requires that the police describe the place to be searched with sufficient specificity in the warrant. It has two primary aims. One is to make sure that the police search the right place. The other is to ensure that probable cause exists to believe that the evidence sought to be found is in fact at the place to be searched.

The Supreme Court, finally, also requires that a warrant based on probable cause be issued only by a "neutral and detached magistrate." This rule seeks to interpose an orderly, deliberate, and "independent" procedure between the police and the citizenry. One of the protections of the warrant process is that the probable cause decision should be made by an official who, theoretically at least, is independent of the police. See generally LaFave, *Search and Seizure*, vol. 2, sec. 4.2.

138   The case that includes the affidavit by James Marion Compton and discusses the constitutionality of the warrant and search of the McSurelys' home is *United States v. McSurely*, 473 F.2d 1178, 1185 (1972).

139   Testimony of Sheriff Perry Justice, Trial Transcript, December 9, 1982, pp. 54–62.

140   The Speech and Debate clause of the U.S. Constitution reads: "They [senators and representatives] shall in all Cases, except Treason, Felony and Breach of Peace, be privileged from Arrest during their Attendance at the Session of their respective Houses, and in going to and returning from the same; and for any Speech or Debate in either House, they shall not be questioned in any other Place." U.S. Constitution, art. I, sec. 6, clause 1.

The Supreme Court has long held that the speech and debate clause is to be "read broadly to effectuate its purposes." *United States v. Johnson*, 383 U.S. 169, 180 (1966), citing *Kilbourn v. Thompson*, 103 U.S. 168 (1880), and *Tenney v. Brandhove*, 341 U.S. 367 (1951). It has included in its protection not only literal speech and debate, but also other legislative acts such as voting, committee hearings, and issuing subpoenas concerning a subject "on which legislation could be had." See *Kilbourn*, p. 204; *Doe v. McMillan*, 412 U.S. 306, 311–13, 317–18 (1973); and per quotation, *Eastland v. United States Servicemen's Fund*, 421 U.S. 491, 506 (1975), quoting *McGrain v. Daugherty*, 273 U.S. 135, 177 (1927). See, generally, Tribe, *American Constitutional Law*, 2d ed. (1988), sec. 5-18. In addition, aides are protected for conduct that would enjoy immunity if performed by a senator or representative. Senator McClellan for himself, and Adlerman, O'Donnell, and Brick as his aides, claimed all of their actions with respect to the McSurelys fell within the protection of the speech and debate clause. See *Gravel v. United States*, 408 U.S. 606, 616 (1972); and *Eastland*, p. 507. It should be noted, however, that the Court has repeatedly insisted that the speech and debate clause be subject to "finite limits" (*Doe v. McMillan*, p. 317), refusing to stretch its protective umbrella "beyond the legislative sphere" to conduct not "essential to legislating." *Gravel*, pp. 621, 624–25.

140   The court also was unanimous in holding that the McSurelys' charge that the federal defendants had acted to encourage state officials to continue their course of conduct was insufficient to state a claim of conspiracy and should have been dismissed. *McSurely v. McClellan*, 553 F.2d 1277 (D.C. Cir. 1976) (en banc).

141   On the split decision in the U.S. Court of Appeals for the D.C. Circuit on the Fourth Amendment issue: Five judges read the safe-keeping order narrowly, insisting that it was a preservation, not secrecy, order. "The purpose of the court order was to preserve the documents for the use of whoever might eventually have a rightful interest in their use." Ibid., p. 1310. The Senate subcommittee, these five judges argued, did have such a rightful interest in the documents. Furthermore, the foundation of the Fourth Amendment is the protection of a person's "reasonable expectation of privacy." According to these judges, "When the documents left the possession of the McSurelys on 11 August 1967 any expectation of privacy in those documents vanished" (p. 1316). They pointed out that the McSurelys, in their many trips through the lower courts, repeatedly asked that the documents be returned to them or impounded, and they were repeatedly refused.

The other five judges on the Court of Appeals argued just the opposite. They said it was clear that it was not up to Thomas Ratliff to decide who may have access to the documents—that issue was to be determined by the courts. Furthermore, they noted, this very court (though not the full panel of ten) had addressed the issue before when they reversed the McSurelys' contempt convictions. Although the prior decision was not binding on the current case because it did not involve the same parties, these five judges declared it to be "pertinent" (p. 1290). The prior court, at least, had said that even though the McSurelys no longer had possession of the documents when Brick obtained them, the Fourth Amendment protected against not only physical intrusion and seizure, but also the "uninvited eye."

141   The Supreme Court case setting the standard for qualified immunity is *Harlow v. Fitzgerald*, 457 U.S. 800, 818 (1982). For more on qualified immunity, see discussions of the First Amendment (*Hobson v. Wilson*) and the Third Amendment.

141   The case dismissing Thomas Ratliff's motion to dismiss on grounds of immunity is *McSurely v. McClellan*, 697 F.2d 309 (D.C. Cir. 1982).

142   Rule 25(a)(1) of the Federal Rules of Civil Procedures allows, upon court order, substitution of "proper parties" in the case of the death of one of the original parties to the suit. This allows the suit to proceed; damages, if any, are then assessed against the new party. In this case, the appeals court ruled that the widows had properly been substituted to stand in their deceased husbands' stead—with damages, if any, to be assessed against the husbands' estates.

142   Testimony of Thomas Ratliff, Trial Transcript, December 14, 1982, pp. 191–94.

143   The final case is *McSurely v. McClellan*, 753 F.2d 88 (D.C. Cir. 1985).

FIFTH AMENDMENT

Right to a Grand Jury Indictment: Rudy Linares

150   Rudy Linares's quotations are from the transcript of an interview broadcast by ABC News on "20/20," show 948, December 8, 1989, p. 2.

151   Rudy Linares's remarks to reporters and the quotation from state's attorney Cecil Partee are from an article by United Press International, April 27, 1989.

151   Many jurisdictions use a more rigorous standard than probable cause for determining when the evidence is sufficient to indict—the prima facie case standard. A prima facie case is defined as the existence of evidence, which "if unexplained or contradicted, would warrant a conviction by a trial jury." Kamisar, LaFave, and Israel, *Modern Criminal Procedure*, p. 953.

For federal prosecutors, bound by rules which limit their ability to ferret out useful information from otherwise uncooperative witnesses, the grand jury's subpoena powers are its main attraction. These powers allow the grand jury to "summon practically anyone it wants, and, through the statute providing for the immunization of witnesses . . . compel a summoned person to testify or risk going to jail for contempt." Thomas P. Sullivan and Robert D. Nachman, "If It Ain't Broke, Don't Fix It: Why the Grand Jury's Accusatory Function Should Not Be Changed," *Journal of Criminal Law and Criminology* 75 (1984): 1047, 1048.

It is for this reason that commentators have termed the

grand jury process both the "shield" and the "sword" of the criminal justice system. Kamisar, LaFave, and Israel, *Modern Criminal Procedure*, p. 634. The grand jury acts as a "shield" when, as in the case of Rudy Linares, it interposes itself between the accused and the government. It acts as a "sword" when it uses its investigatory authority to fight crime, as it did during the 1970s Watergate period.

152   As of January 1989, the number of grand jurors required by Illinois law was reduced from twenty-three to sixteen.

153   When an accusation was initiated by the grand jury itself, its charging document was called a "presentment." (Under current federal law, there is no provision for the use of a presentment). Kamisar, LaFave, and Israel, *Modern Criminal Procedure*, p. 914. When the accusation was the result of evidence put before it by the Crown's representative or prosecutor, the charge was called an "indictment." Historical information can be found in ibid., pp. 693–95; and Levy, *Origins of the Fifth Amendment*, pp. 3–42.

153   The quotation from Gouverneur Morris can be found in Frank B. Latham, *The Trial of John Peter Zenger, August 1735* (New York: Franklin Watts, 1970), p. 61.

153   *Hurtado v. California*, 110 U.S. 516 (1884), held that due process of law does not necessarily require an indictment by a grand jury. In other words, as stated in the text, the right to a grand jury indictment has not been incorporated against the states.

153   Information about various state practices can be found in Kamisar, LaFave, and Israel, *Modern Criminal Procedure*, pp. 974–77.

Prosecutors often choose to proceed by grand jury indictment rather than a preliminary hearing because of certain advantages in the grand jury system. For example, public participation is particularly important in a controversial case or when an uncertain prosecutor wants community input and support. It allows him to get the layperson's reaction to the credibility of witnesses before deciding whether to use them at trial. The secret grand jury proceeding is especially useful when there is concern that testifying in public twice would be too difficult for a witness, like Tammy Linares; or for the victim of a crime, as in a rape or child abuse case; or when the prosecution wants to keep the identity of an undercover informant secret as long as possible. Secrecy also prevents the grand jurors from being pressured by those under investigation (as they might be in an organized crime case), and assures them no one will second-guess their decision.

(The above is based on the authors' interviews with prosecutor Scott Nelson and Linares's defense attorney, Dan Coyne.)

154   The case that held that hearsay evidence may be presented to the grand jury is *Costello v. U.S.*, 350 U.S. 359 (1956).

The case that declined to extend the exclusionary rule to the grand jury (thereby allowing the presentation of unconstitutionally obtained evidence) is *United States v. Calandra,* 414 U.S. 338 (1974).

The quotation from the chief judge of the New York Court of Appeals, Sol Wachtler, appeared in the *New York Times,* February 28, 1990, p. B1.

Double Jeopardy: *Green v. United States*

162   Although allowed at the time of Green's case, mandatory death sentences have since been outlawed by the Supreme Court as "cruel and unusual punishment" under the Eighth Amendment. *Woodson v. North Carolina,* 428 U.S. 280 (1976); *Roberts v. Louisiana,* 428 U.S. 325 (1976). The ban on mandatory death sentences extends to a prisoner convicted of murder while serving a life sentence without possibility of parole. *Sumner v. Shuman,* 483 U.S. 66 (1987).

162   The case in which Green was granted a new trial is *Green v. United States,* 218 F.2d 856, 859 (D.C. Cir. 1955).

162   The prohibition against double jeopardy has been called "the most ancient" of all Bill of Rights protections and its roots have been traced back to Greek and Roman law. See Peter Westen and Richard Drubel, "Toward a General Theory of Double Jeopardy," *Sup. Ct. Rev.* (1978):81. While its appearance in America can be traced to English common law, one scholar has suggested that the inclusion of double jeopardy protection within the Constitution has helped it develop more quickly in America than in England. Hunter, "The Development of the Rule Against Double Jeopardy," *J. Legal Hist.* 5 (1984):1.

In 1969, the Supreme Court incorporated the double jeopardy clause against the States. *Benton v. Maryland,* 395 U.S. 784 (1969).

163   The Supreme Court case in which a double jeopardy claim similar to Green's was rejected in the Philippine Islands is *Trono v. United States,* 199 U.S. 251 (1905).

163   The district court case rejecting Green's double jeopardy claim is *Green v. United States,* 236 F.2d 708 (D.C. Cir. 1956).

164   Green's Supreme Court case is *Green v. United States,* 355 U.S. 184, 197 (1957).

165   The Supreme Court has continued to grapple with these difficult technical questions in defining the parameters of double jeopardy protection. For example, the question of what constitutes the "same offense" is particularly poignant in the case where a drunken driver kills someone. In 1987, Thomas Corbin crossed the double yellow line on a New York State highway and killed the driver of an oncoming car. He was immediately charged with, and pleaded guilty to, driving while intoxicated and failure to keep right. When the local prosecutor later tried to prosecute Corbin for criminally negligent homicide, Corbin claimed double jeopardy. The Supreme Court upheld his claim. *Grady v. Corbin,* 110 S. Ct.

2084 (1989). The Court ruled that, under the double jeopardy clause, a second trial is barred whenever the government would have to prove the same *conduct* for which the defendant had already been prosecuted.

Right Against Self-incrimination: *Baltimore City Department of Social Services v. Bouknight*

169   Letter from Errol L. Bennett, M.D., assistant chief of orthopedics, Francis Scott Key Medical Center, to Denise Ippolito, social worker, March 3, 1987, Joint Appendix to the Briefs for Petitioners and Respondants, *Baltimore City Dept. of Social Services v. Bouknight*, 110 S. Ct. 900 (1990) (No. 88-1182), p. 12 (hereafter Joint Appendix).

170   Historical information is largely drawn from Levy, *Origins of the Fifth Amendment*. John Lilburne, quoted in Levy, *Origins of the Fifth Amendment*, p. 273.

170   Matthew 27:11–14.

171   John Lilburne, quoted in Levy, *Origins of the Fifth Amendment*, p. 276.

171   The description of the right to remain silent as one of the "landmarks in man's struggle to become civilized" is from Erwin Griswold, *The Fifth Amendment Today: Three Speeches by Erwin N. Griswold* (Cambridge: Harvard University Press, 1955), p. 7.

171   Some of those targeted by the McCarthy-era anti-Communist investigations cited another provision of the Bill of Rights for protection. When ten screenwriters were subpoenaed by the House Un-American Activities Committee, they argued that the First Amendment right to freedom of speech contained an implicit right to silence and privacy. After the courts rejected that claim, the so-called "Hollywood Ten" chose to go to jail rather than make a Fifth Amendment argument (in part because they did not believe they had committed any crime) that almost certainly would have succeeded. See Joseph Rauh, "The Privilege Against Self-Incrimination from John Lilburne to Ollie North," *Constitutional Commentary* 5 (1988):405.

A more recent Fifth Amendment debate erupted in Washington during the Iran-Contra scandal, when Vice Admiral John Poindexter and Lieutenant Colonel Oliver North asserted the right and refused to testify before a congressional committee. One columnist urged them to forego their constitutional right to silence in favor of their "patriotic duty to testify" about the affair. William Safire, "Face Down in the Mud," *New York Times*, December 22, 1986, p. A23, col. 1.

Eventually, both Poindexter and North were granted limited immunity for their congressional testimony. This immunity, however, did not bar subsequent federal prosecution for their activities. *U.S. v. Poindexter*, 698 F. Supp. 300 (D.D.C. 1988), *appeal dismissed*, 859 F.2d 216 (D.C. Cir. 1988), *cert. denied*, 109 S. Ct. 1638 (1989).

For additional information on the evolution of the privilege against self-incrimination in the United States, see Laurence A. Benner, "Requiem for Miranda: The Rehnquist Court's Voluntariness Doctrine in Historical Perspective," *Washington University Law Quarterly* 67 (1989):59, 84–92.

171   The description of the difficulties of "hunting up evidence" is from Sir James Fitzjames Stephen, *History of the Criminal Law of England*, quoted in Edward Bennett Williams, *One Man's Freedom* (New York: Atheneum, 1977), p. 125.

171   Legal philosophers continue to ponder the justification for the privilege against self-incrimination. For a qualified defense of the privilege, see R. Kent Greenawalt, "Silence as a Moral and Constitutional Right," *William and Mary Law Review* 23 (1981):15. For a critique of common arguments in its favor, see David Dolinko, "Is There a Rationale for the Privilege Against Self-Incrimination?" *UCLA Law Review* 33 (1986):1063.

172   The citation for the Miranda decision is *Miranda v. Arizona,* 384 U.S., 440, 460 (1966). On March 13, 1963, Ernesto Miranda was arrested at his home and taken in custody to a Phoenix police station, where he was identified by the complaining witness. The police then took him to "Interrogation Room No. 2," where he was questioned by two police officers. Miranda was not advised that he had a right to have an attorney present during the interrogation. Two hours later, the officers emerged from the interrogation with a written confession signed by Miranda. At trial, Miranda was found guilty of kidnapping and rape. Miranda's appeal, along with three similar ones, were heard together by the Supreme Court.

In a five to four decision, the Court held that the Fifth Amendment privilege against self-incrimination extended not only to courtroom testimony, but to statements made during a police interrogation by a suspect in police custody. To ensure that custodial confessions are the product of free choice, and not state coercion, torture, or psychological abuse, *Miranda* requires police officers to recite a series of now-familiar warnings to a person held for questioning: that the person has a right to remain silent, that any statement made can be used as evidence against him, that he has the right to the presence of an attorney, and that if he cannot afford one, a lawyer will be appointed for him prior to any interrogation. Ibid., p. 444.

In the years since that landmark ruling, the Court has narrowed the application of *Miranda*'s protections. In 1984, for example, the Court created a "public safety" exception that in certain circumstances allows police questioning *before* a suspect is given the *Miranda* warnings. *New York v. Quarles,* 467 U.S. 649 (1984).

Scholars have debated and scrutinized *Miranda*'s impact both on the behavior of criminal suspects and on the criminal justice system. One prominent study conducted shortly after the *Miranda* ruling found little short-term effect on the pattern of police interrogations and the frequency of suspect confessions. For example, see Michael Wald, Richard Ayres, David W. Hess, Mark Schantz, and Charles H. Whitebread, "Interrogations in New Haven: The Impact of Miranda," *Yale Law Journal* 76 (1967):1519, 1615–16.

For more details about the original case, see Y. Kamisar, "Miranda: The Case, the Man, and the Players" (book review), *Michigan Law Review* 82 (1984):1074

173 The description of Jackie Bouknight's feelings toward Maurice is from a psychodiagnostic evaluation by Joseph M. Eisenberg, Ph.D., July 27, 1987, Joint Appendix, p. 25.

175 The quotation about extorting information from the accused is from *Fisher v. U.S.*, 425 U.S. 391, 398 (1976), quoting *Couch v. U.S.*, 409 U.S. 322–28 (1973).

175 Further to the discussion of Fifth Amendment exceptions: When a grand jury investigating corruption subpoenaed business records of a self-employed person, the Supreme Court held that the act of turning over the records would admit their existence, his possession of them, and their authenticity, and was therefore protected by his right against self-incrimination. *U.S. v. Doe*, 465 U.S. 605 (1984).

But in *California v. Byers*, 402 U.S. 424 (1971), the plurality cites examples of other information the government might request that receives no Fifth Amendment protection, such as income tax returns and contents of consumer products.

176 The legal aid lawsuit is *L.J. by and through Darr v. Massinga*, 699 F. Supp. 508 (D.Md. 1988).

178 The quotation from Justice Brandeis is from *Olmstead v. U.S.*, 277 U.S. 438, 479. (Brandeis, J., dissenting).

178 The Maryland Court of Appeals' decision is *In re Maurice M.*, 550 A.2d 1135 (Md. 1988).

179 Jackie Bouknight's case in the Supreme Court is *Baltimore City Department of Social Services v. Bouknight*, 110 S. Ct. 900 (1990).

The dissent argued that Jackie, as Maurice's mother and not simply a state-appointed "custodian," should retain broad rights against self-incrimination notwithstanding her connection with the CINA program. The dissent also took issue with the majority's description of Maryland's child welfare regulations as noncriminal, since they "cannot be separated from criminal provisions that serve the same goal." Ibid., pp. 912–13 (Marshall, J., dissenting). Even if the state were to refrain from prosecuting Jackie based on her responses in a civil proceeding, the dissent said. She remained entitled to Fifth Amendment protection.

Due Process of Law: *Fuentes v. Shevin*

185 Substantive due process refers to a set of rights considered fundamental, even though they are not explicitly articulated

in the Bill of Rights. The government may not violate these rights, regardless of how fair its procedures are. Justice Frankfurter defined substantive due process as "those liberties of the individual which history has attested as the indispensable conditions of an open as against a closed society." *Kovucs v. Cooper*, 336 U.S. 77, 95 (1949) (concurring opinion). Thus, in a 1952 case, Frankfurter found the forced stomach pumping of a criminal defendant to be "conduct that shocks the conscience" and violated the due process guarantee of liberty. *Rochin v. California*, 342 U.S. 165, 172 (1952).

Beyond some notion of bodily integrity, substantive due process is controversial because of its malleable content. As L. Tribe noted, "References to history, tradition, evolving community standards, and civilized consensus, can provide suggestive parallels and occasional insights, but it is illusion to suppose that they can yield answers, much less absolve judges of responsibility for developing and defending a theory of what rights are 'preferred' or 'fundamental' under our Constitution and why." Tribe, *American Constitutional Law*, pp. 777–78. Thus, substantive due process has taken on different meanings.

In the early 1900s, when courts' sympathy with free market theories was prevalent, substantive due process included the "liberty" to buy and sell labor unimpeded by government regulations. Many minimum wage and other workplace reforms were nullified by this constitutional barrier. See, e.g., *Lochner v. New York*, 198 U.S. (1905), invalidating New York law prohibiting employment of bakery employees for more than ten hours a day or sixty hours a week. The legislative reforms of the New Deal, and the Supreme Court's acquiescence to them, repudiated this view. See also *Nebbia v. New York*, 291 U.S. 502 (1934), upholding New York's fixing of milk prices against a due process challenge.

The controversy over the idea of substantive due process was revived in the 1965 case *Griswold v. Connecticut*, 381 U.S. 479 (1965), in which the Supreme Court found that a state law prohibiting use of birth control impermissibly interfered with the intimate relations of husband and wife. This notion had surfaced forty years earlier when the Court had reversed the conviction of a teacher for violating an English-language-only statute and stated that "liberty" for due process purposes meant "not merely freedom from bodily restraint but also the rights of the individual to contract, to engage in any of the common occupations of life, to acquire useful knowledge, to marry, to establish a home and bring up children, to worship God according to the dictates of his own conscience, and generally to enjoy those privileges long recognized at common law as essential to the orderly pursuit of happiness by free men." *Meyer v. Nebraska*, 262 U.S. 390, 399 (1923). This notion of liberty is also the basis of the constitutional right to choose abortion. *Roe v. Wade*, 410 U.S. 113 (1973).

For more on the concept of substantive due process, see the discussion of the Ninth Amendment.

186   *Fuentes v. Shevin*, 407 U.S. 67 (1972). *Fuentes* was handed down during a period of expansion of the interests in "liberty" and "property" protected by the due process clause. The Supreme Court case *Goldberg v. Kelly*, 397 U.S. 254 (1970), expressly adopts the language of some influential law review articles that speak of government's largesse in terms of being an "entitlement" rather than a "gratuity." Ibid., p. 262, n. 8, citing Charles A. Reich, "Individual Rights and Social Welfare: The Emerging Legal Issues," *Yale Law Journal* 74 (1965):1245; Charles A. Reich, "The New Property," *Yale Law Journal* 73 (1964):733. "For the first time, the Court recognized as entitlements interests founded on neither constitutional nor on common law claims of request but only on a state-fostered (and hence justifiable) expectation, as opposed to a mere hope, which was derived from 'an independent source such as state law' or from 'mutually explicit understandings.'" Tribe, *American Constitutional Law*, p. 686.

      Therefore, once the state chooses to affirmatively confer benefits (and create legitimate expectancies) by statutory enactment, it must abide by the requirement of procedural due process in withdrawing such entitlement. See, e.g., *Perry v. Sindermann*, 408 U.S. 593 (1972) (interest in "implied tenure" at state university). The Court will examine the specific statute in question to determine whether a protected interest has been created; broad discretionary latitude and procedural frameworks will generally not suffice, the Court being most impressed by "explicitly mandatory language." *Hewitt v. Helms*, 459 U.S. 460, 472 (1983); see also *Greenholtz v. Inmates of Nebraska Penal and Correctional Complex*, 442 U.S. 1 (1979) (existence of parole system does not of itself create liberty interest; "unique structure and language" of statute created protectible interest, however).

186   The case involving the garnishment of wages is *Sniadach v. Family Finance Corp.*, 395 U.S. 337 (1969).
      The case involving the termination of welfare benefits is *Goldberg v. Kelly*, 397 U.S. 254 (1970).

187   The quotation characterizing the Bill of Rights as intended to protect the "fragile values of a vulnerable citizenry" is from *Fuentes*, p. 91, n. 22, quoting *Stanley v. Illinois*, 405 U.S. 645, 656 (1972).

188   In determining "what process is due," the Court's recent doctrine has involved a balancing of the interests at stake. This "utilitarian" approach requires that the court consider "first, the private interest that will be affected by the official action; second, the risk of an erroneous deprivation of such interest through the procedures used, and the probable values, if any, of additional substitute procedural safeguards, and finally, the government's interest, including the function involved and the fiscal and administrative burdens that the additional substitute procedural requirement would entail." *Mathews v. Eldridge*, 424 U.S. 319, 334–35 (1976).

"Takings": *Poletown Neighborhood Council v. Detroit*

192   The Supreme Court incorporated the Fifth Amendment's takings clause against the states in *Fallbrook Irrigation District v.
Bradley*, 164 U.S. 112, 158 (1896).

192   The Michigan state constitutional takings clause is Michigan
Constitution, art. 10, sec. 2.

193   For a discussion of takings for "public use," see generally
Curtis J. Berger, *Land Ownership and Use*, 3d ed. (Boston: Little, Brown, 1983), chap. 18, esp. pp. 1015–31.

Another seemingly intractable issue is that of so-called
"regulatory takings." These are instances where government
regulation of property goes so far that it "will be recognized
as a taking" for which "just compensation" must be made.
Pennsylvania Coal v. Mahon, 260 U.S. 393, 415 (1922). See,
e.g., *Penn Central Transportation Co. v. New York City*, 438 U.S.
104 (1978), where New York law regulating certain uses of
landmark buildings was held *not* to constitute a taking as applied to Penn Central (Penn Central was prevented from placing a fifty-three-story structure over Grand Central Station).

193   The Michigan "quick take" statute is Uniform Condemnation
Procedures Act, Michigan Comp. Laws Ann. 213.51–213.77.

The city was acting pursuant to the state's Economic Development Corporations Act. Michigan Comp. Laws Ann.
125.1601 et seq., which gave it the power to condemn property for transfer to a private corporation "to alleviate and
prevent conditions of unemployment . . . assist and retain local industries . . . to strengthen and revitalize the economy of
this state." (Michigan Comp. Laws Ann. 125.1602).

Similar legislative enactments address the problem of urban renewal in authorizing condemnation of "blighted"
areas. One of the novel aspects of *Poletown*, of course, was
that the community was *not* "blighted," as that term is commonly understood in the law of eminent domain. Some scholars maintain, however, that the state's exercise of its eminent
domain powers is coextensive with the rest of its "police
powers," and that there is no reason for any greater limitations in this area, as long as the ordinary purpose of government—the maximization of welfare—is being pursued. See,
e.g., William B. Stoebuck, "A General Theory of Eminent Domain," *Washington Law Review* 47 (1972):553.

193   The "calamitous proportions" of Detroit's economic problems are from *Poletown Council v. Detroit*, 410 Mich. 616, 647
(1981) (Ryan, J., dissenting).

194   Mayor Young's statements about the effect of a plant closing
are from Testimony of Coleman Young, *Poletown Neighborhood Council v. City of Detroit*, no. 80-039-426 CZ, Trial
Transcript, December 1, 1980, pp. 30–51 (hereafter, Trial
Transcript).

196   Mayor Young's comments about the name "Poletown" are
from Testimony of Coleman Young, Trial Transcript, pp.
46–47.

197 The quote from Mayor Young about Ralph Nader is from a video documentary on the Poletown controversy, *Poletown Lives!*

200 The *Poletown* case at the trial level is *Poletown Neighborhood Council v. City of Detroit*, no. 80-039-426-CZ, December 8, 1980, Third Judicial Circuit of Michigan, Judge George T. Martin, p. 9.

201 The *Poletown* case in the Michigan Supreme Court is *Poletown Neighborhood Council v. Detroit*, 410 Mich. 616 (1981).

201 Actually, some legal scholars had been anticipating this "reverberating clang"—the death knell of the public use limitation on takings—for some time. See, e.g., Comment, "The Public Use Limitation on Eminent Domain: An Advance Requiem," *Yale Law Journal* 58 (1949):599. A prior case, presenting facts similar to the *Poletown* controversy, involved condemnations to make way for New York's World Trade Center. *Courtesy Sandwich Shop v. Port of New York Authority*, 12 N.Y. 2d 379, 190 N.E. 2d 402, 240 N.Y.S. 2d 1 (1963), *app. dismissed*, 375 U.S. 78 (1963). As the Twin Towers will attest, the defendants prevailed in that case as well.

All quotations from Father Joseph Karacevich are from the documentary *Poletown Lives!*

SIXTH AMENDMENT

Right to an Impartial Jury:
Machetti v. Linahan

215 The convictions and death sentences of Rebecca Machetti and John Eldon Smith were upheld by the Georgia Supreme Court in *Smith v. State*, 222 S.E.2d 308 (1976).

Machetti's petition for a writ of habeas corpus (state habeas) was filed in the Superior Court of Baldwin County, Georgia, on January 9, 1979. It was denied on May 9, 1979.

Machetti then petitioned for a writ of habeas corpus (federal habeas) in the U.S. District Court for the Middle District of Georgia, Macon Division. The district court's decision denying Machetti's petition is *Machetti v. Linahan*, 517 F. Supp. 1076 (M.D.Ga. 1981).

Machetti appealed the district court decision to the U.S. Court of Appeals for the Eleventh Circuit. It reversed the lower court and found Machetti had been deprived of her Sixth and Fourteenth Amendment rights to an impartial jury trial in *Machetti v. Linahan*, 679 F.2d 236 (1982).

215 The case that held that the way in which the death penalty was administered at the time was "cruel and unusual punishment" is *Furman v. Georgia*, 408 U.S. 238 (1972).

215 The case in which the Supreme Court upheld Georgia's death penalty law (enacted after its previous statute had been struck down in *Furman*) is *Gregg v. Georgia*, 428 U.S. 153 (1976). For more on *Furman* and *Gregg*, see the discussion and notes on the Eighth Amendment.

215   Further to the discussion of the function of grand jury and trial jury, and the number of jurors: Traditionally the grand jury is a body of twenty-three people drawn from the local community that approves the bringing of criminal indictments; see the Linares story, discussed under the Fifth Amendment. The trial jury, or "petit" jury, decides the trial verdict after hearing all the evidence in the case. Trial juries traditionally consisted of twelve members, but the Constitution permits juries of less than twelve; see *Williams v. Florida*, 399 U.S. 78 (1970) (six-person jury in robbery case). It is not uncommon for federal and state juries to consist of six persons. The Supreme Court has, however, found that a five-person jury violates the Sixth Amendment. *Ballew v. Georgia*, 435 U.S. 223 (1978). Also, the parties may agree to a jury of less than twelve members. Federal Rules of Civil Procedure 48, Federal Rules of Criminal Procedure 23. See generally Lloyd E. Moore, *The Jury: Tool of Kings: Palladium of Liberty*, 2d ed. (Cincinnati: Anderson, 1988).

216   Further to the discussion of racial disparity: it has long been held that the systematic exclusion of blacks from a jury violates equal protection, regardless of a Sixth Amendment fair cross-section claim, although a defendant is not necessarily entitled to a jury of his or her *own* race. *Strauder v. West Virginia*, 100 U.S. 303, 305 (1880); *Peters v. Kiff*, 407 U.S. 493 (1972). See Kamisar, Lafave, and Israel, *Modern Criminal Procedure*, 7th ed. (St. Paul, Minn.: West Publishing, 1990), p. 1304. Once an initial showing of discrimination is made, the state must show that certain exclusions or disparities did not flow from discrimination. *Avery v. Georgia*, 345 U.S. 559 (1953). In *Castaneda v. Partida*, 430 U.S. 482 (1977), such a showing was made when 79.1 percent of a county was Mexican-American, but over an eleven-year period only 39 percent of those summoned to grand jury service were Mexican-American. See also Federal Jury Selection and Service Act of 1968, 28 U.S.C. sec. 861, et. seq. (designed to ensure selection from fair cross-section of the community).

    The Sixth Amendment does not, however, guarantee that the final makeup of the jury represent a racial cross-section. Even if drawn from a representative pool, the composition of the jury may depend on "peremptory challenges," which an attorney may use to dismiss prospective jurors after voir dire. See Federal Rules of Criminal Procedure 24(b) (three to twenty peremptory challenges in federal court). Prosecutors may eliminate jurors of a certain race from the petit jury through peremptory challenges without violating the Sixth Amendment fair cross-section requirement. *Holland v. Illinois*, 110 S. Ct. 803 (1990). But see *Batson v. Kentucky*, 476 U.S. 79 (1986) (using peremptory challenges to exclude blacks from a jury violates equal protection).

216   In a fair cross-section claim such as Machetti's, which focuses solely on the composition of the venire, discriminatory pur-

pose is irrelevant. But in other cases, such specific intent has been shown. See *Amadeo v. Zant*, 108 S. Ct. 1771, 1774 (1988) (county clerk memo showed deliberate plan to underrepresent blacks and women by 5–11 percent). Although there is no magic number, the *Machetti* court noted that disparities high enough to make out a fair cross-section claim ranged in other cases from 13–38 percent. *Machetti*, 679 F.2d at 241. The standard is identical to that for equal protection challenges (ibid., p. 241, n. 6, quoting *U.S. v. Perez-Hernandez*, 672 F.2d 1380, 1384, n. 5 [11th Cir. 1982]).

216   The Supreme Court case that declared the opt-in statute unconstitutional is *Taylor v. Louisiana*, 419 U.S. 522 (1975).

217   Further to the discussion of habeas corpus: often called "the great writ of liberty," a writ of habeas corpus allows prisoners to challenge the legality of detention (as opposed to their guilt or innocence). Prisoners may petition for the writ after conviction in an effort to seek release. The writ is issued by the court, after the prisoner petitions, and orders the person detaining the prisoner to bring the prisoner before the court. The writ of habeas corpus is protected in the Constitution, art. I., sec. 9, which provides: "The Privilege of the Writ of Habeas Corpus shall not be suspended, unless when in Cases of Rebellion or Invasion the public Safety may require it."

This postconviction remedy is not a vehicle to reconsider the merits of the case, but allows a prisoner to challenge a conviction or sentence that was egregiously flawed, usually by the presence of jurisdictional or constitutional error. See Donald E. Wilkes, Jr., *Federal and State Post-conviction Remedies and Relief* (Norcross, Ga.: Harrison, 1983), p. 10. A prisoner may file habeas relief either in state court (pp. 215–22) or in federal court (28 U.S.C. 2241). The discovery of new evidence is a common ground for seeking the writ.

In 1787, trial by jury was protected in the Constitution, art. III, sec. 2, which provides: "The Trial of all Crimes, except in Cases of Impeachment, shall be by Jury, and such Trial shall be held in the State where the said Crimes shall have been committed." When the Bill of Rights was ratified in 1791, the Sixth Amendment guaranteed the right in *federal* court. The constitution of every state entering the Union subsequently protected the right to a jury trial in criminal cases. In the 1967 case *Duncan v. Louisiana*, 391 U.S. 145 (1968) the Supreme Court incorporated the Sixth Amendment right to trial by jury against the states and guaranteed a jury trial for all serious offenses that would be tried by jury if in a federal court.

217   In addition to the fair cross-section claim, Machetti made numerous other claims, including: (1) ineffective assistance of counsel; (2) violation of Machetti's right against self-incrimination; (3) violations of due process because she contended she had been drugged with Thorazine during her trial

and because she contended Maree had a deal with the prosecution (that if he testified against Machetti at trial the state would not seek the death penalty against him), which was not disclosed to the jury as required; (4) the death penalty as administered in Georgia violated her Eighth Amendment right against cruel and unusual punishment, because it was disproportionate to her role in the crime, racially discriminatory (anyone who killed a white victim was more likely to be sentenced to death), and discriminated against poor people. No court, state or federal, awarded relief on any of these claims in Machetti's case. (The Eleventh Circuit did not reach them.)

217   In drafting what became the Sixth Amendment, Madison proposed to expunge the trial-by-jury clause of the original Constitution, which had met with criticism in the Virginia and other conventions (as not strong enough) and to replace it by a longer and more detailed clause providing for trial by an impartial jury of the vicinage, and affirming the requirement of a unanimous verdict for conviction "and other accustomed requisites." Francis Howard Heller, *The Sixth Amendment to the Constitution of the United States: A Study in Constitutional Development* (Lawrence, Kans.: University of Kansas Press, 1969), pp. 29–30. For more on this, see F. Frankfurter and T. Corcoran, "Petty Federal Offenses and the Constitutional Guarantee of Trial by Jury," *Harvard Law Review* 39 (1926): 917, 962–82.

218   Historically, the jury has ancient roots as a check on the over-zealous prosecutor. When a man's freedom, life, or property was at stake, the institution of trial by jury developed as a check on the king's arbitrary power. The grand jury developed by the twelfth century. The trial jury developed later, originally to resolve property disputes, but by the fourteenth century it had become the principal institution for criminal cases as well. See Levy, *Origins of the Fifth Amendment*, pp. 3–42.

Jury trial came to America with the English colonists. Their resentment of royal interference with their system of justice can be seen in the Declaration of Independence. Among the grievances listed against the king are "his depriving us in many cases, of the benefits of Trial by Jury" and "transporting us beyond seas to be tried for pretended offenses."

218   The quotation from Justice Thurgood Marshall is from *Peters v. Kiff*, 407 U.S. 493, 503, 504 (1971).

219   Supreme Court decisions held that excluding those unalterably opposed to capital punishment was permissible (since they would not be able to apply the law properly), but excluding those who only expressed reservations or religious scruples was prohibited by the Sixth Amendment. *Witherspoon v. Illinois*, 391 U.S. 510 (1968). This has proven to be a very difficult distinction for courts to make.

220 The case that held Missouri opt-out statute unconstitutional is *Duren v. Missouri*, 439 U.S. 357 (1979).

In order to have succeeded, the district court found, Machetti would have had to raise the claim on the direct appeal of her conviction, back in 1975, not in her "collateral attack" (postconviction petitions under habeas corpus). *Machetti v. Linahan*, 517 F. Supp. 1076 (M.D.Ga. 1981).

221 The Eleventh Circuit decision denying John Eldon Smith a new trial is *Smith v. Kemp*, 715 F.2d 1459, 1476 (11th Cir. 1983) (opinion of Hatchett, Circuit Judge, concurring in part, dissenting in part.)

Right to Confront:
Coy v. Iowa

John Avery Coy refused to speak with the authors.

225 The account of the assault is based on the depositions of Kathy Brown and Linda Thompson, August 21, 1985, and on the trial testimony of Kathy Brown and Linda Thompson in the case of *State of Iowa v. John Avery Coy*, Criminal no. K-6962, Iowa District Court for Clinton County, Judge L. D. Carstensen, November 14, 1985, pp. 37–94 (hereafter Trial Transcript).

229 Testimony of Mr. Brown, Pre-Trial Hearing, *State of Iowa v. John Avery Coy*, Criminal no. K-6962, September 16, 1985, p. 55.

John Coy argued that the evidence seized in the Bingham home could not be used against him at trial because it had been obtained in violation of his Fourth Amendment right to be free from unreasonable searches and seizures. However, the Fourth Amendment (indeed all of the amendments in the Bill of Rights) protect only against action by the government or the government's agents—that is, someone acting at the direction of a government official. *Burdeau v. McDowell*, 256 U.S. 465, 475 (1921) (origin and history of the Fourth Amendment clearly show that it was not intended as a restraint upon activities other than those of governmental agencies). Officers Smith and Speakman, Mr. Brown, and his neighbor all testified that Brown and the neighbor entered the Bingham house on their own initiative, without the knowledge of the police. The police were therefore free to use the information Brown gave them, just like any other information obtained in the course of an investigation. Coy may have had a case for trespass against Brown, but the search warrant and police search of the Bingham home did not violate Coy's Fourth Amendment rights. Therefore, the evidence obtained from the search could be used against him.

For more on search and seizure, see the discussion and notes on the Fourth Amendment.

230 Iowa Code Ann. 709.8(1) (West 1979 and Supp. 1989) sets forth the crime of Lascivious Acts with a Child: "It is unlawful for any person eighteen years of age or older to per-

form any of the following acts with a child with or without the child's consent unless married to each other, for the purpose of arousing or satisfying the sexual desires of either of them: 1. Fondle or touch the pubes or genitals of a child. . . ."

232 The Iowa statute authorizing the screen, Iowa Code Ann. 910A.14 (West Supp. 1989), reads in pertinent part: "A court may . . . order that the testimony of a child . . . be taken in a room other than the courtroom and be televised by closed circuit equipment in the courtroom to be viewed by the court. Only the judge, parties, counsel, persons necessary to operate the equipment and any person whose presence . . . would contribute to the welfare and well-being of the child may be present in the room with the child during the child's testimony.

"The court may require a party be confined to an adjacent room or behind a screen or mirror that permits the party to see and hear the child during the child's testimony but does not allow the child to see or hear the party. However, if a party is so confined, the court shall take measures to insure that the party and counsel can confer during the testimony and shall inform the child that the party can see and hear the child during testimony."

Critical to the fundamental guarantee of a fair trial is the protection of the trial process from contamination by irrelevant or prejudicial factors. See *Estelle v. Williams*, 425 U.S. 502, 503–6 (1976). A court must therefore closely scrutinize any courtroom practice or arrangement that might dilute the presumption of innocence, which is a basic component of a fair trial. See ibid.; see also *Estes*, 381 U.S. 532 (1965). If a procedure is found to be "inherently prejudicial," a guilty verdict will not be upheld if the procedure was not necessary to further an essential state interest. *Holbrook v. Flynn*, 475 U.S. 560, 568–69 (1986). Coy argued that the use of the screen was "inherently prejudicial" and therefore violated his right to due process of law as guaranteed under the Fourteenth Amendment. Analogizing his plight to a case in which the Supreme Court held that forcing a defendant to appear in court in prison garb would prejudice him in the minds of the jury, Coy's lawyers argued that the state's interest in protecting child witnesses was insufficient to override Coy's due process claim. The screen's use, the lawyers asserted, would inevitably brand Coy in the minds of the jury "with an unmistakable mark of guilt" (citing *Estelle*, 425 U.S. at 518 [Brennan, J., dissenting]). The Supreme Court of Iowa decided against Coy, finding that the jury "likely concluded the screen was being used to reduce the trauma necessarily attached to the children's testimony" and that the screen had not prejudiced the jury. *State v. Coy*, 397 N.W. 2d 730, 733 (Iowa 1986).

The issue was raised on appeal to the U.S. Supreme Court. But because the Supreme Court ultimately disposed of the case on Sixth Amendment grounds, it did not reach the due process issue.

233 Testimony of Kathy Brown and Linda Thompson, Trial Transcript, November 14, 1985, pp. 41.2.

236 Testimony of John Avery Coy, Trial Transcript, November 18, 1985, pp. 316–17.

237 John Avery Coy's case in the Iowa Supreme Court is *State v. Coy*, 397 N.W.2d 730 (1986).

239 Further to the interrelationship between the constitutional right to confront and the evidentiary rules of hearsay: Where the evidence in question appears indispensable and yet is available only in the form of hearsay, the rules of evidence may allow admission of such out-of-court statements where they possess sufficient "indicia of reliability." *California v. Green*, 399 U.S. 149, 161–62 (1970). Also, see generally Jack B. Weinstein and Margaret A. Berger, *Weinstein's Evidence Manual: A Guide to the United States Rules Based on Weinstein's Evidence* (New York: Matthew Bender, 1987), p. 14. The Supreme Court has consistently held that the admission of out-of-court statements pursuant to generally recognized hearsay exceptions does not, per se, violate the Sixth Amendment. *Weinstein's Evidence Manual*, sec. 14.03.

The Court has declined, however, to map out the precise relationship between the hearsay exceptions and the Sixth Amendment right to confront, holding only that although they "stem from the same roots . . . it has never equated the two." *Dutton v. Evans*, 400 U.S. 74, 86 (1970). To do so would, in the words of Justice Harlan, "transplant the ganglia of hearsay rules and their exceptions into the body of constitutional protections." *California v. Green*, p. 173 (Harlan, J., concurring).

237 In *California v. Green*, the Supreme Court upheld admission into evidence of a *prior* recorded statement of a witness, despite the witness's claim in court that he could not recall the events detailed in the prior statement and therefore could not be cross-examined. The Court held that the witness had been subjected to adequate cross-examination at the time the prior statement was recorded—that is, at a preliminary hearing.

In *United States v. Owen*, 108 S. Ct. 838 (1988), the Court resolved the issue, left open in *Green*, of whether a defendant's right to confront is violated when effective *in-court* cross-examination is prevented by a witness's claimed memory loss. The Court held that if the *opportunity* for cross-examination is presented, the Sixth Amendment is not violated, even if cross-examination is made ineffective by the witness's memory loss (p. 842).

238 *Coy v. Iowa*, 108 S. Ct. 2798 (1988). The decision in the *Coy* case was six to two. Justice Scalia delivered the opinion of the Court; Justice O'Connor wrote a concurring opinion in which Justice White joined. Justice Blackmun wrote a dissenting opinion in which Justice Rehnquist joined. Justice Kennedy did not take part in the decision.

238 Justice Blackmun's dissenting opinion, joined by Chief Justice Rehnquist, argued that Coy's trial offended neither the

confrontation clause nor the due process clause. Citing Wigmore for the proposition that, by the time the Sixth Amendment was passed, the right to confront had merged with the right to cross-examine (p. 2807), Justice Blackmun argued that "the ability of a witness to see the defendant while the witness is testifying does not constitute an essential part of the protections afforded by the Confrontation Clause" (p. 2805). He thus found no defect in the courtroom setup in *State v. Coy*.

Further, Justice Blackmun noted, if the admission of "hearsay" statements—that is, statements made out of court—do not violate the confrontation clause, then it cannot be that the right to confront witnesses face to face is indispensable. Indeed, he pointed out, a blind witness could constitutionally have testified against Coy (p. 2808). Finally, Justice Blackmun argued that the policy finding made by the state that the trauma posed by testifying was severe ought to have been sufficient to legitimate the statute (pp. 2828–32).

On the due process issue, Justice Blackmun opined that the procedure used in this case was unlikely to have produced any "subconscious effect on the jury's attitude toward [Coy]" (p. 2810).

239 The Supreme Court held that since "other types of violations of the Confrontation Clause are subject to . . . [a] harmless error analysis . . . [it could] see no reason why denial of face-to-face confrontation should not be treated the same." *Coy*, 108 S. Ct. at 2803. "Harmless error" analysis allows an appellate court reviewing a lower court decision to find that an error appearing in the record is "harmless"— that is it did not prejudice the "substantial rights" of the defendant (Federal Rules of Criminal Procedure, p. 52), and thus to affirm conviction. In *Chapman v. California*, 386 U.S. 18 (1967), the Court for the first time held that harmless error doctrine could be applied to errors involving *constitutional* rights if the reviewing court is able to "declare a belief that . . . [the error] was harmless beyond a reasonable doubt" (p. 24).

240 The Court thus remanded the *Coy* case to the Iowa court to determine whether the violation of John Coy's right to confront the witnesses against him was in fact "harmless" in this case. The Iowa court determined the error was not "harmless," and therefore Coy was entitled to a new trial.

240 The case upholding the use of closed-circuit television is *Maryland v. Craig*, 58 U.S.L.W. 5044 (1990).

Right to Compulsory Process: *In re Myron Farber*

245 Much of the factual information in this story is drawn from Myron Farber's book *Somebody Is Lying* (New York: Doubleday, 1982).

246 Information about the effects of d-tubocurarine can be found in A. Gilman, L. Goodman, T. Rall, and F. Murad, eds., *The Pharmacological Bases of Therapeutics*, 7th ed. (New York:

Macmillan, 1985); and John C. Krautz, Jr., and C. Jelleff Carr, *The Pharmacologic Principles of Medical Practices* (Baltimore: Williams and Wilkins, 1961).

248   Myron Farber's articles appeared in the *New York Times* on January 7 and January 8, 1976. A third article appeared on March 7, 1976.

251   The case in which the Supreme Court rejected a reporter's claim of a First Amendment privilege is *Branzburg v. Hayes*, 408 U.S. 665 (1972). In *Branzburg*, the Court examined and dismissed empirical studies that asserted the importance of confidential sources to reporters (p. 694, nn. 32, 33). See also Note, "The Reporter's Confidentiality Privilege: Updating the Empirical Evidence After a Decade of Subpoenas," *Columbia Human Rights Law Review* 17 (1985): 57, 77 ("Reporters continue to rely heavily upon confidential source information in uncovering, developing, and confirming news stories.")

252   The New Jersey "shield law," N.J.S.A. 24: 84A-21 and 21a, provided in part:

[A] person connected with, or employed by news media for the purpose of gathering . . . or disseminating news for the general public . . . has a privilege to refuse to disclose, in any legal or quasi-legal proceeding or before any investigative body, including, but not limited to, any court . . .

a) The source . . . from or whom any information was procured [;] . . . and
b) any news or information obtained in the course of pursuing his professional activities whether or not it is disseminated.

It is reprinted in *In re Farber*, 78 N.J. 259, 269, n.2 (1978).

253   The Supreme Court has rarely ruled on the compulsory process clause, preferring instead to deal with defendants' access to witnesses through the confrontation clause or due process clause. Until 1967, the Supreme Court had addressed the compulsory process clause only five times, and only perfunctorily. Peter Westen, "The Compulsory Process Clause," *Michigan Law Review* 73 (1974): 71, 108.

The most renowned case involved the treason trial of Aaron Burr in 1807, in which Chief Justice Marshall, sitting as trial judge, found that Burr could subpoena President Jefferson for supposedly incriminating evidence. *U.S. v. Burr*, 25 F. Cas. 30, 35 (No. 14, 692d) (CC Va. 1807), cited in *Pennsylvania v. Ritchie*, 480 U.S. 39, 55 (1987).

The modern formula is: "Our cases establish, at a minimum, that criminal defendants have a right to the government's assistance in compelling the attendance of favorable witnesses at trial and the right to put before a jury evidence that might influence the determination of guilt." Ibid., p. 56; cf. *U.S. v. Nixon*, 418 U.S. 683, 709, 711 (1974) (clause may require production of evidence).

253   The quotation from Chief Justice Earl Warren is from *Washington v. Texas*, 388 U.S. 14, 19 (1967), the case that incorporated the right to compulsory process against the states.

254 The case in which the Supreme Court upheld the right to compulsory process over President Nixon's claim of executive privilege is *U.S. v. Nixon,* 418 U.S. 683 (1974).

254 A court has inherent power to sanction anyone connected with a case for civil or criminal contempt. Civil contempt is designed to secure compliance with a subpoena or other request of one of the parties to a civil suit. A person subject to civil contempt may be fined or imprisoned, but may immediately vacate the punishment by complying. See Kamisar, LaFave, and Israel, *Modern Criminal Procedure.* 7th ed., p. 637, n. a. For more on civil contempt, see discussion and notes on the Fifth Amendment *(Bouknight).*

If civil contempt fails or appears futile, the court may then utilize criminal contempt, which is like a criminal trial and is separate from the underlying proceeding. Criminal contempts are acts that obstruct the administration of justice or tend to bring the court into disrespect. Criminal contempt is an independent proceeding, which is immediately appealable regardless of the status of the underlying trial, but civil contempt is not. *Doyle v. London Guarantee & Accident Co.,* 204 U.S. 599 (1907).

255 The statements by Myron Farber and Judge Trautwein at the contempt hearings are from Transcript of Proceedings, *In the Matter of Myron Farber and the New York Times Co., Charged with Contempt of Court,* Superior Court of New Jersey, Law Division, Bergen County, July 24, 1978.

257 The decision of the New Jersey Supreme Court upholding Dr. Jascalevich's right to compulsory process over Myron Farber's claim of privilege is *In re Myron Farber,* 78 N.J. 259 (1978).

Right to Counsel: *United States v. Cronic*

263 The description of a check-kiting scheme is from an instruction given by the Honorable Thomas R. Brett in *United States v. McKinney,* CR-85-69 (N.D. Okla. 1985); *aff'd United States v. McKinney,* 822 F.2d 946 (10th Cir. 1987), as quoted in *United States v. Cronic,* CR-80-21-P, Brief of Appellant.

265 Judge Eubank's quotation regarding appointment of counsel is from *U.S. v. Cronic,* no. 80-1955, Tenth Circuit, Appellant's Brief, June 24, 1985, p. 5 (citing Trial Transcript, p. 23).

265–266 For a more detailed explanation of the good faith defense to mail fraud in the Tenth Circuit, see *United States v. Washita Construction Co.,* 789 F.2d 809 (10th Cir. 1986).

266 The Supreme Court quotations regarding the history of the right to counsel are from *Powell v. Alabama,* 287 U.S. 45, 60–65 (1932).

When the right to counsel in criminal prosecutions was proposed as a constitutional amendment in 1789, the enforcement of the provision generated virtually no debate. As a result, federal judges "were left free to shape the right as they thought best." William Merritt Beaney, *The Right to Counsel in American Courts* (Westport, Conn.: Greenwood Press, 1972), pp. 8–26.

The Supreme Court did not hand down an in-depth interpretation of the right to counsel until 1938, when in *Johnson v. Zerbst,* 304 U.S. 458, it found a constitutional right to counsel for all federal felony prosecutions. Until then, one legal scholar commented, "there was no feeling . . . that defendants who pleaded guilty, or those who failed to request counsel, had a constitutional right to be advised and offered counsel, or that a conviction without counsel was void" (p. 32).

267 The Supreme Court quotations regarding the importance of the right to counsel are from *United States v. Cronic,* 466 U.S. 648 (1984).

267 *Gideon v. Wainwright,* 372 U.S. 335, 344 (1963). In the decades prior to *Gideon,* the Supreme Court had recognized some aspects of the right to counsel under the Fourteenth Amendment due process clause (as opposed to the Sixth Amendment counsel clause). In 1932, the Court relied on the due process clause to rule that indigent defendants facing capital punishment had a constitutional right to counsel. In *Powell v. Alabama,* the famous "Scottsboro" case, the court reviewed the fate of seven poor, illiterate black youths accused of raping two girls on a train. After being seized from the train and whisked away by a sheriff's posse, the youths were quickly tried, convicted, and sentenced to death. No lawyer was specifically assigned to their defense until the morning of their trial.

While the specific ruling in *Powell* refers to capital cases and destitute defendants, Justice Sutherland's opinion offers a stirring argument for a general right to legal representation at trial: "The right to be heard would be, in many cases, of little avail if it did not comprehend the right to be heard by counsel. Even the intelligent and educated layman has small and sometimes no skill in the science of law. . . . He lacks both the skill and knowledge adequately to prepare his defense, even though he has a perfect one. He requires the guiding hand of counsel at every step in proceedings against him. Without it, though he be not guilty, he faces the danger of conviction because he does not know how to establish his innocence" (pp. 68–69).

268 The Supreme Court case holding the *Gideon* rule applicable to all criminal cases is *Argersinger v. Hamlin,* 407 U.S. 25 (1972).

268 The Chief Justice's comments are from Warren E. Burger, "The Special Skills of Advocacy: Are Specialized Training and Certification of Advocates Essential to Our System of Justice?" *Fordham Law Review* 42 (1973): 227, 230.

268 The case in which the trial attorney admitted his client's guilt to the jury is *Wiley v. Sowders,* 647 F.2d 642 (6th Cir. 1981).

268   The case in which the defendant's trial attorney testified for the prosecution is *Virgin Islands v. Zepp,* 748 F.2d 125 (3rd Cir. 1984).

268   The quotation about sacrificing "unarmed prisoners to gladiators" is from *Cronic,* p. 657.

268   The Supreme Court's recognition of a right to "effective" assistance of counsel is cited in ibid., p. 654, quoting *McMann v. Richardson,* 397 U.S. 759, 771, n. 14 (1970).

268–269   The Tenth Circuit case holding that Cronic did not receive effective assistance of counsel under the Tenth Circuit test is *United States v. Cronic,* 675 F.2d 1126 (10th Cir. 1982). The Supreme Court case rejecting the Tenth Circuit case is *United States v. Cronic,* 466 U.S. 648, 665 (1984). The companion case to Cronic setting forth the test for ineffective assistance of counsel is *Strickland v. Washington,* 466 U.S. 668 (1984).

270   The first quoted remarks from Judge Eubanks are cited in *United States v. Cronic,* 839 F.2d 1401, 1402 (10th Cir. 1988). The second quoted remarks from Judge Eubanks are from Hearing Transcript, *United States v. Cronic,* Case no. CR-80-21-E, March 26, 1985, (hereafter Hearing Transcript), p. 73.

270   Testimony of Chris Colston, Hearing Transcript, p. 73.

270   Remarks of Judge Eubanks, Hearing Transcript, p. 171.

270   The Tenth Circuit case holding that Cronic did not receive effective assistance of counsel under the new *Strickland* test is *United States v. Cronic,* 839 F.2d 1401 (10th Cir. 1988).

272   The Tenth Circuit case finally dismissing Cronic's conviction is *United States v. Cronic,* 900 F.2d 1511, 1512 (10th Cir. 1990).

The mail fraud statute at issue in *Cronic* criminalizes "a scheme to defraud" and a "scheme to obtain money by means of false or fraudulent pretenses, representations, or promises." Although they overlap, the two are considered separate offenses. The "scheme to defraud" offense focuses on the intended end result, not on whether false representations were necessary to effect the result. The second offense, on the other hand, focuses on the *means* by which money was obtained and requires false representations as an essential element of the crime. The indictment against Harrison Cronic charged both offenses. But the government allowed the jury to be instructed regarding the offense of obtaining money by false representations only. Under the law, a bad check in itself does not constitute a false representation. No separate false representations were charged or proved at Harrison Cronic's trial. Thus, there was not sufficient evidence to support the one offense that was submitted to the jury. The conviction was therefore overturned. Furthermore, dismissal on grounds of "legally insufficient evidence" is one of the few exceptions to the usual double jeopardy rule. In most cases, defendants who are acquitted may not be retried for the same offense; but defendants who succeed in getting a reversal on appeal may be retried. (See discussion on the Fifth Amendment.) If, however, a conviction is overturned because the evidence was not legally sufficient to convict in the first place, the defendant may *not* be retried for the same offense. *Burks v. United States*, 437 U.S. 1, 18 (1978). Hence, Harrison Cronic went free.

SEVENTH AMENDMENT

Right to a Civil Jury: "Complexity"

275 The quotation regarding the California IBM litigation is from James S. Campbell, "The Current Understanding of the Seventh Amendment: Jury Trials in Modern Complex Litigation," *Washington University Law Quarterly* 66 (1988): 64.

276 The case with approximately eleven hundred plaintiffs is *Bernstein v. Universal Pictures, Inc.*, 79 F.R.D. 59 (S.D.N.Y. 1978).

276 The case contemplating a two-year trial is *In re U.S. Financial Securities Litigation*, 609 F.2d 411 (9th Cir. 1979).

276 The Alexander Hamilton quotation is from *Federalist* No. 83, *The Federalist Papers*, p. 495.

276 The Supreme Court quotations regarding the importance of the civil jury are from *Dimick v. Schiedt*, 293 U.S. 474, 486 (1935); and *Jacob v. City of New York*, 315 U.S. 752, 753 (1942).

277 Although juries do sometimes practice "black box" justice, they are usually not given free reign. For example, in criminal cases involving obscenity statutes, the jury, as "trier of fact," must apply "contemporary community standards" in inquiring whether the work in question "appeals to the prurient interest." *Roth v. United States*, 354 U.S. 476, 489 (1957). The jurors are permitted to "draw on knowledge of the community or vicinage from which [they] come" in reaching their conclusions. *Hamling v. United States*, 418 U.S. 87, 105 (1974). Nevertheless, the Court has made clear that juries do not have "unbridled discretion in determining what is 'potentially offensive.'" *Jenkins v. Georgia*, 418 U.S. 153, pp. 160–61 (1974), holding that the film *Carnal Knowledge* could not "as a matter of constitutional law" be obscene.

277 The Alexander Hamilton quotation is from *Federalist* No. 83, *The Federalist Papers*, p. 505.

277 *In re U.S. Financial Securities Litigation*, quoting Carl Becker.

278 For further discussion on the right to a civil jury as the "right to an irrational verdict," see Jeffrey Oakes, "The Right to Strike the Jury Trial Demand in Complex Litigation," *University of Miami Law Review* 34 (1980): 243; Note, "The Right to an Incompetent Jury: Protracted Civil Litigation and the Seventh Amendment," *Connecticut Law Review* 10 (1978): 775.

279 The controversial footnote 10 is in *Ross v. Bernhard*, 396 U.S. 531 (1970). The critical interpretation of the *Ross* footnote is fairly substantial. See, e.g., Note, "The Right to a Jury Trial

in Complex Civil Litigation," *Harvard Law Review* 92 (February 1979): 898; Note, "Unfit for Jury Determination: Complex Civil Litigation and the Seventh Amendment Right of Trial by Jury," *Boston College Law Review* 20 (March 1979): 511; Comment, "Complex Civil Litigation and the Seventh Amendment Right to a Jury Trial," *University of Chicago Law Review* 51 (1984): 581. While many courts will advert to "the practical abilities and limitations of juries," only one case, *In re Japanese Elec. Products Antitrust Litigation,* 631 F.2d 1069 (3d Cir. 1980) (discussed in the text) has suggested that complexity of facts *alone* can provide the basis for a court to proceed without a jury. In general, though, the continued vitality of the third *Ross* factor is "indeed open to question." *Phillips v. Kaplus,* 764 F.2d 807, 814, n. 6 (11th Cir. 1985), noting that "on several occasions since *Ross,* the Supreme Court has considered the Seventh Amendment question without once considering the practical abilities and limitations of juries."

Litigants cannot take refuge in pre-*Ross* Supreme Court precedent either—in prior cases the Court has rejected the notion that complex facts and difficulty of proof alone will suffice as a basis for a court to act in its "equitable" capacity. *United States v. Bitter Root Development,* 200 U.S. 451 (1906); *Curriden v. Middleton,* 232 U.S. 633 (1914). The only line of cases that calls into question the practical abilities and limitations of juries deals with so-called "equitable accountings"—that is, actions for an accounting between parties, where the "accounts between the parties are of such a complicated nature' that only a court of equity can satisfactorily unravel them." *Dairy Queen, Inc. v. Wood,* 369 U.S. 469, 478 (1962). In practice, given the availability of "special masters" to handle nettlesome accounting questions, "it will indeed be a rare case" in which this narrow exception will be utilized to invoke the court's equitable jurisdiction (*Dairy Queen,* p. 478). In fact, one court notes that the equitable accounting exception has been limited by *Dairy Queen* "practically to the point of extinction." *In re U.S. Financial Securities Litigation.* See *Phillips,* distinguishing situations where winding up of partnership affairs will necessarily involve an equitable distribution of assets from *Dairy Queen,* where "the party [was] attempting to disguise a legal claim for damages by asking for an accounting" (p. 814). One commentator suggests that the mention of "practical abilities and limitation of juries" may only be a reference to the *Dairy Queen* equitable accounting exception. James William Moore, *Moore's Federal Practice,* 2d ed. (Albany: Matthew Bender, 1988), vol. 5, 38.11 [10], n. 14.

The case that found footnote 10 to be of "constitutional dimension" is *In re Boise Cascade Securities Litigation,* 420 F. Supp. 99 (W.D. Wash. 1976).

279   Further to the rejection of footnote 10: "While it is unclear as to what was meant by the inclusion of the third factor, we do not believe that it stated a rule of constitutional dimensions.

After employing a historical test for almost two hundred years, it is doubtful that the Supreme Court would attempt to make such a radical departure from its prior interpretation of a constitutional provision in a footnote." *In re U.S. Financial Securities Litigation*, p. 425. One commentator remarks that footnote 10 is "so cursory, conclusory and devoid of cited authority or reasoned analysis that it is difficult to believe it could have been intended to reject such established historical practice or Supreme Court precedent." Martin H. Redish, "Seventh Amendment Right to Jury Trial: A Study in the Irrationality of Rational Decision Making," *Northwestern University Law Review* 70 (1975): 486.

279   The antitrust case in which the judge discussed the "fair cross-section" issue is *ILC Peripherals v. International Business Machines*, 458 F. Supp. 423, 448, (N.D. Cal. 1978).

280   The quotation regarding the "intelligence of the citizens" is from *In re U.S. Financial Securities Litigation*, p. 430.

280   The quotation regarding the AT&T jury is from *SRI Intern v. Matsushita Elec. Corp. of America*, 775 F.2d 1107, 1128 (Fed. Cir. 1985) (additional views of Markey, C.J.).

280   The comment regarding a complexity exception for judges is from *Moore's Federal Practice*, vol. 5, par. 38.02 [1].

    For courts avoiding the complexity issue, see, e.g., *Cotten v. Witco Chemical Corp.*, 651 F.2d 274, 276 (5th Cir. 1981) (court does not rule on Seventh Amendment exception, but notes that if such an exception existed, the issues would need to be so complex that a jury *could* not render a rational verdict); *Rosen v. Dick*, 639 F.2d 82 (2d Cir. 1980) (Second Circuit reserving question of whether exception is available); *City of New York v. Pullman*, 662 F.2d 910, 919 (2d Cir. 1981) (not reaching issue of whether complexity exception is ever appropriate, court held that elements of scientific testimony would not take otherwise "simple and discrete" legal issues out of jury's hands).

280   The Third Circuit case upholding a complexity exception is *In re Japanese Elec. Prods. Antitrust Litigation*, p. 1084.

280–281   The Ninth Circuit case rejecting the complexity exception is *In re. U.S. Financial Securities Litigation*, p. 416. The Ninth Circuit affirmed its explicit rejection of the complexity exception in *Davis and Cox v. Summa Corp.*, 751 F.2d 1507, 1516 (9th Cir. 1984).

281   The final quotation comparing the civil jury to rock music is from *Moore's Federal Practice*, vol. 5, 38.02 [1] at 15.

EIGHTH AMENDMENT

Cruel and Unusual Punishment: *Tison v. Arizona*

288   The prison official's quotation about Gary Tison is from Testimony of Dan Deck, *State of Arizona v. Tison*, no. 9299, Aggravation Hearing and Sentencing, Superior Court, Yuma, Arizona, March 14, 1979, p. 132.

288–289   The Tison brothers' quotations about their childhood are from the Pre-Sentence Report in *State of Arizona v. Tison*, no. 9299.

290   The dialogue during the escape is from Testimony of Ed Barry, *State of Arizona v. Raymond Tison*, no. 9299, Superior Court, Yuma, Arizona, February 28, 1979 (hereafter Trial Transcript), pp. 123–24.

294   Testimony of Kathleen Ermentraut, Trial Transcript, p. 221.

298   The felony-murder rule originated in sixteenth-century English common law, *People v. Burroughs*, 678 P.2d 894, 905 (Cal. 1984) (Bird, C.J., concurring), and was designed to deter the commission of felonies. Usually, a murderer must both intend to kill and actually cause the death of another person. But neither is required for a conviction of felony-murder, because the accused is thought to have sacrificed the usual safeguards and endangered the public by committing a felony in the first place. Most states have some version of the felony-murder rule, but have limited it to dangerous felonies such as rape or robbery, or have provided the passive accomplice with a defense. The Model Penal Code and a few states have abolished the felony-murder rule by statute or judicial decision.

298   The quotation from Raymond Tison about the plea bargain is from *State of Arizona v. Tison*, no. 9299, January 25, 1979, p. 308, reprinted in James W. Clarke, *Last Rampage* (Boston: Houghton Mifflin, 1988).

299   *Furman v. Georgia*, 408 U.S. 238 (1972), was actually the culmination of a lengthy and comprehensive campaign led by the NAACP Legal Defense and Educational Fund to invalidate the death penalty.

      In 1963, Justice Arthur Goldberg's dissent in a routine Supreme Court denial of cert. indicated that at least some on the Court were willing to hear constitutional arguments against the death penalty. In *Rudolph v. Alabama*, 375 U.S. 889 (1963), a rapist was sentenced to death. Justice Goldberg argued that the Court should take the case to decide whether a death sentence for one who had "neither taken nor endangered human life" violated the Eighth Amendment and the Fourteenth Amendment due process clause. The Court declined to take the case, but Justice Goldberg's opinion sparked the legal campaign that culminated in 1973 with *Furman*.

299   At the time the Bill of Rights was drafted, most homicides in the American colonies were automatically punishable by death. Until the 1960s, the Supreme Court had always said that the Eighth Amendment did not prohibit this historically accepted punishment. See, e.g., *Trop v. Dulles*, 356 U.S. 86, 99, (1958). This did not mean that any punishment short of death was allowed, since the Supreme Court invalidated certain punishments as disproportionately harsh under the Eighth Amendment. See, e.g., *Trop v. Dulles* (deprivation of U.S. citizenship for court martial, wartime desertion); *Weems v.*

United States, 217 U.S. 349 (1910) (twelve years of hard labor for falsifying public records).

Furthermore, in *McGautha v. California,* 402 U.S. 183 (1971), the Supreme Court found that an unguided jury could impose the death penalty consistent with due process, although the systematic exclusion of jurors who objected to capital punishment fell short of due process. *Witherspoon v. Illinois,* 391 U.S. 510 (1968). Although the death penalty appeared constitutional before *Furman,* Justice Harlan's comment in *McGautha* laid the groundwork for later challenges to state systems of capital punishment: "To identify before the fact those characteristics of criminal homicides and their perpetrators which call for the death penalty, and to express these characteristics in language which can be fairly understood and applied by the sentencing authority, appear to be tasks which are beyond present human ability." *McGautha,* p. 204.

The *Furman* opinion was unusual, some would say incomprehensible, because the official majority opinion was a mere paragraph devoid of discussion, which was followed by 230 pages of concurring and dissenting opinions written separately by each justice.

Justice Brennan's concurrence found the death penalty inherently degrading to human dignity and arbitrary in its application (p. 257). Justice Marshall's concurrence agreed, stating that the death penalty did not comport with society's evolving standards of decency, and he noted that seventy nations had abandoned it (p. 314). These two justices have retained their absolute view in all capital punishment cases from *Furman* to the present day.

Justice Douglas's quote about the whim of one man is from *Furman,* p. 253. Justice Douglas also stressed indications that the death penalty was imposed disproportionately on minorities and the poor (pp. 248–57).

Justice White wrote that ten years of exposure to hundreds of death penalty cases led him to the inescapable conclusion that "there is no meaningful basis for distinguishing the few cases in which [the death penalty] is imposed from the many cases in which it is not" (p. 313).

Chief Justice Burger's dissent restated the historical acceptance of capital punishment and emphasized that the Court should defer to the forty states that then allowed some form of capital punishment and the *McGautha* decision, issued the year before, to define the hazy boundaries of cruel and unusual punishment.

299   Justice Stewart's quotation analogizing the death penalty to being struck by lightening is from *Furman,* pp. 309–10.

299   *Gregg v. Georgia,* 428 U.S. 153 (1976). Justice Stewart wrote the majority opinion, joined by Justices Powell and Stevens. Justices White, Rehnquist, and Blackmun, and Chief Justice Burger concurred in the judgment. Justices Brennan and Marshall each wrote dissenting opinions.

The new Georgia death penalty statute provided specific guidelines for the sentencing jury. Before a jury could sentence a defendant to death, it had to make specific findings of at least one statutory aggravating aspect of the crime or criminal. It could also consider other aggravating and mitigating circumstances of the crime. Aggravators include prior offenses, multiple victims, avoidance of arrest, motive of pecuniary gain, and murders that are particularly heinous. Mitigators typically include the absence of aggravators, emotional disturbance, minor participation in the killing, youth of the defendant, and duress. In addition, there would be an automatic appeal to the Georgia Supreme Court, which was required to review whether the sentencing was affected by prejudice and to compare the sentence to those imposed in similar cases.

300   Those concerned with the "original intent" of the Framers point out that at least three clauses of the Bill of Rights contemplate capital punishment. The Fifth Amendment provides: "No person shall be held to answer for a *capital*, or otherwise infamous crime, unless on a presentment or indictment of a Grand Jury . . . nor shall any person be subject for the same offence to be twice *put in jeopardy of life or limb* . . . nor be *deprived of life*, liberty, or property, without due process of law" (emphasis added).

Also, it is indisputable that the death penalty existed in the American colonies when the Bill of Rights was drafted. According to Justice Black, "The Eighth Amendment forbids 'cruel and unusual punishments.' In my view, these words cannot be read to outlaw capital punishment because that penalty was in common use and authorized by law . . . at the time the Amendment was adopted." *McGautha v. California*, p. 226 (Black, J., concurring).

On the other hand, also in common use and authorized by law at the time were public flogging, branding with a hot iron, and slitting, nailing, and cutting off of ears. As Justice Brennan put it: "Indeed, if it were possible to find answers to all constitutional questions by reference to historical practices we would not need judges. Courts could be staffed by professional historians who could be instructed to compile a comprehensive master list of life in 1791. Cases could be decided based on whether a challenged practice . . . could be located on that great list." William J. Brennan, Jr., "Constitutional Adjudication and the Death Penalty: A View from the Court," Oliver Wendell Holmes Lecture, Harvard Law School, September 5, 1986, pp. 21, 23.

300   Further to the death penalty as deterrent: Many studies have attempted to discover whether the possibility of the death penalty discourages criminals significantly more than other punishments, such as life in prison. See *Gregg*, p. 184, n. 31; D. Archer, R. Gartner, and M. Beittel, "Homicide and the Death Penalty: A Cross-National Test of a Deterrance Hypothesis," *Journal of Criminal Law and Criminology* 74 (1983): 991. Because the forces that encourage and discourage crimes are complicated, often indiscernible, and ill suited to scientific

experimentation, a conclusive answer has been declared, at least by some, to be unattainable. See James Alan Fox and Michael L. Radelet, "Persistent Flaws in Econometric Studies of the Deterrent Effect of the Death Penalty," *Loyola L.A. Law Review* 23 (1989): 29, 31.

300 Further to the death penalty as retribution: In support of the goal of retribution, the Court also cited Justice Stewart's concurring opinion in *Furman:* "The instinct for retribution is part of the nature of man, and channeling that instinct in the administration of criminal justice serves an important purpose in promoting the stability of a society governed by law. When people begin to believe that organized society is unwilling or unable to impose upon criminal offenders the punishment they 'deserve,' then there are sown the seeds of anarchy—of self-help, vigilante justice, and lynch law." *Gregg*, p. 183, quoting *Furman v. Georgia*, p. 308 (Stewart, J., concurring).

Justice Marshall, dissenting in *Gregg*, argued: "This statement is wholly inadequate to justify the death penalty. . . . It simply defies belief to suggest that the death penalty is necessary to prevent the American people from taking the law into their own hands" (p. 238).

301 The case that outlawed the death penalty for the crime of rape is *Coker v. Georgia*, 433 U.S. 584 (1977). The Court canvassed the state laws and jury results as it did in *Gregg*, only this time it found the imposition of the death penalty to be relatively uncommon for rape, as opposed to murder.

301 *Enmund v. Florida*, 458 U.S. 782 (1982).

302 The Tisons' case in the Supreme Court is *Tison v. Arizona*, 481 U.S. 137 (1987). Justice O'Connor wrote the majority opinion in which Chief Justice Rehnquist and Justices White, Powell, and Scalia joined. Justices Brennan, Marshall, Blackmun, and Stevens were in dissent.

302 A person is reckless when he or she "consciously disregards a substantial and unjustifiable risk" of harm. Model Penal Code 2.02 (General Requirements of Culpability). Reckless homicide under the code constitutes manslaughter, which is more serious than negligent homicide and is usually less serious than murder. Model Penal Code 210.2–.4 (Murder; Manslaughter; Negligent Homicide).

NINTH AMENDMENT

Rights Retained by the People: Privacy

315 The quotation from Franklin D. Roosevelt is reprinted in "The Bill of Rights," Milestone Documents in the National Archives, National Archives and Records Administration, Washington, D.C., 1986.

316 The case upholding the right to study a foreign language under the due process clause is *Meyer v. Nebraska*, 262 U.S. 390 (1923).

316   The case striking down forced stomach pumping under the
       due process clause is *Rochin v. California*, 342 U.S. 165
       (1952).

316   The case describing substantive due process rights as "deeply
       rooted" is *Moore v. East Cleveland*, 431 U.S. 494, 503 (1977).
       The case describing those rights as "implicit in the concept of
       ordered liberty" is *Palko v. Connecticut*, 302 U.S. 319 (1937).

316   For more on substantive due process, see the discussion of
       Fuentes under the Fifth Amendment, and accompanying
       notes.

316   Justice Holmes's quotation is from *Baldwin v. Missouri*, 281
       U.S. 586, 595 (1930) (Holmes, J., dissenting).

317   Chief Justice Rehnquist's quotation regarding "so much au-
       thority" is from *Richmond Newspapers v. Virginia*, 448 U.S.
       555, 606 (1980) (Rehnquist, J., dissenting).

317   The quotation from the confirmation hearings on Justice
       Rehnquist is from Laurence H. Tribe, "Contrasting Constitu-
       tional Visions: Of Real and Unreal Differences," *Harvard Civil
       Rights–Civil Liberties Law Review* 22 (1987): 95, 103.

317   *Griswold v. Connecticut*, 381 U.S. 479 (1965).

319   The Alexander Hamilton quotation is from *Federalist* No. 84,
       The Federalist Papers, p. 513.

319   James Madison's statement to Congress is reprinted in
       Griswold, pp. 489–90.

320   The examples of post-*Griswold* Ninth Amendment cases are:
       Freeman v. Flake, 405 U.S. 1032 (1972) (schoolboys and long
       hair); *Williams v. Board of Education*, 388 F. Supp. 93
       (S.D.W.Va. 1975) (fundamentalists and schoolbooks); *Burns v.
       Swensen*, 430 F.2d 771 (8th Cir. 1970) (felons and maximum
       security); and *Tanner v. Armco Steel Corp.*, 340 F. Supp. 532
       (S.D. Tex. 1972) (healthful environment).

321   Robert H. Bork, *The Tempting of America* (New York: Free
       Press, 1990), p. 183. He argues that James Madison could
       have drafted a more explicit provision if the Framers wanted
       judges to have so much discretion.

321   Tribe, "Contrasting Constitutional Visions," pp. 100, 108.

321   After *Griswold*, the Ninth Amendment was mentioned only
       one more time in a majority opinion by the Supreme Court.
       In *Richmond Newspapers v. Virginia* 448 U.S. 555 (1980), the
       Court upheld a claim to a public right of access to criminal
       trials. In response to the state's argument that no such right
       is spelled out in the Constitution, the Court wrote, "Notwith-
       standing the appropriate caution against reading into the
       Constitution rights not explicitly defined, the Court has ac-
       knowledged that certain unarticulated rights are implicit in
       enumerated guarantees." In a footnote, the Court cited the
       Ninth Amendment as support.

321   *Roe v. Wade*, 314 F. Supp. 1217 (N.D. Texas 1970), *aff'd in
       part*, *Roe v. Wade*, 410 U.S. 113 (1973).

322   *Hardwick v. Bowers*, 760 F.2d 1202 (11th Cir. 1985), *rev'd*, *Bowers v. Hardwick*, 478 U.S. 186 (1986).

323   *Webster v. Reproductive Health Services*, 109 S.Ct. 3040 (1989).

323   Chief Justice Rehnquist's quotation is from *Roe*, p. 173.

TENTH AMENDMENT

Powers Reserved to the States: Minimum Wage

327   The best-known example of a case involving a state law enacted to protect workers that was struck down by the Supreme Court is *Lochner v. New York*, 198 U.S. 45 (1905). In *Lochner*, the Court struck down as an abridgment of liberty of contract, and therefore a violation of due process, a New York law that limited the hours a bakery employee could work to ten per day and sixty per week.

The federal effort to desegregate the schools began in earnest in *Brown v. Board of Education*, 347 U.S. 483 (1954), and has continued. Some of the 1960s cases are *Gross v. Board of Education* 373 U.S. 683 (1963) (invalidating minority-to-majority transfer plans); *Griffin v. County School Board*, 377 U.S. 218 (1964) (rejecting a county's attempt to close its public schools rather than comply with a desegregation order); *Green v. County School Board*, 391 U.S. 430 (1968) (rejecting freedom-of-choice plans); and *Swann v. Charlotte-Mecklenburg* 402 U.S. 1 (1971) (requiring de jure segregation before a federal court may order a set board to adjust the racial composition of its schools).

This phenomenon of states providing individuals more protection in state constitutions and statutes than the Supreme Court accords under the federal constitution took on added importance in the 1980s when the Court generally took to reading those protections more narrowly. See William J. Brennan, Jr., "State Constitutions and the Protection of Individual Rights," *Harvard Law Review* 90 (1977): 489; Collins, Gale, and Kincaid, "State High Courts, State Constitutions, and Individual Rights Litigation Since 1980: A Judicial Survey," *Hastings Constitutional Law Quarterly* 13 (1986): 599.

An example of this trend is the New York case *New York v. Kern*, 75 N.Y.2d 638 (1990), in which the New York Court of Appeals ruled that under New York's *state* constitution *defense* lawyers cannot dismiss prospective jurors because of their race, while the *federal* constitution prohibits only the prosecution from doing so. *Batson v. Kentucky*, 476 U.S. 79 (1986).

328   The James Madison quotation is from *Federalist* No. 45, *The Federalist Papers*, pp. 292–93.

329   *Hammer v. Dagenhart*, 247 U.S. 251 (1918).

331   *United States v. Darby*, 312 U.S. 100 (1941).

331   *Fry v. United States*, 421 U.S. 542 (1975).

332   *National League of Cities v. Usery*, 426 U.S. 833 (1976).

333   *Garcia v. San Antonio Metropolitan Transit Authority*, 469 U.S. 528 (1985).

After the *Garcia* decision, Congress amended the Fair Labor Standards Act (FLSA) in an effort to alleviate some of the financial burden on the state employers, while preserving the benefits to workers. The amendments allow state and local governments to award "comp time" at a time-and-a-half rate to employees who have worked overtime, provided some form of employee agreement has been reached prior to performance of the work. Public safety, emergency, and seasonal workers may accrue up to 480 hours of comp time before their employers are required to make overtime cash payments, while all other public employees are limited to 240 hours of comp time before the FLSA's cash overtime requirements are triggered. P.L. 99-150.

According to Labor Department estimates, 13.8 million state and local government employees were brought within the FLSA's coverage as a result of *Garcia*. According to an economic impact study (included in the Labor Department's final regulations implementing the amendments), the *Garcia* decision would have cost public employers an additional $733 million between April 1986 and March 1987 if the amendments had not been enacted. The amendments are estimated to have saved employers $517 million in overtime costs over the same period. Current Developments, Daily Labor Report, no. 13, A-14, 1-21-87, Bureau of National Affairs, Inc.; Washington, D.C., 1987.

Under amendments to the FLSA enacted in 1989 (P.L. 101-157), the federal minimum wage was raised from $3.35 per hour to $3.80 per hour effective April 1, 1990, and will increase to $4.25 per hour on April 1, 1991.

EPILOGUE

337   The Supreme Court flag burning case that set off a nationwide controversy is *Texas v. Johnson*, 109 S.Ct. 2533 (1989). For further information on the flag burning controversy, see notes to First Amendment (*Missouri Knights of the Ku Klux Klan*).

338   The Supreme Court quote regarding "freedom to differ" is from *West Virginia State Board of Education v. Barnette*, 319 U.S. 624, 642 (1943).

338   The quote from Justice Holmes regarding the Constitution as an experiment is from *Abrams v. United States*, 250 U.S. 616, 630 (1919) (Holmes, J., dissenting).

339   The final sentence of the *Epilogue* refers to another quotation from Justice Holmes:

Thus only can you gain the secret isolated joy of the thinker, who knows that, a hundred years after he is dead and forgotten, men who never heard of him will be moving to the measure of his thought.

O. W. Holmes, *The Profession of the Law*, 1886.

Bibliography

Adams, Charles Francis, ed. *The Works of John Adams*. Boston: Little, Brown, 1856.

Bailyn, Bernard. *The Ideological Origins of the American Revolution*. Cambridge: Harvard University Press, 1967.

Beaney, William Merritt. *The Right to Counsel in American Courts*. Westport, Conn.: Greenwood Press, 1972.

Bell, Griffin B., and Ostrow, Ronald. *Taking Care of the Law*. New York: William Morrow, 1982.

Bickel, Alexander M. *The Morality of Consent*. New Haven: Yale University Press, 1975.

Bollinger, Lee C. *The Tolerant Society: Freedom of Speech and Extremist Speech in America*. New York: Oxford University Press, 1986.

Bork, Robert H. *The Tempting of America*. New York: Free Press, 1990.

Brennan, William J., Jr. *Constitutional Adjudication and the Death Penalty: A View from the Court*. Cambridge: Harvard University Press, 1986.

Buranelli, Vincent, ed. *The Trial of Peter Zenger*. New York: New York University Press, 1957.

Bush, Douglas, ed. *The Portable Milton*. New York: Viking, 1977.

Chafee, Zechariah, Jr. *Free Speech in the United States*. Cambridge: Harvard University Press, 1942.

Clarke, James W. *Last Rampage: The Escape of Gary Tison*. Boston: Houghton Mifflin, 1988.

Curry, Thomas J. *The First Freedoms: Church and State in America to the Passage of the First Amendment*. New York: Oxford University Press, 1986.

Dershowitz, Alan M. *The Best Defense*. New York: Random House, 1982.

Donner, Frank J. *The Un-Americans*. New York: Ballantine Books, 1961.

Farber, Myron. *Somebody Is Lying*. New York: Doubleday, 1982.

Feldman, Daniel L. *The Logic of American Government: Applying the Constitution to the Contemporary World*. New York: William Morrow, 1990.

Friendly, Fred. *Minnesota Rag*. New York: Random House, 1981.

Friendly, Fred W., and Martha J. H. Elliott. *The Constitution: That Delicate Balance*. New York: Random House, 1984.

Garraty, John A., ed. *Quarrels That Have Shaped the Constitution*. Rev. ed. New York: Harper & Row, 1987.

Gilman, A., L. Goodman, T. Rall, and F. Murad. *The Pharmacological Basis of Therapeutics*. 7th ed. New York: Macmillan, 1985.

Griswold, Erwin N. *The Fifth Amendment Today: Three Speeches by Erwin N. Griswold*. Cambridge: Harvard University Press, 1955.

Gunther, Gerald. *Constitutional Law*. 11th ed. New York: Foundation Press, 1985.

Hamilton, Alexander, James Madison, and John Jay. *The Federalist Papers*. Edited by Clinton Rossiter. New York: New American Library, 1961.

Hand, Learned. *The Bill of Rights*. Cambridge: Harvard University Press, 1958.

Harris, Richard. *Freedom Spent*. Boston: Little, Brown, 1976.

Hart, Henry M. *Hart and Wechsler's The Federal Courts and the Federal System*. Westbury, N.Y.: Foundation Press, 1988.

Heller, Francis Howard. *The Sixth Amendment to the Constitution of the United States: A Study in Constitutional Development*. Lawrence, Kans.: University of Kansas Press, 1969.

Howe, Mark DeWolfe. *The Garden and the Wilderness: Religion and Government in American Constitutional History*. Chicago: University of Chicago Press, 1965.

Jefferson, Thomas. *Writings*. New York: Library of America, Literary Classics of the United States, 1984.

Kamisar, Yale, Wayne H. LaFave, and Jerold H. Israel. *Modern Criminal Procedure*. 6th and 7th ed. St. Paul, Minn.: West Publishing, 1986 and 1990.

Kammen, Michael. *A Machine That Would Go of Itself: The Constitution in American Culture*. New York: Alfred A. Knopf, 1986.

———. ed. *The Origins of the American Constitution: A Documentary History*. New York: Penguin, 1986.

Ketcham, Ralph, ed. *The Anti-Federalist Papers and the Constitutional Convention Debates*. New York: New American Library, 1986.

Krantz, John C., and C. Jelleff Carr. *The Pharmacologic Principles of Medical Practice*. Baltimore: Williams and Wilkins, 1961.

Kurland, Philip, and Ralph Lerner, eds. *The Founders' Constitution.* Vol. 5. Chicago: University of Chicago Press, 1987.

LaFave, Wayne R. *Search and Seizure: A Treatise on the Fourth Amendment.* St. Paul, Minn.: West Publishing, 1978.

Latham, Frank B. *The Trial of John Peter Zenger, August 1735: An Early Fight for America's Freedom of the Press.* New York: Franklin Watts, 1970.

Levy, Leonard W. *Emergence of a Free Press.* New York: Oxford University Press, 1985.

————. *Freedom of Speech and Press in Early American History: Legacy of Suppression.* New York: Harper & Row, 1960.

————. *Origins of the Fifth Amendment: The Right Against Self-Incrimination.* New York: Macmillan, 1986.

Lockhart, William B., Yale Kamisar, Jesse H. Choper, and Steven H. Shiffrin. *Constitutional Rights and Liberties.* 6th ed. St. Paul, Minn.: West Publishing, 1986.

Magee, Douglas. *Slow Coming Dark: Interviews on Death Row.* New York: Pilgrim Press, 1980.

Meiklejohn, Alexander. *Political Freedom: The Constitutional Powers of the People.* New York: Harper and Bros., 1948.

Meltsner, Michael. *Cruel and Unusual: The Supreme Court and Capital Punishment.* New York: Random House, 1973.

Meltzer, Milton. *The Right to Remain Silent.* New York: Harcourt, Brace, Jovanovich, 1972.

Moore, James William. *Moore's Federal Practice.* 2d ed. Albany: Matthew Bender, 1948.

Moore, Lloyd E. *The Jury: Tool of Kings, Palladium of Liberty.* 2d ed. Cincinnati: Anderson Publishing, 1988.

Morland, Howard. *The Secret That Exploded.* New York: Random House, 1981.

Padover, Saul K. *The Living U.S. Constitution.* 2d rev. ed. by Jacob W. Landynski. New York: New American Library, 1982.

Powers, Richard Gid. *Secrecy and Power: The Life of J. Edgar Hoover.* New York: Free Press, 1987.

Prettyman, Barret. *Death and the Supreme Court.* New York: Harcourt, Brace & World, 1961.

Rutland, Robert Allen. *The Birth of the Bill of Rights.* Boston: Northeastern University Press, 1983.

Schwartz, Bernard. *The Bill of Rights: A Documentary History.* 2 vols. New York: McGraw-Hill, 1971.

————. *The Great Rights of Mankind: A History of the American Bill of Rights.* New York: Oxford University Press, 1977.

Syrett, Harold C., ed. *The Papers of Alexander Hamilton.* Vol. 1, 1768–1778. New York: Columbia University Press, 1961.

Tribe, Laurence H. *American Constitutional Law.* 2d ed. Mineola, N.Y.: Foundation Press, 1988.

Unger, Sanford J. *The Papers and the Papers.* New York: E. P. Dutton, 1972.

Weinstein, Jack B. *Weinstein's Evidence Manual: A Guide to the United States Rules Based on Weinstein's Evidence.* New York: Matthew Bender, 1987.

Wilkes, Donald E. *Federal and State Postconviction Remedies and Relief.* Norcross, Ga.: Harrison Company, 1983.

Williams, Edward Bennett. *One Man's Freedom.* New York: Atheneum Press, 1977.

INDEX

Page numbers in *italics* refer to illustrations.

417

Congress OF THE United States

begun and held at the City of New-York, on
Wednesday the Fourth of March, one thousand seven hundred and eighty nine.

THE Conventions of number of the States, having at the time of their adopting the Constitution, expressed a desire, in order to prevent misconstruction or abuse of its powers, that further declaratory and restrictive clauses should be added: And as extending the ground of public confidence in the Government, will best ensure the beneficent ends of its institution.

RESOLVED by the Senate and House of Representatives of the United States of America, in Congress assembled, two thirds of both Houses concurring, that the following Articles be proposed to the Legislatures of the several States, as amendments to the Constitution of the United States, all, or any of which Articles, when ratified by three fourths of the said Legislatures, to be valid to all intents and purposes, as part of the said Constitution; viz.

ARTICLES in addition to, and amendment of the Constitution of the United States of America, proposed by Congress, and ratified by the Legislatures of the several States, pursuant to the fifth Article of the original Constitution.

Article the first.... After the first enumeration required by the first Article of the Constitution, there shall be one Representative for every thirty thousand, until the number shall amount to one hundred, after which the proportion shall be so regulated by Congress, that there shall be not less than one hundred Representatives, nor less than one Representative for every forty thousand persons, until the number of Representatives shall amount to two hundred, after which the proportion shall be so regulated by Congress, that there shall not be less than two hundred Representatives, nor more than one Representative for every fifty thousand persons.

Article the second. No law, varying the compensation for the services of the Senators and Representatives, shall take effect, until an election of Representatives shall have intervened.

Article the third. Congress shall make no law respecting an establishment of religion, or prohibiting the free exercise thereof; or abridging the freedom of speech, or of the press; or the right of the people peaceably to assemble, and to petition the Government for a redress of grievances.

Article the fourth. A well regulated militia, being necessary to the security of a free State, the right of the people to keep and bear arms, shall not be infringed.

Article the fifth. No soldier shall, in time of peace be quartered in any house, without the consent of the owner, nor in time of war, but in a manner to be prescribed by law.

Article the sixth. The right of the people to be secure in their persons, houses, papers, and effects, against unreasonable searches and seizures, shall not be violated, and no Warrants shall issue, but upon probable cause, supported by oath or affirmation, and particularly describing the place to be searched, and the persons or things to be seized.

Article the seventh. No person shall be held to answer for a capital, or otherwise infamous crime, unless on a presentment or indictment of a Grand Jury, except in cases arising in the land or naval forces, or in the Militia, when in actual service in time of War or public danger; nor shall any person be subject for the same offence to be twice put in jeopardy of life or limb; nor shall be compelled in any criminal case to be a witness against himself, nor be deprived of life, liberty, or property, without due process of law; nor shall private property be taken for public use, without just compensation.

Article the eighth. In all criminal prosecutions, the accused shall enjoy the right to a speedy and public trial, by an impartial jury of the State and district wherein the crime shall have been committed, which district shall have been previously ascertained by law, and to be informed of the nature and cause of the accusation; to be confronted with the witnesses against him; to have compulsory process for obtaining witnesses in his favor, and to have the assistance of counsel for his defense.

Article the ninth. In suits at common law, where the value in controversy shall exceed twenty dollars, the right of trial by jury shall be preserved, and no fact tried by a jury, shall be otherwise re-examined in any court of the United States, than according to the rules of the common law.

Article the tenth. Excessive bail shall not be required, nor excessive fines imposed, nor cruel and unusual punishments inflicted.

Article the eleventh. The enumeration in the Constitution, of certain rights, shall not be construed to deny or disparage others retained by the people.

Article the twelfth. The powers not delegated to the United States by the Constitution, nor prohibited by it to the States, are reserved to the States respectively, or to the people.

ATTEST,

Frederick Augustus Muhlenberg, Speaker of the House of Representatives.

John Adams, Vice President of the United States, and President of the Senate.

John Beckley, Clerk of the House of Representatives.
Sam. A. Otis Secretary of the Senate.